EXTREME ECONOMIES

EXTREME ECONOMIES

WHAT LIFE AT THE WORLD'S MARGINS
CAN TEACH US ABOUT OUR OWN FUTURE

RICHARD DAVIES

FARRAR, STRAUS AND GIROUX • NEW YORK

Farrar, Straus and Giroux
120 Broadway, New York 10271

Printed in the United States of America
Originally published in 2019 by Bantam Press, an imprint of Transworld Publishers Ltd,
Great Britain
Published in the United States by Farrar, Straus and Giroux
First American edition, 2020

Maps by Lovell Johns Ltd; charts and illustrations by Global Blended Learning.

Library of Congress Control Number: 2019951666
ISBN: 978-1-250-17048-4

Our books may be purchased in bulk for promotional, educational, or business use.
Please contact your local bookseller or the Macmillan Corporate and Premium Sales Department
at 1-800-221-7945, extension 5442, or by e-mail at MacmillanSpecialMarkets@macmillan.com.

www.fsgbooks.com
www.twitter.com/fsgbooks • www.facebook.com/fsgbooks

10 9 8 7 6 5 4 3 2 1

To Dr Richard Boyd and Mr Anthony Courakis, with thanks

CONTENTS

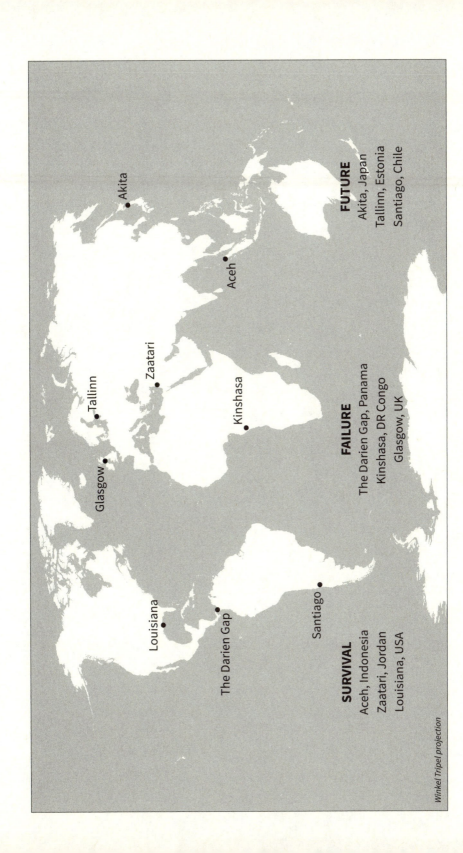

Akita

Aceh

Zaatari

Tallinn

Kinshasa

Glasgow

Louisiana

The Darien Gap

Santiago

FUTURE
Akita, Japan
Tallinn, Estonia
Santiago, Chile

FAILURE
The Darien Gap, Panama
Kinshasa, DR Congo
Glasgow, UK

SURVIVAL
Aceh, Indonesia
Zaatari, Jordan
Louisiana, USA

Winkel Tripel projection

Introduction

Economics in extreme places

Nature is nowhere accustomed more openly to display
her secret mysteries than in cases where she shows tracings of her
workings apart from the beaten paths.

William Harvey,
De Motu Cordis, 1628

RESILIENCE ON THE BEACH

As Suryandi recounts the morning of 26 December 2004, his strongest memories are of the terrifying sounds the tsunami made. It was a Sunday, and he had been busily preparing his restaurant, situated in prime position on the beach at Lampuuk, Aceh, for the coming day's trade. When he heard a petrified fisherman shouting that a thick fog was rising from the ocean on the horizon, he headed down to the water's edge to see what the commotion was about. The reef, usually underwater, was exposed, and out on the edge of the bay two fishing boats had run aground in a spot that was normally a deep channel. He stood and watched until he saw the wave hit a headland a mile to the north. It sounded like a bomb had exploded, and Suryandi knew he was in trouble. He ran for his motorbike and opened the throttle, flying inland up narrow village lanes. By that point the air was full of screams and prayers, he says. There was no time to stop and check on his family and friends as he pushed on for higher ground. Behind him he could hear the wave. It sounded like an aircraft was chasing him.

Tsunami survivors in Aceh remember three waves and say the second was by far the worst. Suryandi watched it from the broadcasting tower of a local television station, which he had climbed up after racing inland. Water from the first wave had engulfed everything, he says, but homes and gardens remained, shops and cattle sheds were still intact. The second wave thundered in like the first, but was accompanied by sharper sounds of demolition – loud snaps and crunches – as trees were uprooted and buildings were destroyed. The third wave was far quieter, its rumble quickly giving way to a deep whooshing as the sea water began to drain back to the ocean. As the water receded, the local mosque appeared, but nothing else did. Every home was gone, every business flattened; all the fishing boats were smashed and the cattle had been swept away. Then, a final sound fell on Lampuuk, which Suryandi describes as the worst experience of his life – there was complete silence.

Today on Lampuuk beach, Suryandi has a new restaurant. It is called Akun and sits, like the first one, in prime position at the head of the bay. His speciality is fresh fish, cooked over the glowing embers of coconut shells and served with local pickles. Like other Acehnese tsunami survivors, Suryandi ignored advice to relocate away from the coast and instead returned quickly to his village to rebuild his life. He started with nothing, building a shack made from driftwood into a thriving business. His account of that terrible day, on which he lost his mother, fiancée and many of his friends, is one of grief and mourning. But like other Acehnese, he has another story to tell: one of ingenuity, determination and, in a way, triumph. Suryandi faced an extreme challenge, the type of which few people have come up against, yet through resilience and adaptation he bested it. My mission in Aceh was to find out how locals had rebuilt their communities so quickly, what role the economics played in their astonishing resilience, and what the rest of us could learn.

THREE EXTREMES: SURVIVAL, FAILURE AND FUTURE

The idea that the extremes of life offer important lessons is an idea widely used by scientists. In the field of medicine its founding father is Dr William Harvey, a London-based anatomist working in the seventeenth century. Harvey saw the value in examining odd and rare cases, with the remarkable life story of Hugh Montgomery a fine example. As a child, Hugh suffered a riding injury: the left side of his torso smashed so badly when he fell from his horse that his ribcage fell away, leaving part of his heart and lungs uncovered. Miraculously the boy survived – a metal plate in place of ribs was used to protect his vital organs. By carefully removing the plate, Harvey was able to examine Hugh, and recorded how the movement of his heart came at the same time as the pulse in his wrist. It gave the doctor a unique window on human anatomy and was evidence for a controversial idea he was seeking to prove – that blood circulated continuously around the human body.

Harvey was mocked by his peers, but as centuries passed, the importance of his most famous finding – blood circulation – became clear and the value of his methods respected. Other medics showed those who survived following bodily damage could offer valuable insight. In 1822 a young Canadian, Alexis St Martin, survived an accidental shooting and lived with a hole in his abdomen; direct observation of how his digestive system worked became an important foundation of gastric physiology. And in 1848 a railroad labourer in Vermont, Phineas Gage, miraculously survived an explosion which propelled a metal rod through his skull; the record of his life following the accident – how his abilities and moods changed – became a groundbreaking study of how the brain works. The miraculous resilience of these extreme patients – all damaged in some way, yet all surviving – offered lessons that could be applied when thinking about how more normal, healthy human bodies functioned.

A related tradition exists in engineering. It began in the mid-1800s after a series of tragic industrial and transport accidents. The Industrial Revolution had pushed materials to their limits – in the UK, factories collapsed and boilers exploded; France was shaken by a rail tragedy in which a train derailed due to a snapped axle, claiming 52 lives. These disasters became public scandals, dominating politics and spurring a new branch of scientific investigation as engineers began to conduct in-depth studies of why things were going so wrong. The Scots excelled in this discipline and foremost among them was David Kirkaldy. Trained as an engineer, Kirkaldy devoted much of his life to studying why materials buckled and bent under pressure. He saw such value in the examination of failure that he designed a huge hydraulic machine to push metal samples until they snapped and sheared, and curated a small museum in which to display the fragments. When Britain suffered its worst disaster of the nineteenth century – the 1879 collapse of the Tay Bridge – it was Kirkaldy who was called in to get to the bottom of what had gone wrong.

David Kirkaldy's idea that we can learn from extreme failure echoes today. Anyone who has crossed London's Hammersmith Bridge or the Eads Bridge over the Mississippi has relied on his testing machine, which was used to check components for both. Modern scientists evaluating cutting-edge new materials do the same thing, putting samples in contraptions much like Kirkaldy's, testing them to destruction and then picking over the fragments. The core property of a material is known as its 'potential': it could be the ability to bear a load or to withstand pressure; the capacity to bend and stretch; being able to conduct heat or insulate from it. When a material fails, these latent properties are lost – rubber loses its elasticity, metal loses its strength – and the potential is gone. Kirkaldy's big idea was that to understand potential fully – its limits, how it can be lost, how it can be protected – we need to collect and examine fragments of failure.

The final motivation for studying extremes comes from an idea set out in 1928 by the economist John Maynard Keynes. Concerned that society was in the grip of a bout of pessimism about the economy, Keynes set out a largely optimistic long-term vision. Part of his argument was that we can get a glimpse of the future today, if we know where to look. The trick was to identify a sustained trend – a path most people are following – and look at the lives of those experiencing the extremes of that trend. At the time, Keynes thought the sustained trends would be an increase in material wealth and a reduction in the need to work. To zoom forward in time, he said, we need to find those whose lives are like this already: those with the most wealth, and those enjoying lots of leisure. Keynes called people who are living at the extreme limit of the trends shaping the economy 'our advance guard'. They are a useful way to think about the economic future because they are 'spying out the promised land for the rest of us and pitching their camp there'.

NINE ECONOMIES

The nine places that feature in this book are all societies where these three types of extreme experience – survival, failure and future – play a definitional role in people's lives. The first part of the book takes its inspiration from William Harvey and features places where people have proved resilient in the face of extreme damage and trauma. Aceh, where I met Suryandi, was the region hit hardest by the tsunami waves of 26 December 2004. The villagers lost everything, yet it was the site of a rapid economic rebound. The Syrian families I met in Zaatari, northern Jordan, had left behind their homes and businesses as they fled their country's civil war. Yet they too rebuilt, establishing a vibrant new life in this vast and controversial settlement which became the world's biggest and fastest-growing refugee camp. The prisoners I met in Louisiana left everything behind when they entered their new home, the biggest penitentiary in the US's most incarcerated state. Even here, there is a kind of economic resilience, as people barter and trade to get by. For these people, natural disaster, war and imprisonment wiped away everything that went before. Yet in all three places people survive and even thrive, often relying on the economy to do so.

Next I visited places I think David Kirkaldy would have investigated had he been an economist – three economies that have failed. The second part of the book starts with the Darien Gap, a site of such enviable location and natural riches that it has been a target for entrepreneurs since the 1500s. Today the territory remains a lawless no-man's-land, has a reputation as one of the most dangerous places on earth, and is the scene of devastating environmental degradation. Kinshasa, capital of the Democratic Republic of the Congo, has such potential that it should be Africa's best megacity. But it too is a place of failure; home to 10 million people, it is the poorest major city on earth. Glasgow once vied with London for the title of Britain's leading city, with so many breakthroughs in science, engineering and the arts that there was no better place to live at the start of the twentieth century. But Glasgow unravelled, losing everything as it became Britain's most troubled city, a dubious honour it retains today. In each of these places vast potential – whether natural, human or industrial – has somehow gone to waste, with economics often at the core of the problem.

Finally, I visited three places John Maynard Keynes would have looked at if he were alive today and following his own advice on how to take a peek at the economic future. As 2020 approaches, it seems the world is again in the grip of economic pessimism. Across the globe, most countries face three trends: ageing populations, the flux caused by new technology, and a rise of inequality. The trends are generally seen as unavoidable and capable of inflicting serious damage on the economy: they will be tests of resilience and may drive some economies to failure. So I followed Keynes's advice and sought out cities that were as old, advanced and unequal as possible. Akita, in northern Japan, is a frontier of ageing; Tallinn, Estonia's capital, is a frontier of technology; Santiago, Chile's capital, is a frontier of inequality. The majority of people in the world will soon live in places that feature a mixture of the stresses and opportunities seen in these three cities today. This means life for the 'advance guard' of these economies is a window on our own likely future. I visited them to understand the economic forces there, compare them to those underlying resilience and failure, and see whether it all added up to grounds for hope about the future, or fear.

A Note on Data

Since the challenge was to find and visit global extremes, the places I travelled to were picked in as quantitative and objective a way as possible to ensure they were the most striking examples of their kind. More details, facts and figures on each economy and how it was selected are given in each chapter. Wherever possible I have used data downloaded from official national statistical agencies or international institutions. My notes, together with references to research and further reading, are at the end of the book. A selection of interactive graphs, notes and data sources is available at the book's website: www.extremeeconomies.com.

SURVIVAL

THE ECONOMICS OF RESILIENCE

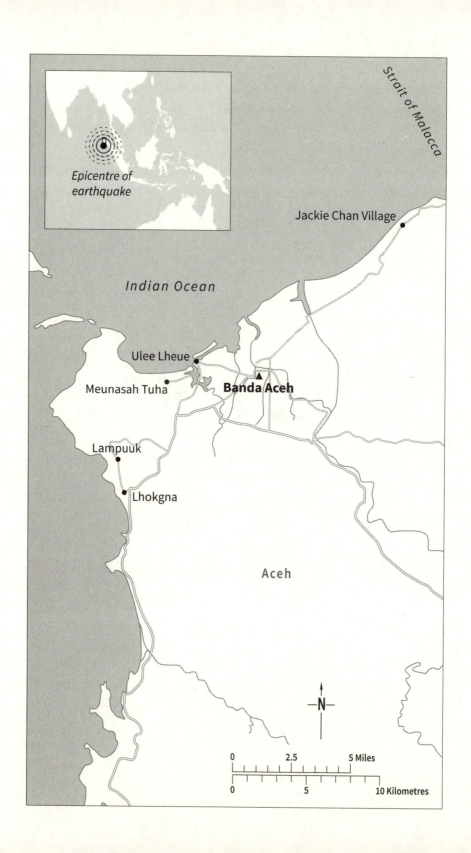

Strait of Malacca

Epicentre of
earthquake

Indian Ocean

Jackie Chan Village

Ulee Lheue

Meunasah Tuha

Banda Aceh

Lampuuk

Lhokgna

Aceh

—N—

| 0 | 2.5 | 5 Miles |

| 0 | 5 | 10 Kilometres |

1

Aceh

An enemy lays waste a country by fire and sword,
and destroys or carries away nearly all the moveable wealth
existing in it: all the inhabitants are ruined, and yet in a few years
after, everything is much as it was before.

John Stuart Mill,
Principles of Political Economy, 1848

DEVASTATION

THROW THE KEYS AWAY

'The earthquake did not feel that bad,' says Yusnidar, 'but then my son Yudi went down to the sea. He said there were fish all over the beach and there was a wave coming.' The shoreline is just 500 metres from where Yusnidar and her family lived in the centre of Lhokgna, a tiny village on the far north-west coast of the province of Aceh, Indonesia, so they knew they needed to move fast. They were fortunate, Yusnidar, now in her late sixties, says: as headteacher of the local primary school she had a decent income and the family, well off by local standards, all had motorbikes. Her son, Yudi, sped off to pick up his sister from a nearby house while his mother, unaware of how bad things were about to get, took the time to grab a few treasured possessions including a small bag that held room keys to the guest house the family owned. With her bag in hand, she jumped on to the back of her husband Darlian's bike, and they tore off in search of higher ground.

Those motorbikes saved their lives, Yusnidar reflects. Without them the tsunami wave that destroyed Lhokgna on the morning of 26 December 2004 would have caught the family, as it did so many of their neighbours. Now retired, Yusnidar is still comfortably middle class. She wears a crisp shirt, her dark hair is held back by a thin white band, and she plays with a thick gold bangle that rests halfway up her left forearm as she recounts the tsunami and its impact. Many years of dealing with tourists has given her good English: 'We were the first in the village to set up a homestay,' she says, explaining how the couple took in their first guests – initially providing accommodation free of charge to surf explorers – in 1981. They soon turned it into a business, which gradually expanded as the couple added extra buildings when times were good. The additional income from the guest house allowed them to pay for high school and university educations for their kids.

The terrain rises quickly here as you move inland, soon becoming dense jungle. The track they fled up that day still exists: retracing their route, it is possible to get a few hundred feet above sea level after just a couple of minutes. This meant Yusnidar and Darlian were safe, as were their three children. But you cannot see the beach or the village from the hillside, which is covered in dense jungle, and after sheltering there for a few hours the parents decided to walk back down and assess the damage. 'I picked up my bag of keys to go and check on my home and the guest house,' she recalls. But Yudi, then 22, had already ventured down the hill to the edge of the village, and he stopped her. 'He shouted at me: "No, Mumma!"' She pauses, sighing. 'He said there was nothing. No house, no buildings, no homestay. All gone.'

Under-estimating the severity of the situation in the village would have been easy to do. This was no normal disaster – the forces unleashed that morning had rocked the earth on its axis, destroyed five million homes and claimed almost 230,000 lives. The people of Lhokgna, its twin village of Lampuuk and the town of Banda Aceh were the first and hardest hit. What happened in these places that morning was terrifying. What has happened since is a story of stubborn survival, resilience and rebuilding that illuminates the basic building blocks of economics.

As she finishes her account of the disaster, Yusnidar makes a lobbing motion with her hands, as if she is throwing something away. Her treasured bag of keys, the years of work and investment it embodied, had become a relic of a life, a village and an economy that had been wiped away. She threw the bag into the jungle and walked down to Lhokgna to start again.

THE DAY THE EARTH CHANGED SHAPE

Tectonic plates usually move extremely slowly, shifting at most 8 cm in a year. (Glaciers, which can move over 15 km in a year, are thousands of times faster.) But just after 8 a.m. that day, things sped up as, around 50 km off the western coast of Aceh, the Indian Plate fell 30 metres in a few seconds, driven down by the opposing Burma Plate. From this epicentre a long thin rupture started to appear and, like a giant zipper being closed across the ocean floor, it drew the plates together quickly. Starting off the coast of Aceh it stretched 400 km to the north, moving at nearly 10,000 km per hour, or nine times the speed of sound.

The vibrations created an earthquake known as a 'megathrust'. It had a magnitude of 9.1, releasing 40 zettajoules of energy, enough to sustain global energy consumption for 80 years, and equivalent to 500 million Hiroshima atomic bombs. The shock that started just 50 km from the coast of Aceh was so big that the earth wobbled on its axis and even changed shape (our planet is now a more perfect sphere and spins faster, so we have slightly shorter days). It was the kind of thing that happens perhaps every 500 years.

Earthquakes often cause tsunamis, so something on this scale could be expected to cause a large wave. But scientists examining the seabed have recently discovered why things were so extreme in this case. Alongside the main faults, a series of secondary ruptures appeared, forcing huge chunks of the seabed up into space occupied by the ocean, and creating waves that were bigger and faster than any tsunami on record. The fishing villages of Aceh's north-west coast, Lhokgna and Lampuuk, were directly in its path. As in other parts of the world, the waves rose up and slowed as the waters shallowed. Here they reached 90 feet.

The waves killed 227,898 people across 14 countries, with Aceh being hit first and hit hardest. In Lhokgna and Lampuuk, more than 90 per cent of the villagers perished – the population fell from 7,500 to just 400. The Rahmatullah mosque was the only building that survived on this stretch of coastline, as every home, hostel and restaurant was destroyed. Yet within just a few months the Acehnese were rebuilding their lives and their economy, resulting in a remarkably fast rebound. Today, stories like Suryandi's are

Killer waves: the 20 worst tsunami disasters on record

Deaths caused by tsunami waves, 20 highest since 1900

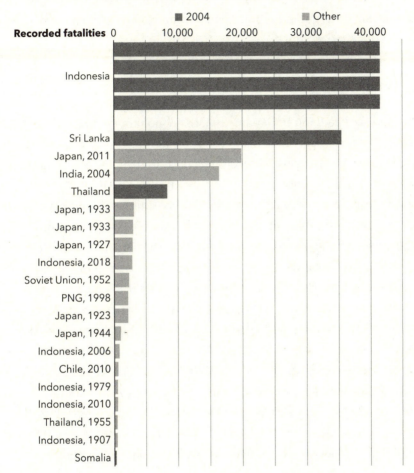

Source: Emergency Events Database (EM–DAT)

common in this unique place: people are back on the beach, living as they did before.

The extremes in the first part of this book are places where an economy survives and comes to thrive despite all the odds. On this definition, Aceh is a fascinating place to study. In this little-known corner of Indonesia, the people were put to unmatched stress, and many were encouraged to move away from their decimated coastline.

Yet they stayed put, rebuilt quickly and soon started to thrive. I went to Aceh to meet the people to understand what drives the human urge to rebuild, how we should measure the strength of an economy, and to ask locals about the source of human resilience in the face of such a devastating shock.

THE STORY OF ACEH

Around the headland in Banda Aceh, the regional capital, the disaster was devastating. Almost 170,000 people (around 55 per cent of the population) lost their lives. Ulee Lheue is a pretty suburb with neat rows of houses enclosed by tropical trees, ferns and palms; it is also low lying, close to the sea and completely flat. After wrapping around the headland, the tsunami waves would still have been 10 metres high here, and they destroyed every home in the neighbourhood. Yet today the streets run as they did then, parallel to the plot of the local mosque and right down to the shore. The house at the very end of the road, closest to the water, is a metre above sea level at most and would have been the first here to be flattened by the wave. Its owner then, as now, is a jolly local policeman called Mohammad Iqbal.

You can see why the family likes living here – the area around the mosque is a hub of activity. Mohammad's brother-in-law cycles up as we talk. He has built a mobile display cabinet, placed it on top of a side car and attached it to the side of his bicycle, from which he sells fruit and jewellery – freshly cut pineapple, melon and mango along with the large *aqiq* rings set with chunky gemstones that Acehnese men favour. His son, also Mohammad Iqbal, speaks good English and explains that he lost his mother, brother and sister in the disaster. The younger Mohammad is the first person to say something I end up hearing a lot: 'Welcome to Aceh. Remember that the letters in our name stand for Arabic, Chinese, European and Hindu.' The story – that this is a special place founded by traders – is strong in the minds of the Acehnese, a people who understand the history of their land and regard it as exceptional.

THE PEPPER CAPITAL AND VERANDA TO MECCA

Aceh's location, so devastating in 2004, has through most of its history been an economic asset. As maritime trade began to flourish in the fifteenth century, Banda Aceh became the gateway to the Malacca Strait, the channel that links the Pacific and Indian Oceans and is the primary shipping lane joining India and the west with China, Japan and the east. Cargoes from the Spice Islands – pepper, nutmeg, mace, cloves, ginger and cinnamon – were shipped up the strait and then on to ports in Sri Lanka and India as they headed west to Europe. They were light and their uses in curing meat and making medicines made them hugely valuable: nutmeg was worth more than its weight in gold in Britain, and London dockers would happily be paid in cloves. The spice ships navigating the Malacca Strait were like floating buckets of cash, and offering them safe harbour, as Banda Aceh did, was a lucrative business.

As well as controlling a strategic port, the Acehnese became powerful exporters, selling nutmeg and cloves, together with betel nuts, which can be chewed to give a caffeine-like high. But the big money here came from the global pepper boom. Pepper vines thrived when planted along Aceh's west coast, and by the 1820s the region was producing up to 10,000 tonnes a year, half the world's supply. Local farmers stopped cultivating rice and instead sent pepper south, trading it for lower value rice plus gold to settle the difference in value of the crops. Trade meant Aceh became richer than other parts of Sumatra, allowing it to maintain supreme maritime strength. For its control of shipping and the products of its land, the Acehnese came to understand that their end of the island was superior.

Others recognized the value of Aceh too, leading to centuries of battles and warfare between the Acehnese and rivals who sought control of the Malacca Strait. The early enemy was the Malacca Sultanate based across the water on the Malay Peninsula (modern-day Malaysia). Later, as European powers explored the east, Britain became an important protector, guaranteeing Acehnese independence in order to prevent the strategic region falling into enemy hands. But in 1871 the UK stepped back, allowing the Dutch to invade and claim the whole of Sumatra. The Acehnese resisted, and hostilities continued until after the Second World War. As part of the post-war peace process Aceh was bundled up with the rest of Sumatra and made part of the new Republic of Indonesia. It was a merger the Acehnese never agreed to, fuelling an independence struggle with regular battles between GAM (Gerakan Aceh Merdeka, the Acehnese guerrilla army) and Indonesian forces.

One of the fears about our economic future is that ageing, technology and inequality will lead to greater divisions: between the old and young, those with skills and those lacking them, the rich and the poor. The importance of understanding divisions, and how they widen or heal as an economy evolves, was another reason to visit Aceh. Its unique history meant the place had its own fault-lines, competing claims and factions that pre-existed the tsunami. This idyllic-looking spot was a land where peace talks had failed, a large military presence operated alongside an active rebel army, and which had a population who identified as Acehnese first and Indonesian second. Would the pressure of rebuilding exacerbate these divisions or would the challenge bring people together?

RESILIENCE

THE COFFEE KING

'The water was eight metres when it passed through here,' says Sanusi, 52, pointing to the roof of a nearby two-storey building to emphasize the point. His cafe – Sanusi Coffee – is at the heart of Lampaseh, a suburb of Banda Aceh around 15 minutes by motorbike from the west coast. He is smartly dressed, with an impressive bushy moustache, and his business is buzzing around us: at the main bar a stream of commuters swings in and out for takeaway espressos; outside, customers sip iced green tea and pick from plates of snacks under awnings providing welcome relief from the blistering sun. Sanusi explains that he did not outrun the tsunami – the roads here became too congested to escape by motorbike – but survived by shimmying up the trunk of a coconut tree. By the time he slid down, his business had been washed away, taking with it a safe containing his life savings. Sanusi returned home to find his house flattened, and his wife and eldest son dead. He recalls sitting traumatized for a day or so, doing nothing.

Within a couple of days he had decided to rebuild his coffee shop. 'This is what I do,' he says, 'and I had my surviving children and customers to think of.' After losing his house, much of his family and all his savings, how would rebuilding be possible?

One thing the tsunami waves did not destroy was Sanusi's knowledge of the coffee business. He started as a teenager, working for a wholesaler: 'I learned about trade pricing, and where to source the best beans.' Sanusi orders a young helper to bring us a bag of raw green coffee beans for a demonstration, selecting examples of plump ones that will make it to his roasting facility and the thinner ones that will be discarded. His suppliers, high up in Aceh's mountainous Gayo region, were unaffected by the disaster, so maintaining a supply of coffee was no problem. As we talk, he carefully continues to pick at the bag of beans, separating good from bad. The Acehnese don't drink alcohol but guzzle coffee, and Sanusi knows the business better than anyone. Determined to rebuild, what he needed was cash.

In any other situation Sanusi would have been the ideal candidate for a bank loan: an entrepreneur who knew his supply chain inside out and had a track record of turning coffee beans into profit. But the local banks had been destroyed, and the international aid agencies that started to arrive were focused on housing and sanitation rather than on business loans. His savings were gone and new funds impossible to find.

Then a customer, an academic from Jakarta who regularly visited Aceh, came to his rescue, loaning him 5 million rupiah (then around

$500, or £300). Using this to pay labourers and order new equipment, Sanusi Coffee was operating again within just five months of the disaster. 'Rebuilding this place was not just for me – look,' he says, proudly gesturing towards street vendors selling snacks to his customers (*peunajoh*, a sticky rice ball wrapped in banana leaf, is the most popular). Next he points to another stall that has set up outside, selling portions of rice and various curries to be taken home wrapped up in palm leaves as *bonkus* – Acehnese takeaway. His place has become a lesson in how even the smallest assistance can go a long way when combined with knowledge, skill and effort. A local hub once again, Sanusi Coffee is its own thriving mini economy where one business supports another. As the local coffee king finishes his account, he sits back and gives a rueful smile. In front of him are two neat piles of coffee beans: good ones on the left, bad on the right.

A LIFESAVING TRADITION

Banda Aceh's old market, Basar Aceh, is a fantastic place to shop. Fruit stalls are piled high with tropical offerings including scaly purple snake fruit, hairy red rambutan and the spiky green durian, like a bloated green rugby ball, that the Acehnese adore. (Supposedly the king of fruit, it smells like a wet dog; local hotels display signs asking guests not to bring them on to the premises.) It is the run-up to Ramadan – prime wedding season – and the haberdasheries are packed with women comparing material for dresses and their first sets of curtains; down tiny side streets an army of tailors can be seen, their sewing machines whirring as they work. Bridal gowns with plenty of lace are the current style, says one shopkeeper, explaining that newlyweds' taste in curtain material is more perennial: they like to buy deep-red fabrics reminiscent of the colours of the Acehnese flag. At the heart of Basar Aceh is the key to this economy – the shops that buy and sell jewellery and gold.

Harun Keuchik Leumicek, the head of the local gold traders' association, sits in a private room at the back of his shop in the old market. The place is cool, quiet and pleasantly pungent; a sink in the corner is stacked with red and blue tubs of Brylcreem, the shelf above it lined with various bottles of eau de cologne. Harun, in his seventies, is as natty as he is fragrant, dressed in black silk trousers cut wide like culottes, black snakeskin leather shoes and a short-sleeved batik shirt with a fiery red motif. His right ring finger carries the large blue gemstone that is common among Acehnese men; his left wields a giant diamond, which is not. The walls of his lair display awards for his expertise in gold and from a previous life in journalism. He adjusts his solid-gold Rolex, explaining that a centuries-old tradition was one reason local families were able to bounce back from tragedy so quickly.

'Whatever the purpose of their trip, the first thing people do at the market is check the price of gold,' says Harun. In Aceh, gold is king; the Acehnese have their own nomenclature for gold ingots, and their own system of weights and measures (the basic unit, the mayam, is around 3.3 grams). When an Acehnese person asks a jeweller for the gold price it is akin to a western shopper checking their bank account. Banks are not widely used in Aceh, Harun explains: 'Here people put their trust in gold.' Since savings are often held as gold ingots or weighty jewellery, the market price tells them how well they are doing, and whether it is a day to scrimp or splurge.

Gold also acts as a kind of informal insurance mechanism, explains Sofi, the 36-year-old heir to the busiest gold shop in the market. When preparing for marriage a man will need to ensure he builds up a stash of gold ahead of the day. This payment – known locally as 'the price of marriage' – is different from a dowry since it is given to the wife and held by her, rather than by her father. The going rate in Banda Aceh is 20 mayam (around 40 million rupiah, or $2,800, or £2,200), almost enough to exchange for one of the solid bangles that glow in Sofi and Harun's display cases. In an economy buffeted by the ups and downs of farming and fishing, the people are used to buying gold after bumper harvests or fishing seasons and selling it after lean ones. That culture means a woman's gold is both her personal treasure and plays a functional role as the family's financial buffer. The annual wage for a labourer here would be around 30 million rupiah; wearing a gold bangle is like having enough cash on your wrist to employ a builder for a year.

The gold-based system of saving and insurance is ancient, informal and unregulated. It worked quickly and efficiently in the months after the tsunami. The gold traders were the first shops in Basar Aceh to re-open – Harun and Sofi were both up and running within three months. They sold no gold and instead became bulk buyers of ingots and jewellery, allowing customers to generate funds for rebuilding. While some lost gold in the disaster, I meet many survivors who were able to sell jewellery they were wearing. And they got a fair price: while in many markets a rush of sellers would depress the local price, gold is a global commodity. Harun and Sofi were able to buy at the international price, confident that they could ship the gold to contacts in Jakarta who would buy it. This traditional form of finance insulated Aceh and provided its entrepreneurs with rapid access to cash.

This traditional system is the first example of a theme that came up in all the extreme economies I visited: informal systems of trade, exchange and even currency are hugely important. When the formal economy is damaged, it is often informal and traditional systems of trade, exchange and insurance that spring up first, and become the source of resilience. A key lesson is that we need to understand and value them more. The Acehnese financial system is a prime example: the kind of set-up that is seen as outdated and inefficient by western experts, it worked quickly and efficiently. The contrast with the western financial system, in which banks' own borrowing (their 'leverage') tends to amplify turbulence rather than dampen it, could not be sharper.

BACK TO THE BEACH

As the people in nearby Banda Aceh were struggling to their feet, restaurateur Suryandi's village, Lampuuk, lay in tatters. After working for an international charity for a few months clearing rubble and timber to unblock roads, he went to work at a restaurant in the town. Tents were soon erected in Lampuuk, creating what the locals called the 'refugee camp' where the village had been. Suryandi felt drawn to his old village and so moved back, taking the only job there was – fishing. 'I got seasick and bored,' he says, and after three months bobbing around on the Indian Ocean he decided to rebuild his restaurant.

His first challenge was getting permission. On the day of the tsunami the local fishing chief had screamed about divine retribution and the idea had caught on, especially among village elders in Lampuuk who had agreed that the tsunami was a message about lax morals on the beach. 'The problem was never with western tourists,' says Suryandi. The concern was that young locals were spending too much time flirting on the sand and too little working, studying and praying. The elders decreed that the beach must close indefinitely.

To bring about a relaxation of the new regulation, the beach entrepreneurs made an economic case: there was too little work in the village, and re-opening the beach would create jobs. The meetings went on for three months until the elders relented, on one condition. In the chaotic days after the tsunami, some locals whose bodies had been washed inland had been buried far from their home village, violating beliefs about what constitutes a good burial. To rectify things, the entrepreneurs would have to exhume these corpses and return them to Lampuuk. Once this gruesome task was complete the beach re-opened, but there were still problems: some villagers were superstitious, some were traumatized, others were simply afraid. The beach, once the focal point of village life, remained deserted.

Suryandi went back immediately and, lacking a rich benefactor, rebuilt his hut using scrap wood washed up on the shore. Then foreigners working for aid agencies came to his rescue in an unexpected way. There was no aid money for his cafe, he recalls, 'But those aid workers saved me – they were not scared of the sea and became my first customers.' Once locals heard that foreigners were frequenting the shoreline they gradually ventured back too. Suryandi operated from his shack until he had saved 15 million rupiah in profits, enough to put up a proper building. Today his Akun restaurant sits in prime position at the head of the bay next to the safe swimming water. A new outfit next door rents out arm bands and life jackets. The beach is now popular again, the economy so much improved that a building like his would cost at least 100 million rupiah to buy today, he says.

DESTRUCTION AND GROWTH

After a while you start to understand that the rapid rebuild is a common story here. One night I meet 61-year-old barber Yusuf in a cafe and we chat while eating *Aceh Mei* – instant noodles souped up with extra vegetables and spices. He didn't escape the wave but was engulfed by it, waking up in the afternoon of 26 December fully 8 km from his home with dead bodies either side of him. He had been laid out in a line of victims. His right leg was broken in a number of places but he managed to stand. 'When I got up the local villagers thought I was a zombie,' he says, laughing. Back from the dead, his barber shop was open within a year.

The speed of the rebuild and the fact that informal networks of trade and traditional finance sprang up before external help arrived are striking. A bigger surprise is that the local economy did not just rebound but improved. Akhyar Ibrahim is a serial entrepreneur who runs a private school and a business training institute, and owns and manages a series of rice fields. An engineer by training, the 61-year-old shows me around the house he designed and built in the late 1980s. An unorthodox design, based around many central columns, it withstood the tsunami. Over green tea and crackers he mulls over how the disaster changed things. 'Regarding the economy, things are very much better now.' Akhyar lost the second of his five sons in the disaster but, he continues, 'Lifestyles are better too. The tsunami had huge costs, but it also had benefits.'

The idea that the tsunami brought benefits to the region can be hard to believe. Everything here – from the personal trauma of lost friends and relatives, to the evidence of the region's physical devastation on show in the local museum – points to a place that was smashed and beyond repair. Yet in many ways things did get better in Aceh following the tsunami. A good chunk of this is down to a stronger economy. For an economist, a short-term boom here is less surprising than for most: the perplexing truth, seen across the world, is that natural disasters can make an economy grow faster. Understanding why this is the case helps to demystify Aceh's miraculous recovery and illuminates the most important measure used in economics.

SHAKING THE FOUNDATIONS

The first attempt at a systematic measure of the size and strength of an economy was set out by William Petty in the 1650s. Petty was a polymath: a surgeon and professor of anatomy at Oxford, a gentleman-farmer, an agricultural and maritime inventor (he designed an automatic grain planter and an early catamaran, and came up with a proposal for attaching engines to boats), and a leading civil servant. (He would have known about Aceh, since during his lifetime the English and Dutch were pitched in major battles for control of the seas, including the Malacca Strait.) The three Anglo-Dutch wars between 1652 and 1674 were costly, with the taxes to fund the conflict falling on landowners, including Petty. He thought this unfair, and so set out to measure Britain's economy more accurately and work out who should bear the burden of taxation. His central argument was that while assets such as land and buildings were one part of a nation's wealth, the annual flows of money associated with the world of work – wages, together with firms' income and profits – were the original source of a country's economic might. They were being overlooked, and business owners and workers should pay more tax.

Petty's argument that policymakers needed an accurate measure of economic strength that considered every source of income and every sector of an economy never really caught on. For 250 years economists studied single sectors, tracking the volume of industrial production, the tonnage of coal mined, or the value of manufacturing exports. Economic analysis and policy were done in a piecemeal way, with no all-encompassing measure. Then, in the 1930s, the US economy suffered a huge recession that became the Great Depression, which spread across the globe. The Great Depression is the defining event of modern economics and led to a detailed investigation of the sources of economic growth. It was necessary to devise a master measure of everything the economy does. A group at Cambridge University came up with the solution, producing a set of economic accounts for the UK in 1941. This marked the beginning of the modern focus on gross domestic product, or GDP.

GDP is a measure of the monetary value of a nation's economy, and can be thought of as a camera capturing an economy through three alternative lenses: the first lens picks up production, the second captures income, while the third focuses on spending. When something is produced, GDP rises; when income accrues as a worker's wages or firm's profits, GDP rises; and when money is spent by a person, company or government, GDP rises. Perhaps the most important thing about GDP is that its three lenses capture live activity rather than past achievements: factories, shops or homes that were built and sold last year count for zero in this year's GDP. All these things are important physical assets, but since they are not part of this year's production, income and spending they represent the activity of the past. GDP aims to capture what a country's residents are doing now, rather than what they have done previously.

The 2004 tsunami destroyed physical assets on a huge scale. In the twin villages of Lhokgna and Lampuuk every house was destroyed; across Aceh 139,000 were lost. Large factories collapsed and around 105,000 small businesses and their buildings were wiped out. In the harbour at Banda Aceh fishing boats were smashed into driftwood – 14,000 across the region met the same fate – and the riverside huts used by fishermen to clean and sell their catch were washed away. On the beachfront, every cafe was obliterated; the parasols and surfboards would never be seen again. All of these things were important, the result of years of work. But having been produced and purchased in the past, none of them counted as the kind of 'current activity' captured by GDP. On that terrible morning when the tsunami wrought its destruction, the size of Aceh's economy as measured by GDP did not shrink.

Of course, economic potential had been lost: the wiped-out factories and restaurants took with them jobs as factory workers and waiters, for example. But offsetting this loss of capacity for production and income generation was the fact that rebuilding a village or town means lots of fresh activity. Take housing: in the four years following the disaster, 140,000 new homes were built in Aceh. Each one meant builders needed to spend on materials such as bricks, wood and electrical wire, and they had to pay the wages of the workmen who use them. All this generates income for companies – the builders' merchant, the concrete supplier and the haulier – and for tradesmen such as the bricklayer, joiner and electrician. Once the job is finished, a new house has been produced. Construction means a rush of the three types of activity – producing, earning and spending – that contribute to GDP. As accounts like Suryani's and Sanusi's show, the determination of the Acehnese meant an immediate urge to rebuild homes, schools, shops and roads. This, in part, explains the puzzle of why an economy, measured by GDP, will tend to grow in the aftermath of a natural disaster, even one at the extreme scale seen in Aceh.

THE AID BOOM

While traditional forms of saving helped provide immediate capital to some entrepreneurs, outside help was needed to pay for the mass reconstruction. Cruise around the villages here on a motorbike for a few days and you can see exactly where the cash came from. Approaching Lhokgna from the south, the coast road crosses a steel-truss bridge carrying the logo of the US donor agency, USAID. As you enter the village, all the houses – detached bungalows on small plots – have a similar design on their front wall: the dark-green circle enclosing two crossed swords beneath a palm tree, which is the emblem of Saudi Arabia, a major donor of funds for housing. Half a mile north to Lampuuk a road turns inland; this street, the one Suryandi fled up on the day of the tsunami, is lined with properties bearing the star and crescent of Turkey above the porch. The Turkish-donated houses are the best, locals say, since they came with fully equipped kitchens.

Overall $6.7 billion was spent in Aceh in the four years following the disaster. The cash created its own turbulence, a kind of mini boom. The aid agencies brought their own workers on decent salaries who had money to spend; they hired many locals and made huge orders of brick, concrete and timber for reconstruction. This demand surge pushed up prices: inflation rose from around 5 per cent in 2004 to 20 per cent in 2005 and topped 35 per cent the following year. Business owners still grumble about this because it eroded their profit margins: the cost of essential staples like sugar, rice and coffee surged but it was hard to raise the prices customers were charged. But in the main these are remembered as good years for the economy. Aid-agency cash supported local jobs and wages, and flowed to local businesses. Aceh, now an aid economy, was buoyant.

Today the fading emblems, flags and logos painted by foreigners on the things they donated are the main reminder of their work. After four intense years of activity the aid agencies withdrew in 2008. The number of foreign workers in Aceh fell from 8,000 to a few hundred and job opportunities for locals plummeted. In 2009 the Indonesian government agency overseeing the aid effort was shut down, having done its job. Inflation in Aceh went back to the national average as the tide of aid money receded.

Sucking all that activity out of an economy – the spending, the wages, the construction projects – is a recipe for a big drop in GDP. Since this measure of the economy is based on activity, development economists worried that while the rebuild had created short-term activity the economy would shrink in GDP terms, suffering a recession. What happened next was mysterious. Despite the loss of all the aid-agency spending and all the job cuts, economic growth continued to rise: having grown 19 per cent during the four-year aid boom, the economy expanded by 23 per cent over the next four years. Where was all the new spending, income and production coming from?

BUILDING BACK BETTER: ROADS, MACHINES OR IDEAS?

If you are in search of a hot meal in Lhokgna, Dian's restaurant is the place to visit. She is always open and sells delicious marinated fish and curries in generous portions. Sitting at one of the tables on a quiet night she puts Aceh's improved economy down to something less palatable: sewerage. Some things are worse today, she says: the traditional houses were preferable in style to the new ones (they were wooden and had upper floors with balconies, whereas the replacements are concrete bungalows). But the big change is having your own toilet. Before the disaster the village lacked a basic sewerage system, with the nearby river providing clean water and taking dirty water away. The modern homes have plumbed-in bathrooms, cutting out time-consuming walks to the river.

As the rebuild continued, the notion of 'building back better' became a well-known phrase, referring to the policy of using modern designs and materials to improve the local infrastructure. The new coast road built by USAID is wider than the old one, and the steel-truss bridge it crosses at Lhokgna is higher and longer than its stone-column predecessor, the remains of which protrude from the river like broken teeth. Mid-way between Lhokgna and Banda Aceh, a family-run factory that once processed coconuts into paste and cooking oil has been retooled as a cement plant with a row of gleaming mixer trucks parked outside. The raw material comes from a large cement factory a few minutes' drive down the coast. Owned by

Lafarge, a French company, it was destroyed in 2004 and re-opened in 2010 with 30 per cent higher capacity. While there is some quibbling over the precise design of the houses, the aid-funded rebuild left Aceh with better roads, bridges and factories than those that were lost. All of this improved the potential for trade and tourism.

But the ongoing benefits of the aid effort went further than pure cash, and many were informal or unintentional. Take use of technology, which survivors say shifted hugely after the tsunami. For Suryandi the arrival of outsiders using mobile phones improved things for entrepreneurs. The beachfront restaurateurs invested in basic burner-style mobiles, using them to call in help if there are lots of customers at the beach, or if the kitchen needs fresh supplies. Yusnidar says the diffusion of motorbikes has improved life: before the tsunami only richer families had them, but money earned during the aid boom means that every family has at least one, with better-off families owning a car. These changes modernized Aceh, making it easier to get ready for work, to know where you need to be and to get there quickly.

The disaster led to subtler changes that have influenced both the economy and wider society, explains Zuhir, a village chief. Zuhir is 43 and says his job is hard because most of the village elders died in the tsunami. Before the disaster the elders set the rules that the chief would then enforce. Vital information – on property rights and customs – was passed down by word of mouth, so that today it can be impossible to resolve disputes. 'Important information died out with the elders,' says Zuhir. Like many in Aceh's smaller conurbations, he mourns the loss of village-specific traditions that had been maintained by elders and are now lost for ever.

Despite this loss, new ideas and customs have arrived that have made things better, Zuhir says, 'people in Aceh have become more open'. It is a sentiment I hear across the region. Take the Acehnese view of the Dutch. Before the tsunami locals say it varied from unmasked hatred to a sort of unfriendly mocking. (Someone being deceitful or sly could be accused of 'being Dutch' here, the slur a reference to the Dutch tendency to send spies to the region to live among the

Acehnese.) Now most people welcome the historical enemy, in part because they helped with the aid effort, but also because there is a sense that old rivalries died out with the tsunami. The same applied on the micro level at which village rivalries and feuds play out. Before the disaster it would be rare for someone to open a business in a village unless they had been born there, now this is common.

This evolution of Aceh explains why the region saw growth even after the short-term boost of aid money had worn off. With improved sanitation, transport and communications, local workers became more efficient. They were speeding along better roads to work in factories with safer machines with a higher capacity, making them more productive and better off. But the ripple and echo of aid was much wider, and some of it unintended. Just as much of Aceh's initial economic resilience was informal, the ongoing strength rested on adopting the technologies and tastes of the aid workers who briefly lived in the region.

Another example of shifts in expectation is education, the local chief says. An education market has sprung up: an entire street in Banda Aceh running parallel to the main strip is now devoted to the kinds of cramming schools seen in other parts of Asia. Publicly funded education runs from 8 a.m. to 1 p.m. and then the kids head to these private places for the afternoon. Nina, a Lhokgna businesswoman, says she would like to send her toddlers to these booster schools. It is partly because aid-agency work made clear how important a degree was, and partly because the economy is stronger, so people can afford it, she explains. But it is also because priorities have changed: having seen the physical world destroyed in a single morning, locals put a higher value on investing in themselves. 'We put people first now,' she says.

A CHRONIC ILLNESS IS CURED

In a region that had been struggling for its independence for centuries, the upheaval of the tsunami was bound to have implications.

In the immediate aftermath it seemed as if the fighting would get worse. A group of GAM freedom fighters scrambled down to Lampuuk from their forest hideouts in the first few hours after the wave. A former rebel soldier, Armiya, then 23, was among them and says the village was underwater for no longer than 45 minutes: 'We were on the beach looking for survivors by 11 a.m.' But three days later, Indonesian forces arrived in large numbers to help. Officially still at war, they set their sights on the devastated rebel army. Restaurateur Suryandi describes a horrific few days stuck in a low-lying village where the sea water did not drain immediately. He spent his time tying dead bodies to the few remaining trees to prevent them floating away, while all around him armed groups were shooting at each other. At least three bystanders died in the gunfight, he says.

Things soon swung the other way. Discuss the tsunami in Aceh and after a while a western phrase – 'MOU' – will come up. Signed on 15 August 2005, the Memorandum of Understanding – essentially a peace accord – has resulted in the most stable period since before the first Dutch invasion in the 1870s. With the eyes of the world briefly on Aceh, big hitters from the world of humanitarian aid initiated peace talks, brokering a new deal where others had failed. The rebels stood down 3,000 fighters, handed in 840 weapons, and retired their uniform and insignia. In exchange, the Indonesian Army withdrew all troops from Aceh and released political prisoners. The MOU also enshrined a series of new rights. Aceh would have its own legislature, court system, flag and anthem. It would use Indonesia's currency, but official interest rates could differ from the rest of the country. The local government was given the power to raise taxes locally and retain the revenue from sales of natural resources, including oil. The settlement created a country within a country. While modern Aceh lies on Indonesian soil, it has its own special kind of sovereignty.

Peace improved life in Aceh, particularly for young men. 'Before the MOU parents wanted to keep their sons inside,' says Yusnidar, recalling how she worried about her boys. Others agree that young men had a grim time: claiming neutrality was unacceptable to both the rebels and the Indonesian Army, and anyone caught on their own could be conscripted or interrogated by either side. Boys from Lampuuk and Lhokgna were prevented from travelling through an area known as Keudee Bieng, a hot spot for fighting. The inability to travel locally limited their education by blocking the route to the universities in nearby Banda Aceh.

The uncertainty of war was a major drag on the economy, says Suryandi. Aceh had been a militarized zone since 1990, with the military police prone to shutting down the restaurateurs at any time and imposing a curfew that destroyed the evening meal trade. Yusnidar agrees, saying that her homestay business dried up in some years as surfers stayed away, fearful of the military action. Locals say there was never really a problem for foreigners but in one incident a surfer suspected of being a rebel soldier was kidnapped, blindfolded and taken to the hills to be interrogated by the Indonesian Army. The man was in fact a Japanese tourist and was released the same day, but the tale got into the bloodstream of the international surf community whose trips to Lhokgna had been a crucial source of spending in the village.

Put it all together – better homes and roads, new ideas from abroad, and a long-lasting peace – and you start to understand why people who still mourn the human loss of the tsunami also prefer life after it. Local tycoon Akhayar and his wife offer a tour of the tsunami-withstanding home they designed, pointing out a mark on the kitchen wall that shows the water level (it is around 1.7 metres) on the day of the disaster. The proud father shows family photos, telling me where his sons are studying, and pointing to the boy lost in the disaster. It was a terrible day, he reflects, but the deep changes it led to – a more open and outward-looking society, a cathartic peace process that ended years of fighting – are valued by the people here, as is the expanded economy that provides more work, income and opportunity than before the disaster.

FAULTLINES

THE POWER OF IDEAS

Fragilities remain in Aceh. Arriving from the west, the risk you read about is the rise of Sharia Law. The Islamic legal system was becoming more popular here before the disaster and religious feeling grew in the aftermath. The duty to impose Sharia was made part of the secular law in 2006, and a new criminal code requiring corporal punishment was adopted in 2015. Since then Aceh has become a place where people receive public whippings for transgressions. The western media has followed this, publishing photos of the whippings, with tourism websites expressing concern over equal treatment of women and the new requirement to wear headscarves. To a westerner skimming the internet, Aceh can seem a scary place, and not one to visit.

But just as Aceh shows how tradition can lie at the root of economic resilience, the region also shows how the informal and unseen – in this case the legend and narrative of a place – can act as a root that tempers sharp swings in political or religious approval. 'You have to remember the story of Aceh,' says Eka, the head of a public high school on the outskirts of Banda Aceh. The playground is taken up by a basketball court and is surrounded by dense jungle; nearby a steep hill is marked as the evacuation route the children should take if another tsunami wave strikes. Eka, 37, grew up in Lhokgna and went to university in Banda Aceh. She wears a silver hijab with a tailored pinstripe jacket over her dress. 'Our region was built by women; this guarantees us an equal role,' she says. The new and stronger-form religious laws have to contend with older foundation stories, including the lives of two heroines who define what it is to be Acehnese.

This maritime place has ships, trade and warfare at its core, with the ancient port of Banda Aceh boasting the world's first female admiral, Laksamana Malahayati. Appointed to lead the sultan's fleet in the late 1500s, she successfully defended the Malacca Strait, hunting down and killing enemy captains, and building a reputation so strong that she negotiated directly with Queen Elizabeth I about British access to the trade route. She was killed in action against the Portuguese. Today the region's main commercial port carries Malahayati's name.

While the admiral's legend is strong, Cut Nyak Dhien is an even greater military hero. Born to an aristocratic family, she rose to lead the Acehnese resistance against the Dutch in the 1890s. Her exploits – hiding in the woods to ambush and defeat large onrushing armies – are famous, and in 1964 she was posthumously made a National Hero of Indonesia, the country's highest honour, her image soon appearing on stamps and bank notes. In a complex tussle of ideas these old stories about the fight for freedom seem to blend with Islamic teaching, creating a unique Acehnese version of Sharia. The big fear outsiders have for Aceh seems to be a red herring when you spend time here: 'Our women are fearless,' says Eka. 'We do what we like, religion is no problem here.'

THE DARK SIDE OF HUMAN RESILIENCE

Just as Lhokgna and Lampuuk show how rebuilding an old village can happen astonishingly quickly, a place known as 'Jackie Chan Village' shows that building a new one takes much longer. Formally named the Friendship Village of Indonesia-China, the catchier nickname caught on after the Hollywood actor visited this new conurbation to see the reconstruction effort.* In many villages that had been flattened the approach was gradual and organic, with brick homes gradually replacing the stick and tarpaulin shelters the villagers had put up on their old plots. In Jackie Chan Village the government had more ambitious plans: reasoning that elevation

---

* *Kampung Persahabatan Indonesia-Tiongkok* in Indonesian.

brings safety, they sought land that was empty and high up, and built a brand-new village 500 metres up the side of a mountain.

The blueprint included all the public services and amenities a village could need. Near the grand gated entrance to the village there is a mosque, and at the top of the hill there is a large school; in the middle there is a large open market terraced neatly into the steep hillside. The market, at the new village's heart, was designed as a hub for local commerce, complete with an access road to allow vehicles carrying produce in and out, numbered pitches for the stallholders and tin roofing to provide shade. This top-down plan had its benefits, says the local chief Darmanain, sitting on a bamboo bench in the shade of a tree loaded with deep pink *jambu air* (rose apples). There was strict government control of the budget and timing of the build: a Chinese contractor brought in 36 of their own master builders who oversaw a team of 2,000 locals, with the workforce building over 600 houses in just 14 months. It was quick, efficient and the dwellings are good quality, he says, beckoning to his own place in the centre, near the market. Jackie Chan Village was also intended to make life in Aceh a little more equal. The majority of the people allocated homes here were not locals but disadvantaged families previously living in cramped rented accommodation in Banda Aceh.

The attempt to engineer a new and egalitarian village was a nice idea but nothing has changed for the people here, the chief explains. The residents of the village still do low-end jobs in Banda Aceh; they now own homes but are stuck on top of a hill miles from the economic activity of the town, and lose time and money to their daily commute. The market is barren and empty, with weeds growing where the stalls should be. With the adults all commuting for work, the only people to be seen in the village are a lone teenager and a puzzled elderly Chinese man who speaks no Acehnese or Bahasa Indonesian. The families given these houses were poor, unskilled and troubled before the tsunami, and these facts have not changed. As the chief explains, he invites us to pick some rose apples from his tree, but with no market to sell the fruit, they have been on the branch too long and are rotten to the core.

REBUILDING ACEH

The speed with which the Acehnese rebuilt an economy in which physical infrastructure had been decimated illuminates two aspects of how we think about the economy. The first of these is GDP, the central concept used to track whether or not an economy is 'growing'. Many people are critical of using GDP as a measure of economic success, favouring other metrics including fairness and happiness. And measuring economic strength through the lens of GDP certainly has perplexing results in that an economy can grow faster after a disaster. But that oddity, which some take as evidence of the cold, callous nature of economics, is because GDP is all about current human activities – spending, wages, income, producing goods – rather than the value embodied in physical assets such as buildings and factories. Far from being a mean or cold measure, economists' favourite yardstick is a fundamentally human one.

The Acehnese tsunami survivors I met, who said their economy and society improved following the tsunami, were always talking about an increase in the activities – making new products, taking new jobs, buying new consumer goods – that economists track in a growing economy. But while GDP and the benefits of economic growth are in line with the way regular people think and talk about their economy, my interviews in Aceh were the first look at an important problem. So much of what happened in places like Lohkgna and Lampuuk was informal – from loans granted by friends to cash sales of gold – and goes unmeasured and unassessed. When the formal economy is razed to the ground, this underlying network of trade is easier to see. I left Aceh thinking that economists' lens on a growing economy, GDP, is the right one. Far from being out of line with what people think of as a strong economy, in its motivation GDP is a fine but incomplete measure – it aims for the right thing, but because so much of the activity that defines an economy is hidden from view, we pick up only part of the picture.

The second aspect illuminated by Aceh is a reminder of where true human resilience lies. The philosopher and economist John Stuart Mill wrote in 1848 that it was common for communities to rebound after a war or disaster had 'laid waste' to their economy, and noted that most people would regard this as surprising. The source of the unexpected resilience, Mill thought, was the fact that walls, bridges and warehouses – physical capital – matter less than the ideas, skills and effort of the people who make up a country or community, since it is the people who will be called on to rebuild what has been lost.* Aceh is a modern disaster that proves Mill's point. The people here lost every physical asset but the tsunami survivors retained skills and knowledge from before the disaster, and rebuilt quickly as a result. As the global economy faces new challenges, Aceh suggests that human capital and the extent to which it is damaged or protected by economic change will be a key determinant of success.

With an eye to the divisions in society that economic change can bring, Aceh offers an important warning. This place has seen a complete revolution in its economy and society since 2004: there are new types of houses, roads and bridges; the shops sell new brands and styles of goods; the ways people date, play, trade and pray have changed. But coffee magnate Sanusi is once again a coffee magnate; restaurateur Suryandi is back selling barbecued fish from his prime spot on the beach; and while Yusnidar, who opened the first homestay in Lhokgna, has retired, the best hotel in Lhokgna is now owned by her son. The same is true for those at the bottom of the economic scale. The families who once squatted in Banda Aceh now live in a ghost village with a desolate market and rotting fruit on the trees. Life has changed completely here, and hardly at all. Human capital is

---

* In 1662 William Petty, in an argument criticizing the use of excessive prison sentences, made a similar point: the wealth of a place springs from its people (and therefore putting so many in jail makes a country poorer).

resilient, and that means economies are easier to rebuild than we might think, and divisions in them harder to change.

Despite the remaining fractures, Aceh is an optimistic place, even where things seem bleakest. As the road that borders Jackie Chan Village descends the mountain, row after row of deserted streets pass on the right and a steep drop appears on the left. Then the track veers sharply to reveal a set of tiny terraces cut into the hill, each holding a trestle table and a bench. The manager of this makeshift cafe, a 13-year-old boy, appears. Each day after school he buys drinks and snacks from a shop at the foot of the mountain and carries them up here to sell. Born to a poor family in the year of the tsunami, the young entrepreneur says business is good: most people live at sea level and are prepared to pay a premium for the view his cafe affords. While he pours a Sprite over ice, the trees in the forest below shake as a family of macaques plays in the canopy. Beyond this, the rooftops of aid-agency housing appear, a patchwork of colour-coded roofing reflecting the donor countries' flags. Then the rice fields of lowland Aceh begin, and a rich green carpet runs out all the way to the deep-blue ocean of the Malacca Strait.

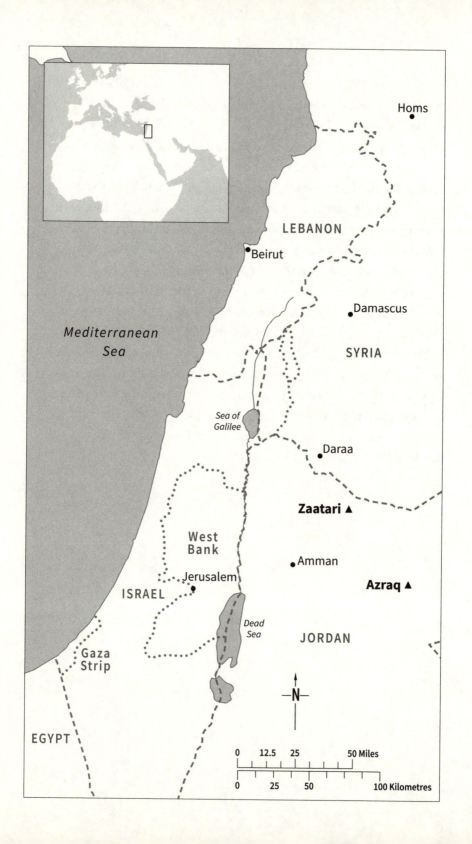

2

Zaatari

A musician must make music, an artist must paint,
a poet must write, if he is to be ultimately at peace with himself.
What a man can be, he must be.

Abraham Maslow,
Motivation and Personality, 1954

ZAATARI EMERGES

THE FOX

They call him the Fox because of his eyes. Khaled's gaze flicks from side to side as he scans the horizon, looking for danger or opportunity. He needs to be alert. As the kingpin of a syndicate of renegade traders he leads a precarious existence. If caught, Khaled and his gang could be expelled from Jordan and sent north to face the war in Syria.

His risky life brings its rewards. At the end of each day Khaled takes home 20 dinars (around $28, or £22). It is roughly double what a young professional – a 30-year-old engineer, say – can expect to make in Amman, the Jordanian capital. It is lucrative because it is illegal: his team are smugglers, and their contraband consists of food, cigarettes, electronic equipment and medical supplies. The borders he navigates are those of Zaatari, the world's fastest-growing refugee camp. Khaled is 15 years old.

The smuggling game is new to him. Until 2013 Khaled lived in a town called Dael, in southern Syria. He spent his days in school, just like 94 per cent of Syrian kids did before the war. Unlike parched and dusty Jordan, Syria is a lush country with plenty of water, and the farmers of Dael are known for their olives and grapes. Before the war, with a population close to 30,000, Dael was about the size of Ithaca, Sevenoaks or Pontypridd – hardly a metropolis. But in March 2011 the residents protested against Bashar al-Assad, making Dael a target of heavy bombing in the war that followed. They had no choice but to flee south over the border and to attempt to rebuild their lives, just as the people of Aceh did after the 2004 tsunami.

The Syrian refugees of northern Jordan and the Acehnese tsunami survivors both experienced devastating personal loss, and the destruction of their society and economy. The life stories of the people living in the Zaatari camp, as with the villagers of Aceh, are shocking and brutal. Yet as in Aceh, when you spend time in Zaatari, after a while a sense of optimism, a confidence in the human ability to prevail against all odds, begins to grow. For Zaatari is the site of another extreme, a miraculous trading post that has survived despite all the odds. It is a place defined in part by what the refugees have lost, but also by the rapid emergence of a vibrant and innovative economy, a business hub packed with start-up firms that quickly became so successful that it was exporting goods to surrounding Jordanian towns.

I expected the refugees' stories to offer related but distinct lessons to the tsunami survivors'. In Aceh, the outside help that came was advisory in nature: people were told not to go back to the beach-front living, but they soon returned to low-lying land that they knew well and had controlled for centuries. For Syrian families, things were different: seeking safety they moved to new land, and as refugees in a foreign country were subject to tight controls. Outsiders – the Jordanian authorities and the international aid agencies – were not advisers but rulers, making decisions that had a huge influence on the refugees' lives. While they may have lost less in terms of the sheer numbers of fatalities, when it came to life choices, agency and self-determination, it seemed that the Syrians lost far more.

Informal trade is common in refugee camps, but official data from the Zaatari camp – the number of companies springing up there – quickly marked it out as astonishing, so I travelled to the camp with the intention of finding out how and why the refugees managed so much trade when their economic lives – where they shopped, what they ate and what they wore – was supposed to be under strict control. As I interviewed the camp's ingenious group of entrepreneurs about their lessons on how to rebuild when your economy collapses, I started to hear stories about a second camp – a feared place seen by the Syrians as the bubbling Zaatari camp's evil twin. The stripped-back economics of the two camps shows how informal trade helps to satisfy the refugees' needs, for both simple goods and services and for the deeper and definitional values of choice and agency. The twin camps also show how outsiders, even those with good intentions, can drive a group of people to misery when they misunderstand the human value of an economy.

BUILDING ZAATARI

Until the summer of 2012, anyone heading east from Mafraq, a small town in northern Jordan, would see nothing for hundreds of kilometres. Highway 15 leaves the town and cuts its way through the desert, eventually hitting the Iraqi border and continuing on to Baghdad. Today things are different. After driving for only 10 minutes a city, but in miniature, appears on the right. Close up, it becomes clear that it is no illusion – the white houses really are tiny. A haphazard web of electricity cable hangs precariously overhead. There is barbed wire all over the place and Jordanian guards sit tending to their guns. This is Zaatari, a pop-up town that thousands of displaced Syrians now call home.

The Zaatari camp was formed in July 2012 as Daraa, a region in southern Syria, became the early epicentre of the Syrian civil war. Daraa had been home to 100,000 people, and as the bombs fell they were forced to flee. It is over 50 km from the centre of Daraa to the site of the refugee camp, a good 12-hour walk even for a healthy adult. Many refugees explain they had much longer journeys, travelling from towns and villages far beyond Daraa. As the families walked through the night the older children helped, carrying belongings and their younger siblings on their backs. As the fighting intensified, thousands started to arrive every day. Zaatari's population boomed. By April 2013 it had grown to over 200,000 people and became the biggest and fastest-growing refugee camp in the world.

Then something unexpected happened. As the daily flow of new refugees hit 4,000, the organization in charge of the camp – the United Nations High Commissioner for Refugees (UNHCR) – ran out of manpower. So many people were arriving that they were forced to rationalize their operation, focusing on just a few essentials: health

A displaced world: the 10 largest refugee camps

10 camps ranked by peak size between 2010 and 2016

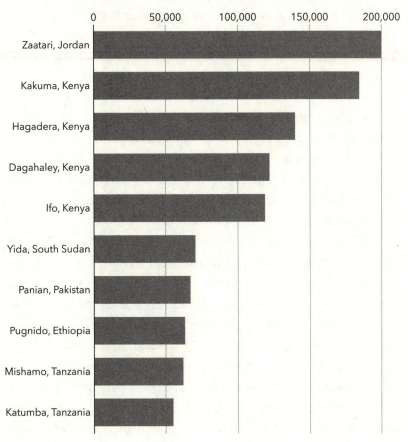

Source: UNHCR, see notes

and vaccinations, food and water, and security. They ceded control of much that is rigorously enforced in other camps: details such as how houses should be laid out, and the number of shops and traders that are permitted. Without close administration, Zaatari became a lawless place, with fights breaking out. At the same time an informal economy flowered as Syrians, determined to re-create a little of the economic life they had left behind, set up mini versions of the companies they had run at home.

At first the shopkeepers operated from tents. Then, when the UNHCR provided wooden caravans for the refugees to live in, the entrepreneurs got hold of these, cut the sides out and created small kiosks. Soon there were outlets everywhere: grocers, a tobacconist, wedding-dress rentals, shops selling pet birds and others selling bicycles; there was even a billiard hall that catered to teenagers. By 2014, when the camp was just two years old, it had over 1,400 businesses. With one company for every six adults, shops were more common in Zaatari than in an established economy like the UK. Kiosks kept on popping up at an incredible rate; today there are 3,000. Other refugee camps have companies inside them too: the Dagahaley settlement in Kenya is a similar size and has around 1,000, for example. But that camp is 20 years old. The scale and speed of business creation in Zaatari make it one of a kind.

As an economy Zaatari performs well. In its turbulent early years, the refugee camp achieved an employment rate, at 65 per cent, that was higher than France's. By early 2015 the unauthorized businesses that the Syrian arrivals had set up were estimated by the UNHCR to be generating 10 million dinars per month – close to $14 million. This did not happen by design but by accident, with outsiders doing little to help and often acting to thwart entrepreneurs in the camp. All this means Zaatari is an economic puzzle worth unpicking. How did people who arrived in the dead of night, carrying little other than the children on their backs, create all this? And what does Zaatari tell us about the importance of the economy in our own lives and what the state should and shouldn't do to help?

THE SMUGGLER KIDS

It takes some time to realize how vital Khaled and his band of child smugglers are to Zaatari. The first thing that becomes clear is who they are up against. Day one in the camp means a visit to the Jordanian security force, the Syrian Refugee Affairs Directorate (SRAD). Inside the SRAD compound burly officers chain-smoke and check

the passes of visitors. They also patrol the borders of the camp, trying to stop contraband going in or out. These Jordanians, often
retired army men, are locked in a daily game of cat and mouse with
the Syrian smuggler kids.

The geography of Zaatari stacks the border-control game in the
kids' favour, making it a hopeless task. The camp is a huge oval, a
little over two kilometres from north to south and three kilometres
from east to west. When you walk down one of the rows of makeshift
homes for long enough, the dwellings abruptly end at a smooth
single-track road that forms a ring around Zaatari and marks the
camp's perimeter. Unlike at the main gate, there is no barbed wire
here, and there are no guards or checkpoints. Beyond the ring road
there is desert and nothing to see but a few Bedouins tending to their
tents and goats. If you are prepared to trek through the dust you can
easily get into Zaatari, or out of it.

The porous borders are not the only factor in favour of smuggler
children like Khaled. It is easy to blend in because Zaatari is a place
to which families fled, and there are kids everywhere. The camp has
an even split of men and women; they marry young and have lots of
children. More than 6,000 babies were born in Zaatari in the camp's
first four years, and 45,000 of the refugees here are under 18. The
smooth tarmac of the ring road is a rare luxury and a valued surface
for playing ball games. Tiny kids charge around unsupervised; teenagers speed up and down on bicycles. Spotting smuggler children
among this pack would be impossible.

The lives of Khaled and his gang are a lesson in the power of
informal – in this case illicit – supply chains to spring up organically,
seemingly from nothing, when a group of potential customers lack
something they regard as essential. The reason smugglers are so
important is that they satisfy the huge demand for goods brought in
from the outside. Rana Hoshan's home is towards the fringe of the
camp. She wears a blue hijab over a black dress and explains, while
preparing a dinner of tabbouleh salad and kibbeh, a kind of meat
pasty: 'We have tinned beef, which we don't want; we don't have

shampoo, which we do want. The kids help make the exchange.' The smugglers play the role of border shippers, meaning that Zaatari can be thought of as having imports and exports just like any other economy. And like any other economy, the camp must have an economic engine that explains its drive. In Zaatari the fuel comes from a huge store within the camp, called Tazweed.

A STRANGE SUPERMARKET

Tazweed is a supermarket from another dimension. In a regular economy you take money to a shop and buy the things that you want. In Zaatari's extreme economy things work in exactly the opposite way. The refugee families head to Tazweed without any cash; they then buy things that they do not want and at the end of the day they end up with money. It is a bizarre chain of events. Understand it, and the mystery of the camp becomes clear.

The supermarket is privately owned and run. It pays tax and rents the land it sits on. There is another, Safeway, located 3 km away at the other end of the camp. This is a piece of careful economic design by the UNHCR. The idea is that having two supermarkets will prevent a monopoly from fleecing the customers. It should mean a better deal for donors that help fund food supply, principally the UN's World Food Programme (WFP) and supporting charities such as Save the Children. It should also mean a better deal for the refugees that shop there.

The supermarkets are located at the borders of the camp – right up against the external ring road. With the houses concentrated at the centre of the camp, this can mean a long walk for anyone wanting to shop there. Thankfully some of the Bedouin farmers who live in the nearby desert own pickup trucks and use them to perform an informal taxi-bus service inside the camp. As Abu Bakr, a Bedouin in his fifties, stops, five women pile into his truck. There is no more space inside so we ride on the back, which is already partially filled with tools, grain and a six-year-old Syrian girl, Nasim. Her mother speaks some English and explains that the girl's name means 'fresh', or 'breeze'.

The Tazweed building is simple and austere – it is essentially a large farm shed: steel girders form the skeleton to which sheet-metal walls and a corrugated iron roof have been bolted on. It is dingy inside, with strip bulbs lighting the aisles. In place of shelving, the interior structures are created by stacking up produce, including a glowing golden wall built from huge cans of Hayat's vegetable ghee, imported from the United Arab Emirates. Elsewhere there are massive partitions built using bags of wheat, sugar and salt.

Despite the rugged no-frills appearance there are plenty of options for the discerning shopper. Tea is a big part of Syrian culture and Tazweed offers a choice of Indian Toledo tea, selling for 1.29 Jordanian dinars ($1.80) for 100 bags, or loose Alghazaleen tea leaves from Sri Lanka, at 2.40 dinars for 500 grams. There are at least ten types of pulses and beans to pick from. There are snacks, including tubs of halva, a spread similar to tahini and made from crushed sesame seeds. Near the checkout there are culinary luxuries: sachets of chicken soup and beef-flavoured noodle pots. This standard retailers' trick – tempting you with additional items just before you pay – makes it all seem very familiar.

The big difference is that Tazweed's shoppers have no cash. Instead they are using electronic cards loaded with credit. Each customer's bill is totted up and debited from these cards as they are presented at the checkout. Atef Al Khaldi, a friendly 50-year-old retired Jordanian army officer, runs Tazweed. He beckons us to follow him through a secure compound behind the supermarket, past a large fountain with the name of the company carved into it, and to his office, to show us how he manages food supply in the face of a constantly changing refugee population. On his computer screen he shows the month's plans set out by the WFP, whose staff keep track of refugee numbers. With other camps opening to relieve population pressures in Zaatari, by 2016 the population fell to 80,000. Atef's screen shows 73,000 beneficiaries for credit, and that this month the cards will be loaded with a total of 1.4 million dinars. The WFP then reimburses Tazweed and Safeway in respect of the credit spent in each store. The system is designed so that money flows directly from the donors to the supermarket owners, without passing through the refugees' hands. Zaatari is intended to be a cashless economy.

Atef explains that each month a family's card is reloaded with 20 dinars per person. This includes kids, so that a couple with three children will receive 100 dinars per month. When Tazweed first opened there were huge queues, crushes and arguments. He explains how everyone arrived at the same time, as soon as the credit was granted: 'Just imagine what it is like when everyone has been waiting for one month to get food.' So the supermarkets asked the WFP to stagger the payments. Atef's computer screen shows that on 2 November families with nine or more members will have their card topped up. A couple of days later those with eight members will get new credit, then those with seven, and so on. This means there are no more crushes, but a steady flow of customers. 'This system is good for dignity and respect,' says Atef optimistically. 'The people can choose what they want to buy.'

While the refugees can choose which supermarket to shop at, their freedom is crimped by other aspects of the e-card system. Each of the cards has information stored on it in five separate 'wallets'. These are like mini bank accounts containing funds that are allocated to different things. As the camp prepares for the harsh desert winter, Unicef has loaded one of the wallets with 20 dinars to allow the refugees to buy warmer clothing. Knowing this, Atef will order the clothes from his suppliers so that Tazweed is stocked up with coats, hats and gloves. Refugees cannot transfer cash between wallets, so aid money designated for food cannot be spent on clothes, and the winter clothing allowance cannot be spent on food.

This top-down economic engineering seems like a sensible system. By controlling the flow of electronic credit, the authorities know how much food is going to be bought each month. And specifying exactly what can be bought with credit is a way of directing donor money. The refugees here do not drink, but men who can afford cigarettes smoke constantly. Since donors would be unable to justify giving people cash to buy cigarettes, the authorities use a system that prevents this, providing choice and buying power, but for only a limited list of items. For items the donors will not fund, Tazweed has a small selection of items that can be bought using cash. 'There are no cigarettes, but we do have luxuries,' says Atef, 'like shampoo.'

ZAATARI'S MOST LIQUID ASSET

At Rana Hoshan's makeshift Zaatari home the family sit on mats, drinking tea and soda, and discussing life in the camp and what it was like back home in Syria. Suddenly, a pair of arms poke through the window and a plump smiling baby is plopped in Rana's lap. A second later an identical chubby infant wearing matching clothes is delivered head first through the window. Everyone cheers. Samaher, the mother of these bemused twins and a long-time friend of the family, newly arrived from Syria, appears promptly in the doorway.

Rana and Samaher, both in their mid-thirties, are educated women. Back in Syria Rana was a teacher and Samaher, who has an English degree, worked in a college. They explain the problem with the supermarket system. They want shampoo and toothpaste for the kids, and wipes and tissues for the babies. But these and other necessities – haircuts, for example – are outside the e-card system. On top of this, many of the brands on offer – particularly the oils and beans – are inferior to Syrian ones, they say. But it is the overbearing rules on health and safety that they find the most annoying. Yoghurt is a big part of the Syrian diet: kids eat it in the morning with vegetables; in the evening everyone digs in to labneh as a side dish. Often these yoghurts are homemade and sold cheaply by a Syrian woman to her neighbours. This is banned in Zaatari on health grounds. Instead, the authorities encourage the use of dried milk and powdered yoghurt, but the women say these are low quality and cost far too much.

The formal economy of Zaatari is artificial, under the complete control of outsiders and, as a result, fails the basic test of any well-functioning market – to be a place where demand meets supply. It isn't just that the supermarkets lack crucial items the refugees badly want; they are also filled with row after row of things no one is buying. This includes tins of Sun Shine and Sunny Sea, both brands of tuna, and a whole Italian section with pasta, spaghetti and various tomato sauces. These are hardly staples of the Syrian diet. Most bizarrely, Brazilian coffee prepared for use in a cafetière is on sale. Syrians drink Arabic coffee and if they are splashing out they want Turkish, which they regard as the best. These products are here to satisfy an aid worker's spreadsheet, rather than the Syrian refugees' tastes and desires.

Tazweed and Safeway do sell things that the refugees find useful. There are plenty of tins of fava beans and *foul moudamas* (fava beans cooked with vegetable oil and spices), which are selling well, and a butcher is cutting fresh meat for waiting customers. But the refugees say that the prices are wrong. One example is malfouf, a large green cabbage-like plant the leaves of which Syrians boil, roll up and stuff with mince and vegetables to make *malfouf mihshi*. The vegetable is a hugely popular staple: tasty, cheap and traditional. At Tazweed you can buy two large malfouf heads for 1 dinar; outside the camp a dinar buys you ten of them.

It is easy to find huge price differences between the Zaatari camp and the outside world, once you start looking. The powdered milk on sale in the camp is vastly expensive: a 2.25-kilo bag of Anchor milk (imported from New Zealand) costs 9 dinars and would wipe out almost half of an adult's monthly e-card credit allowance. A small can of Del Monte canned tomatoes for half a dinar is pushing it when farmers outside Zaatari offer a huge bag of fresh ones for half the price. The location of the supermarkets adds to these exorbitant costs: cans of oil and ghee and bags of wheat and salt are heavy, and the refugees are often old, injured or accompanying children. Shopping at the supermarket can mean paying a Bedouin like Abu Bakr or an off-duty smuggler kid to lug your stuff home.

So the residents of Zaatari don't like the supermarkets much, despite the efforts of well-meaning managers like Atef. But since the e-cards holding monthly food allowances are worthless anywhere else, the Syrian families must use Tazweed and Safeway to do their shopping. The refugees live in an artificial economic system where they have the freedom to make some choices for themselves, but only within the boundaries set by the governmental agencies that run the camp.

At least, that is the plan. Approaching the checkout in Tazweed something strange becomes apparent. The contents of the trolleys are weird. Some people have gone for an understandable basket of items: a mixture of canned goods, tea and coffee together with fresh vegetables and meat. But lots of others are buying huge quantities of just one item, and nothing else. And the powdered milk – which everyone says is a rip-off – is flying off the shelves. Suddenly the puzzles of Zaatari – from Khaled's huge profits to the vast number of pop-up kiosks here – all click into place. This is not a controlled economy, it is a cash-based one. The refugees have found a way around the cards.

Turning the annoying and patronizing e-credit into cash is simple, once you know how to do it. Families buy a large bag of powdered milk for 9 dinars on their e-card and sell it immediately to a smuggler for 7 dinars in cash. The smuggler then slips out of the camp, past the SRAD guards, and resells the milk for 8 dinars to Jordanians driving past, who are happy to buy at this price. Once the dealing is done, the Jordanian outside the camp has saved a dinar on milk (buying at 8 rather than 9 dinars it would normally cost outside the camp) and the smuggler has made a dinar by buying at 7 and selling at 8. But most importantly it means that 9 dinars of electronic credit sitting within a constrained economic system have turned into 7 dinars of hard cash the family can use as they please. This money can be spent on anything that the camp offers. And thanks to the ingenuity of its residents, Zaatari offers a lot.

THE ZAATARI SCHOOL OF BUSINESS

Economists view a country's 'start-up rate' – the number of new firms divided by the number of existing ones – as an indicator of how business-friendly a place is. In the US the start-up rate is around 20 to 25 per cent in a given year; in entrepreneurial hotspots it can reach 40 per cent. In Zaatari the start-up rate for 2016 was 42 per cent. The Syrian refugees have set up so many businesses that if the camp were a country it would rank as one of the friendliest places for companies in the world. The entrepreneurs of Zaatari are welcoming, sociable and happy to share their business tips.

The first rule when doing business in the camp is a familiar one: location is vital. The main strip that takes you deeper into the camp is a road the UNHCR refers to as Market Street 1 but that everyone else calls the Champs-Elysées. (Charities that operate in the camp have their bases near by; the nickname is in part a pun related to the fact that the road starts near a French aid agency's hospital.) A diverse clientele ranging from newly arrived refugees to off-duty aid workers constantly trawls up and down the street and can choose from a host of goods and services: a decent coffee, a haircut, wedding-dress rental, a falafel wrap or chicken shawarma takeaway.

A few hundred metres into the camp most people turn left off the Champs-Elysées as they head to the housing districts to the east. This bustling strip – formally Market Street 2 – is known as 'Saudi Shop' (the firms here operate out of caravans donated by Saudi Arabia). The stores close to the main junction sell durable wares: clothes, televisions, DIY materials and bicycles. Further along Saudi Shop activity starts to thin out and the street becomes Zaatari's version of an out-of-town retail park, offering metal posts, tools and wood to refugees seeking to build an extension to their houses.

Mohammed Jendi owns the biggest store on Zaatari's main streets, a large clothing emporium located on Saudi Shop. His first business tip is the importance of precise information on customer demand, and the way he goes about it is professional: he explains how he surveys his friends and neighbours to find out what they want and need before stocking his store. In the first few months of the camp, conditions were really desperate, and all the refugees wanted was thick and warm clothing to make it through the harsh winter. But as things improved, the refugees began to want to express individual tastes. So Mr Jendi now offers men an array of colourful tracksuits, sports jackets, and jeans in various cuts. Women can choose from a wide selection of shawls, handbags and high heels.

A little further down Saudi Shop we find what I am told is the best bicycle store in Zaatari. The store's owner, Qaseem Al Aeash, explains that his success is also down to the desire for individuality. The refugees are not allowed cars or motorbikes, but the camp is packed with bicycles. This includes 500 sturdy two-wheelers donated by the Netherlands. The donated bikes are loved and can go for up to $200 when sold. The only problem with Dutch bikes is that they all look the same: they are all the same design and started off black or dark blue.

So Qaseem helps his customers pimp their bikes, spraying them bright colours and adding bells and pinstriped grips. His own steed is a beauty: designed to look like a motorbike, it is bright yellow with red stripes and reflectors, twin exhaust pipes stuck to the sides and dual speedometers. I comment on the large VIP sign he has stuck to the back: 'Of course,' says Qaseem: 'I am a businessman.'

The refugees had to adapt when they came to the camp, and they often run businesses that are related only loosely to what they did back at home. Mr Jendi says he knew little about clothing – he ran a small supermarket back in Syria – but he knew about retail. Qaseem Al Aeash was a mechanic and found himself in a refugee camp with no cars. He first tried working as an electrician, providing and mending lighting in people's homes, before switching to bikes. A neighbouring entrepreneur, Tarek Darra, explains how he repurposed his skills too. Before becoming a refugee he designed houses; in Zaatari he works as a carpenter, running one of the main joineries in the camp.

But Mr Darra rues his decision to set up as a carpenter, explaining that the trade is struggling. The problem, he says, is that his products are too durable. Refugees' lives are tough and money is tight, so possessions are cared for and made to last. Once people have a bed, shelves and cupboards, they do not need his help with woodwork again. 'You should always try to set up a business where people keep coming back,' he says glumly. Mr Jendi agrees: he must keep switching the styles and colours of the clothes he sells to stoke demand.

This on-the-ground wisdom is exactly the sort of lesson taught to budding entrepreneurs on MBA courses, who study the success of companies such as Rolls-Royce – who, in addition to its car manufacturing business, sells aircraft engines to airlines and makes money servicing them – and, more recently, in the business-school obsession with subscription models for music, clothes and food, all designed, as the Syrian entrepreneurs have done, to keep the customer coming back. As I talk with Qaseem, he is soldering away, mending the dynamo on a longstanding customer's bike. This is the beauty of the bike business, he says: once you sell someone a bike, you know you have a future customer for cycle maintenance.

Zaatari's entrepreneurs keep a close eye on costs and have some rare advantages in doing so: electricity supplies are often informal spurs from the main grid – a practice that is banned but means free power – and there is no tax collected inside the camp. Zaatari, in its own accidental way, is akin to the kind of state-subsidized enterprise zone that governments, most notably China, use to stimulate activity. While not sustainable in the long term, it does offer a lesson in how an economic hub can be launched by lowering entrepreneurs' costs and barriers to entry. Once off the ground, the business community in Zaatari explained how they seek their own efficiencies too: one of the secrets of Hasan Al Arsi's success as a baker is economies of scale, he explains. Knowing that *knafeh* – miniature pastry nests with nuts nestling inside – is a strong seller, he makes huge quantities of these and other baked sweets at his main bakery. Doing these big batches keeps costs down, and his employees then transport trays of baked goods to his four outlet kiosks dotted across Zaatari. Offering a taste of Syria is so popular that he is opening a fifth outlet soon. This hub-and-spoke method of cooking and selling food is exactly the so-called 'dark kitchen' model now being pursued by Travis Kalanick, the founder of Uber.

Other entrepreneurs pull on the refugees' nostalgia for their lost homeland too. Hamid Harriri's sweet shop mainly sells knockoffs including 'Chiko' chocolate eclairs, an imitation of the Cadbury's version. But his most prized candies are the real thing: sugar-coated almonds called *mlabbas* that he imports from Syria. Hamid explains that Damascus is famed for these sweets and that people like to give them as gifts during the Eid celebrations at the end of Ramadan.

The shopkeepers all agree that while the yearning for Syria helps them sell, it is also a risk. As the war shifted to Aleppo, almost 500 kilometres north of Daraa, some Syrians in Zaatari heard that their villages were safe. They began heading back in 2015, and many shopkeepers say that the numbers in the camp are dropping below official estimates because of this. When friends leave Zaatari for this reason the refugees are happy. The camp authorities, concerned about the resources needed in an overcrowded camp, are more comfortable with Zaatari shrinking too. But for the Syrians there is a tension that comes with this transience. A declining population, meaning fewer customers and fewer jobs in the camp's informal economy, is a big worry for those who must stay.

And people are leaving the camp for less happy reasons too, the refugees say. The Jordanian government and UNHCR have understandably never looked fondly on the bustle of the Champs-Elysées, which after all rests on the conversion of homes to businesses and flipping aid credit, via smuggling, into hard cash. In response to Zaatari's uncontrolled growth they opened a new camp in 2014. This new town, in many ways Zaatari's twin, seems to act as a dark force on the psyche of the refugees here. They don't mention the other camp much, and when they do they lower their voices. Some of the refugees I speak to say they would rather face the war in Syria than be sent there. It is perhaps the greatest risk that the rule-breakers and smugglers in this entrepreneurial hotspot face. Step out of line in Zaatari, and you could be sent to Azraq.

INSIDE AZRAQ

FROM OASIS TO MIRAGE

That the Syrian refugees are so fearful of Jordan's second-biggest camp is an irony: for millennia the little town of Azraq was a haven. The site of the only oasis in the arid land that now forms eastern Jordan, its name means 'blue' in Arabic. The water here travelled for hundreds of kilometres through aquifers – channels of porous rock running under the desert – and met with rivers to form deep pools. There were palm trees and eucalyptus groves, migrating birds, buffalo and wild horses. It was the kind of lush and fertile land that the Syrian refugees describe when they talk about home.

The water made Azraq a place for rest and recuperation. Traders would stop there, watering their camels and picking up supplies as they travelled the incense road transporting frankincense, myrrh and spices from South Arabia (modern-day Yemen) to Europe via Syria and Turkey. Soldiers have rested in Azraq too, with the Romans building a fortress, Qasr al-Azraq, there in the third century. The castle became Lawrence of Arabia's 'Blue Fort', used as a refuge in the winter of 1917–18, ahead of his final assault on the Ottoman stronghold at Damascus.

Today Azraq is no oasis. The Jordanians began to tap the springs in the 1960s to feed arid Amman and ran them dry within 20 years. The buffalo and wild horses are long gone, the birds land elsewhere on their migration. But some things have not changed: the fort still stands, and there are a few hardy travellers (Azraq is included in a 'castle loop' that tourists with cars can drive around). And the town's modern purpose is the same: R & R for those engaged in trade and war. Hundreds of oil tankers – all of them with Mercedes-Benz cabs – line the nearby motorway as the drivers stop for food. Off-duty military men from the nearby air base mill around, or sit drinking coffee.

The Azraq camp is 25 km outside town and at the end of 2018 was home to around 40,000 Syrian refugees. These two places, Azraq and Zaatari, dwarf the other camps that Syrians can end up in. (Mrajeeb Al Fhood, a camp close to Zaatari that houses around 4,000, is the norm for the constellation of small satellite camps.) It is these two huge camps that Syrian refugees talk about, discuss and debate. Like its twin camp, Azraq is a place of extremes, but its extremes are often the opposite of Zaatari's.

To find that the refugees feared Azraq was puzzling, since everything I had read about the place before arriving in Jordan sounded good. The new camp was built to a strict design, the fruit of meticulous planning rather than the haphazard way that Zaatari, built under emergency conditions, had been allowed to mushroom. Newspaper reports and official documents explained how the authorities had 'learned lessons' from Zaatari. This meant that instead of grouping houses around a central core – presumably seen as dense and chaotic – Azraq housing was designed to spread between a series of separate 'villages' with plenty of space between them. Much was made of the new camp's village structure, and it sounded much nicer than the austere language of 'Districts' and 'Market Streets' used to describe Zaatari.

The launch of the camp, in April 2014, hailed other improvements too. The homes were sturdier: proper structures with foundations fixed into the ground, and much larger than the cramped caravans and flimsy tents of Zaatari. The electricity supply was said to be better, with every household connected to a proper grid capable of providing enough power to run fridges, lights and fans. These benefits came with a cost – $63.5 million was spent on roads, buildings and power lines – and the investment in Azraq seemed like an impressive commitment to creating a true sanctuary for Syria's refugees.

In truth the most impressive thing about Azraq is the success of the PR campaign surrounding it. The reality became clear when I met my friendly press minder there – the only place in Jordan where this was required. The minder's main job was to steer conversation, and our car, away from a part of the camp called Village 5 and to tell us repeatedly there was nothing interesting to see there. The fact that my permission letter said I could conduct interviews everywhere 'except Village 5' and the fact that the local SRAD chief flew into a rage when we asked about this mysterious place told us otherwise.

The truth about Azraq is that it is more like a huge open prison than a network of connected hamlets. The atomistic village system may once have been designed to foster community among smaller groups, but when I visited it was there to enforce segregation. Village 5 is not a refuge; it is a huge open pen surrounded by secure fencing and used to hold refugees, including children, arriving from towns known to be ISIS strongholds. The much-touted electricity supply is poor: thousands of homes are not connected to the grid and those that do have a link are hardly better off since the power supply often fails. It quickly became clear that it was best to follow a simple rule of thumb in Azraq: when you are told something official, the opposite tends to be true.

VILLAGES AND PRISON BLOCKS

The notion that Azraq is a better place for refugees quickly evaporates when you see the camp's front gate. The entrance to Zaatari is hardly friendly, but the guards' rifles are the kind of thing a farmer might own, and hang loosely over the shoulders of teenagers and young men who chat and smoke. The gate at Azraq is that of a military base. The guards have large sub-machine guns strapped tightly to their chests and wear immaculately polished boots. No one is chatting or smoking, the fences are high and sturdy-looking, and next to the gate an armoured truck sits under a sun shade.

After a 90-minute wait our minder arrives to escort us to the camp. There is still nearly 2 km to drive before, over the brow of a hill, the settlement finally comes into view. It is built on land that forms a huge shallow bowl. The homes are arranged on these gentle banks, with hospitals and a large mosque in the bottom of the bowl, in the centre. From afar you can see the strict urban planning, with rows and columns of houses that form a perfect mathematical grid. The Syrian refugees' homes gleam silver and white against the oranges and reds of the desert floor. From a distance the geometric symmetry and order give it a kind of minimalist beauty.

Up close the camp is less pleasant. Its grid system is nothing like a real village, either in Syria or anywhere else in the world, and in urban design – as in so much else in here – the desire to control the refugees' lives has won out. In Zaatari, where the artificial economy has been replaced by a thriving informal one, shops sell all manner of kit for DIY and gardening; refugees have painted the outside of their homes in bright colours and put murals on the walls; many have planted small gardens. Here there is none of that: the walls are all pristine in white and grey, the ground too dry for anything to grow. The space, cleanliness and order soon become disturbing, giving it a forbidding feel. Azraq also has a ring road of sorts, but outside it there are no trees, Bedouin camps, farms or houses. One little girl stands alone, perhaps half a mile out into the desert, pushing a toddler in a full-size metal builder's wheelbarrow. It looks as if she is lost in the desert. This forlorn place is just an hour-and-a-half's drive from Zaatari, but it is worlds away.

A VERY DIFFERENT ECONOMY

Nasreen Alawad is a 39-year-old refugee with soft, kind eyes. She wears a long black robe, with a pale-blue headscarf; her voice is unusual – a high falsetto – and she speaks good English. Like most Syrian refugees, Nasreen is a Sunni Muslim. Many of the female refugees shake hands but she prefers not to, and the first time we meet she teaches me how best to greet women here: a slow movement to touch your own chest with your palms, centrally, just below the throat. Nasreen is bubbly, likes to laugh and gossip, and enjoys probing visitors about their family and love lives. She fled from Syria on New Year's Day 2013.

Back in Syria Nasreen had been a schoolteacher; having studied for a master's degree in English from Damascus University, she moved south to a home in Al Shaykh Maskin, a small satellite town 23 km north of Daraa, where she taught for ten years. Her hometown, strategically located on the Damascus–Daraa highway, has been another focal point of the war. Nasreen, her husband Samir and their 14-year-old son Mohammed were wise to leave when they did. In 2014 their hometown was the setting for the battle of Al Shaykh Maskin, a fight involving thousands of troops and an estimated 200 casualties. A second ferocious battle followed there in 2016.

The marketplace that Nasreen takes me to is Azraq's only shopping hub and is relatively new. At first the authorities refused to allow a market of any kind, because it had not been included in the masterplan, but bitter complaints forced them to relent. Rather than allowing the market to form organically, they decreed that there should be exactly 100 shops and that they should be set out, as the homes are, in a strict grid. The news of Zaatari's business success had travelled fast in Jordan, so local entrepreneurs lobbied to be able to supply goods to the Syrian arrivals. To ensure things were fair, each of the shacks was given a number and they were divvied up equally: odd numbers may only be used by Syrian entrepreneurs, while even ones are solely for Jordanians.

We visit Azraq's newest business, a pet shop owned by a young Syrian, Mohayed Maraba, who is selling birds. Mohayed explains that the shop is just one week old, but that back home in Homs he had ten years' experience in pet shops. Canaries are the most popular pet birds, he says, because of their pleasant song, so he has found suppliers in Amman that can bring them to the camp. He sells a bird and a cage for 18 dinars and like the entrepreneurs of Zaatari is hoping that this is the start of repeat sales: 'First you sell the birds, then customers come back to buy the seeds.' Nasreen beams as a little bird chirps away. She says it is a good idea – she will try to save up for one. But the outlook seems bleak; the footfall here is awful. Apart from us, the only other person in the market is a rotund World Health Organization worker, and the only store receiving his custom is the sole shawarma shack.

Later, as we drive to Nasreen's home, she explains that Azraq's meticulous planning does have upsides and that her family is a good example: they have been allocated a house close to the road because her husband's war injuries make it hard for him to walk. We meet Samir, sitting on a mattress at the entrance to their home. This is all he can do, he says, explaining how he was wounded.

Samir fled Syria with Nasreen and Mohammed. But a few days later, once his wife and child were safely hidden in a neighbouring village, he went back to Al Shaykh Maskin to collect clothes and valuables. While he was there an air strike hit the neighbourhood; 11 of his neighbours' homes were destroyed. One wall of Samir's house collapsed in the blast, and a metal girder contained in the wall crushed his leg. He rolls up his loose tracksuit trousers to reveal a limb covered in shiny scar tissue and criss-crossed with lines of stitches from the multiple operations he's had. When he walks he hobbles and leans heavily on a stick. This is why allocating houses in an organized way is so important, says Nasreen: in Zaatari's uncontrolled economy, a housing market has sprung up which is driven by money and power, rather than need.

But on the other side of this bargain are the costs of a centrally engineered and artificially divided economy. Azraq's rules are so rigid that economic forces have been squeezed out of the camp entirely. The market is not just badly laid out, homogenous and dull; it is also desolate, empty and depressing. The rule that splits the shops fifty-fifty between Syrians and Jordanians has not created the equitable and harmonious trading hub the authorities imagined; it simply prevents shops bunching together, and from shrinking or expanding with business fortunes as they do in less rigidly controlled markets.

On Zaatari's main strip every inch of space is used up, with tiny cubby-hole stores popping up to fill the gaps between larger kiosks. At Azraq setting up shop requires a formal application with paperwork to be filled in. Only the better educated can jump these hurdles. Most of the buildings stand empty and unused, gradually gathering sand blown across them by the desert wind.

There is no informal or underground market here either. The camp is miles from the nearest Jordanian settlement and its remoteness isolates it from the outside world, making it much harder to ferry things in and out, legally or otherwise. In Zaatari anything not needed spawns a buzzing informal export trade; anything in short supply is quickly imported. Here, where there are no such market forces, there are huge surpluses of some items and shortages of others. Mattresses are a case in point. Samir and Nasreen's home is like a palace of mattresses: they have at least 50, and have created a huge U-shaped foam sofa around the perimeter of their main room. Everyone has lots of foam mattresses, since every family is given a set when they arrive. But families leave too, and because there is no informal market for trading unwanted things, people donate them to friends. As refugees come and go, the number of mattresses in Azraq steadily increases.

Most importantly, the tight security at the camp makes it much harder to smuggle out high-value items; even if it were possible, the remote location means there are few passers-by to sell to. The trading trick used at Zaatari to flip supermarket credit into cash does not work here; the e-card system works as it was designed and the camp is cashless.

The result, in a world where food and shelter are provided, and informal trade has been choked out of existence, is a striking lack of meaningful work. Some adults can boost their income by engaging in what the authorities call 'incentive-based volunteering'. But these roles – paid jobs by another name – are scarce. Of the 22,000 working-age adults living in the camp in 2016, only 1,980 had jobs, an employment rate of just 9 per cent. One group of men I met in the market had been employed by the camp authorities to keep the place clean, in exchange for official pay of 1 to 2 dinars an hour. But with no trade taking place in the market, there was no need to clean: no packaging to recycle, no discarded malfouf leaves to sweep up. So the men spent the afternoon sitting on the floor with nothing to do, in the shade of one of the many empty shop units. A couple were talking, but most just stared out across the desert.

THE PYRAMID OF LIFE

Abraham Maslow would have had firm opinions about which of the two refugee camps, Azraq or Zaatari, was a better place to rebuild a life uprooted by war. Maslow was born in Brooklyn in 1908, the eldest son of immigrants from Kiev. From humble beginnings he became an influential figure in psychology, teaching at Columbia University in New York City and rising to be president of the American Psychological Association. His most influential work, 'A Theory of Human Motivation', was published in 1943, when Maslow was 35. The ideas he develops in the paper help to explain why many of the refugees in Azraq are so miserable and why those in Zaatari fear being moved there.

Maslow's theory is that every human being has five basic needs: physiological needs (by which he meant food, water and shelter), and needs for safety, love, esteem and self-actualization. These five needs, he said, determine much of what motivates us. Equating them with

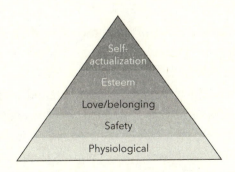

vitamins, he argued that every one of them is needed for a healthy and happy life.

While each of the needs Maslow identified are vital in his theory, they do follow a hierarchy, and although he did not use diagrams, psychology textbooks often set out the five needs as a pyramid, with the most basic needs at the bottom.

Many of the people I met in Zaatari and Azraq had suffered extreme shocks at the base of Maslow's pyramid. For some, food was a problem. Samaher, the mother of the baby twins I met in Zaatari, had explained how she bought six green tomatoes the night before she fled. The tomatoes were all that she and her eldest child, then two years old, had for two weeks while travelling. But for most, the chief motivation was at the pyramid's second level – safety. Maslow wrote that a human in extreme danger can be said to be 'living almost for safety alone'. Perhaps he put that a bit mildly. For the refugees in Zaatari and Azraq, the focus on safety was total: they picked up their children and ran from Syria because they knew that if they did not they would die.

This period of hunger and extreme fear was short lived for the refugees. Once in the camps they were safe, and while the food might not be ideal they would not starve. With their foundational needs fulfilled, they quickly look to move up the pyramid, searching for love and belonging by seeking out friends, family and neighbours from their towns and villages in Syria. This layer of the pyramid has been badly damaged. Every family has lost someone. Those who have died are sometimes the elderly; sometimes they are children; but most often they are husbands. There are thousands of widows in the camps. But the survivors find their friends and, like the Acehnese after the tsunami wave, they soon set out to re-create more of their precious life, including their economy.

It is here that many get stuck in Azraq and where Zaatari, despite its chaos and unfairness, seems a more human model. Maslow wrote that satisfaction comes from esteem that is 'soundly based on a real capacity, achievement and respect from others'. Azraq, an isolated town with a 9 per cent employment rate, is therefore unlikely to be a happy place or one that helps satisfy the need for the esteem of one's peers. Consistent with this, Syrian refugees who are out of work report feelings of isolation and boredom, a lack of self-esteem and a loss of identity.

ZAATARI SUNSET

This is not to say that Zaatari, with its thousands of firms and strong culture of work, is anything close to ideal. In a place that offers so much work, some people – young men in particular – end up working extremely hard. On my last day in Zaatari I stroll through the camp with Ahmad Shabana, a 28-year-old refugee who has been my guide during my visits. We stop at the first shop on the Champs-Elysées for a quick coffee. It is a tiny hut no more than 3 metres wide, painted mint green, and is run by two smiling young refugees, 21-year-old Khaled Al Harriri, and his friend Moath Sherif, 16. They call it Kushk Qahwah, which roughly translates as 'Little Coffee Shack'. Moath hands me a cup and refuses payment. They use only Turkish coffee, he says, because it is the best quality, and have mixed it with *hel* (cardamom), a health-giving spice.

Moath is working happily but when I ask whether he goes to school his face drops. He has not been to school since leaving Syria. He would like to, but the two friends need to run the shop. Khaled agrees: he had finished his schooling by the time the war started, and had planned to continue studying, improve his English and complete a university degree. But life is harder in Zaatari than it was back at home, and his family needs the money, so there is no time for more education.

Many of the children here work. Some, like Ali, aged 12, are apprentices learning their family trade (Ali will be a baker) and still attend school. Others work in much harsher conditions as agricultural labourers. Adults in Zaatari are allowed to leave the camp to take up

short-term employment (15-day stints are permitted) if they successfully apply for a work permit. But some families cannot wait. So each
morning at dawn, hundreds head out of the camp to work illegally
on nearby farms. Those who are caught can be sent back to Syria
or to Azraq. Often the eldest boy in a family will join his father, sneaking out to work illegally. Many boys have lost their fathers in the
war and have become the sole breadwinner, heading out to the fields
alone.

Ahmed is 14 and has been working in the fields for two years. His
family fled from their village close to Daraa after a bomb, dropped
on the second day of Ramadan in 2012, sent a piece of shrapnel into
his sister Esra's chest, piercing her heart. She was nine years old. Now
Ahmed spends his days digging, sowing seeds and picking tomato
crops with his father. They set off for the fields around Zaatari at
5 a.m. The cold and early starts mean that Ahmed is regularly ill, his
mother says. Together, father and son earn 10 dinars per day, far more
than the UN allowance, and enough to allow the rest of the family
something approaching a normal life. Ahmed's 17-year-old sister Waad
and ten-year-old sister Alia both attend one of the schools that have
been set up in the camp. But Ahmed is like Khaled, the kingpin of
the smugglers: school is no longer a possibility for them and they are
forced to grow up quickly.

FREEDOM OF THE CITY

Yet, for all Zaatari's weaknesses, it has a vibrancy that the refugees
here value. Walking through the streets we discuss the colourful
artwork on refugees' homes, and the bright tones that the shops are
painted in. Ahmed explains the importance of self-expression here,
and how each colour has a different meaning for Syrians. Some of
the refugees have used the employment and resources that Zaatari
can provide to satisfy Maslow's final need, 'self-actualization',
expressing their own potential, talent and individuality. I mention
Qaseem's bright-yellow bicycle, with its stickers, bells and stripes.

'It is good, yes, but not the best bike,' says Ahmed. 'The best bicycle in Zaatari is a Rolls-Royce.'

After 20 minutes of searching we find Youssef al-Masri down a backstreet, babysitting his newborn grandson, Khalil. Youssef is in his late forties, with long grey hair tied in a ponytail, and is the only man in Zaatari who wears a bandana. He worked as a hospital technician administering anaesthetics in a surgical ward in Syria, fleeing when he was conscripted by the army to work in a military hospital. His 'Rolls-Royce' is a huge contraption made from the frames of multiple bicycles. It is the size and shape of a car; it looks a little like a Ford Model T, and is painted gold. The car is pedal powered, with an extended chain that powers the front wheels as the driver pedals. Look closely and you can see the skeletons of other bikes that make up the axles and frame. But stand back and focus on the red leather seating, adjustable wing mirrors and sun shade, and you can see why they call it a Rolls.

It is Friday, and as we sit and talk to Youssef the call to prayer suddenly starts. 'We must go,' says Ahmed. We put down our drinks and start to jog through the streets. This trip is unplanned, and so I am not sure if it is safe – there were rumours of ISIS activity in Syrian refugee camps – but by now we are part of a stream of men pushing through the streets and it is too late to turn back. The small mosque – Zaatari has 120 – is a flat-roofed building with a single rectangular room, much wider than it is deep. There are carpets on the floor and the older refugees sit at the edges, resting their backs on the wall. As we remove our shoes and step inside, Ahmed starts to look serious: 'Put your camera away and stay very close to me.'

After attending the mosque, it is as if the rules of Zaatari have changed. Ahmed and I no longer have to ask permission and exchange niceties before entering shops or homes; instead, we are dragged into them by refugees keen to talk. In just a few hours I discover hidden places I hadn't been able to access: a billiard hall, a US-style barber's shop. Bundled into a house, I spend an hour with a schoolteacher, his sons and their English dictionary. They are desperate to go through words they are having difficulties with: we go through alphabetic-ally, getting stuck on 'dweeb', which is very hard to translate, and end on 'dwelling'. Journalists and filmmakers are not allowed to stay in the camp overnight; it is considered too dangerous. But next time I come, they say, I must stay with them here in Zaatari.

The clock is ticking now – visitors must vacate the camp by 3 p.m. – and some of my new friends have promised the best food in Zaatari, and the best place to eat it. Back on the Champs-Elysées we pick up hot grilled-chicken wraps and fizzy orange sodas. Then we go to find the only hill in the camp, seeking out the most elevated home in Zaatari. One of the boys from the mosque pops inside to talk to the owner, and with his permission we clamber up the side of the house and sit on the tin roof, eating our chicken and looking down over the camp.

A VIEWPOINT ON ZAATARI

This is a view of a refugee camp that outsiders rarely see. The photos of Zaatari you find online tend to be taken from planes, giving a bird's-eye perspective that makes the camp look like a grubby brown wasteland. Down in the heart of the camp, life seems chaotic: the roads are haphazard, none of the walls are straight. Here, high up but close to the camp, the order becomes clear: the ring road as a perimeter, the main arteries, the regularity of the mosques and cor-ner shops. Carts carrying fruit and vegetables can be seen travelling the outer streets, selling produce to those who are too old or injured to walk to the market. Down one nearby backstreet a man carries a sack of food, calling out to anyone who has decided to head back to Syria to sell any small surplus they have. Down another a newlywed bride and groom stand in the flatbed of a pickup truck; as the driver pulls away small children chase and cheer.

Zaatari arose from nothing to become the world's largest refugee camp in an incredibly short space of time. Seen from inside it is clear that Zaatari has become a city in its own right. Like any city, it is troubled at times and it can be turbulent. But it is a place where people can rebuild and adapt, re-creating some of what they had back in Syria. Their lives are far from what they dreamed of: Mohammed Jendi did not set out to run a clothing emporium – he was a grocer; Qaseem Al Aeash did not grow up planning to pimp bikes – he was a car mechanic. But these entrepreneurs, their staff, customers and competitors take pride in what they do, and the informal economy of Zaatari means that over 60 per cent of people have jobs. The work can be hard and cold, and for some it comes at the expense of their education. But employment also generates a sense of respect, esteem and, for many, enjoyment.

The lesson of Aceh was that we should cherish a strong economy, since growth is about activities – making, earning and spending – that matter to everyone and are fundamentally human. Zaatari offers a related lesson: we should think of the value of thriving markets in a deeper and more human way too. Markets are often described by economists as a tool or an 'allocation mechanism', a way to get goods and services from suppliers selling them to the consumer demanding them at the right price. Markets, in other words, are there to fulfil our basic needs for food, clothing and housing. When they go wrong, or change, it is these – the more basic needs in Maslow's hierarchy – that are under threat.

This shallow view of trade and exchange is dangerous. It is what makes artificial markets such as Azraq's seem sensible and allows us to miss the true costs of trends that cause economies and their markets to shift and change. In Azraq central control ensures equitable outcomes, guaranteeing that the distribution of important resources is fair. But while refugees in Azraq do not go cold and they do not go hungry, they are left wanting. What they are missing are all the higher needs that are satisfied when trade arises organically, firms are set up as a matter of choice, products bought as a matter of taste. On this deeper view, markets are not just a means to an end but ends in themselves that provide agency, vocation and life satisfaction.

This perspective is often ignored, as the cases of these two camps show. The Zaatari camp is by no means perfect, but it is vibrant; the Azraq camp is something from a post-apocalyptic nightmare. Yet official bodies such as Jordan's SRAD and the UNHCR – the organizations with the power to change these camps – saw the emergence of uncontrolled and unregulated Zaatari as an aberration. So they built Azraq to a model, an idealized camp that had learned the lessons from errors made in Zaatari. Visiting these economies, talking to the people who live there, and seeing them through the lens of the human needs outlined by Abraham Maslow suggests the official conclusions were the wrong way round. The camps offer the first glimpse of a theme that is central to the failures of the three economies in the second part of this book – that even benign policymakers can get economic planning badly wrong.

By 4.30 p.m. on my final day in Zaatari my curfew had been broken. As we hastened to leave the camp, the sun was setting. It was getting cold, and the refugees were battening down doors, preparing for the harsh desert winter night. Approaching the main gate to leave, I noticed a dozen boys huddled tightly together, pushed up against a wire fence. It was an unnerving sight: they were straining, shoving their faces against the mesh and poking their arms through it.

My guide Ahmad explained what was going on – yet another informal trade had sprung up to satisfy a strongly felt need. The fence the young boys were pushing their arms through was not an external one to keep them in, but a barrier designed to keep them out. The other side of the wire is a compound, inside the camp, where various aid-agency offices are based – and these places have Wi-Fi signal. The aid workers regularly change their passwords and try to keep them secret. But the kids find them out somehow, and when they do a brisk trade ensues as the knowledge is sold to anyone wanting to access the internet. The going rate is a dinar. A couple of teenagers, perhaps 14 years old, were pushing their phones through the wire to get close to the buildings and catch a signal, and told us they are using

Facebook and WhatsApp to send messages to their friends and relatives back in Syria, and to find out if they are OK. We asked some younger boys if they were doing the same thing. No, they said, looking at us as if we were idiots; they are playing video games. Their current favourite, a game of territory and war, is called Clash of Clans.

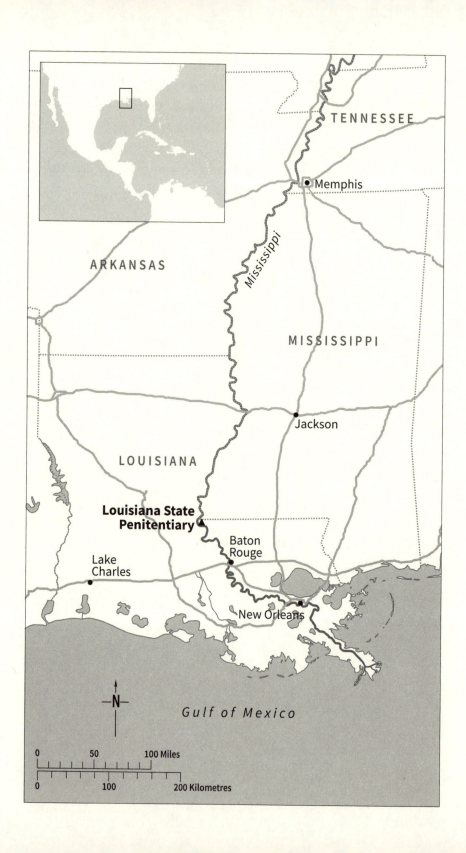

3

Louisiana

Currency is to the science of economy what the squaring of the circle is to geometry, or perpetual motion to mechanics.

William Stanley Jevons,
Money and the Mechanism of Exchange, 1875

ECONOMICS BEHIND BARS

THE ROAD TO ANGOLA

New Orleans seems like a promising place to start a journey. From here the US's greatest river twists north, the never-ending oxbows of the Mississippi defining the ragged borders of ten states, from Louisiana in the south to Minnesota in the north. The legendary Highway 61 travelled by musicians seeking fame and fortune – Robert Johnson in Clarksdale, Mississippi; Johnny Cash and Elvis in Memphis, Tennessee – starts in New Orleans too and goes all the way to the Canadian border. The iconic river and road make this city, Louisiana's largest, seem like a place of opportunity and freedom.

For those born in New Orleans, life's road is often much shorter. After a couple of hours driving north on Highway 61 the swamps and cypress trees of low-lying Louisiana disappear as the road begins to undulate through hills. A turning to the right leads to the pretty town of Jackson with its antique shops, neat lawns and white picket fences. Turning left on to Highway 66 the road swoops and rolls past Baptist churches, plastic letters on their signs spelling out messages – JESUS IS RISEN, and GOD'S NOT DEAD – to the passing traffic. Then the highway stops, abruptly, at a dead end. There is a large wire gate and a security tower. This is the entrance to Louisiana State Penitentiary, the 'Alcatraz of the South', a place known by prisoners, guards and locals as 'Angola'. If you are a black man born in New Orleans, there is a one-in-14 chance you will end up behind bars. If you end up in Angola, there is a good chance you will never leave.

There are 2.1 million prisoners in the US – by far the highest number of any country in the world. That so many are in jail is not because the country has a large population (China's population is more than four times that of the US, and its prison population considerably smaller) but because the incarceration rate is so high. In 2017 the US had 568 prisoners per 100,000 residents, a far higher rate than any other large country. The population of Texas is half that of the UK, while the state's prison population is larger than those of the UK, France and Germany combined. But it is Louisiana that stands out. The state has almost 34,000 prisoners, 94 per cent of them men, resulting in an extraordinarily high male incarceration rate of 1,387 per 100,000 residents, which is more than double the national average. Louisiana is the capital of US incarceration, and Angola is the state's only maximum-security jail. It is the country's largest, covering an 18,000-acre site that is larger than Manhattan. At any one time around 5,200 men are imprisoned here. And most are here to stay: the average sentence for an inmate in Angola is 92 years; over 70 per cent of them will never be released.

Like disaster zones and refugee camps, prisons are places where an individual's past has been vaporized – inmates lose social standing and every aspect of their previous economic life. The vital difference is that the trauma suffered by tsunami survivors and Syrian refugees was quickly followed by help from outsiders. Sometimes badly designed and poorly targeted, aid and assistance is nevertheless there to help them rebuild and prepare for their future lives. A life sentence in a US penitentiary is not like this. Convicts' crimes mean that their lives are contained and controlled by design. Many of the men in Louisiana's prison system will never leave it. Their future, as free people, is over.

Prisons should, in theory, be places like the Azraq refugee camp – artificial societies where the human urge to trade and construct an informal economy are suppressed. Yet across the world underground economies flourish in prisons and history seems to suggest it has always been so. In one of the first published accounts of prison life, George Laval Chesterton, the governor of a central London jail, wrote in the 1850s that 'From one end of the prison to the other, there existed a vast illicit commerce' in which inmates would trade 'wine and spirits, tea and coffee, tobacco and pipes . . . even pickles, pre-

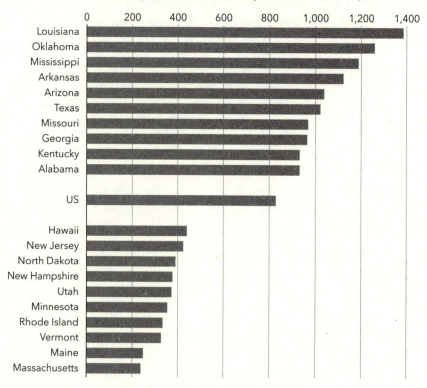

United States of Incarceration

Male imprisonment rate per 100,000 residents, top and bottom 10 states, and US

Source: Bureau of Justice Statistics (2019), data for 2017

serves, and fish sauce'. Prisons tend to hold their own hidden extreme economy, secret markets where people trade and exchange despite all the odds. So I went to Louisiana to meet prisoners currently living in Angola, ex-convicts who had made it out of this jail and those who had been incarcerated in other state facilities.

I wanted to find out if there was an underground informal trade in the state's prisons and, if so, how it was possible to build an economy when prisoners have so little agency, control and choice over their lives. By studying the emergence of economic life on such barren ground I hoped to learn more about the DNA of economic resilience – to hear the elements in setting up an economy that are truly vital, and those we can do without. I expected to hear about the emergence of underground barter economies, with prisoners swapping basic goods and services. Instead, I found a pair of parallel market economies that are sophisticated and run on informal currency systems that are modern, innovative and perfectly suited to their needs. The first step was to head northwest from New Orleans to Baton Rouge, Louisiana's state capital, in search of Angola's most famous former prisoner.

PRISONER C-18

Wilbert Rideau is a small man – around 5 ft 8 in, with a slight frame. Now in his late seventies, he looks more like 60. Wearing a chequered button-down shirt with the sleeves rolled up a little, faded grey jeans and New Balance trainers, he could pass as an academic from LSU, the nearby state university that dominates this part of town. We meet at Coffee Call, a favourite neighbourhood cafe, and Wilbert sends me inside for a plate of beignets. We sit down to share them and he starts to recount the 42 years he spent as a prisoner in Angola.

Wilbert committed his crime, a murder, when he was 19 years old. Brought up in Lake Charles, a small Louisiana city close to the border with Texas, he developed a habit for petty theft in his early teens. At 17, after being caught handling the proceeds of a robbery committed by his elder brother, he was sent to a penal reform school for five months. After this stint he dropped out of regular school and took up a job as a porter in a local fabric shop. His dream, he writes in his memoir, *In the Place of Justice*, was to get to California.

He is wiry today, and police photos from 1961 show a scrawny youth. He was bullied and picked on. This drove him to buy a knife and a gun. But he did more than just protect himself: there was a bank next to the fabric shop and at closing time he went inside, intent on robbing it. He bungled the job – the manager was able to call the police – and so he fled, taking with him the manager and two clerks and ordering them to drive him. His plan was to release the hostages in the nearby countryside and escape west, towards the state border and Texas. But his hostages escaped and as they fled he shot two of them and stabbed another, Julia Ferguson, who later died. Convicted of murder and sentenced to death, he arrived at Angola with the label C-18. The C stood for condemned, with 18 denoting his place on the death-row list. His fate would be the electric chair.

In the end Wilbert avoided execution. He lived in isolation on death row for over a decade and read books voraciously during this time, becoming interested in journalism and starting to write his own pieces. By the mid-1970s he was living in the main prison and writing for *The Angolite*, the penitentiary's in-house monthly magazine. Under Wilbert's 20-year editorship the magazine won many national awards. He first made his name as a prison reporter with a column he called 'The Jungle'. The very first topic he chose, and one Angola's magazine would turn to again and again under his editorship, was the working of the prison economy.

PRISON ECONOMICS 101

Serving prisoners and ex-convicts say the first law of prison economics is unsatisfied demand and the innovation that it stimulates. Cut off from the outside, prisoners find themselves lacking staples previously regarded as essential, and unable to make choices – over clothing and toiletries, for example – that they had previously taken for granted. The urge to get hold of simple material goods is strong, and prisoners I meet describe the first few weeks inside as a shock during which time they learn the rules of their new world and adapt to the reality that they have lost not only their freedom but also their possessions. Today in Louisiana new inmates receive basic supplies: standard-issue clothing, a bar of soap and some lotion. But there are lots of day-to-day items they lack and want: deodorant, decent jeans, better sneakers. It was the same in the 1960s, Wilbert says: while you got simple provisions, a lot of effort went into getting hold of extra comforts.

Some goods are available via official channels, but getting hold of them takes a huge amount of time. Books are one example. Many of the men at Angola – particularly those over 30 – tell me they like to read. They are allowed to purchase books and can be sent new ones by friends and family. But when a prisoner in Angola orders a book or is sent one, it can take six months, or longer, to reach them, since censors need to check the content. The delay is an example of a general theme in the Louisiana prison economy: it operates in a time warp.

Time works differently in Louisiana prisons in part because sentences are so long. The 92-year average sentence in Angola is longer than in neighbouring Mississippi's state penitentiary, and longer than San Quentin, which houses California's toughest inmates and its death row. Even at ADX Florence in Colorado, called the 'Alcatraz of the Rockies' because it houses the US's most dangerous criminals, the average sentence is only 36 years.

The huge number of prisoners and their extraordinarily long sentences reflect that Louisiana, perhaps the most troubled state in the US, is an extreme place. It is poor. It has an average income that ranks towards the bottom of the nation, and poverty and obesity rates that are close to the top. The educational system fails its students, with 26 per cent of them – and 34 per cent of black students – not graduating from high school. Louisiana life is violent: there were 477 murders in 2014, the latest year for which the FBI published data. The murder rate, at over ten per 100,000 people, is more than double the US average, making Louisiana the murder capital of the US, a position it has held every year since 1989.

Most of the murders in Louisiana are committed with guns, and ultimately come down to drugs. Everyone convicted gets a mandatory life sentence, as do any accomplices or friends who were at the scene and who are charged with second-degree murder. But even non-violent crime can mean a huge sentence in Louisiana. The state

ratchets up mandatory sentences for repeat offenders at an extraordinary rate, the upper limit doubling with each conviction: stealing
a car, for example, carries a mandatory sentence of up to 12 years
as a first offence and 24 years for a second. On top of this there
is another rule – a kind of 'four strikes and you're out' – which means
a fourth offence can have a mandatory minimum of 20 years and
a maximum of life in jail. I meet one ex-Angola resident, Louis, who
spent 20 years in Angola on a drug charge. He explains his case
isn't the worst: Timothy Jackson, a man caught stealing a jacket
from a shop more than 20 years ago, is set to spend the rest of his life
in Angola.

In many prisons, simple goods that are cheap and insignificant
on the outside can have huge value inside; in facilities like Angola,
the ultra-long sentences take this to another level. In his memoir,
Mr Rideau explains how tiny improvements can transform a prisoner's life. Like the other men on death row he was confined to a
small cell. Three of the walls – the back and two sides – were brick. The
front wall was a grid of bars, offering no privacy as guards and other
prisoners walked past, and allowing in a cold draught during winter.
Getting hold of a blanket or a curtain to hang over the bars could
have a transformative effect on an inmate's life. When your world
shrinks to a three-sided box, a piece of cloth that will grant you
privacy and warmth becomes a fundamental need you will work
hard to satisfy.

SLAVE FARMING

One way for an inmate to improve his lot in Angola is through official work. Another nickname for the penitentiary is 'the Farm'; soon
after passing the main gate it becomes clear why. After a car park full
of employee vehicles and a small grey outer block holding female
prisoners, the forest disappears and the road becomes a long straight
driveway that continues on through fields planted with crops. It is
April and almost time to plant cotton, which the inmates will harvest

in late September and early October. They toil all year, including August when temperatures can rise to around 38 °C (above 100 °F). The farmland here is productive – the best in Louisiana, official reports on the prison claim.

Angola takes its name from the slave plantation that previously existed on the site. The land had been owned by Isaac Franklin, of Franklin and Armfield, one of the US's largest slave-trading firms. Franklin traded heavily with the Portuguese, with the result that many of the slaves he owned were Kongo people enslaved in West Africa. They were shipped to the US via Luanda, Angola's main port, the site of a Portuguese colony and major slavery operation. Franklin owned four huge slave farms in this region of Louisiana, and named this one Angola after the colony from which the slaves had set sail. The name stuck when the site was bought and converted into a penitentiary by a Confederate Army major awarded the private contract to house the state's prisoners following the Civil War.

Today between 2,500 and 3,000 acres of Angola's farmland are devoted to arable farming. There are grass crops here: corn and wheat together with sorghum used for animal feed and in making ethanol fuel. There are soybeans, the oil and protein from which is used in food products from animal feed to tofu. And, as there have been for the past 200 years, there are cotton plants.

For the Department of Public Safety and Corrections, the arm of the state government that oversees prisons, the agricultural output of the Angola farm is an important source of food for Louisiana's prisoners. In addition to staple crops, fruit and vegetables are grown here, including tomatoes, cabbage, okra, onions, beans and peppers. This produce cuts food costs across the state prison system. The farming operation also raises revenue. Like many other US states Louisiana owns a government-run company, Prison Enterprises, which sells goods produced by inmates. Prison Enterprises brought in almost $29 million in 2016, with much of the revenue coming from the agricultural produce of Angola. That revenue goes to help defray some of the costs the Louisiana government faces in running Angola, which has an annual budget of around $120 million.

ALL WORK AND NO PAY

The prisoners' official work schedule is designed to take up most of their day. Inmates cannot refuse to work, and the vast majority have a job of some kind (exceptions are men on death row or in solitary confinement, or those who have an illness or other medical exemption). There is a clear hierarchy of jobs, and those in the fields are at the bottom. One current prisoner explains why being sent out 'picking greens' is the worst gig in the prison: the shift is eight hours and it is hot, hard work. The men work in parallel lines tossing waste plant matter to their side. Accidentally hitting another prisoner with a discarded stalk can cause a fight; cutting your own hand while picking can be taken as an attempt at self-harm, leading to a tedious investigation. Those who serve a full decade without breaking any rules – fighting or self-harm could both set the clock back to zero – are awarded 'trusty' status. These prisoners get prized jobs such as working as a caddy at the guards' golf club, or as a cleaner at the small museum devoted to the history of the penitentiary located just outside the main gates.

The official payroll here works on a different scale from the outside world. Pay in the penitentiary ranges from 2¢ to 20¢ per hour. Most of those involved in picking greens or other basic farm work seem to be on 4¢ per hour, giving them a weekly wage of $1.60. At this pay rate a convict must work for 181 hours to earn $7.25, the federal minimum hourly wage in the US. Those on the highest pay, 20¢ per hour, can be quickly demoted. One lifer explains how his trusted status was revoked and his pay put to the bottom of the scale when he was accused of taking a wrench from the workshop, something he says he did not do. Whatever the truth, with good behaviour he can expect an annual raise of 4¢, making it back to 20¢ per hour by 2021. Work in Angola is hard, mandatory and not lucrative.

Once cash has been earned a prisoner can spend it at the commissary, of which there are seven in Angola. These official shops are a lifeline for prisoners seeking material comforts. In Angola they carry Russell Athletic sweatshirts, Fruit of the Loom T-shirts and boxers, and Frogg Togg sports towels. They also hold a range of footwear: Rhino work boots, New Balance tennis shoes and two types of Reebok sneakers. The other big category is food. The inmates are served three meals a day but grumble that it is tasteless; the commissary offers snacks that make up for this: sweet and hot Asian sauce, Texas Tito's jumbo whole dill pickle and jalapeño-flavoured cheese curls. The quantities Angola orders reveal the scale of the operation: a recent document sets out a tender for 3,000 boxes – 312,000 packets – of 'Cool Ranch'-flavour Doritos. The commissary is clearly doing a good business.

The official shops are a source of irritation too. Some prisoners complain about shortages; others say that quality is bad. The prisoners know that they are a captive market with no way to switch suppliers. While Prison Enterprises specifies that goods must be new and undamaged, there are suspicions that items are defective and that inmates are getting a raw deal. The biggest complaint is the prices. The prisoners are convinced they are being ripped off, paying more in the commissary than they would in the outside world, and their cost of living rising faster than their wages.

They have a case here, since the disparity between the price of goods and the wages prisoners are paid has become sharper over time. The pay scales used in Angola today have been held at the same level since at least as far back as the 1970s, a step that is both cost-effective and politically expedient. The impact of this policy is a reminder that without sustained pay rises inflation compounds over time to erode workers' purchasing power hugely. A packet of Bugler, a strong blend of rolling tobacco favoured by inmates, is a good example. In the 1970s it retailed at less than 50¢, so a trusty on 20¢ could earn a packet in half a day. Today a pouch of the tobacco in the same light-blue package and emblazoned with the same logo – a boy with his bugle – costs around $8. Someone on 20¢ an hour would need to work a full week to buy a pack.

Louisiana is not alone in requiring its prisoners to work on pay scales that bear no relation to the cost of goods they might want to buy. Legally speaking, prisoners do not need to be paid at all (the Thirteenth Amendment prohibits all forms of slavery and involuntary servitude, 'except as punishment for crime'). Prisoners in Georgia make furniture and road signs, and receive no payment. In Alabama car licence plates are made by a company called Correctional Industries that pays inmates between 25¢ and 75¢ per hour. In Missouri, convicts are paid $7.50 a month for full-time work, an hourly rate of around 4¢. The UK's system is less extreme, but similar. Pay rates start at around £10 ($13) for a 35-hour week and the same complaints arise: favourite canteen purchases – a bag of salted nuts, noodles, breakfast cereal – all sell for over £2. Earning one of these items on prison pay can be almost a full day's work.

TOWNS WHERE PRICES DON'T WORK

In many ways a prison's official economy is like that of a regular town. In Angola there is a world of work, with jobs and pay, promotions and demotions. And there is a world of shopping, with consumer goods and stores to buy them from. In any normal economy these two worlds are linked together by prices: things are expensive in Manhattan and Mayfair because many people are rich, and they are cheap in the Bronx and Brixton where many people are poor. Prices, in other words, say something about the local economy. In Angola, and in other prisons, the official price system has been intentionally broken. Prisons are economic systems in which the cost of goods bears no relation to wages or the buying power of the workforce.

The economic challenge prisoners face is different from those in Aceh and Zaatari. In those two places the economy had been obliterated, and the task was to build a new one in its place, with informal trade acting alongside the assistance of outsiders. A prisoner's old

economic life is gone too but is immediately replaced by a new artificial and engineered one in which the most important connections
of a market economy – the prices that link work and pay, demand
and supply – have been severed, intentionally, by the authorities. The
official prison economy exists but it may as well not, leaving the prisoners to build their own underground markets.

With warnings of economic Armageddon in the future, Louisiana's underground prison markets, another example of economic
survival against all the odds, may be useful case studies. A high-
security prison is perhaps the most barren soil to seek growth and
innovation, so the trades that occur here help illuminate what people
need and what they can manage without when building an economy
from scratch. In Angola, the urge to build functional markets that
provide goods, roles and identity is the root of a thriving hidden
economy with many different jobs or, as the Louisiana old-timers
call them, 'hustles'.

THE HUSTLE ECONOMY

WHEN PECANS TRUMP GREENBACKS

In the underground prison economy things that might seem simple
are hard, and things that might seem impossible can be pretty easy.
The case of John Goodlow and his pecans illustrates why. For 20
years Goodlow was the pecan king of Angola, explains Wilbert
Rideau. Pecan nuts are grown widely across the South, and home-
made pecan candies, which look a bit like a flapjack, are a favourite
treat in Louisiana. The recipe starts with condensed milk, heated on
a low burner to create a thick syrup; pecans and butter are then
stirred in and the mixture cooked until sugar crystals form, before it
is poured into a tray and cooked. Once cool, Goodlow would cut
them into large pieces. They were the best pecan pralines ever, says
Wilbert – 'better than those outside'. John Goodlow's 'candies', large

squares of the stuff, were valued at $2 in Angola. He probably could have raised his prices, says Wilbert: they were so sought after he had often pre-sold a whole batch before he had even finished cooking it.

The fact that making pralines was possible in a maximum-security prison is surprising. Cooking them requires lots of ingredients, as well as pots, a hotplate and an oven. Complex on the outside, this would seemingly be impossible inside. 'Prisoners are never power-less,' says Wilbert Rideau, explaining an aspect of prison life that few on the outside understand. 'They always have the power of rebel-lion, violence, and just screwing up operations and making life hard for the management.' The power prisoners have means management often cooperate and facilitate certain requests, he explains. Prisons are places where on low-level matters power is shared, and where there is room for simple trade-offs to be made. In this place of cooperative control, getting hold of a pan can be fairly easy.

But some things that are mundane and common on the outside are outlawed in a jail. The same refrain – 'security and safety' – is drilled into prison guards, and anything that raises the probability of escape or violence is banned. Many are obvious: weapons, drugs and cigarette lighters are off limits, and mobile phones, which can be used to organize drug deliveries, are forbidden. But a whole host of innocent-seeming items are classed as contraband too: some savoury spreads (e.g. Marmite) contain yeast and can be used in illicit brewing operations; chewing gum and reusable adhesives (e.g. Blu Tack) can be used to make an imprint of a key or lock; baby oil can be used to make an inmate's arms slippery, rendering them impossible to restrain.

Physical money itself counts as contraband. The official prison economy works a little like the one in the Zaatari refugee camp: cash cards are loaded with prisoners' wages, which can be used to buy things at the commissary. This keeps hard cash out of prisoners' hands and is a way to deprive powerful inmates of resources that could help them bribe guards. The logic means cash is treated as top-level con-traband, and any prisoner with 'trusty' status caught handling it would lose their privileges.

The lack of cash is a problem for prisoners operating one of the relatively innocent businesses to which guards tend to turn a blind eye. There are lots of these: in addition to baking pecans, prisoners sell fried chicken, and offer a host of grooming services from haircuts to tattoos to shirt-pressing that allow prisoners to look their best – important ahead of a visit from relatives. These prisoner entrepreneurs can offer the goods or service but cannot accept cash as payment for it. One Angola inmate tells me that a prisoner with a spotless record for good behaviour would be unlikely to take a $5 bill as payment, even if the item being sold is worth as little as $2. Money is too risky to hold, making US prisons one of the few places on earth where the dollar is not accepted. Lacking money, prisoners are pushed towards the most primitive of markets, a barter economy in which goods are swapped rather than bought and sold with money.

INVENTING MONEY BEHIND BARS

The problem with barter is that it can be hard to find a swap that works. Very often the person who wants what you are offering will not own the thing you want. Economists have called the rare situation in which a swap will work out the 'double coincidence of wants' ever since William Stanley Jevons explained the problems with barter, and how money solved them, in a book published in 1875, *Money and the Mechanism of Exchange*. Jevons, born in Liverpool and having studied at University College London, was a founder of modern economic theory and regarded currency as the lifeblood of an economy. The problem with barter, he explained, applied to both primitive economies and more advanced ones:

> There may be many people wanting, and many possessing those things wanted; but *to allow of an act of barter, there must be a double coincidence, which will rarely happen.* A hunter having returned from a successful chase has plenty of game, and may want arms and ammunition to renew the chase. But

those who have arms may happen to be well supplied with game, so that no direct exchange is possible. In civilized society the owner of a house may find it unsuitable, and may have his eye upon another house exactly fitted to his needs. But even if the owner of this second house wishes to part with it at all, it is exceedingly unlikely that he will exactly reciprocate the feelings of the first owner, and wish to barter houses. [emphasis added]

GOOD MONEY, BAD MONEY

To further illuminate what is going on, Jevons outlined four separate roles that money can play. First, money is a medium of exchange, something that everyone accepts and 'lubricates the action of exchange'. Second, it is a 'measure' – the way that prices are set out today. Third, it is a 'standard' by which prices in the future may be set. Finally, it is a way to 'store' value – something that can transport economic value over long distances or through time.

We are used to thinking of currency as something that is officially designated: government-backed slips of paper with a monarch's or president's face on them. But because lots of things have the properties Jevons set out, lots of things can become a circulating currency. When a currency emerges in this unofficial and organic way, it often has particular physical properties that make it suitable. The desirable characteristic was explained by Austrian economist Carl Menger, a friend and rival of Jevons, in 1892. He called it *Absatzfähigkeit*, which was translated as 'saleableness' but today we might call it 'marketability'. Since a currency will be used over and over again in trades the key for Menger was to find an object that could change hands hundreds of times without losing value. Consumer goods – clothes, shoes or books – would be bad things to use as currency since once they are bought they become second-hand and their price drops. Commodities – salt, sugar or grain – are much better currencies: second-hand salt is as good as new.

Further, a commodity tends to make a good currency if it is 'divisible': if it can be easily chopped up and used in smaller trades. Diamonds would make a bad currency since splitting a large diamond into two destroys much of the value. Another key criterion is durability. Food commodities that rot or spoil, such as milk, wheat or butter, would make a poor currency. And finally ease and cost of transport matters. Cotton, which is divisible and durable, may seem like a good informal currency, but it is so light that it lacks value in small quantities: any meaningful trade would require transporting huge sacks of it.

FROM WOODPECKERS TO MACKEREL – WEIRD MONEY

Societies have chosen to use all sorts of strange things as currency. On Rossel Island, which lies 240 km south-east of Papua New Guinea, a currency based on ndap shells developed: they were light and durable, and varied sizes gave 22 different values that could be divided and combined to come up with any price. The US's indigenous Yoruk people, based in northern California, valued woodpecker scalps highly, and used them in head-dresses. The scalps became a form of currency: the large pileated woodpecker was worth more than the small acorn woodpecker, giving the tribe a currency that had small and large denominations. Others have used any light, durable and divisible commodity: salt was used in Rome, ancient China and modern Ethiopia; the Aztec kingdom of Central America used chocolate (cacao beans).

Prisons have a rich tradition of inventing informal currencies too. In London's Cold Bath Fields prison the 'vast illicit commerce' of the nineteenth century was lubricated by using cigarette papers as currency. In modern UK jails (where, as in Angola, cash is banned) inmates often use shower gel capsules or rosary beads – both easy to get hold of – as their informal cash. Small, light, divisible and durable, handfuls of capsules and beads fit perfectly the descriptions set out by the nineteenth-century economists.

In the US there are many different types of prison: public and private, long and short term, and the rules for what goes on in them vary state by state. This means there are variations in the menu of goods circulating, and in which of them is most suitable as money. Postage stamps are small, light and highly durable, and have been used as currency in many US prisons. But stamps are considered so close to hard cash that their use is often banned. When stamps are not an option, packets of ramen noodles are often used. In these prison economies this edible currency is given the nickname 'soup'. In recent years a popular currency has been canned mackerel. Each can costs around $1.40, and cans are light, durable and long-lasting. These 'EMAK' (edible mackerel) currencies have become so common in the US's vast prison population that some have suggested they have influenced prices for mackerel in the outside world.

The most obvious prison currency, something always saleable and easily divisible into defined smaller units, is tobacco. For over a century the underground trading in Angola ran on it. By getting round the difficulties of barter and the danger of using contraband dollars, cigarettes and rolling tobacco became a currency to rely on. Then, after 100 years of currency stability, everything changed. In 2015 Angola banned smoking, with tobacco and cigarettes both becoming contraband. Around the same time an aggressive new designer drug, Mojo, began to infiltrate the prison, and many men became hooked instantly. The underground economy was rocked. Its currency was now illegal, yet there was huge demand for this new drug. The foundations of the prison economy had shifted: what many men wanted changed, as did the way they could pay for it. The response in Angola, and across Louisiana's prisons, was to adapt rapidly, inventing a new currency, one that is as high-tech as the designer drug it is often used to purchase.

OLD FARM, NEW DRUGS

On my second trip to Louisiana I arrange to meet an ex-convict in his mid-thirties, recently released after 16 years in state prisons, including Angola. 'Most people in the prison system are looking for some stimulant or kind of way to get high,' he says. 'It is a way to kill time.' But there is a more specific reason Mojo – a type of synthetic cannabis – took off so quickly: 'It changes so much that it is hard for them to drug test for it. So it's a highly valued commodity and a lot of people want it.' Continual adjustment and refinement of the compounds used in synthetic cannabis means there are thousands of variants, making the task of designing an accurate detection test for the drugs fiendishly difficult.

The first death linked to synthetic cannabis in Louisiana was recorded in 2010 and the state's governor banned the chemicals used in Mojo the same year. But the difficulty of detecting the drugs meant they became a drug of choice for groups subject to regular testing including college athletes, military personnel and prisoners. Mojo use quickly affected college football and basketball teams, and the drug became particularly popular in the US Navy. In 2011 there were more than 700 investigations into cases of its use by seamen; it was so popular that naval hospitals became leaders for research into the impact of its recreational use. The drug – a new product that inmates needed and would work tirelessly to get hold of – was also a huge shock to informal prison economies.

Louisiana prisoners remember Mojo first appearing in 2010 or 2011. The ex-convict in New Orleans remembers the rumours circulating: 'Everyone was like: "Man, this is synthetic weed," and they said, "You can smoke it and pass the drugs test." But in my mind I was like, "They test you for THC, so if it is not THC that is getting you high, what is getting you high?" ' It was a wise decision to be cautious, he recalls. 'I said no, but they all started smoking it. Some started having seizures, some were having aneurysms, and people were freaking out and getting paranoid and scared. I saw a dude get butt naked and jump in a dumpster – and he refused to come out. They were going crazy on it. But they loved it.' The first rule of prison economics is unsatisfied demand, and on this measure Mojo had become king in Louisiana's prisons. The desire was huge. The challenge was how to get it in, and how to pay for it without getting caught.

THE WORKING LIFE

Prisoners in Angola call the guards 'free people'. They also use the phrase to describe anything on the outside, referring to 'free people's clothes' and 'free people's food'. When pressed on what they would wear or eat outside they don't mention a specific garment or dish, tending instead to reply, 'I don't know – whatever I wanted.' What the prisoners miss on the inside is the freedom to choose.

The reality for many free people living in this part of rural Louisiana is that the choice of career is limited. A couple of big manufacturers remain: the paper mill based in St Francisville that employs around 300 people, and the River Bend Nuclear Station, owned by Entergy, that employs close to 700. These offer well-paid roles. Wages at the mill average over $60,000 and engineers at the plant can earn over $100,000. But these jobs tend to require either a college degree or technical training; the nuclear plant hires a lot of ex-military people, often trained by the US Navy. Many here fail to graduate from high school.

For those with no degree or technical training the options are thin. Agriculture was once a big employer of unskilled workers in Louisiana but less than 2 per cent of jobs are in the farm sector now. Local job advertisements show what remains: openings in retail, with around 50 posts up for grabs at Home Depot and Dollar General or at the fast-food restaurants that fringe Highway 61, with jobs on offer at Sonic and at Wendy's, Burger King and Pizza Hut. Many of these posts start near the federal minimum wage of $7.25 and offer few benefits.

Or there is Angola, which with its 1,600 staff is by far the largest employer in the region. The penitentiary is constantly hiring, and the terms are decent by local standards. In 2017 a cadet at Angola started on $11.71 per hour, an annual salary of a little over $24,000. After six months of good performance cadets can become sergeants, earning $13.03 per hour. Benefits include 12 days of paid leave, a health plan (the penitentiary will pay for half) and the chance of a 4 per cent performance-based annual pay rise. By comparison with what else is on offer, working at Angola is a good gig.

But the town of Simmesport, home to many of Angola's workers, shows the reality of life as a prison guard. People living here are nicknamed 'river people' by prisoners because each morning and afternoon a special private craft – the Angola Ferry – sets out across the Mississippi from within the penitentiary, cutting out a lengthy drive to the nearest bridge. Simmesport is a long way from the antebellum luxury of St Francisville or Jackson on the east of the river. The houses are prefabricated and stand atop cinder blocks. Older buildings are made of corrugated iron sheets and are badly rusted. Decaying trucks and tractors lie in ditches, broken boats sit rotting on overgrown lawns. The only buildings in a good state of repair are the churches.

POROUS BORDERS

The economic situation outside the prison means security is a problem. 'These kids are young and uneducated,' says one recently released prisoner, describing young cadets on low pay. 'They can triple their wages by bringing things in.' The scarcity of basic items inside means huge gains are possible for those willing to smuggle contraband. The recent tobacco ban shows just how powerful the laws of supply and demand can be. As soon as it was announced, prisoners realized there would be short supply and the price of a packet of cigarettes spiked, peaking at $125 in the weeks following the ban. A recently released Angola prisoner tells me he could get $40 or $50 for a pack 'any time he wanted' if the cigarettes could be smuggled in.

But smuggling Mojo is an even more tempting economic opportunity. In the free world synthetic cannabis is dirt cheap. Supply is plentiful because illegal laboratories find it easy to produce, and

demand is low because the side effects put off most recreational drug
users. A large bag can be bought for less than $10. Inside prisons, per-
ceptions are different: the fact that synthetic cannabis will knock
you out all day is seen as a good thing, not a bad one. Prisoners will
happily pay $5 for a tiny heap of Mojo to put in a bong. The mark-up
for a smuggler can be 100 times the outlay.

Mojo also poses a lower risk to the smuggler than other drugs.
Sniffer dogs can miss bags of plant matter sprayed with synthetic
cannabis – the smell is different to marijuana and changes with the
chemicals used. Another option, recently discovered in UK jails, is
to spray liquid JWH-018 on to letters sent in by an inmate's family.
The paper looks and smells innocent – like a regular note from a
child or girlfriend – but can later be torn up and smoked. Smuggling
is not risk-free, and in early 2018 a group of young Angola cadets and
sergeants were busted attempting it. But if you are seeking a quick
buck synthetic cannabis is the way to go.

A NEW MONEY MYSTERY

The way the smugglers get paid is a conundrum. The underground
economy in which old-timers and trusty prisoners are involved can
certainly generate kick-backs for guards in the form of food, laundry
or car tune-ups at the prisoners' auto workshop. But these things are
difficult to offer in high-value chunks. And old-timers tell me their
informal currency quickly morphed from cigarettes to coffee and
other items from the commissary after the tobacco ban – currencies
that are of no real use outside the penitentiary. This means that prisoners running serious hustles like Mojo smuggling don't use the default
currencies. A former prisoner familiar with the system explains: 'You
know, I could give you $20 in commissary, or I could give you $5 in
cash. You are going to take the cash. That is something you can actually
send home – that you can actually do more stuff with – it is how you
persuade the guards to bring the other contraband in.'

The use of dollars inside the prison is a puzzle. Anyone running a major drug operation is going to need to shift large cash balances, but dollar bills are something sniffer dogs can detect. The notion that cash is being transferred to the outside world is also surprising, since digital payments between accounts can be traced. In fact, it turns out drug traders and smugglers face none of these risks because Louisiana prisons have a remarkable new currency innovation, something far better than tobacco or cans of mackerel. The new currency means dollar notes are not being handled, and bank accounts are not being linked. 'Cash is contraband, but people have got cash,' my contact explains, 'but it is not cash like cash in hand. It is untraceable. It is all based on numbers. People pay each other with dots.'

INVISIBLE MONEY

The new 'dot' payment system is the latest in the ever-evolving system of prison currencies. Like Mojo it started with a technological innovation, an idea that Blockbuster Video, founded in Texas in 1985, came up with in the mid-1990s. Like other retailers the company operated a gift-certificate system akin to book tokens, allowing a parent or friend to give credit at Blockbuster stores as a gift. But gift certificates are annoying: customers can lose them and worse, from a shop's perspective, they create petty remainder balances after a purchase and these low amounts (often $2 and below) are redeemable for cash. That means when a parent buys a $20 gift certificate, the child using it might only generate the store $18 of sales.

So in 1995 Blockbuster launched the first store card. Plastic and shaped like a credit card, it could be loaded with dollars. Unlike a paper gift certificate, it was durable, allowing parents and relatives to make periodic uploads as part of an allowance. The card formed a so-called 'closed loop' between the person loading the credit (the parent), the company providing the goods (Blockbuster) and the person consuming them. Other stores quickly followed suit, with Kmart launching a similar card in 1997. By the late 1990s most retailers had adopted some form of gift-credit system using plastic cards.

Financial firms spotted an opportunity and soon offered their own cards. This second generation of cards followed the same core principle: money had to be pre-loaded for anything to be spent. But a vital change was made. The new cards were an 'open-loop' system: the person with the card was not restricted to a specific store but could spend the money anywhere, or even withdraw it as cash. The initial idea was that the cards would be used by young adults – parents loading college kids' cards with a monthly allowance – or as a modern alternative to traveller's cheques.

The use of pre-paid cards has rocketed in the US in the past 20 years. They were the fastest-growing form of payment in the 2000s and usage tripled from 3.3 billion transactions in 2006 to 9.9 billion in 2015. While the innovation was a hit, the initial customers the financiers had in mind – well-to-do parents, cash-rich retirees on trips to Venice – was way off. Pre-paid cards are favoured by people with a poor credit history, usually because they have overdue debts or are recent immigrants. Users are most likely to be African-American, female, unemployed and have no college degree. They are predominantly used in the South, with Louisiana's neighbour Texas the epicentre.

The name of the prisoners' new currency takes its name from the popular Green Dot brand of these cards, which carry the Visa or MasterCard logo and can be used to make purchases wherever regular credit and debit cards are accepted. The user sets up an account name for the card, but no proof of address or ID is needed and so an alias can be used. They then buy a second card, this one a single-use scratch card called a MoneyPak, which is used to load the debit card with credit of anywhere between $20 and $500. Both cards can be bought pretty much anywhere: at Walmart, CVS or any other pharmacy. Scratching away the back of a MoneyPak reveals a 14-digit number. This number, the 'dots', is the vital link, carrying up to $500 of buying power. The user goes online, logs in to their account and enters the 'dots', and the credit appears, instantly, on their debit card.

The process is a little fiddly, but it also has features that make it a powerful new method for making illicit transactions. The person buying the Green Dot card can pay in cash, as can the person buying a $500 MoneyPak, so there is no trace of who owns them. The beneficiary of the credit does not need to see or even be in the same location as the MoneyPak; all they need to know are the numbers. Texting someone the 14-digit 'dots' using a contraband phone, or sending them a photo or letter with the numbers, or simply communicating the numbers over a telephone call will do. The dots are a currency close to cash: an instant, simple and safe transfer of value over long distance.

To make a large cash payment a prisoner asks a friend on the outside to buy a MoneyPak and to pass on the dots once they have done so. These 14 digits, as good as hard cash, can then be exchanged with a guard or another prisoner for something in the prison, including drugs. By exchanging dots instead of cash, the prisoners keep their hands clean. The free people on the outside – one buying the MoneyPak, the other receiving its value on a Green Dot card – do not need to meet each other, know each other or link bank accounts. Using pre-paid cards in this way creates an informal currency that is durable, divisible into payments as small as the MoneyPak minimum of $20 and is accepted everywhere. It fits precisely the standards for a good currency that Jevons and Menger set out centuries ago.

MONEY AND TRADE – FOR BETTER OR WORSE

There are broader lessons too, from this extreme currency invention. Many policymakers regard the rise of online banking as a way to tackle illicit trade and money laundering because banking digitally – using apps or the internet to make payments between accounts – leaves a trace. This, the theory goes, should mean digital economies are easier to police than cash-based ones. Some countries are even considering banning paper money entirely as a way to shift all banking online and clean up their economies. Yet an understanding of how currency innovation works suggests these hopes are credulous: from remote islands to high-security prisons, money invention is informal, organic and – as Louisiana's prisons show – can now be untraceable. The new digital 'dot' currency is reportedly already being used to launder cash across national borders.

Despite the clear damage illicit prison markets can do, an ex-convict in his thirties defends the underground prison economy: 'I've got friends inside. This is how they support their families on the outside.' He explains that those who are not trusty prisoners have limited access to improve their lot inside state prisons. 'So they sell drugs, they run tickets and they gamble; this is how they make their money.' Veterans who have spent decades in Louisiana's prisons defend their economy too, insisting that underground exchanges are a way to keep life inside the prison calm. Simple trades – haircuts, pecans, books, shirt-pressing and even tattoos – that once used tobacco as currency and now use mackerel, noodles or coffee, are a way to make the ultra-long Louisiana sentences a little easier to bear.

PARALLEL PRISON ECONOMIES

For those concerned about the future, the hidden economies of the Louisiana prison system offer a vital lesson, which builds on life in Aceh and Zaatari. It stems from the power of the informal economy in enabling a society to recover from a shock, and the extraordinary levels of effort and innovation that people will commit to establish a trading system if theirs is damaged, destroyed or limited in some way.

Louisiana's prisons have parallel economies. There is the illicit-drug economy that runs on its untraceable dot currency, and alongside it a more innocent marketplace where basic necessities are mediated with some agreed item – currently coffee – acting as a currency. Trades in both economies work because of the most basic law of prison economics – that a prison is a place defined by unsatisfied needs, tastes and demands – that Wilbert Rideau set out. Both economies are self-built, organic and highly innovative. Both show that a currency, the provision of which can seem like the ultimate role of the state in an economy, can be established completely. Prisons show that the human urge to trade and exchange informally is impossible to repress – solutions to future challenges are as likely to come from informal markets as formal ones.

REAL GENTLEMEN

The value that trade in prisons creates means that obliterating it, if it could be achieved, would come at a cost. One reason is that the skills men pick up in underground prison economies can be used once they are released. On my last day in Louisiana I head to the Real Gentlemen Barbershop in New Orleans' Seventh District for a haircut. My barber is Daniel Rideau, now 42, who has spent two lengthy stints in Angola: the first for drug offences, the second for identity fraud. His co-founder, Jerome Morgan, is a local celebrity: sentenced for first-degree murder at age 17, he lived at Angola for 20 years until new evidence revealed that he had been wrongfully convicted and led to his release. Both men started cutting hair in Angola's underground economy. Their new shop, nestled between a record store and a cafe, is a first-class affair: deep leather chairs, swirling barber's poles. The going rate for a haircut is $35.

Both men say that Angola taught them a work ethic they lacked as teenagers. Crime in New Orleans, they say, rests on deeper problems: a lack of role models, an absence of decent jobs, and low expectations for what young black men can achieve. 'At 19 you don't have any job opportunities, especially when you come from an impoverished neighbourhood,' Daniel says. 'So you have to make a conscious decision to go and work at McDonald's or in a hotel, changing sheets. And that is a hard decision for someone to make at 19.' Today they both extol the virtue of work. In addition to the barber's shop they are working on a book about their time inside, and have taken on a young apprentice: 'You are put on this earth to work, period,' says Jerome.

Another example of the value of informal trade is the fact that adjusting to release can be hard. Freedom after years inside is bitter-sweet, old-timers say, because of the loss of the prison network and the roles and purpose it provided. In central New Orleans I visit an organization called the First 72+ that aims to tackle exactly this problem. Housed in a small building that was once a bondsman's office, this is a 'transition house' designed to help those from Angola with their first three days of freedom. Set up by Norris Henderson, who spent 26 years in Angola, and Kelly Orians, a local lawyer, the house helps men deal with the loss of role, purpose and routine, offering them a new network and assistance in setting up anew.

Inside the building an entrepreneurs' club for ex-convicts is meeting, with a group of men in their early thirties discussing new ventures. Many lost their twenties to the prison system as the result of a theft or robbery – 'in at 18 and out at 32' is typical – but today they are discussing how to rebuild, and comparing notes on their businesses. One has recently started a gardening venture and says the next step is to buy his own vehicle. Another, who spent much of his time inside mending the penitentiary's vans and buses, has started an auto-repair business in New Orleans. As well as a place to talk and compare notes, the club offers the men seed funding, with a pool of capital they can draw on to invest – in a new machine, or tools – and repay once sales have been made. In Louisiana, a third of prisoners will be back inside within three years of release, and this kind of project – providing sustainable economic opportunities – is a crucial way to cut this depressing statistic.

Another man at the business hub, Darryl, tells me that the only business he knew as a kid was drugs. In prison he took formal courses, learning how to make lenses for eyeglasses and qualifying as an optical technician. On release he has set up a business doing just this, and shows me the thick blank lenses he starts with, the machine he uses to heat and shape them to each customer's needs, and the wide range of frames that he offers. The fact that eyewear giant Lux-ottica owns many brands, including Arnette, Oakley, Ray-Ban and

Persol, shows the industry is ripe for challengers, he says. Darryl's knowledge of the industry is intricate and sophisticated, his product looks sleek and professional, and his sales are rising. The intelligence and drive of Darryl and his fellow entrepreneurs are a reason for optimism but also a marker of the huge waste so many decades lost in prison represent.

And directly across the road from the tiny transition house, a massive new building shows the scale of the challenge reformers like Mr Henderson and Ms Orians face. Dominating the skyline with tinted windows that gleam in the afternoon sun, it looks like the headquarters of an investment bank or law firm. The shiny behemoth is Louisiana's newest jail, where an investment of $145 million has created capacity for another 1,438 prisoners. With the prison system overflowing, convicts end up staying in local jails like this one for a while, before being transferred to Angola or other long-term penitentiaries. Payphones in the new jail are located near windows that allow a line of sight down to Perdido Street, which means that local families can drive here, park up and wave to their relatives while talking to them on the phone. They have given this trick a nickname: prison FaceTime.

Louisiana, it turned out, was a good place to end an investigation of three extreme economies marked by surprising survival; three places where markets, currencies, trade and exchange exist despite all the odds. As well as being home to incredible stories of resilience this state is a reminder that the world's most advanced countries are failing. Driving away from Perdido Street, I hit Tulane Avenue. This is the thoroughfare that links the French Quarter of New Orleans with the great Highway 61, and it would be easy to picture a tree-lined avenue on which cafes playing jazz music morph slowly into blues bars. Instead, it is a depressing place, a catalogue of economic malaise. There is public under-investment: the hospital looks worn out, drunk ex-servicemen sleep at a bus stop outside the veterans' centre, the court looks like a prison and its walls are filthy. The private sector's offering is rotten: nothing but dingy shop-fronts with neon signs offering debt relief and bail bonds to the families of those awaiting trial. There are huge derelict plots full of weeds and rubbish. On the main street a pothole the size of a large paddling pool is filled with stagnant water.

Economies don't always bounce back; people aren't always resilient. Sometimes things get worse and stay that way. Fraying Louisiana was a taste of what was to come when I visited the world's most extreme examples of economic failure: Darien, Kinshasa and Glasgow.

FAILURE

THE ECONOMICS OF LOST POTENTIAL

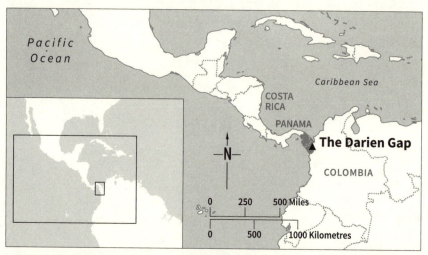

Pacific
Ocean

Caribbean Sea

COSTA
RICA

PANAMA

The Darien Gap

COLOMBIA

N

0   250   500 Miles

0   500   1000 Kilometres

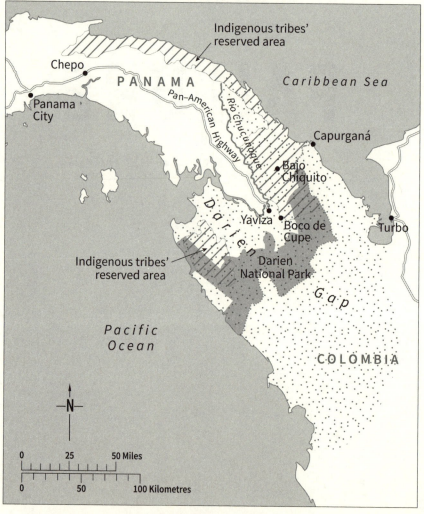

Indigenous tribes'
reserved area

Chepo

P A N A M A

Caribbean Sea

Río Chucunaque

Pan–American Highway

Panama
City

Capurganá

Bajo
Chiquito

Yaviza

Boco de
Cupe

D a r i e n

Turbo

Indigenous tribes'
reserved area

Darien
National Park

G a p

Pacific
Ocean

COLOMBIA

N

0   25   50 Miles

0   50   100 Kilometres

4

Darien

Trade will increase trade and money will beget money . . .
Thus this door to the seas and the key to the universe with anything
of a reasonable management will of course enable its proprietors to give
laws to both oceans, and to become arbitrators of the commercial world.

William Paterson,
A Proposal to Plant a Colony in Darien, 1701

Darien, Thou, Land, devourest men,
and eatest up thy inhabitants.

Francis Borland,
History of Darien, 1779

ALONE IN THE GAP

THE WORRIES OF HIGH OFFICE

In many ways the Panamanian village of Bajo Chiquito is an idyll. Located amid lush green jungle, the villagers' wooden homes sit on high stilts and consist of one large shared room where hammocks swing slowly in the breeze under a thick thatched roof that keeps the family dry. The village is built on a raised hillock that overlooks the shallow Rio Tuquesa, a river with a stone bed and crystal-clear water. The people living here are members of the indigenous Embera tribe whose tiny villages are dotted throughout this part of the jungle. The residents of Bajo Chiquito make the most of their river: mothers and toddlers bathe, wash clothes and play in the shallows watched by herons on the far bank; further upstream there are splashes of excitement from a group of teenagers fishing with home-made harpoons. As the day passes an impressive catch piles up on the riverbank.

Juan Velasquez, the village chief, is sitting outside his home, holding forth on life in Bajo Chiquito while his future son-in-law listens intently. The young man is from a neighbouring village a few miles upriver but when he marries Juan's daughter he will move here into a newly built home, the materials for which will be funded by felling some of the valuable hardwood trees that surround the village. Juan was elected as chief just four months ago but is already weighed down by the responsibility, which includes both the economic management of the village and its security. A thin path leads from the river, up the hillock and into the village – Juan's home sits near this entrance. 'We don't feel safe here,' he says, beckoning to the path and explaining that uninvited outsiders pass through the village most days.

Bajo Chiquito is remote – a few days' hike from the nearest road – yet it sees a steady flow of foreigners. They arrive at any time of day and without warning, Juan says. Most days just a few pass through but some days the village, which has a population of just 300, is overrun by hundreds. As we talk the outgoing chief, Nelson, wanders over. He agrees that foreigners and the security threat they pose are the main problem any Embera leader faces.

As if on cue, Juan's eyes tighten and his focus sharpens. He raises his eyebrows and looks over my shoulder, beckoning me to do the same with a little flick of his head. Six men have walked into the village and these newcomers look totally out of place. The Embera are a short and stocky people: few of the men are much over 5 feet, and the women are shorter. After having an early morning wash in the river most men are bare chested, wearing nylon basketball shorts, with bare feet, or simple plastic clogs to protect their toes. The new arrivals are tall and thin, and wear jeans and Nike trainers. One of them is wearing a red Arsenal football shirt. 'We don't know who they are or where they are from,' Juan says. A tiny place in the middle of a vast jungle, Bajo Chiquito has no walls and porous borders. 'We have no way to protect ourselves if people decide to invade.'

I had travelled to Bajo Chiquito to try to understand the economics of the Darien Gap, a patch of dense jungle and rainforest formally overlapping with Panama and Colombia, separating the continents of North and South America. This little-known land, as with the other places in this part of the book, is an extreme not because of its surprising resilience, but because of its astonishing failure. Darien, Kinshasa and Glasgow are, on paper, places that should be world-leaders, sites of unrivalled prosperity. In Darien's case there is considerable potential in the land's natural wealth: the gold that lies underground, and the rare and valuable timbers, including rosewood, that pack its pristine rainforests. But the asset that makes Darien stand out is its location – it is a bridge between the Americas and the Atlantic and Pacific Oceans. This strategic location means Darien has been known about for hundreds of years, with early adventurers planning a trading hub here that would have linked continents and seas – the sure-fire economic success that would follow making this land a 'key to the universe'.

Yet today Darien is a forgotten place, undeveloped economically and known only for its risk and danger, if it is known at all. In large parts it is a world where rules, regulations and government oversight are at a minimum. The result is a lawless place, inhabited by men and women on the run, including drug smugglers and freedom fighters, as well as the indigenous tribes. The reason these groups are here is the rainforest – it is impenetrable and hugely valuable. It is also shrinking fast: globally, deforestation continues apace with 2016 the worst year on record for tree loss – in both Colombia and Panama, the two countries that are supposed to oversee Darien, the rate of deforestation has increased sharply since. I trekked into the Gap to find out why it had never properly developed, to meet the people living and trading in this little-known geographic crossroads, and to understand the economic forces that meant trade had not protected their incredible land but had put it at risk.

LAND OF DANGER AND OPPORTUNITY

The Gap got its name because it is the only interruption in the great Pan-American Highway. That road is said to be 30,000 km long, and to link the northern part of Alaska with Argentina's southernmost province, Tierra del Fuego. In truth, the highway is not 'Pan-American' at all because there is a gap in the road. The northern section ends in Yaviza, Panama, and the southern section starts around 112 km east at Turbo in Colombia. The Darien Gap sits between the two. The landscape here is stunning, with mile after mile of rainforest threaded with hundreds of rivers. Passable only by canoe and on foot, it is known by locals as *El Tapón*, or 'the stopper'.

Officially the Darien Gap is four-fifths Panamanian, with the remainder lying over the Colombian border. The border between Panama and Colombia is a few days' hike into the rainforest and can be crossed freely if you can get to it. But it is best to think of Darien as a territory of its own. Panama proper, and with it Central America, ends in the region's west; Colombia and South America start on

its eastern fringe. The area in the middle is a place where national-
ities are fluid, with people moving in and out at will. Panama's border
force, the *Servicio Nacional de Fronteras* or 'Senafront', maintains a
presence in most villages, even tiny ones like Bajo Chiquito, but
exercises little control in the wilderness. Farms here are infamous
for building airstrips used by light aircraft carrying cocaine. Close to
Yaviza, one local points out a straight section of the Pan-American
Highway, explaining that locals know to keep off it at night, since
Colombian drug smugglers sometimes land their planes on the main
road.

The Gap's challenge, now and historically, is security. Much of its
fearsome modern reputation stems from the activity of Colombia's
guerrilla army in a civil war that lasted over 50 years. The Revolutionary Armed Forces of Colombia (*Fuerzas Armadas Revolucionarias de
Colombia* – FARC) formed in 1964 as a group of fighters loyal to the
Colombian Communist Party and officially disbanded in 2016 as part
of the Colombian peace accord signed that year. During the war FARC
became best known for the way its funds were raised: kidnap and ran-
som, extortive 'taxation' of villages and towns, and drug smuggling.
Between 1958 and 2016 the Colombian conflict resulted in an estimated 260,000 deaths, with FARC held responsible for around 12 per
cent of them and designated a terrorist group by many countries.

It explains why Juan, the chief of Bajo Chiquito, was so concerned
when six outsiders arrived unannounced in the village. The uninvited guests the Embera fear most are the Colombians involved in
the narcotics trade. They call the smugglers *gente de la montaña*, or
'mountain people', and know that the men, often former FARC
members, can be armed and vicious. Only a few weeks after Juan
was elected as chief four people had died in a gunfight between a
gang of narco-guerrillas and a Panamanian border patrol force deep
in Darien's jungle. Other villages had fared worse: Pena Bijagual,
around 16 km away, was abandoned by the Embera after a gang of
drug smugglers invaded. The sight of six unknown men marching
into this tiny village in the Gap was enough to get the heart racing.

As it turned out, we had nothing to fear from the new arrivals in Bajo Chiquito. The group appearing from the dense jungle was not a Colombian drug gang, but a friendly group of young Nepalese men. They, along with other young men and women from India, Senegal, Cameroon and Venezuela I would meet across the Gap, were economic migrants on a brutal and life-threatening route to the US that uses the Darien Gap as a way into Panama. The migrants' challenge, and that of the indigenous tribes, are linked and have economics at their core. And while meeting them was a surprise, with history in mind their epic journey is fitting. Darien is a place where economic seekers – poor, ambitious, enslaved and dispossessed – have sought shelter, solace and a fresh start for hundreds of years. The illegal migrants are the latest in a line of people who have bet everything on Darien. While for some the undeveloped wilderness of the jungle here spells danger, for others it is a land of irresistible potential. That potential once made long-forgotten Darien the hottest topic in Britain.

AN EXTRAORDINARY GOOD HARBOUR

THE BUCCANEERS

By the 1600s Britain was growing rich on trade: from Cardiff to London, from Southampton to Glasgow, every part of the island had a port that was humming. Merchants started to build grand homes, and imports from overseas allowed the British diet to improve. Potatoes, which had arrived from South America in 1585, were taking off as a staple; coffee shops spread quickly after the first was opened in the 1650s; weird and tasty foods such as tomatoes and broccoli were becoming increasingly available for the wealthy and adventurous.

As well as new things to buy and eat, trade provided an ample supply of exciting and shocking stories. Some of the best tales were about a Welshman, Henry Morgan, who amassed a private army of thousands, raiding cities in Cuba, Panama and Venezuela, destroying buildings and torturing locals as he went in search of gold. The popularity of tales involving trade and exploration meant that Darien became well known when a pair of books by buccaneer friends William Dampier and Lionel Wafer were published in the 1690s. More than just bestsellers, these books about Darien ended up changing European history.

Dampier and Wafer were bright men. Samuel Taylor Coleridge called Dampier 'a pirate of exquisite mind' and Wafer was a trainee surgeon who had been promoted quickly, becoming the senior medic on the ships he sailed on. Wafer's account is particularly exciting. Both men are part of an expedition aiming to hike across Darien and get to the Pacific coast, but disaster strikes when a clumsy pirate accidentally shoots Wafer in the knee, scorching it with gunpowder. Left in the jungle, he befriends a native tribe who heal his injury with a paste made from exotic plants chewed in their mouths. But they then begin to suspect his role in the recent death of an Indian guide and build a large fire on which to burn him alive. Wafer avoids this fate by teaching the tribe European medical treatments and is instead celebrated as a demigod. After promising the tribe's chief he will return to marry his daughter – the only way he is allowed to leave – Wafer then treks alone through the jungle before finding his shipmates on the Caribbean coast and setting sail for Cartagena. It is like the script of a Hollywood blockbuster.

The original Darien hiking tales were read aloud in European coffee shops to great excitement. They made the place seem like a paradise. Wafer's audiences heard of land that abounded with 'brooks and perennial springs' and of ground in which crops would 'grow very luxuriantly, considering the exceeding richness of the soil'. The 'delightful groves of trees' are classified in minute detail, with descriptions of many valuable types of wood. The food Wafer ate sounds mouth-watering: he describes barbecuing 'nourishing and well-tasted' hogs followed by the ultimate luxury of the day, the pineapple: ''Tis very juicy; and some fancy it to resemble the taste of all the most delicious fruits one can imagine mix'd together.'

Darien's natural resources excited Britons, while its strategic location created a kind of mania in this age of trade and exploration. The accounts and maps that started to appear made clear that Darien was the narrowest part of the Central American isthmus and that it was traversed by large rivers. The river system was intoxicating to entrepreneurial traders because it opened up the possibility of trading not just along the Caribbean coast, but crossing the Americas to trade along the Pacific shore at nearby hubs of shipbuilding and commerce such as Guayaquil, in modern-day Ecuador, which were at the time controlled by the Spanish. Landing a fleet at Darien was thought to be easy since at one spot – Golden Island – there was a deep and protected inlet. According to Wafer it was an 'extraordinary good harbour'.

HOW DARIEN MADE THE UK

The descriptions of Darien were too much for one country in particular to resist. Scotland's political and merchant class had become convinced that establishing a trading colony overseas would boost the nation's ailing economy. They acted fast, quickly interviewing Wafer and Dampier to extract more information. A publicly traded company set up to support such exploration had drawn in £500,000 from investors rich and poor – around half the entire country's capital at the time. On 14 July 1698 a fleet of five ships led by the *Unicorn* and the *Endeavour* and carrying around 1,200 people set out to find Golden Island and establish Scotland's first colony. The diaries that survive show the adventurous settlers were spellbound by Darien's beauty. Wafer, it seemed, had been right. They named their country New Caledonia and set to work building its capital, New Edinburgh.

This hopeful expedition, now known as the Darien Disaster, was Scotland's greatest economic catastrophe. The goods the Scots had brought to sell at trading posts along the way included consumer items of the time – wigs and combs, slippers and pipes – which were worthless in the Caribbean. Unable to trade, they were forced to rely on their wits for food. The sea was teeming with fish but each ship had carried only one small net; the population of the land crabs that could be caught and eaten dwindled fast. The settlers quickly turned to drink, draining the plentiful supplies of brandy. A catalogue of fevers – smallpox, plague, cholera, dysentery, typhoid, yellow fever and malaria – took over. As one survivor, Walter Harris, put it in his account, 'men fell down and died like rotten sheep'.

Although another fleet of ships was sent carrying supplies, things got worse. The Scots abandoned Darien for Jamaica, but many died on the journey while others left destitute were forced to sell themselves as slaves there. More than 2,000 of the 2,500 Scots that set out for Darien died and only one of 16 boats sent there survived. For Scotland, the colonial plan could not have gone any worse. Rather than create a new Scottish Empire, the Darien expedition bankrupted the country, leading to a financial rescue package in 1707 that made Scotland part of England's domain. While other colonizing countries – most notably Spain – have built small settlements here and pockets of trade have flourished at times, to travel in modern Darien is to discover a land that is quiet, deserted and undeveloped. Three hundred years on from the Scottish disaster that created the United Kingdom, Darien remains untamed.

OPPORTUNITY LOST

AT THE END OF THE ROAD

Panama City is ugly – a mess of cheap-looking high-rise apartment blocks clogged with traffic. But as you head east towards Darien things change quickly. After around 30 minutes the buildings disappear and the Pan-American Highway becomes a single-track road that undulates gently and curves through lush farmland. Crowds of

vultures picking at the carcasses of animals mown down by speeding trucks become more regular, the huge birds taking to the air as
we speed by. As we pass the remains of a giant squashed snake I ask
my driver what type of snake it was. He shrugs his shoulders and
says, 'You don't ask, you just kill it before it kills you.'

The Gap used to be much wider: until the 1960s the Pan-American
Highway ended at Chepo, a small town 60 km east of Panama City. The
smooth road extends further today, and after Chepo the agricultural
land that borders the road is replaced by mile after mile of teak forest,
the huge leaves of the trees making an impenetrable canopy in deep
green. Families sit at brightly coloured bus stops, everyone trying to
keep out of the sun, which by 10 a.m. is burning hot. The men all wear
sunhats made from light-yellow straw, with deep-brown bands and a
perfectly circular brim, the front of which is turned up like a bonnet.
(The 'Panama' hat is from Ecuador.) The women carry yellow and
orange parasols. Every kilometre or so a farmer sits at the side of the
road with a massive pile of plantain to sell. Well-worn pickup trucks
buzz up and down, collecting the crops before heading back to the city.

After a couple of hours the teak forests end and a large archway
over the road appears. Senafront guards in smart uniforms inspect
vehicles meticulously, but this spot, Agua Fría, is effectively the border of the Darien Gap, known as the end of the territory over which
the Panamanian authorities have full control. Things change immediately after we pass under the arch: the smooth tarmac becomes a
bumpy track covered in grit and dust. There are few cars and buses,
and the traffic is mainly industrial: massive trucks trundle up and
down the track, laden with huge, deep-red tree trunks. Many drivers
have removed their trucks' exhausts – a trick that gives the vehicles
more power – and the engines make a deafening scream as they roll
past. Formally Panamanian soil, signs of South America can already
be seen here: the dark bands in the men's hats are thicker, and more
of them wear the brim turned down, Colombian style.

With little warning the road stops at the river port of Yaviza.
A wooden sign at the side of the highway commemorates the 12,580

unbroken miles between here and Alaska. The pontoon into the river is busy as dugout canoes piled high with plantain are being unloaded and their contents stacked meticulously on the backs of trucks parked at the riverside. The main street is 200 metres or so long with cantinas and pool halls along both sides: they blast out Panamanian pop music, known as *típica*, day and night. The singers are all male and the lyrics are always similar, a local explains – tales of love, loss and loneliness. Yaviza is a town that smacks of under-employment – there are lots of drunks, lots of prostitutes. As a stroke of luck there is also a local econo-mist who is able to describe how the road, river and port go a long way to explaining the problems here in what was once the capital of Darien's economy.

FROM HUB TO SPOKE

'Yaviza's best days are in the past,' says Hermel Lopez, a local in his fifties who studied economics in the US. Previously a government adviser, Mr Lopez became exasperated by Yaviza's run-down condi-tion and has set up a community centre to offer training and advice to local businesses. He is also raising funds for a Darien museum to be centred here. The town has a rich history, he explains, and its decline is indicative of the economic problems faced by Darien. Just next door are the ruins of a fort built by the Spaniards who controlled Panama until the collapse of the Spanish Empire in the 1820s. Span-ish officers were stationed in Yaviza to guard the gold that had been mined deep in the jungle before being transported downriver by boat.

With no roads in the region, rivers were the main form of trans-port and continued to determine trade flows until the 1960s. Yaviza's position was perfect. Rivers flowing from the higher ground to the north-east drain to here, and the Rio Chucunaque acts like a high-way, linking Yaviza with hundreds of small towns and villages. In Yaviza merchants and wholesalers would trade with the people from these settlements, buying goods until their own larger boats were full. From here they would sail south to the Pacific and then west, up the coast to Panama City. The river-based connections meant that while Darien could trade with the capital, it had its own separate river-based economy with Yaviza at its heart.

Signs that Yaviza was once the site of a far stronger economy can be seen all over the town. The people here are poor and under-employed, they wear frayed clothes and, with too much time on their hands, many spend all day hanging around the bars. But on the main streets the houses have a faded grandeur: they have two stor-eys, with first-floor verandas looking down over the thoroughfares and the river. The wooden boards used to make external walls are thick and well cut; they have weathered nicely and are carved with intricate patterns. By comparison the newer homes are small and cheap, consisting of concrete walls with a tin roof slapped on top, requiring little skill to build.

Yaviza's port, built when times were better, is too big for the town's paltry modern economy. Sitting on a bend in this remote river it is industrial in design, with a large unloading area and fortified gantries to allow the packing of heavy goods on to large vessels that once stopped here. The trade that remains today – a traditional dugout canoe stacked with plantain every few hours – does not justify this infrastructure. The town has more than 30 bars, one local tells me, because the port used to be much busier. Walking the backstreets reveals that most are open but empty. A desolate place built on the riches of a long-lost river trade, this is a failed town that lost its eco-nomic network and was unable to regain it, something seen in both Kinshasa and Glasgow. Fortunes started to tip against Yaviza when innovations in transport worked against the town, turning it from the hub of its own economic system into a distant spoke of Panama City's.

THE HIGH COST OF A LOW REPUTATION

Darien's wild reputation has cost Yaviza dearly, explains Mr Lopez. The way the Pan-American Highway was completed is a case in point. After hearing the authorities in Panama had decided a road should link Chepo with Yaviza, the locals here, fearing isolation, requested that the new road be built by two teams: one would start in Yaviza, the other in Chepo, and they would meet in the middle. The plea was ignored and the highway was extended in one direction only, starting from Chepo in 1963 and eventually reaching Yaviza in the 1980s. The road runs parallel to the Chucunaque River, and as it reached each new village and town it became the easiest way to access Panama City, making river travel redundant. Year by year, Yaviza's connectivity and influence fell while towns to the east gained. Large ships were no longer needed at the port, and the jobs of shipbuilders, mechanics, captains, crew and port workers vanished.

The Embera captain of a large dugout canoe explains another reason why being out on a limb is such a problem as he watches his crew – two young men – unload plantain. The men have sailed from Boca de Cupe, a village deep in the Gap, and make the trip once per fortnight. They load the village's boat with plantain, bought from local villagers for 8¢ per fruit, and travel six hours downriver to get to Yaviza where the going rate for a plantain is 10¢. Other villages across Darien do the same thing, creating fierce competition at the port and allowing truck owners who buy from them to dictate their terms. (Often, the chief says, the truck drivers refuse to pay at all, and will only reimburse the villager after selling the fruit to a wholesaler.) By the time the plantain arrive in Panama City they sell for between 25¢ and 50¢, he complains; his margin of just 2¢ per fruit is hardly worth the effort once you add in the cost of fuel and staff. The captain's problem is the length of his supply chain and the huge number of parties involved, each one taking a cut; as we mull over his troubles he asks if we know of any more direct routes to Panama that might help him avoid all the middlemen. But Yaviza is trapped at the end of the road. There is only one way out.

SELLING NATURE

In a town stripped of work, the people of Yaviza do what they can. Most of the jobs involve extracting value from the environment in some way. At the oversized port, young men in pairs head out in flimsy-looking canoes, their only equipment a paddle and a plastic bucket. They dredge sand and grit from the river bed, before hauling it up the steep bank. Along the edge of the river, piles of various grades of sand and grit are sold to local builders who pay 20¢ per bucket. Others harvest wood, sneaking into the forest to find valuable cocobolo trees. The tree – rosewood – is a protected species but the locals know that a Chinese trader in the town will buy it for export. Then there are the *campesinos*, migratory cattle herders who roam across public land grazing their cattle and selling the meat before moving on to new pastures. Upriver, deep in the Gap, gold is still being found by teams that blast riverbanks with water and mercury to release the valuable flakes from the sediment. The environment is an asset, and for many people living in Yaviza getting by is only possible by chipping a bit off and selling it.

The damage that results has disastrous long-term implications, says Alvin Bellorín, the local Roman Catholic priest. A missionary originally from Nicaragua, the 37-year-old has been in Yaviza for six years of a ten-year stint. The jungle is receding rapidly, he explains, as loggers take trees and *campesinos* convert the forest to pasture. Father Bellorín enjoys taking walks along the river and says it has changed during his short time in Darien. The loss of jungle and constant dredging of the river for sand and grit has changed its flow and the banks are eroding. As if to prove his point, a walkway near by that once skirted the riverbank now drops over a cliff and into the river; further up, concrete blocks that were once parts of buildings now rise out of the water. The Spanish fort is precariously close to the collapsing bank, and looks as if it will be the next thing to go. It has stood for almost 300 years.

The environmental erosion evident on the ground in Darien can be seen using a much wider-angle lens, explains Samuel Valdez, who until 2016 was the national director of protected areas in Panama, overseeing 117,000 acres of land across the country. 'The rich bio-diversity should be an economic resource for people here,' he says, emphasizing the value to environmental tourism and carefully managed logging programmes. Instead, he explains, resources are being exploited in a devastating way. Aerial photos of this part of Panama from the 1960s show dense jungle stretching all the way to Chepo, where the Darien Gap used to start. With the completion of the road deeper into Darien, people have moved in and a huge area of rainforest has been destroyed. Between 1990 and 2010 alone, Panama lost 27,050 hectares of forest cover a year, on average – a total loss equivalent to the size of over 750,000 football pitches. 'In Darien,' Mr Valdez says, 'the environment is in intensive care.'

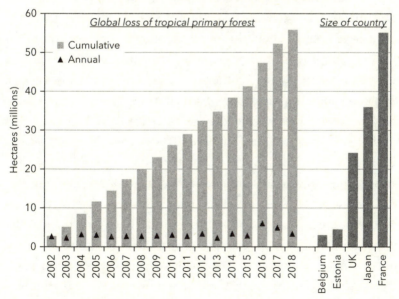

The world's disappearing tropics

Annual tropical primary forest loss, 2002–2018, cumulative and annual. Land mass of selected countries.

Source: World Resources Institute

THE TRAGEDY OF THE JUNGLE

THE PROBLEM WITH FREE EXCHANGE

In their own ways the resilience of the communities in the first part of the book showed the best of economics. These are places where people start with nothing but build an informal economy in which they innovate, often inventing an unofficial currency, creating markets from scratch and trading to each other's mutual benefit. This reaction to economic devastation whether due to disaster, war or incarceration seems innate, and it shows how an informal or underground marketplace can allocate scarce resources, help people define roles and identities, and give meaning to life.

Places like Darien show that informal economies are not always benign. Absent of rules and regulations, markets can arise that destroy resources, reduce the value of a human settlement and undermine its long-term prospects. The puzzle is why, in a region where everyone knows the environment is being degraded, the people of Darien can't manage the economy in a way that stops it happening. Economists have worried about this problem, often called the 'Tragedy of the Commons', for centuries. Darien's extractive jungle economy is a striking modern example of those concerns and a reminder of why, despite economists' tendency to be enthusiastic about the power markets have to create value, they cannot be trusted to do so.

The fact that trade might be destructive was first set out by William Forster Lloyd in a pair of lectures delivered at Oxford University in 1832. Lloyd was ordained as a Church of England minister and worked on problems in mathematics before switching to political economics, where he became particularly concerned about the implications of rapid population growth. He described a plot of public land – 'the common' – on which farmers were free to graze their cattle, and observed that the pasture would end up 'bare worn' from overgrazing. This, for Lloyd, was a puzzle: 'Why are the cattle on a common so puny and stunted?'

The root of the problem, Lloyd explained, lay in the calculation each farmer makes when deciding whether to allow cattle on to a field. If the farmer owns the land he will consider the full implications of his actions: he knows that each extra cow will eat more grass, taking this nourishment away from the rest of the herd. At some point the farmer knows his private land is 'saturated' and that adding another cow to the pasture will make his other heifers go hungry. Since this is a cost the farmer bears directly, he will seek out another field for the cow in question.

On 'common' or publicly owned land the calculation changes. The downside of adding an extra cow to a field harms not only the farmer's cattle; the loss of pasture is spread across every animal on the common ground, including the cows that the farmer does not own. Since the cost is not fully borne by the farmer, he tends to downplay it, and will add an extra cow to a public field that he would not add to a private one. Since every other farmer with access to the public land does the same, the common fills up with cattle, the grass is overgrazed and the cows end up under-nourished. Lloyd's story, about a hypothetical farmer, is a perfect description of land used by *campesinos* in Darien today.

THE VILLAGE OPTIMIST

Given that informal and unregulated economies are a key part of the resilience shown by people in the most difficult and pressurized economies on earth, the prediction that free trade will so often be self-defeating is a depressing one. Thankfully, the work of a much more recent economist – Elinor Ostrom – offers a more optimistic view. Rejected by UCLA's PhD course in economics because her mathematics was not strong enough, Ostrom pursued a doctorate in political science instead. She used her outsider status, and went on to develop her own unique brand of analysis based on detailed field studies of life in villages across Africa, Asia and Europe, and became the first female winner of the Nobel Prize in Economics in 2009. Ostrom, who died in 2012, observed that in many situations, communities do manage to look after common resources without depleting them or resorting to laws or restrictive regulations that block trade. Her work shows why informal and unregulated trade that operates outside government control works perfectly well in some villages but is disastrous in others.

The green pasture and dense forests of Törbel, an Alpine region of Switzerland, were one example Ostrom highlighted, pointing to a clever tradition that ensures conservation of the forest, the village's source of winter fuel. The locals work as a team to fell, haul and chop trees, stacking the wood into piles, each of which is given a number. They then run a sweepstake to determine who gets which stack. Since each family knows they could get any pile they all work hard to ensure that every bundle of wood contains sufficient fuel to get through the winter. Similarly every family knows that any over-felling will come back to bite them because it will mean less wood for the following winter. The unwritten tradition aligns incentives perfectly: villagers take neither too much nor too little, and they share it out fairly.

In parts of rural Japan communally owned land is often managed using similar norms. The villages of Hirano, Nagaike and Yamanaka, nestled around a lake at the foot of Mount Fuji, are another example Ostrom investigated. The communities share the common forest running up the side of the mountain, which provides wood for fuel, game meat to eat and fertilizer (from the decaying plants on the forest floor) for growing vegetables. The forest also controls the flow of water down the side of the mountain, preventing flooding and soil erosion. The problem was that from the seventeenth century onwards, Japan experienced a logging boom driven by construction needs (a growing population needed houses, temples and shrines, and military fortifications, all using timber). Across the country forest turned to *genya* (barren land), with more soil erosion and more frequent landslides. So the villagers came up with a system of self-regulation that was fine-tuned to the local environment. Local tradition now dictates the exact dates on which different types of tree can be felled, limiting both the length of the harvesting window and the number of loggers that can cut trees at any one time. The forest returned, the ground firmed up and the villages were saved.

The question for the communities living in Darien is whether they will survive, by making free exchange work in their favour, or fail, by depleting their natural resources until there is none left. Here, Ostrom's research can help: decades of field trips allowed her to pin down a set of factors that support self-governance and help stop damaging trades that put common resources such as forests and rivers at risk. Clear boundaries around environmental assets are helpful, since they demarcate exactly what is private and what is shared, regular meetings at an assembly hall or forum allow villagers to debate and resolve any conflicts amicably. A relatively stable population helps too, because it means reputation becomes important: in a place where people tend to stay put, anyone violating local traditions knows they face a big cost – the ire of their neighbours for years to come.

Overall, the fact that communities often do conserve common economic resources made Ostrom an optimist about unregulated markets. She was a realist though, observing that even informal economic systems were rarely completely rule-free, needing sticks as well as carrots. Japanese villages, for example, use informal forest 'detectives' who patrol the land, hand out fines (often paid in *sake*) and can confiscate equipment from those felling trees at the wrong time. And there were other settings, she found, where 'rampant opportunistic behaviour' would limit what a remote community lacking the power to monitor and punish its members could achieve. The problem for Darien is that it is precisely one of those settings.

VILLAGE FLUX

Ostrom's first rule – clearly defined borders – is supposed to hold Darien. While much of the Darien Gap allows public access, it is not a complete free-for-all. The Panamanian government has reserved large tracts known as *comarcas* for the use of the Embera, Wounan and Kuna tribes. While outsiders have the right to travel across these areas, the lack of roads and the presence of tolls and checkpoints where roads do exist prevent over-use and prohibit visitors from taking logs, meat or other natural resources as they pass through. The wood is a source of fuel for the tribes, and cash from selling it is used to fund important purchases such as outboard motors for dug-out canoes, and the concrete blocks and corrugated roofing that are needed when building homes for newlywed couples.

To ensure that neighbouring villages do not deplete wood from these common areas, the exclusive territories are covered by a licensing system specifying the amount of wood that each village can collect and sell. In addition, there is the Darien National Park, extending to 575,000 hectares and registered as a UN World Heritage Site, where the most pristine 'primary' rainforest cannot be logged by anyone, surrounded by a protective buffer zone to avoid any confusion. On paper the set-up seems to offer the best of both worlds, allowing villagers to self-regulate, doing what they wish with their land, and underpinning this with a cap on trade that acts as a kind of environmental safety net.

But while official borders may be well defined in Darien, in practical terms they are not, and many of Ostrom's other conditions fail here. Far from being stable, explains local activist Hermel Lopez, the Gap is a place of population flux and unauthorized migration. Darien is a magnet, the only part of Panama in which every ethnic group in the country is represented. The people who have been here longest are the Afro-Darienistas, says Hermel: the descendants of freed and escaped slaves, they have high social rank, often owning and running businesses. The small supermarkets and corner shops dotted over the parts of Darien that have roads are all run by Chinese-Panamanians, the descendants of labourers shipped here in the 1850s to work on railroads and in the 1900s to dig the Panama Canal. Even two of the 'indigenous' tribes are relatively recent migrants: both the Embera and Wounan migrated from western Colombia in the late eighteenth century. Those with looser ties include nomadic *campesino* cattle herders and *colonos*, a class of migratory farm labourers from the north. The latest arrivals are large teams of Colombian construction workers, here to improve the highway.

Little love is lost between the ethnic groups that share this land. The Afro-Darienistas have founders' bragging rights. They and other established locals regard running shops as low-grade work, and look down on the Chinese-Panamanians who do so, referring to them as *chinitos*, or 'little Chinese'. The feeling seems to be mutual: at the minimart in Yaviza customers throw their money at the owner, who chucks the change back. There are no smiles or pleasantries accompanying this exchange. The Embera and Wounan were once part of the same tribe but split and now claim overlapping territories, making them rivals. Everyone seems to loathe the Hispanic *campesinos* and *colonos*.

In successful unregulated markets, locals cooperate, Ostrom had observed. But there is no coordination among those involved in farming or forestry in the Darien Gap, explains Jose Quintana, a local who owns a 4x4 truck and offers a local taxi service to villages deep in the jungle beyond Yaviza. The recent swings in the market for nyame, a starchy root similar to a potato, are a case in point. In 2016 there was a local shortage, and farmers could get up to $50 per 100 pounds of the root vegetable. Responding to this opportunity, every farmer planted nyame, Jose explains, resulting in a massive surplus that pushed the price down to $9. But 100 pounds of the crop costs a farmer $2 to dig up and prepare for the market, another $2 to transport it to El Real, a river port, and a further $2 as payment for the captain of a boat to take it to Yaviza for sale. After accounting for tools and the farmer's own labour, it was not worth it, so local fields that were once dense rainforest were full of unharvested nyame being left to rot.

The problem is not just a lack of community spirit, Jose explains, but that the various groups in Darien actively undermine one another's plans. As we head towards Piji Basal, a tiny Embera village in the National Park, Jose waves his hand proudly at a field he owns and has planted with cocobolo trees. In 15 years the trees will be ready for felling, the rosewood providing a payout large enough to fund his children's education. But until then he must guard them, he says, because anyone around here might take them.

Jose's concern is a lesson in what makes informal markets fail that comes straight from Ostrom's groundbreaking economics. Even unregulated free markets need a rudder – a kind of community spirit, a shared goal that drives cohesion. If they lack this, some informal referee – like Japan's forest detectives – is needed to enforce local norms. The Darien Gap lacks both cohesion and oversight – when someone behaves badly there is little chance of a legal solution, and it is unlikely that a neighbour will intervene. With so much population flux, locals often don't know who the wrongdoers are. And with drug gangs and plenty of guns in the area, it is safer not to make any accusations.

LIFE AND LIMB

Just outside Piji Basal we finally get to pristine primary rainforest. It is mesmerizing: water drips constantly from branches and vines, and the air is hot and misty. It is midday but almost dark, the path lit by small rays that cut through various layers of canopy. The ground is slippery, covered by a thick mat of decaying leaves that makes it easy to lose your footing. The roots of trees offer some stability underfoot but we quickly see our first deadly *fer-de-lance* snake – and after that every root becomes a dangerous python.

After a two-hour hike we track down a team of experts, led by Samuel Valdez, investigating the habitat of some of Panama's rarest birds. The devastating exploitation of natural resources starts, he says, with a paradoxical problem – a lack of logging equipment. Species like the giant kapok, whose foliage rises high above the canopy, can be over 100 feet tall. These and other hardwood species are incredibly heavy and require specialist tools to fell and vehicles to haul, but the Embera villagers with the logging rights own only their tiny dugout canoes. Rather than rent the equipment or club together to buy it, the Embera chiefs sell the licence they have been granted to specialist logging companies. With this paperwork in hand the loggers have a legal right to operate in the reserved territories, quickly building tracks deep into the jungle to sites where the most valuable species grow. Once there, they are supposed to adhere to the quotas, recording every tree felled and leaving a numbered tag on its stump.

The tragedy of Darien is that it offers lessons not just in the failure of informal markets, but also shows that well-intentioned rules and regulations can end up amplifying the damage done. One problem is the fact that logging quotas are not respected, say the local experts. Walking through a logging zone deep in the Gap, it seems that perhaps two out of every ten stumps have been tagged. Even if the quotas are respected, the system causes massive wastage, explains Hermel Lopez. A company facing a weight limit on the amount of wood it can take from the forest will take only the best. Consequently the legal loggers in Darien take only the straightest trunks, casting aside the remainder of the felled trees so that only a fraction of each is used. The quota system is designed to protect the forest but does the opposite because the professional loggers regard the branches of these great trees – themselves huge pieces of wood – as rubbish. 'Walk in the forest and you will see,' says Mr Lopez, looking bleak: 'The limbs lie on the floor.'

From here follows a series of unintended consequences of the timber trade – every one of them negative. Deep in the jungle we find tracks the logging companies have built. They are not the thin rural lanes I had imagined but wide and reinforced roads to allow huge trucks carrying lumber in and out. As each logging track is built it acts like a tapped vein, draining the forest of lifeblood. With the dense jungle smashed away it is easy for unscrupulous locals searching for contraband wood to get in and out with a pickup truck. Then the *campesinos* follow, setting their cattle to graze on land that was previously rainforest. Since it is poor pasture they keep moving, ensuring the final destruction of the forest as they go.

Recognizing the deforestation problem, the Panamanian government put in place a system of reforestation subsidies, starting in 1992. Landowners planting trees would receive subsidized credit and tax cuts to boost the profitability of timber plantations. The new set-up – Panama's Law 24 – would align the public and private benefits, encouraging landowners to plant more trees to the advantage of everyone. The raw economics worked, Mr Valdez explains, creating a massive reforestation boom. But the policy was badly designed, rewarding any tree planting rather than specifying that native species must be replaced. 'A plantation is not a forest,' he says, 'and now we have a terrible problem – the teak tree.'

Driving through the never-ending teak plantations on the way into Darien, the deep green of the leaves had seemed natural, lush and healthy. But after sleeping in the rainforest, meeting its people and learning how teak trees work, I discovered the plant was something to loathe. *Tectona grandis* is not a native species but an import from Southeast Asia. The tree's leaves are plump, waxy and the size of a large serving dish. This surface area means that teak loses a lot of moisture and draws huge quantities of water from the ground. In the prime rainforest the native upper-canopy trees have small leaves, allowing many layers of secondary canopy, vines and bushes to find enough light lower down to grow. By contrast a teak tree's massive leaves shade the forest floor completely, and when they fall and start to decompose they release an acid that kills insects. Stop at a teak plantation and you find that under the canopy there is nothing, and it is deathly quiet. Drained of water, starved of light and scorched by leaf acid the soil is parched. The ground looks as if it has been doused with petrol and left to burn.

The story of Panamanian teak offers a wider lesson in economics – a seemingly small policy tweak can have a massive impact. The engineered market created an unnatural forest, with teak accounting for fully 80 per cent of the 75,000 hectares of 'reforestation' stimulated by the Law-24 subsidies. By providing investors with an incentive to buy teak plantations, the government unleashed a massive externality – a public cost that teak planters do not take account of – which is born by Panamanians now and in the future via degradation of the environment. This problem goes well beyond Darien's artificial teak markets. Many of the problems of the modern economy – from the excessive use of fossil fuels to the dangerous levels of debt on banks' balance sheets – are the result not of free markets but of engineered ones (fossil-fuel use and debt financing are both stimulated, like teak, by government subsidies). Free markets left to run can cause damage; meddling in them can amplify it.

Occasionally there are glimmers of hope from the Panamanian government. In 2015 a new ministry of environment was created to monitor the country's natural resources. But campaigners and Darien locals worry that the ministry is toothless. The word 'Panama' supposedly means both 'many butterflies' and 'abundance of fish', but this has done little to enamour the country's city-dwelling public to green policies. In recent years politicians have successfully run on explicitly anti-green policies, arguing that environmental protection should not hold back development. The biggest logging firms are owned by serving politicians, and Panama now sells citizenship to anyone willing to invest $80,000 in a teak plantation. For many people in the land of butterflies and fish, the environment carries little weight.

DARIEN'S LATEST BUCCANEERS

REPUTATION MATTERS

The big hope for many of the locals I met in Darien was that they could start to use their natural environment in a sustainable way and build a new economy based on eco-tourism. Marketing the region's flora and fauna is a decent idea: it is one of the most biodiverse places on the planet, with at least 150 species of mammal, 99 native reptiles and 50 types of fish. The bird life – there are up to 900 species, many of them unique – is unmatched on the planet. Neighbouring Costa Rica has shown that it is possible to convert this natural wealth into jobs and income without destroying it, attracting over 1.2 million eco-tourists a year who pay for hikes, guides and birdwatching, bringing in more than $1 billion in revenue.

Here the Gap starts from a blank slate. I saw no real tourists in Darien: only two hippies and their camper van stuck at the end of the highway in Yaviza, and an academic ornithologist deep in the jungle hunting for rare birds. Official data is hard to get but suggests that in the mid-2000s for every 2.4 million tourist visits Panama received per year, just 700 people visited the Darien National Park. 'The problem is still the reputation,' says Hermel, and he is right. This is a beautiful place, but a jungle known to harbour FARC guerrillas is not somewhere you can relax. To make money from outsiders, the locals would need to make Darien accessible and safe. The experiences of Darien's latest group of adventurers – the illegal immigrants trekking through the jungle – show that goal is a long way off.

BUCCANEERS VERSUS PIRATES

Illegal immigrants – all of them heading for the US – enter the Darien Gap on its eastern border, at the Colombian town of Capurganá. The little port was previously a no-go area because of fighting between the Colombian Army and FARC rebels, but following the 2016 peace accord adventurous travellers have returned. There are Americans and Parisians in their twenties and thirties with wispy beards and dreadlocks, and small crews of baby-boomer yachtsmen with blotchy tans, the sun damage from weeks at sea. These western tourists and the locals alike wear shorts and flip-flops and like to party. Reggaeton – an upbeat blend of reggae and house music – booms constantly. Local fishermen head out early and are back for lunch, in time to join in.

Against this backdrop the illegal migrants are a sharp contrast. They are younger – most in their early twenties – and much smarter, wearing jeans and long-sleeved shirts, with their hair cut short. Their matching luggage is a giveaway too: many carry a small military-style backpack in blue or black. The side pockets of their bags are filled with crisps, biscuits and cans of soda. In a town of sun-seeking bohemians and hard-drinking fishermen these young people, who come from India, Bangladesh, Senegal and Cameroon, stand out as urbanites. From Capurganá they start a life-and-death trek through the jungle, without guides, to reach Embera villages like Bajo Chiquito on the Panamanian side of the Gap.

Ever since the Scots perished here, attempting to cross the Gap has been a suicide mission. As I would learn in Darien it still is, so I pressed the groups of migrants on why they are taking the risk. Why don't they just migrate to a bigger city in their own country to find work? 'Impossible,' say a group from Punjab unanimously: 'Too much corruption.' They say that finding a better-paid job requires connections of family and caste, and that no matter how hard they work to educate themselves they will never do better in India. The Nepalese men I had met on the Panamanian side of the Gap said their problem was more acute: 'I know that I can eat tomorrow, the next day and the day after that,' Ashim says. 'But next month, next year – I do not know.' His uncle Jedkan, a tomato farmer, agrees. Food can fall short in Nepal. The Nepalese love the UK but say it is too hard to get in. After having an application to join the Ghurkas rejected, they decided to head for the US. Like the unlucky Scottish settlers tempted here by Lionel Wafer's account of Darien, these young people are driven by economics, and the hope of a better life.

In theory, crossing the Gap should have become safer in recent years. The 2016 peace accord, signed by the Colombian government and FARC, officially ended the conflict. There was an amnesty on weapons and an agreement that former FARC members would not be prosecuted and could continue their support for the communist cause peacefully, as an official political group. With no reason for freedom fighters to hide in the jungle, the hopes in Darien were that the danger would lift as guerrilla fighters left the area.

But members of FARC face their own economic challenges, and they are severe. The soldiers FARC recruited, 40 per cent of whom were women, were often poor and uneducated. Having lived in the jungle for years, they have few skills that are of use in Colombia's formal economy. They also lack popular support, with many people viewing the blanket pardon the guerrillas received as too lenient, and Colombia's largest right-wing paramilitary group announcing that it would not respect the ceasefire and would continue to hunt FARC. This makes hiding in the jungle and running the old illicit economy, based on drugs and extortion, hard to give up. The production of coca, the plant used to make cocaine, had been declining in Colombia between 2010 and 2015. But the peace deal also promised the termination of the narcotics trade, and as this approached, coca planting doubled when local farmers, supported by FARC, rushed to produce one last cash crop.

The economic ripples the ceasefire caused mean the Gap is actually riskier now, explains Kilo, a birdwatching scout we meet at a rangers' station two hours' trek into the jungle. Kilo is a sought-after star of the birding scene, specializing in helping academics and obsessives find the very rarest birds. He is one of the few people in the Darien Gap prepared to trek for days into the deepest prime rainforest and has noticed changes since the ceasefire.

Kilo describes the scene at the foothills of Cerro Takarcuna, a mountain on the Panama–Colombia border. FARC traditionally grouped together in large camps but now, all around the base of the mountain, tiny guerrilla encampments have sprung up, he says. Since disbanding, FARC has splintered and factions are now competing with one another for the trade in shipping drugs and people across the Gap. This all leads to disorder and violence. Locals I spoke to in Yaviza agreed. The presence of FARC was a drag but at least it was organized criminality, with a leader who was known locally. Now the 'mountain people' of the jungle are more like pirates, launching opportunistic raids and seemingly random attacks.

Darien's latest buccaneers, young people from across the world seeking a new life in the US, are easy targets. 'So far ports and airports are the worst for robbery – big problem,' says Gagandeep, a Sikh man in his late twenties from Jalandhar in Punjab, India. By the time they reach the Darien Gap's Colombian border they have already been through many such terminals. The first hurdle, wherever in the world you start out, is to get into the Americas by taking advantage of lax entry controls in many South American countries. The Nepalese travel overland to New Delhi, and then fly to Moscow, then Madrid and enter the Americas at Santa Cruz, Bolivia. The Punjabis also head for New Delhi but fly first to Addis Ababa, then to São Paulo, Brazil. The route from Cameroon goes via Nigeria and the Ivory Coast to Dakar, Senegal. From Senegal migrants fly direct to Quito, Ecuador's capital. It is an expensive trip, and they have been saving for between two and five years. The Punjabis expect to spend $20,000 along the way, with $10,000 reserved for the border between the US and Mexico. Holding them up can prove very lucrative.

DEADLY DARIEN

As they prepare for the hike in Capurganá, the latest Darien buccaneers are undeterred by the risks but take steps to protect themselves. Those from India and Nepal tend to travel in groups of four to eight and are often part of a chain, with friends and relatives in other pods a few days ahead or behind them. This string of connection is vital: they carry smartphones and communicate information about the route using WhatsApp. Those from Senegal and Cameroon come alone or in pairs and often team up with a larger Indian or Nepali group. There is no sign of factionalism. By the time they are here, at the very edge of the Gap, the migrants have been travelling for six weeks. The Punjabis have covered 21,000 km; the Nepalese more. Hardened by life on the road, they are united in their common goal and their shared loathing of the Colombians they encounter along the way who seek to rob them at every step.

The last stage of the migrants' South American journey is to hike through the Gap. It is around 50 km from Capurganá to Bajo Chiquito, the Embera village on the other side in Panamanian Darien. The trek takes anything from four to eight days – if you make it. None of the migrants knew about Darien's fearful reputation before setting off from home, but have discovered it along the way. Gagandeep tells me how a group a few weeks ahead of them went through: the news on WhatsApp from the other side was not good – 'Four went in; only three came out.' Knowing that the hike is risky and arduous, the men hang around in Capurganá for a few days, preparing. They are happy to talk about their trek, cricket, and life back home in Punjab. But it is hardly relaxing: I visit them trapped in a tiny hostel room, fearful of the threatening-looking Colombians hanging around outside.

On the third day we are sitting around eating biscuits when the door bursts open. It is Gagandeep's brother Major Singh and three friends. They are older men, in their late thirties or early forties, and they roll up their trousers to reveal calves and shins covered in deep gashes, scratches and insect bites. They are back in town after an abortive eight-day hike, having slept without tent or tarpaulin for six nights in the jungle. A Colombian local had charged them $150 to guide them through, but once they were miles from the town he attempted to rob them before leaving them to find their own way. As they trekked they say they saw four dead bodies. The corpses were sitting up with their backs against trees, arms crossed over their chests. The men imitate the position of an Egyptian mummy and close their eyes. I ask why they had died. 'No food, no water – lost,' they say.

ANOTHER MARKET FAILURE

Venturing just a little way into the Colombian jungle along the migrant route gives an idea of the hardships the men will soon face. The path is slippery and covered in snake-like roots; what turn out to be tiny jungle crabs cause large and unnerving movements in the undergrowth. Water drips from leaves everywhere, but there are no streams or brooks to drink from. The idea that a city-dweller could become self-sufficient here is a joke. I don't see a single fruit on four separate hikes.

That there is no way to pay for guaranteed safe passage through the gap is another market failure. The trip from Nepal to California via Russia, Spain and Bolivia is surely the longest economic migration on the planet and has a life-threatening risk – the Darien hike – right in the middle. The young migrants are committed and have funds for their mission; the locals, both Embera and ex-FARC, lack money but know the jungle intimately. If there were ever a place for informal trade to flower – one in which local jungle experts would sell their services as guides – it would be here. But in this place of flux reputation does not matter, interactions are one-offs. The negative economic culture Elinor Ostrom feared – one of opportunism, cynical behaviour and mistrust – flourishes in Darien. It is easier and quicker to rob the migrants and leave them to fend for themselves than to take them to the other side.

ANYTHING OF A REASONABLE MANAGEMENT

The Scottish plan to colonize Darien promised that with 'anything of a reasonable management' the men and women who controlled this land would come to great riches. The Darien Gap's potential, both natural and geographic, means that its lure remains strong to economic seekers today. Still, for the most part Darien is unknown, a forgotten place that, by ruining Scotland, helped to create the UK and define the modern history of Europe. Its historical capital, Yaviza, was once the heart of a thriving river trade that is long gone. There are no museums marking the history of this incredible place, and few tourists: Darien, a land of promise and opportunity, has never truly developed.

Today it is a place riven by economic failures. The extractive timber market that eats away at the rainforest is exactly the 'externality' problem early economists worried about – when people don't consider the costs of their actions, markets can cause damage. Darien also shows how hard attempts to correct these problems are: it is a place where informal self-regulation fails and the official state actions to guide markets, in this case the damaging teak subsidies, do more harm than good. And, in the case of the missing trade for safe passage that would make everyone better off, Darien demonstrates how vital markets can fail to flower. The overarching lesson of Darien is a reminder that markets cannot be relied on: they can be damaging, fiendishly hard to correct and can fail to emerge when most needed.

A less extractive model for Darien's economy is possible, says local economist Hermel Lopez. It would start with the infrastructure investment needed to return Yaviza to its former role as an economic hub. With a proper power supply, factories could be set up to process the wood and capture more of its value here. That could help fund scouts who would guard the forests and jungle. The plan makes sense. The Embera chiefs told me the agreements they have signed mean they sell their raw timber for a 'blended' price of 14¢ per foot, whatever the species. But sawn cocobolo (rosewood) has a wholesale price up to 500 times higher ($40–$70 per foot), so someone down the line is making a killing. If the Embera controlled their supply chain and sold a finished product, their return would rise many hundreds of times. For the same income they could cut a tiny fraction of the trees currently earmarked for logging.

As I left Bajo Chiquito, deep in the jungle, these economic improvements seemed a long way off. For Juan, the Embera chief, the need to provide housing meant a few more trees must be felled, at just a few cents per foot, to fund construction. Metres away, huddled under a white tarpaulin, the Nepalese and Cameroonian migrants waited in limbo. None spoke any Spanish, and with no one to help we ran through the words they wanted to know most: 'food', 'price', 'bus station' and 'danger'. What would come next was uncertain but at least they had survived the most dangerous part of the Gap, and the Pan-American Highway was just a few days' walk downriver.

On the other side of the Gap, in Capurganá, the Punjabi group's trek is yet to come and I ask them about their families back at home. 'Our mothers are happy we are on this trip,' says Gagandeep. His friends agree, describing their plans for future lives in California, Texas and New York. Gagandeep shows me a picture of his two-year-old daughter on his smartphone, saying that when he gets to the US he will send back money so that his wife can finish her nursing degree. With the qualification in hand he hopes she will be able to travel to the US legally, bringing the child with her.

Like the other migrants I spent time with in Darien, the men make me promise to visit their homeland. 'Beautiful country, beautiful people, bad government,' says Jasminder, describing Punjab and advising me to visit the Golden Temple in Amritsar. Driven into a killer jungle by the lack of economic opportunity at home, they remain patriots and talk like expert tour guides. Here in Darien they are novices, and they ask for the names of the Panamanian towns they might end up in once they are through the Gap. I give them my map and we say goodbye.

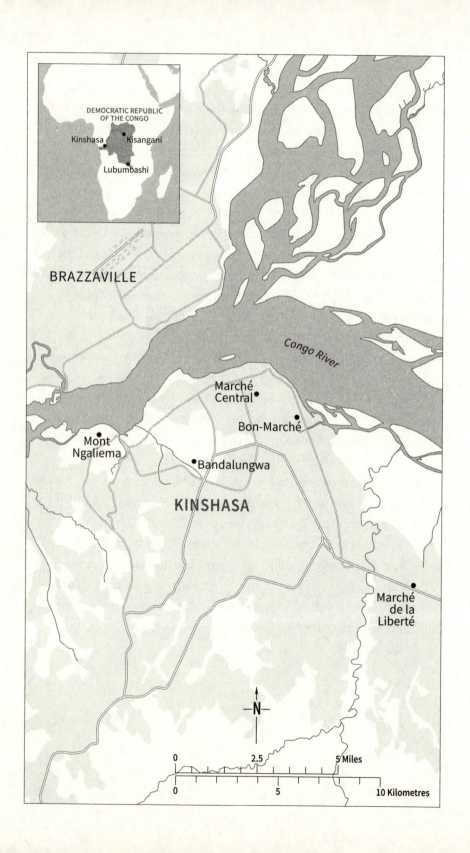

5

Kinshasa

The vegetable and mineral products of this marvellous land are equal in
variety, value, and quantity to those of the most favoured portions
of the globe.

Verney Lovett Cameron,
Across Africa, 1877

One no longer works in the Congo. One no longer produces
in the Congo . . . The Congo can no longer feed and
clothe its own sons.

Joseph–Désiré Mobutu,
1965

FAILURE SQUARED

'We have three levels of society here,' says Father Sylvain Mongambo, a Roman Catholic priest in his early fifties, as we sit down at a small cafe within the compound of Saint-Paul's Church in Bon-Marché, one of Kinshasa's central suburbs. The top layer are those with ministerial and high-level government jobs, he explains. They work in Gombe, a leafy district where foreign embassies are located, and earn salaries that would make them well paid in a rich country (Congolese MPs are paid $10,000 per month, with many perks on top). The second tier are people with a steady private-sector job, those who own their own company or are public-sector workers, such as police officers and teachers. 'These people get by but have little security,' Father Mongambo explains, 'so they use the informal economy as a backup.'

The bottom level consists of people with no official employment. 'This is the biggest level, by far,' the priest says. The country's devastating statistics bear this out. The unemployment rate in the Congo has not been below 44 per cent in the past 20 years; in most years it is over 60 per cent, and in bad years more than 80 per cent of people here have no work.* For most people in Kinshasa steady work is impossible to come by: 'So these people rely on the economy of the street. They do any kind of trade they can think of; they make any kind of business they can.' There are no unemployment benefits and the jobless receive no assistance with housing. 'The fact that they survive,' the priest concludes, 'is truly a miracle.'

Kinshasa, home to 10 million people, is not a city where you would want to be without work. At the last count 77 per cent of

---

* Everyone I met in Kinshasa refers to their country – the Democratic Republic of the Congo – as the Congo, and themselves as Congolese. I follow the local usage in this chapter. The other Congo – the Republic of the Congo – is over the river and referred to as Congo-Brazzaville.

people in the Congo were living on less than $1.90 per day, the international poverty line. There are more people in extreme poverty here than in any other country in the world and there is no hiding it. On my first day in Kinshasa, as I walked to the city's central market a girl, perhaps ten years old, approached wearing a scavenged woman's dress far too big for her, a sandal on one foot and a flip-flop on the other. Amid the layers of sun-bleached plastic that carpets the city floor she spotted a discarded piece of corn and dived on it, devouring the few tiny grains of flesh left on the cob. Street children and scavengers are everywhere in Kinshasa, and I quickly came to realize that for huge numbers of people in this city $1.90 a day is a dream. Many of them live on nothing at all.

Kinshasa's poverty makes the city a unique case of economic failure. Just as Darien should be the site of a hub where those trading by land and sea meet, Kinshasa should be the ultimate source of such trade, sending food, manufactured goods and resources across the globe. Ever since the Dorset-born explorer Verney Lovett Cameron crossed central Africa in the 1870s people have known that the Congo is a place of unrivalled potential. Cameron's account talked of sugar cane, palm oil and tobacco of 'very excellent quality', and described rubber-producing vines 'nearly everywhere' along with an abundance of coal, copper and gold. The Congo has diamonds, tin and other rare metals, the world's second-largest rainforest and a river whose flow is second only to the Amazon. In addition to this natural wealth the city possesses many attributes that should help a modern economy thrive: it shares a time zone with Paris, the people here speak a major European language (French), and the population is young and growing. Not only is Kinshasa the poorest major city in the world, but it should be one of the richest.

The world is urbanizing, making the forces that can drive a city to failure a vital thing for those concerned about the future to understand. Yet Kinshasa is something of a mystery, with most accounts of the Congo's troubles focusing on the war close to Goma in the east, or fraud and corruption at the mines around Katanga in the south.

Like everything in this country those troubles are incomparable, but Kinshasa is thousands of miles from any of this, and I wanted to understand the economics of everyday life for the city's residents: what was holding them back, and what they needed to succeed.

Within minutes of arriving it became clear that the kind of economic anaemia I had seen in the feeble markets of Azraq and Jackie Chan Village and the languid trade of Yaviza had nothing to do with the story of Kinshasa. The city's vitality, as well as its poverty, is impossible to forget. Head south of the embassies and government offices of Gombe and the city buzzes. From Bandal and Kintambo, suburbs close to the centre, to the very poorest districts of Mesina and N'Djili that are further out, the scene is the same: everyone, everywhere, is hustling to make a living. Afternoons here are a special time – a vibrant display of colourful tailored suits, pumping music and sizzling barbecued meat that makes the world's most bustling cities seem stale by comparison. People are getting by in this city, perhaps the world's toughest, and some of them are doing well. If the Kinoise are as resilient and innovative as they seem, why is their economy so weak?

THE GOLDEN RULE

BECOME THE TOP MAN'S SON

Christian Mpongo, 33, has been working in Kinshasa's Marché Central for decades and looks good on it. He sits on a plastic chair outside his shop, sporting a black polo shirt customized with extra pieces of red and green cloth in the shape of flames and vines that run up his chest. Many of the stalls here are empty but Christian's, a food wholesale operation, is busy. Customers come and go, ordering 20 kg sacks of rice, corn and sugar that have been imported to the Congo from Argentina, Thailand and Turkey. As his staff, a team of young porters, lug the sacks to customers' cars or the bus stop, Christian issues gentle commands in Kikongo, his mother tongue.

Christian's success is a first lesson in how the harshness of life in Kinshasa also creates opportunities. He first came to the market as an 11-year-old, and quickly spotted a way to make money. Despite the proximity of such a mighty river, Kinshasa has no proper supply of clean drinking water. Gombe, the rich suburb, is tiny and outside it few homes have taps that are safe to drink from. Selling small plastic bags filled with clean water is a major industry here, and as a teenager Christian worked out a scheme to buy clean water cheaply in bulk, allowing him to make around 1,000 Congolese francs (60¢) each time he sold 20 water sachets. He worked his way up, first as a market porter, then opening his own retail store and finally moving into wholesale trade, which is more lucrative and more stable, he says. It adds up to 22 years of experience in the heart of the city, and he is happy to explain how to get ahead here. 'The first rule of Kinshasa's economy,' he says, 'is corruption.'

His principal concern is tax, and it is shared by everyone I meet: from small stallholders to supermarket-owning tycoons, from manual labourers to university professors, everyone in Kinshasa loathes the tax system. Officially Congolese businesses are supposed to pay tax monthly. The reality is that tax is collected at least once a day in Kinshasa, and many areas have both a morning and an afternoon tax. The rate is high – officially 54 per cent of profits – but what really hurts are all the extra undocumented payments. A restaurateur who runs a cafe and supermarket explains: 'Every day I pay tax, and I must pay a bribe in exchange for a receipt for the tax I have just paid, and then I am forced to offer a "*bon prix*" on the tax official's lunch.' This is daily payment in triplicate, amounting to over a thousand taxes a year.

'To survive, I must become the top man's son,' says Christian, describing how he copes. 'As soon as I find out there is a new government official overseeing the market, I find out his name and go and see him. I find out what he likes to eat, what his wife likes to wear – even what his kids like – and I make sure I get all of this to him.' Knowing someone at the top is vital, because tax here is like a pyramid scheme, with a local official – the top man – at its pinnacle.

Everyone in the pyramid steals a little for themselves as the funds pass through their hands, and if you pay in at the bottom of the pyramid there are hundreds of low-level tax officials competing to claim your cash. Christian's strategy is to create an alliance with those near the apex, cutting out the middlemen to save himself time, money and hassle. 'If my plan works I know my business will survive,' Christian says. 'But if I fail to make the top man happy I will be broken in a few days.'

CONSTITUTIONALLY RESILIENT

Stories like this are troubling, since it soon becomes clear that the people of modern Kinshasa rely on their local, often informal, economy as a safety net. The philosophy of self-reliance – of resilience through trade, barter and exchange – is so common here that it has a nickname: 'Article 15', an ironic reference to an imaginary chapter of the country's constitution. There is a motto for the system too, *débrouillez-vous pour vivre* (do-it-yourself to survive), often shortened to *débrouillez-vous* or simply *Système D*. If you want to survive here, work for yourself, rely on yourself: sort yourself out because the state will not. Popularized decades ago, these thoughts are still Kinshasa's defining ethos.

The little stall run by Fifi Beyelo shows how the system works. Her business, situated towards the edge of the city's central market, is simple: a pair of trestle tables laden with pallets of fresh eggs for sale; two plastic chairs, one for Ms Beyelo and one for her single employee; and two brightly coloured beach umbrellas to keep everything in the shade. Ms Beyelo is in her forties and is well dressed, wearing a black silk top, white jeans and a gold necklace. She has been selling eggs here for 15 years, having set up the stall when she separated from the father of her two children. The Marché Central is regulated, but on its fringes you can quickly set up a stall, or find employment to make a little money. Trade is a safety net in Kinshasa, she says: 'I came to sell in the market when life got hard.'

The footfall here makes it a great spot – hundreds of people pass by as we talk – but Ms Beyelo says times are tough. 'This is a hand-to-mouth business,' she explains. Ten years ago the women could sell 600 eggs a day but demand is now half that. Part of the problem is constant inflation. (Between 2016 and 2018 prices in Kinshasa have risen by over 50 per cent.) The wholesale rate for a pallet of 30 eggs has risen from 5,000 to 7,000 Congolese francs recently (from around $3.00 to $4.50), pushing the stallholders' cost per egg above 200 francs. 'People come with expectations. They think an egg should be 200,' but at this price the women would make a loss.

'Taxes are the other problem,' says Ms Beyelo, explaining the daily charges she must pay. There is a stall fee of 300 francs, a sales tax that, depending on the tax collector in charge on the day, could be 200 or 500 francs, plus a daily *salongo* fee (a cleaning and sanitation charge) of 100 francs. Since they make such a tiny return per egg sold they need to sell a pallet or two each day before they generate any money they can keep for themselves. This is subsistence trading and the women build no capital over time. 'We do this not to save our profit,' Ms Beyelo says, 'but just to make enough to eat.'

The market traders receive few services in exchange for the sales taxes and cleaning fees. Stalls like Ms Beyelo's are not permanent structures but flimsy mobile ones; the pitch they pay to operate from is just the edge of a dirty track. The *salongo* cleaning fee is a joke: the road behind them – in the heart of Kinshasa – looks like a farmyard in winter, with thick mud perhaps half a metre deep. In a city of 10 million the sludge is mixed with plastic, paper, metal wire, food and human waste that a scrawny cockerel is picking from. Every 100 yards or so wooden planks have been laid across the mire so that people can cross the road.

I ask the women if, with service provision clearly so poor, they can refuse to pay: either bargaining to lower their taxes or holding out until the market authorities clean the place up. They shake their heads. 'It is not worth challenging the tax officials,' says Ms Beyelo. 'The daily amounts are set low so that we cannot say we don't have the money, and it is not worth our time arguing about them.' All the Congolese I speak with say the same, and the foreign traders that are here – Lebanese restaurateurs, Indians running phone shops, Chinese tailors – all agree. The tax man calls each day and will cause you problems if you don't comply, so you pay him to go away.

The role of government here can take a while to sink in. This country tends to be held up as the archetypal 'failed state', with western coverage conjuring a government that is absent or passive and making it easy to imagine the Congolese capital as a place of decaying official buildings and unfilled civil-service positions. Kinshasa is nothing like this. The government thrives, with boulevards lined with the offices of countless ministries thronged by thousands of functionaries at knocking-off time. The Congolese state is active but parasitic, a corruption superstructure that often works directly against the interests of its people. The massive informal economy that has risen up, built on the do-it-yourself culture of 'Article 15', is a direct response.

Darien's failure was ultimately down to economic culture: short-termism, opportunism and an absence of cooperation. In Kinshasa, the breakdown is different: the public trust one another, but regard public officials – including teachers and police officers – on a sliding scale of distrust with tax officials at the apex. History echoes strongly in Kinshasa, with the roots of economic distrust and self-reliance down to the legacy of two men: a foreign colonial founder, and a home-grown dictator.

THE KING, AND THE MESSIAH

A ROYAL LIAR

Kinshasa has lies and deception in its bedrock. The city was founded by Henry Morton Stanley, a journalist and explorer born in Wales, most famous for his reaction – 'Dr Livingstone, I presume?' – when he found the Scottish explorer, long presumed dead, close to the modern border of Tanzania in 1871. Stanley returned to central Africa in 1874, publishing an account of his travels that sold well across Europe. Unable to finance a third trip in Britain he nonetheless set off again in 1879, this time funded by the International African Association (IAA), a company bankrolled and controlled by King Leopold II of Belgium. The stated aims of the IAA were philanthropy and scientific discovery, and Stanley crossed the country building roads and setting up steamship ports along the river as he went. His determination to break through impassable ground meant the Kikongo tribesmen called him *Bula Matari*, the 'breaker of stones'. In 1881 Stanley established a trading station on the modern site of Kinshasa, naming it Léopoldville.

The Belgian king had secured the massive Congo Free State, which was privately owned by him rather than by his country, by promising more powerful European nations that he would trade freely with them, develop the land, and provide education and eventually independence. Stanley seems to have bought into Leopold's vision for the Congo, as did Britain's other leading expert on central Africa, Verney Lovett Cameron. Cameron wrote at length about the evils of both slavery and the ivory trade, and championed Leopold's 'philanthropic efforts', giving a rallying call: 'Let those interested in scientific research come forward and support the King of the Belgians in his noble scheme for united and systematic exploration.'

Stanley was no saint: his accounts brag about vicious tactics used in battles with local chiefs and brutal treatment of those under his command. This Welshman was also a firm supporter of free trade among independent African nation states, and later became a campaigner for the abolition of slavery. But Leopold was a liar and narcissist with no interest in humanitarian development, scientific discovery or free trade. The king quickly sought to exploit the people and their environment via the ivory trade. In the end, far bigger revenues came as the result of demand for a new industrial material: rubber.

Charles Goodyear had developed vulcanized rubber in 1839, with John Boyd Dunlop inventing the rubber bicycle tyre in 1887 and the Michelin brothers the car tyre in 1895. The boom in rubber demand that followed saved Leopold, who had been losing money on his Congolese investments. The king sold off sections of his colony to foreign firms, retaining around two-thirds – an area more than 50 times bigger than Belgium – as the *Domaine Privé* that was protected by a private army, the *Force Publique*.

Backed by the *Force Publique*, Leopold's agents set targets for the Congolese whom they forced to collect rubber. With the easiest vines soon tapped, the quotas became impossible to meet but the agents would not relent, cutting off the right hand or foot of anyone deemed not to be working hard enough, or those of their children. Ammunition was costly, so *Force Publique* officers often demanded a hand as proof that someone had been killed when a bullet was fired. Leopold's Congo was an ongoing genocide in which baskets of human hands became a kind of grotesque currency, presented at trading posts as proof of hard work.

Horrific rumours began to filter back to Europe, and in 1900 a British diplomat, Roger Casement, reported that 'the root of the evil lies in the fact that the government of the Congo is above all a commercial trust, that everything else is orientated towards commercial gain'. The Casement Report, regarded as one of the first human-rights investigations, was published in 1904, and by 1908 international pressure finally forced Leopold to hand his colony to the Belgian state. By then rubber extraction had generated 220 million francs (over $1.5 billion in 2018 dollars) and funded a 20-year construction spree, his fondness for palaces, fountains and arches earning Leopold the nickname 'Builder King' in Belgium. Estimates of the human cost vary, but the most reliable suggest that in the Congo around 12 million people, half the population, died.

FROM CRISIS TO SAVIOUR

Belgian control lasted until the Congo gained its independence in 1960. To facilitate the extraction of diamonds and copper, the Belgian state employed locals to build railways that linked the major cities and a road network that connected most towns. But investment in the Congolese themselves was scant: with the Catholic Church providing most of the schooling and no universities established until the mid-1950s. Still, the transport infrastructure connected the country and culturally Kinshasa became a regional hub with some of the first radio stations and most successful recording studios in central Africa. With paved tree-lined boulevards, great food and music the city became known as 'Kin, La Belle'. One senior restaurateur, recalling the city of his youth, explains that Kinshasa was a magnet: 'If you got ill in South Africa you would fly to a hospital here to be treated if you had the money. This used to be easily the best city in Africa.'

Within a year of independence Kinshasa was engulfed in political turmoil known as the 'Congo Crisis'. The country started to break up, with the mine-rich regions Katanga and South Kasai claiming to be independent nations. The country's first prime minister, Patrice Lumumba, and its first president, Joseph Kasa-Vubu, were from different parties and refused to respect one another's authority. Foreign powers acted to destabilize the country too: Belgians tempted by diamond mining supported the breakaway states and Lumumba, seen as a potential ally of the communist USSR, was arrested in 1961 and then murdered by Congolese soldiers funded by the governments of Belgium and the US.

For five years governments chopped and changed. Each new leader made big economic promises, with tax revenues falling short of the spending that resulted and the central bank printing new money to fill the gap, resulting in high inflation. In November 1965, with Kinshasa stuck in another political deadlock, the head of the army, Joseph-Désiré Mobutu, took control in a peaceful coup. The Congo's

'First Republic' was dead, and 35-year-old Mobutu was in charge. His elevation was heralded as a victory against communism, and the end of the crisis.

But rather than follow any existing ideology Mobutu developed his own, 'Mobutuism'. Over time it became a personal cult backed by dictatorial power, giving him a tight grip on the economy and wider society. Mobutu took steps to expunge the country of colonial and western influence via a series of steps he called *Authenticité*. He took a Kikongo word – *nzere*, 'the river that swallows all rivers' – and came up with 'Zaire' as the new name for the country and its river, with its currency also named the zaire. The names of cities and towns were changed – Léopoldville became Kinshasa, Stanleyville became Kisangani. Fashion evolved by diktat, with men asked, and later forced, to drop European-style suits and adopt a kind of tunic, the 'abacost', favoured by Mao Tse-tung. European Christian names were banned, with the president changing his own and becoming Mobutu Sese Seko Kuku Ngbendu Wa Za Banga, or 'The warrior who knows no defeat because of his endurance and inflexible will and is all powerful, leaving fire in his wake as he goes from conquest to conquest'.

The early years of Mobutuism were good. In the summer of 1967 the president's economic plan was launched, with the country's new currency at its core. As a display of economic strength the zaire was launched at a value of 1,000 old Congo francs, exactly twice the value of the US dollar. To protect Mobutu's new currency state finances were to be brought under control with higher taxes, especially on luxury imports including cars and cigarettes. Mobutu's economics made sense, with the plan praised by the international community. By 1968 inflation was down to just 2.5 per cent and, with firms compelled by Mobutu to grant wage rises of 10 per cent or more, the public's spending power rose, the economy expanding by 8 per cent in a year. Praise names were coined for Mobutu: the president was known as 'the guide', 'the leader' and even 'the messiah'.

Yet over the next thirty years Mobutu's policies delivered an

The Congo - bottom of the pack

GDP per capita (constant 2010$), 1960–2016
Rebased so 1960 = 100

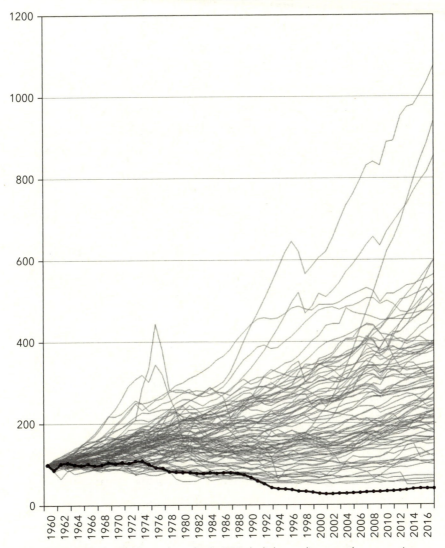

Source: World Bank. The dark line is drawn for the DRC, the light-grey lines are other economies.

economic decline that was deeper than that suffered by any other country in the twentieth century. By 1997 Zaire's currency – the iconic bedrock of the president's plan – had lost 99.9% of its value. With his currency worthless the president fled to Morocco by aeroplane, taking off under a hail of bullets. Suffering from prostate cancer, he died there shortly afterwards.

In his place came the reign of the Kabila family: Laurent-Désiré Kabila took over in a military coup in 1998 but was assassinated in 2001. His son Joseph assumed power. After an 18-year reign – a length which violates the Congo's constitution – Joseph Kabila finally stood down in January 2019, replaced by Félix Tshisekedi, the leader of a rival party, the UDPS. Despite losing the presidency, Kabila retains control with his coalition, the Common Front for Congo (FCC), controlling 84 per cent of senate seats, over two-thirds of the National Assembly and the position of prime minister. Despite the length and ongoing durability of the Kabila family's influence, in the eyes of the Kinoise it is Mobutu that matters most in understanding modern Kinshasa. Mobutu's economics drove this city to two episodes of violent destruction and gave birth to a culture of self-reliance that is at once remarkable and self-defeating.

LESSONS IN DESTRUCTION

Mobutu's first economic failure was a catastrophic agricultural policy that resulted in the Congo, which should be a major food exporter, becoming dependent on expensive foreign imports. The nub of his plan was state control of agricultural prices. Rural peasants did not respond much to prices, the thinking went, and could be offered very little for the food staples (cassava, corn, rice and yam) and factory inputs (cotton, palm oil, lint) that flowed from the rural interior to the cities. With crop prices held down, food would be cheap, allowing industrialists to pay low wages without causing unrest among their workers. Profits would be high, and could be reinvested in plant and machinery as the country industrialized.

This attempt at economic engineering was used all over central Africa, but Mobutu took it to the extreme. The price of maize was set at the equivalent of 2¢ per kilo, so that a couple of fields producing 625 kilos a year would yield just $12.50. Given the hours taken to cultivate it, this was a return of around 6¢ per day. As production began to drop, Mobutu resorted to strongman tactics, fining and jailing farmers who missed their output quotas. But rural families were unable to live on the returns, and stopped growing these crops. The number of cotton-growing households fell from 800,000 in 1960 to 350,000 by the mid-1970s, and their annual output of lint dropped from 60,000 to 8,500 tonnes. Instead of ensuring a cheap input for Kinshasa's linen factories Mobutu's policy forced them to import expensive lint from abroad. Similar patterns were seen with palm oil, corn and rice. By the late 1970s maize was rotting in the countryside, the price the government had agreed too low to justify its harvest. At the same time the country's scant holdings of foreign currency had to be spent importing food to Kinshasa.

Mobutu's second economic legacy was the near complete eradication of industry from the country. His big idea was that Kinshasa would become a manufacturing hub that ran on hydroelectric power from a dam at the Inga Falls, around 200 km south-west of the capital. The flow at Inga – 42 million litres of water per second – is bettered only by the Amazon and, being so close to the equator, is more reliable. The dam was intended to drive turbines that would provide Kinshasa with the cheapest and most reliable source of renewable energy of any major city on earth. Energy-intensive foreign businesses – aluminium smelters, for example – would relocate to Kinshasa, which would have its own steel mill at Maluku. A system of power lines would take electricity to the Shaba region in the south-east, meaning that Zairean mining would flourish too.

Foreign consultants – particularly Italian and Japanese – rushed in, advising Mobutu on his infrastructure projects. Foreign firms snapped up the contracts to do the work that followed. To pay Mobutu's bills Zaire borrowed heavily, planning to use the revenues of

Gécamines, the state mining company, to pay down the debt. Again, the plan made some sense: the president was mortgaging one asset, the mining industry, to invest in others: dams, electricity networks and factories. Western manufacturers set up around Kinshasa, with Renault, General Motors and British Leyland all establishing car plants. A German company built a huge cement factory; new breweries, textiles and tobacco plants went up. Mobutu matched the private investment with more of his own: new planes for Air Zaire, upgraded airports and modern tankers for the state shipping line. Manufacturing grew to take up 11 per cent of national output. In Nigeria, Zaire's regional rival, it was around 3 per cent.

THE MESSIAH AND THE MARKET

Things started to unravel for Mobutu in the mid-1970s, his early failings offering a reminder of the importance of diversification. Back in the late 1950s the Congo had exported both farm produce and minerals so that foreign earnings came from a few different sources. But Mobutu's agricultural failures meant Zaire's success now rested squarely on copper – his plan was essentially a wager that revenues would remain steady and pay for all the new investment. The bet did not pay off, with global copper prices tumbling from $2.20 per pound in 1974 to less than $1 by the mid-1980s, eroding the revenues of Gécamines. The first Inga dam was finished in 1973; the second dam and the power lines that would take electricity to the mines was finished in 1982. With the government lacking funds for upkeep and maintenance, the dams quickly dwindled to a fraction of their promised capacity.

The Maluku steel mill was completed in 1975 at a cost of $250 million (which went to Italian and German firms). The mill had a capacity of 250,000 tonnes and, since national demand was just 30,000 tonnes, significant exports were expected. But neither Mobutu nor his foreign advisers had thought about where the iron ore would come from. Lacking this vital input the mill ran on scrap metal, resulting in steel that was poor quality and expensive. The Maluku mill's output peaked at 7 per cent of capacity in 1975, fell to 3 per cent by 1980 and, lacking power and raw materials, hit zero in 1986.

Kinshasa was supposed to be a riverside industrial hub running on cheap power. Some even made comparisons with the German Ruhr valley. It ended up being a city surrounded by failed investment projects, a metropolis with rolling power cuts in which operating a factory at 10 per cent of capacity was the standard. The failure of Mobutu's agricultural and industrial plans had torn through the city: by the mid-80s the standard of living was three-quarters lower than it had been when the president took the helm. Kinshasa was ready to snap.

THE PILLAGES

Ask people in Kinshasa to name the worst years in this city in living memory and you get the same answer: 'les pillages'. In the early 1990s the city was ransacked, twice, enveloped in a chaos that cost hundreds of lives and reduced the rusting industrial base to nothing. They were so grim they form a kind of low-water mark against which everything else is measured. On both occasions it was state employees – the army – who destroyed much of the city.

The first pillage of Kinshasa took place over two days in September 1991. Public servants, including the army and police, had been suffering, with the government unable to pay their wages. The uprising began at N'Djili International Airport, 25 km south-east of the centre, and spread to Camp Kokolo, the main army barracks. Around 3,000 paratroopers ran riot, smashing windows and looting, with the stores of the many Greek, Lebanese and Portuguese traders targeted. The public began to join in, and by the third day property worth an estimated $1 billion had been damaged or destroyed. With Kinshasa in a state of anarchy, the French and Belgian armies stepped in, calming the city and evacuating foreigners.

The second pillage was worse, locals say. It was triggered by the final failure of the bedrock of the president's economic system, the currency. At launch Mobutu's money was so strong that 1 dollar was worth just half a zaire. But the constant recourse to printing more money whenever it was needed had caused sustained inflation and depreciation, making the currency close to worthless. By early 1993 a single dollar would have bought 2.5 million zaires.

Once again lacking the funds to meet his payroll, Mobutu demanded that the central bank design a new high-value note worth 5 million zaires – and print enough of them to pay the army. But after 25 years this trick – debasing the currency to prop up his regime – suddenly stopped working. A political rival announced that Mobutu's new notes would cause yet more inflation and Kinshasa's shopkeepers agreed, refusing to accept them. Finding that their pay was worthless, the army went on another even more aggressive rampage: 2,000 people died, and the city's factories and warehouses were destroyed. The French ambassador in Kinshasa was killed; foreign diplomats and officials from international agencies fled. The country had been ex-communicated from the global economy. In 1970 income per head had been over $1,000. By the time Mobutu's plane took off, evacuating him to Morocco, it was below $360.

THE FLOW ECONOMY

In a word, everything is for sale, anything can be bought in our country. And in this flow, he who holds the slightest cover of public authority uses it illegally to acquire money, goods, prestige or to avoid obligations. The right to be recognized by a public servant, to have one's children enrolled in school, to obtain medical care, etc. . . . are all subject to this tax which, though invisible, is known and expected by all.

Mobutu Sese Seko, 1977

HOW TO STEAL NICELY

Mobutu had one more economic bequest to Kinshasa – an astonishing view on corruption. The dictator claimed to condemn corruption, but also said that a little graft could be a legitimate source of revenue. In a country with no opposition, his speeches had the status of laws, and in them he advised public servants on how to take from the 'flow' (in Mobutu's original French, the 'traffic') of public life. And he gave commandments on how to avoid public outcry, saying: 'If you want to steal, steal a little in a nice way.'

It was not advice he took to heart, amassing a personal wealth estimated at $5 billion and, as one US politician put it, setting 'a new standard by which all future international thieves will have to be measured'. The pinnacle of his extravagance was Gbadolite, the presidential village he built near his birthplace in north-eastern Zaire. Known as the 'Versailles of the Jungle' it had three palaces, and an airstrip long enough to allow his Concorde, chartered from Air France, to land. There were shopping sprees and dental appointments in Paris; famous pastry chefs carrying birthday cakes were flown in. On a 1982 trip he took his coterie to Walt Disney World in Florida, allegedly spending $2 million – including international donors' aid money – while on the trip. Mobutu's barber lived in New York and was flown first class to Kinshasa once a fortnight, at an estimated expense of $130,000 a year.

FEEDING THE HORSE

The masters of turning Mobutu's 'flow' of public life into money are the city's police force. They are everywhere: on every street corner, at every traffic junction and outside every supermarket. They look smart, wearing royal-blue berets and trousers, with sky-blue shirts that have epaulettes, and carry a large shield-shaped badge on the left arm, with the gold star from the country's flag at its centre. Traffic cops stand out, sporting a bright-orange gilet over their uniforms;

the senior ones don pith helmets. Kinshasa's drivers need policing. There is a culture here of driving as the crow would fly, with these direct routes involving going the wrong way up motorways or around the city's four-lane roundabouts in the wrong direction. But the police are badly paid – their salaries of around $50 a month put them below the international poverty line – and spend much of their time finding ways to boost their income. They call it 'feeding the horse'.

The basic trick is the road block: every journey in this city features at least one, and some feature many. (On one short trip from Gombe to the University of Kinshasa, we are stopped four times.) They are low key and informal: a team of police officers, usually five or six strong, pull a flimsy metal barrier across a main road to ensure traffic must pass through slowly and in single file. Anyone they like the look of is then pulled over for questioning and asked for documents while the state of their car is inspected. There is no way to win at this game. Even if a driver's paperwork is all in order, extra forms can be invented. One group of taxi drivers tells me that even if their cars are in good condition they can be told that their lights or mirrors 'look like they might soon break' and are fined accordingly.

Fines and fees are metered on the spot, and vary from 1,000 francs (less than $1) up to a demand for $20 when we are accused (falsely) of going through a red light. The discussions are mostly friendly, but you can see how things could turn nasty. On one occasion a single policeman seemed to have co-opted a bunch of local strongmen, many of whom appeared drunk and some of whom had rifles, to operate a large-scale block. Thankfully this seemed to be more than the Kinoise would tolerate: people started to shout at the police, demanding to know where their uniforms were, and everyone simply drove off.

The cost of this goes further than the small payments Kinshasa's drivers must make. Because traffic policing is so lucrative, other branches of the force are tempted to get involved. In the summer of 2018 a new law banned unmarked taxis, requiring them all to carry the red, yellow and blue stripes of the country's colours. This created an opportunity for traffic cops, and in the days after the law came into force anyone in a small car, including me, was stopped and accused of operating an illegal taxi (the police ignore diplomats and aid workers, who all drive Toyota Land Cruisers). Since it is impossible to prove definitively that you are not operating a taxi, most people were paying a small fine in order to get moving again. Spotting a valuable opportunity, squads of specialized policemen from armed response units wearing flak jackets and equipped with machine guns decided to get involved, to help enforce the new law. Their motivation was revenue, not road safety, and it meant abandoning the responsibilities they had been trained and kitted out for. The magnetic effect traffic duties have on the police in Kinshasa shows how even low-level corruption has serious costs by encouraging the misallocation of public resources.

THE DIY MEGACITY

For the people of Kinshasa the daily challenge is to avoid the costs that tax officials, traffic police and others impose. The way to get ahead starts with personal greetings which, when dealing with any state employee, must be made in Swahili, a language with its roots thousands of miles away in East Africa. Using Swahili is a signal in Kinshasa: Mobutu was said to favour Lingala speakers and since his demise favouritism has shifted east, with the Kabila family who hail from the far east of the Congo appointing ministers, bodyguards and advisers who have links to Tanzania and Rwanda. For over 20 years this eastern bias has filtered throughout the state, so that even low-ranking clerks in a ministry or security guards at the port will either use Swahili or will take it as a sign of being close to the presidency. Conversations start with a formal hello, 'Salama', to which the official tends to reply 'Pole pole', literally 'Slowly, slowly'. In Kinshasa this means 'explain what you are up to and give me some cash'.

There are various ways to avoid the voracious tax collectors. The Marché de la Liberté is the city's largest formal market, built to honour Laurent Kabila and celebrate the end of Mobutu's dictatorship. Tax influences the way stalls are built, explains Jean-Christophe Bukasa, a tailor in his thirties. His sewing machine is bolted to a rectangular segment that has been cut out from the wooden table-top beneath. This means that when they are not stitching together a shirt or dress the tailors can lift their machines up and out of the table, turning them 90 degrees so that they are no longer flush with the worktop and are not held securely in place. 'When business is slow, we need to prove we are not working,' says Jean-Christophe, carefully lifting and twisting his own sewing machine to its 'off' position as we talk. 'If we do not, they will tax us.'

Others attempt to hold off the government by clubbing together to form a guild or association. In Bandal, a busy district close to the centre of the city, the leaders of a bus drivers' union explain their difficulties. With the Congo's currency weakening, the cost of imported fuel has rocketed in the past year, meaning that they cannot afford to pay the police's fabricated fines. So they organize strikes, bringing Kinshasa to a halt until public outcry forces the police to back down. Further out, the Matadi Road is often the first port of call for new arrivals to Kinshasa. One of the best businesses here is selling mattresses, says young entrepreneur Guelord Nambeka – every newcomer needs something to sleep on. Mr Nambeka sells blocks of foam the size of a double bed for 108,000 francs (around $7). There is sharp rivalry between mattress sellers, he explains, except when they come together to battle the tax man: 'We compete, but it is tax that can beat us,' he explains. 'Forming a cooperative means we cannot be the victim of a big tax.' These innovative strategies are ultimately economic distortion reflecting time spent inventing ways to avoid tax collectors, rather than driving passengers or selling to customers.

PIRATE MARKETS

After a couple of weeks in Kinshasa you begin to realize that the whole place is one huge market. Street by street and district by district, the city is thronged by sellers, and all these urban villages run into one another. Mid-afternoon is familiar in every quarter here: the sun starts to dip, the light turns deep orange, and stalls of every type pop up ready for the commuter rush. The absence of paving, the lack of reliable public transport and the constant agitation of police road blocks make the journey home brutal. But the city works, with the informal economy solving this problem by turning roads into supermarket aisles. Wherever you live in this city and wherever you work, any conceivable item to feed and clothe your family can be picked up without a detour on the way home.

No scrap of land goes to waste in the afternoon's trading. Along every road blankets are laid out by women offering massive brown tubers of cassava, along with *chikwangue*, a bread made by cooking cassava wrapped in leaves. There are pastel-white salt fish and jet-black smoked fish, along with huge varieties of fruit. Men walk in and out of the traffic and pedestrian flow, offering socks, ties, imitation designer jeans and three-piece suits. There are thousands of shoe-shine boys and even more water sellers. Other young boys act as mobile pharmacists, carrying baskets full of herbs and roots chewed to stave off infection. Men offering higher-value items like sim cards and phones or silver jewellery operate from small wooden boxes that act as display cabinet, office and cash register all in one.

All this activity is banned by the state, which has outlawed these '*marchés pirates*'. But as in the informal markets of the Zaatari refugee camp and the underground trade of Louisiana prisons, the stall-holders of Kinshasa respond to economic rules that undermine their basic needs by ignoring them. This is why designing a pop-up form of stall is so important: if the police or other government officials arrive they can disappear in a second, avoiding the payments, both formal and corrupt, that will be levied. In this game of cat and mouse there are thousands of police but millions of traders; the traders win, making Kinshasa one huge pirate market.

Nicole Bwanga and Charlene Matado explain life as a pirate trader. The best place to operate is close to or inside a formal market, to make the most of the footfall. When I meet them, the women, both in their late twenties, have set up shop inside the Marché de la Liberté. Their business equipment consists of three large circular plastic washing-up bowls, and three large sacks. Each bag is full of dark peat containing a mass of wriggling insects that are scooped out and put on offer in the display bowls. Nicole says that women in this business are known as 'Mama Pose' after the name of one of the grubs they sell (pose are the larvae of the palm weevil, the length of an adult's little finger but fatter, with a small black head and chubby white body). They also sell *makoloko*, a giant caterpillar bigger than a thumb, and the small, hairy and luminous *mbinzo*. Nicole mimics how to prepare food with a pose worm, pretending to pull off its head, squeeze out the innards and fry it in an imaginary pan. She is careful not to damage the wriggling grub, which is returned to the writhing mass in the bowl.

Selling insects is a good business, the women explain. The insects are a delicacy, fried with onions, tomatoes and spices, and eaten as a treat. Reflecting this, and their rarity, they command a premium: a small scoop of worms is 4,000 francs (around $2.20). Knowledge of the pose business – the best sources of the larvae and caterpillars – is handed down through families. 'My father taught me how this trade works,' Nicole explains. But it is also fragile. The women came to Kinshasa from Bandudu seeking a better return for their insects, and live in Masina, one of the city's poorest neighbourhoods. They have nine children to feed and clothe between them, including Nicole's young son 'Fils' who is helping them. 'We came to the city thinking life would be easy,' she says, 'but life as a Mama Pose is hard.'

Some of the problems they face are common to any economy. There is rivalry: as we talk, another group of older women fire unfriendly comments at Nicole, claiming that this market is their patch. And there is seasonality: it is late June, the driest month, and times are particularly hard. The women explain that their suppliers collect the insects from trees back in their home province, Bandudu, which is about 400 km away, close to the Kasai River. But with parched land it is harder to find insects at this time and this pushes wholesale prices higher, eroding the women's returns.

Other difficulties are particular to Kinshasa and stem from the city's warped economic rulebook. 'The summer is a tough period for everyone who trades, because of school exams,' the women say. The school calendar has an impact on the economy in Kinshasa due to the informal market for school graduation certificates. The fact that parents need these pieces of paper for their children creates an opportunity for schools, which demand payment. With family income diverted to buying these credentials, the knock-on effect is that spending at the market drops. Nicole shrugs: 'Pose are just seen as too expensive – parents feed their kids rice and beans until the exam certificates have been paid for.'

Pirate traders can be fined heavily for operating inside the market and so the women are constantly on the lookout. As we talk, Charlene's eyes dart around, scanning the walkways for officials. To avoid fines they need to be mobile, quickly tipping bowls of grubs back into their sacks and heading off to a new spot. This way of selling is precarious and uncertain, and I ask the women whether they could formalize things, getting an official spot at the market. They both shake their heads. They only need a tiny spot to operate from, but for each square metre they will be charged $300 per year (the official price is closer to $100 but backhanders push it up). Then there are official daily taxes, unofficial side payments to keep tax collectors happy and the cheap supply of insects that the market officials would demand.

For those without education or the knowledge of a skilled trade, the most easily accessible gig is to service commuters in some way. As millions of Kinoise make their way to the city centre each day, thousands get by working in what Lingala speakers call '*ko teka ndambu-ndambu*', the 'break-up business'. They are street hawkers, and buy up a large wholesaler's pack of some staple – water, peanuts, tissues, cigarettes – divide it into smaller portions and sell these during the commute. The bottom of the rung of the hawking life, seemingly reserved exclusively for women, is breaking up fuel by sifting through giant sacks of charcoal the size of a large sleeping bag to fill smaller 500-gram plastic bags sold as cooking fuel. Like the pirates trading on the fringes of markets, these hawkers are a universal sight in Kinshasa. In a way part of an army of economic exchange, they are also a workforce of loners, with over 80 per cent of this informal industry undertaken by sole traders.

TRADING RISK

More advanced pirateers make money in Kinshasa by helping to off-set the volatility of the Congo's official currency. Foreign-exchange traders are more common here even than water sellers and shoe-shine boys: a bevy of them can be found sitting on plastic chairs outside any legitimate business. The head honcho of foreign exchange on the busy Matadi Road is a man in his early thirties known as 'the president', Kutamisa Papitsho. Like others he started in the 'break-up' trade, selling tissues in the street and saving up to buy his first phone, a $15 Ericsson. 'It was a brick,' he laughs, but a neighbour liked it and offered to buy it for $25. Soon Kutamisa had built a business buying and selling used phones. Things went so well that he was able to use the profit to enrol in university. 'But I had to stop,' he says. 'While I was at classes my staff were eating my profit.' Resigning himself to a life of trading on the street, he moved into the forex business.

Like the sale of sachets containing clean water, this industry results from an acute shortage – the absence of a stable currency. The runaway inflation and rapid exchange-rate depreciations of Mobutu's years are still seen in modern Kinshasa. In mid-2016 one dollar bought you 900 Congolese francs; by the summer of 2018 almost half the franc's value had evaporated, with a dollar buying 1,650 francs.

This creates a problem for Kinshasa's residents: they need Congolese francs to pay any official transactions, including taxes, but they know their country's currency quickly loses its value over time. The thousands of exchange traders allow an informal dual-currency system to operate. People hold both dollars and francs in their wallets: the dollar to store value over time, and francs for small daily transactions. When shoppers go to the market or a restaurant, for example, they first stop to buy some francs from the exchange trader who will be sitting outside.

The exchange traders solve the public's currency problem and make their own living by buying and selling at advantageous rates (in the summer of 2018 most were buying francs at 1,620 per dollar and selling at 1,650 per dollar). Theirs is a risky job involving holding large amounts of a volatile currency, so they manage their capital carefully. 'We try to keep around 60 per cent of our capital in dollars, as a buffer,' says Kutamisa. To gauge the demand for currencies he conducts a clandestine survey, heading into a neighbouring market and posing as a shopper who would like to buy goods in dollars. 'If the shopkeeper is very keen to do this, or will offer a lower price to me when I pay in dollars, I know there must be a shortage of dollars.' This ingenious trick helps him predict currency demand – and calculate how many dollars and francs he should be holding – allowing him to make the most of the afternoon rush.

A PUBLIC–PRIVATE PARTNERSHIP

'It is easy to see informal trading at the bottom – those people are on the street,' says Father Mongambo, the Roman Catholic priest. 'But informal markets underpin life in the middle class too.' By way of explanation he gestures towards the office tower of ONATRA – the Office National des Transports, a state-owned company responsible for rail and river transport. The company's headquarters is one of the biggest buildings in the city, in prime position on the main boulevard in Gombe, and employs thousands of Kinoise who look smart as they show up for work. 'The truth is those people there go unpaid,' the priest says, explaining that members of his congregation can sometimes be owed 11 months' wages. With corruption at all levels making the tax system leaky, together with a huge informal economy that contributes no tax, the Congolese state is threadbare. The transport workers' difficulties are shared by teachers, doctors and the police, who are paid months – years, in some cases – late.

The result is that public-sector workers with full-time contracts also tend to have second jobs as a fall-back option. At the University of Kinshasa a lecturer explains how it works for academics. When wages are not paid classes will be cancelled, as assistant professors disappear. The young teachers are not on strike, holding out for pay as they might in a regular economy; they are working elsewhere – doing their secondary jobs so that they can pay rent and eat. Popular secondary jobs for the highly skilled in Kinshasa include working as translators for aid agencies, or as drivers. This system of portfolio careers has clear benefits and costs. The upside is that second gigs offer a form of income insurance, vital in a city where official government positions cannot be relied on. The downside is yet another misallocation of skill and talent: with university lecturers working as drivers rather than teaching students, a country is not putting its human capital to best use.

You might imagine that a police officer asking for a backhander, a university lecturer moonlighting as a cab driver, or a teacher billing parents for a simple exam certificate would be regarded as a dodgy character, if not a crook. The Kinoise understand that these things should not happen, but recognize that their city's economy demands a more flexible moral code. Stand at any busy junction in the city and you can see how it works. As cars pass by, a traffic cop in his or her orange tunic will make a subtle sign: some will bring the tips of all four fingers and thumb together and then slowly towards their mouths, as if eating a ball of *ugali* or rice, while others mimic sipping from a bottle. The message is clear: 'I'm going hungry' or 'I'm thirsty'.

Some drivers ignore it but many smile and dip into the huge

bundle of 500-franc notes that locals keep stuffed in their dash-boards, offering a couple through the window as they drive past. Return to a parked car and a policeman will often appear out of nowhere, stopping the traffic to allow vehicles to pull out or turn around. Such manoeuvres are impossible without assistance in Kinshasa's dense traffic, so this is 1,000 francs well spent. The public understands that police are paid a salary that keeps them in poverty, and when they are asked politely like this, away from the coercion of the road block, they are generally happy to boost it.

The same phenomenon – the privatization, informally, of the public sector – can be seen in Kinshasa's schools. Constitutionally, free public education at primary level is a universal right, referred to as *gratuité*. But teachers' salaries have always been easier to cut than those of the police or army, and things got so bad in the pillage years that in 1992 teachers, tired of going unpaid, went on strike. The following two years are known as the *années blanches* by educators here: the schools were closed, there were no exams and no high-school graduates.

Things were resolved with the national parents' association agreeing to boost teachers' pay, and a voluntary system of parent-funded bonuses, the *frais de motivation*, was introduced. Teachers' salaries are around $80 a month in Kinshasa, which puts them, like the police, close to the international poverty line (a whole category of teachers, known as the *non-payés*, are not paid by the state at all). The motivation bonuses paid by parents ensure the *non-payés* get paid, and a regular teacher's income is boosted from $80 to closer to $250 a month. Another informal privatization of a broken public service, they are a reminder of how rules work in Kinshasa. Unpopular with parents, the fees were officially banned in 2004 yet in practice they exist in every school and are compulsory.

This direct payment for public services explains why people in Kinshasa are loath to pay the regular taxes that are supposed to fund police salaries and schools. The burden can be great. Even in the poorest districts such as Mesina, parents like Nicole and Charlene, the pirate traders scraping a living selling insects, pay over $100 per child each year to send their kids to school. They are somehow paying for eight of their nine children to go to school. Their resourcefulness, as the priest said, is miraculous.

A RESILIENT RUT

THE PRICE OF BAD GOVERNMENT

Kinshasa's do-it-yourself culture goes much further than the informal economies I saw elsewhere in the world: it is a safety net that covers the whole city. In education, health, policing – even clean water – it is relied on to provide public services the state does not. Yet, like Darien, Kinshasa shows the limits of a human resilience built on informality. This city demonstrates that there are some things that only a functioning state can provide, and the huge costs ordinary people pay when that does not happen.

The starkest example is the simplest of public infrastructure – roads. In the 1950s there were 140,000 km of serviceable roads, with reliable routes between Kinshasa and major cities. By the mid-1970s the Office des Routes had become known as the 'Office des Trous' – the 'department for potholes' – as the network fell to 20,000 km. Under the two Kabila presidencies the slide continued, and the nickname stuck. Foreign aid ensures major roads are smooth; the highway to the airport, for example, was funded by Japan. But even in the centre of Gombe, the richest neighbourhood, the backstreets are dirt tracks. Today the Congo has just 2,250 km of paved roads, a network far thinner than in its neighbouring countries, all of whom are far smaller.

The lack of transport connection has a punishing economic impact. 'The potential for foreign trade here is bigger than any country in the world,' says Sebastian Cuche, the managing director of a large logistics firm based in Kinshasa, 'but the country is not even connected internally yet.' Sending anything heavy overland to the Congo's second city, Lubumbashi, means first exporting the cargo to Angola, then travelling through that country to make use of its better roads, before re-importing goods at a border closer to the destination. The Congolese road, if it were reliable enough to use, would be 2,250 km; instead the route that goods travel is over 5,600 km; it takes a month and costs $18,000 per container. Some cities, like Kisangani, are linked to Kinshasa by river. Moving goods there is cheaper, but it is upstream and still takes a month.

The result of this is a simple economic problem that is one of the Congo's unheard-of scandals. Across the world, ever bigger shipping tankers and fuel-efficient trucks – the modern workhorses of trade – have driven down the cost of transport year after year. But lacking both the ports and road network to accommodate them, the Congo instead relies on air freight, Mr Cuche explains. Low-value yet heavy imported products – everything from toothpaste and shampoo to fruit and vegetables – arrive in the country and are distributed around it by aeroplane, pushing up the prices. The result is that a city that has the lowest income and highest poverty in the world is also one of the most expensive places to live in Africa. The Congo's exports, which must travel out by this costly route, are uncompetitive, starving the country of foreign earnings. Government failure, and the sclerotic transport system it has delivered, impoverishes Kinshasa.

Transport links are so bad that the costs spill over from economic problems into political and social ones. A recent entrepreneurs' roundtable, held in Kinshasa and supported by international donors, brought together female farmers from across the country to discuss proposals for new agribusinesses. They sat down to discuss their ideas, and how they might seek investor funding. The first pitch was from a woman with a small dairy farm in the Masisi mountains who had a proposal to expand her cheese-making business. The region, close to Goma in the east, is one where cattle thrive and where artisans make a Congolese version of Gouda. But the presentation was met with blank stares: the other farmers, even those in neighbouring regions, had never seen or heard of cheese. Outside the flying classes, the country is so disconnected that local produce does not flow internally even over short distances, making this a country in which many know little about how their fellow Congolese live and work.

In addition to facing punishingly high prices for anything imported, the volatility of prices hurts people in Kinshasa, particularly the poorest. On the outskirts of the city I meet a community of people disabled by polio to whom the government has granted a tiny strip of land to live on. Their plot is around 5 metres wide and perhaps 100 metres long, a narrow lane with homes constructed as corrugated iron awnings, leaning from the walls of neighbouring properties. Each dwelling is little bigger than a bed and an open sewer runs parallel to them. Like everyone else in Kinshasa, people here fend for themselves, the men working as tailors, the women bagging up charcoal. Asked what they need from the government to improve their lot, the item at the top of their list is stable prices.

Charlotte Matalie lives on the site and explains the evils of inflation while sitting on the floor, sifting through a large pile of charcoal. She shows me the huge sack that she buys each week, before splitting it up into hundreds of small packages that are sold as cooking fuel on the street. 'Prices can rise overnight,' she explains, 'so sometimes we find that we have sold our small bags at too low a price.' The profit margins on which charcoal baggers operate are so thin that if this happens Charlotte can return to her supplier to find that costs have risen and that she cannot afford her next sack. Inflation cruelly erodes the working capital of a group of people who have close to none. We meet on a weekday, and as we discuss the challenges the community faces a friendly gang of kids run around playing and chatting and missing out on school.

MIRACLE AND DISASTER

Modern Kinshasa is a disaster everyone should know about. Since 1960 – the date of Congolese independence – no country has performed worse in terms of GDP per person, the best single measure we have of economic development. Given the potential of this country and this city, this is surely the most extreme failure of economics in modern times. Yet far from being a city in the doldrums, it is a vibrant place, buzzing, and offers two perspectives that may help as we consider our own uncertain economic futures.

The first is to be optimistic about the power of the informal, underground or pirate economy. Kinshasa shows that the human desire to trade, exchange and build a market can go well beyond small villages, refugee camps or prisons – it can span a megacity the size of London. Despite being on a completely different scale, the place I visited that was most similar to Kinshasa was the Zaatari camp. The people of Kinshasa, let down first by colonial powers, then by Mobutu and the Kabila family, have come to rely on a self-built economy of hawking and gig employment. As with people hit by a natural disaster or fleeing war, the basic needs for food and shelter are at risk in Kinshasa; here the cause is poverty, and the Congolese use illegal pirate markets as a kind of natural defence. The difference is that the malign government has been so long-lasting that a kind of privatization of the state has occurred, with direct, micro-level deals done between citizens and state employees. In Kinshasa the organic and informal economy delves into areas of life, such as policing, that even the most market-orientated countries regard as public or state functions. In its span and depth, the informal economy is greater than we appreciate.

But this city, like the Darien Gap, offers a warning about the limits of all this. The culture of *débrouillez-vous* – to look after yourself, trade informally, and avoid the corrupt and voracious tax collector – is completely rational when public officials like police and teachers demand payment directly. By the same token, asking the people whose neighbourhood you police for a small fee, or the parents of children you teach for an income boost, is natural when public officials can go unpaid for long stretches of time. But these decisions put Kinshasa in a catch-22 situation: mistrust of government means people rely on pirate trading, but the inability to tax these trades means scant money to fund the public services and infrastructure that might improve trust in government. A more cooperative system would surely lead to better outcomes, but as the Prisoner's Dilemma of economics shows, this can be impossible to sustain, and it is possible to get stuck in this kind of negative loop indefinitely. Kinshasa destroys the notion that free markets naturally bounce back or have some self-righting property – a town, city or country can get stuck in a rut and stay there.

The result is a megacity with the infrastructure of a village. Home to 10 million people and located on the bank of the world's most reliable river, it lacks clean water, irrigation and proper sewerage. In a city founded with a promise of lucrative free trade and with the potential for a manufacturing hub driven by cheap hydroelectric power, the failure of government means scant export revenue, punishingly expensive imports, a crumbling electricity grid and rolling blackouts.

At the modern river port I meet Adolf Kitete and his friend Papy, a pair of sharply dressed traders who operate a clever scheme they call 'parity' when conditions are right. 'When there are shortages or political unrest in Kinshasa, prices jump,' explains Mr Kitete. He holds up a small bottle of water as an example: 'This could cost 4,000 francs.' (Over $2, and around four times the regular price.) Across the river in Brazzaville, the capital of the neighbouring Republic of the Congo, prices are steadier (the *cefa* currency is used by six countries and is pegged, quite successfully, to the euro). When a price discrepancy appears, the men head over the river with dollars, swapping them for *cefa* in Brazzaville and buying bundles of jeans or shirts. Once back in Kinshasa the men sell the clothing to hawkers before quickly swapping the volatile Congolese currency they receive for safe dollars.

The river traders are astute businessmen. Jeans can be sold for $20 in Kinshasa but can be found for $8 in Brazzaville, so by taking $100 across the river they can double their money in a day. Taken together, the two currencies, the river crossing and Kinshasa's instability add up to a fine business opportunity, but I ask the men whether they can do better: surely they could boost their profit by taking goods from giant Kinshasa over to tiny Brazzaville on the first leg of the trip? 'No – it is always a one-way trade,' says Papy. 'Kinshasa has nothing that Brazzaville needs.'

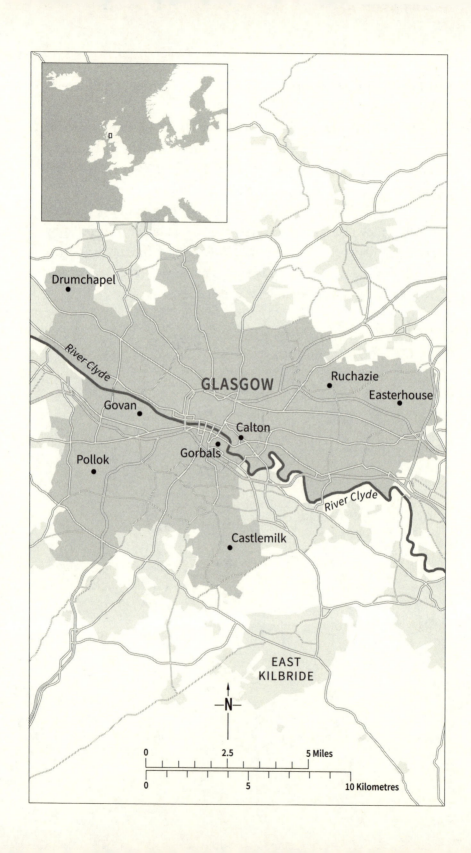

6

Glasgow

Glasgow has wrestled from London her iron shipbuilding; she shares
with Liverpool the great American trade. The energy of her children
has made her the second town in the United Kingdom.

Sir Spencer Walpole,
A History of England, 1878

Mortality rates in Scotland are substantially higher than in England and
Wales . . . Although this unexplained excess level of mortality has
been shown to exist in all parts of Scotland compared with the
rest of Great Britain, it is highest in and around Glasgow.

David Walsh,
History, Politics and Vulnerability:
Explaining Excess Mortality in Scotland and Glasgow, 2016

GHOST RIVER

A START IN LIFE

The shipbuilders of Glasgow were a tough bunch, but even the steeliest of them felt a rush of emotion watching a huge vessel being launched. 'I don't care what people say,' says Jim Craig, a 74-year-old from Govan, an area west of Glasgow's centre that was once the heartland of British shipbuilding, 'when you see a ship you've built sliding into the Clyde you feel a huge sense of accomplishment.' Mr Craig was born on Elder Park Road, a few hundred yards from the main gate of Fairfield, the shipyard where his father worked as a boilermaker. He left school on a Friday in the autumn of 1959 and started at the Fairfield yard the following Monday, his fifteenth birthday. Half a century in shipbuilding – as an office boy, apprentice, welder, foreman and eventually a manager – took him around the world; his last job was in a shipyard in Pittsburgh. He enjoyed working abroad, he says, but his heart, as with all shipbuilders, remained with Fairfield, his first or 'mother' yard. 'Wherever you go in the world, you always had affection for your first yard,' he says. 'If you got the chance, you would go back there. It was a strong attachment, because your mother yard had given you your start in life.'

While he may not have known it at the time, the young Mr Craig was joining one of the last cohorts of a line of workers – the Glaswegian shipbuilder – that revolutionized the global economy. In terms of pedigree, the yards were untouchable, for it was on the banks of the Clyde that steam-powered and steel-hulled shipping was invented, and it was huge Clyde-built ships that, between 1870 and 1910, drove the first globalization of trade. In terms of lasting impact on the modern economy, few cities can compete with Glasgow: Detroit's automobiles may have revolutionized transport but

Glasgow's ships created the interlinked world we live in today. In 1959, when Jim Craig started work, the upper Clyde had eight large yards with a millennium of history between them. Within a decade, the majority had failed.

Today you see no ships being built when you walk the banks of the Clyde: all but two of the yards are gone, and the activity that remains is small scale and military, taking place under hangars. The only boat in sight is the *Glenlee*, a 245-foot steel-hulled tall ship launched here in 1896. Fun for the tourists who hop aboard and kids who race around the deck, her modest size and antiquated technology paints a false picture of the mighty Clyde industry: by the late nineteenth century a fifth of all ships in the world – including cutting-edge steamers over 350 feet long – were being built here. The south side of the river in particular bears the scars of lost industry. The docks where ships would have once sat while being loaded and fitted out are overgrown with weeds; the offices are derelict, with broken windowpanes and red-brick walls covered in graffiti.

Glasgow is an extreme economy because no other city in the twentieth century experienced a decline as severe. To see this, consider the highs and lows. In the late nineteenth century Glasgow was seen as the 'Second City of Empire', and in many ways began to outpace the UK's capital, leading London in art, design and architecture as well as engineering, innovation and trade. Some even referred to it as a 'modern Rome'. Yet a century later, shipping was gone, unemployment rife and in Calton, a Glaswegian suburb, male life expectancy was just 54. (In Swaziland, where 27 per cent of the adult population has AIDS, it is 57.) From a modern Rome, to a place lagging sub-Saharan Africa, Glasgow had slid from being the best city in Europe to the most troubled.

The Glasgow story – the failure of a successful city – is important since so many of us are urbanites. In 1950 just 30 per cent of the global population lived in urban areas, but today more than half of us live in cities. And with 75 per cent of people set to live in cities by 2050, to understand the fragilities of a city economy is, in large part, to understand the risks of the future. I visited Glasgow to meet people who remembered the city when it was still mighty and could explain, first hand, what had gone wrong.

THE GOLDEN CLYDE

THE VIRGINIA DONS

For an example of how Glasgow once led Europe, consider tastes for art. At the turn of the twentieth century the term 'Impressionism' was a slur: critics said the paintings looked unfinished, the technique inferior; Impressionist painters were shunned by the top continental art schools. Yet a small number of art dealers supported them, creating what many now regard as the most important shift in the history of art – because it represents the step from ancient representational art to modernity. Alexander Reid, a Glaswegian who opened his first gallery in 1877, was one of the most influential of these leading dealers. He sold huge numbers of paintings to Glasgow's merchant class, befriending and supporting important artists. (Van Gogh painted just two portraits of British subjects in his lifetime, and both were of Reid.) In 1902, Germany's leading critic advised those interested in art to skip London and head straight for Glasgow.

Art is a particular example of a general rule: pick any arena – from science and engineering to literature and culture – and this city is the origin of an innovation that changed the way we see the world. The units we use to measure both temperature (Kelvin) and power (Watt) take their names from Glaswegian inventors. In addition to cutting-edge art the city's many theatres were known for supporting challenging new work by Anton Chekhov and Henrik Ibsen. It was a connected and dense city with travel made easy thanks to the 1896 launch of the world's third – and most advanced – underground train. In 1927 a local inventor linked cameras in London to a screen in Glasgow's Central Hotel, creating the world's first television broadcast.

Glasgow rose to such stature on the back of international trade. As a port, its location was one of the best in Britain: with favourable winds picking up off Scotland's west coast, sailing from Glasgow to American colonies such as Virginia and Maryland was considerably quicker than setting off from London. In the mid-eighteenth century, local merchants would buy up consumer goods and ship them to America on credit; planters would send tobacco back to repay these debts. A small group of families – the Cunninghams, Glassfords and Spiers – controlled the market and owned chains of stores across the colonies. As a result men like John Glassford and Alexander Spiers became some of the most important merchants in Europe and were given nicknames befitting their status, including the 'Tobacco Lords' and 'Virginia Dons'.

THE GLASGOW PIVOT: FROM TOBACCO TO SHIPPING

American independence cut Glasgow's grip on the tobacco trade and ruined the Virginia Dons, but the city's economic rise was just beginning. The tobacco merchants had invested in Glasgow's infrastructure, deepening and clearing the River Clyde. Entrepreneurial Glaswegians had diversified into other businesses, developing steam-driven power looms that made linen quickly and cheaply. Expertise in metalwork and steam technology gained from the linen trade, together with improved river access, helped spawn Glasgow's second world-leading trade – shipbuilding.

While tobacco initially enriched Glasgow, shipbuilding turned it into a superpower of the Industrial Revolution. The production of ships was hugely lucrative: Glasgow produced over 200 new ships each year, including naval vessels commissioned by the UK, Dutch and Turkish governments. By the late 1860s there was a workforce of 20,000 on the Clyde.

As a city of world-leading innovation and buzzing with employment, Glasgow's plaudits grew, attracting entrepreneurs and investors to the city. When Glasgow held an international exhibition in 1888 almost six million people attended. This was 20 per cent more than the entire Scottish population and included visitors from across the world. Glasgow, it seemed, was destined to become one of the greatest cities of the twentieth century.

THE HOLY TRINITY

At the same time, 300 miles south of Glasgow, an economist at Cambridge University in his mid-40s called Alfred Marshall was working on a book, *Principles of Economics*, that was to become arguably the most influential text in the history of economics.

Marshall was a highly technical theorist but wanted to make his subject accessible, regarding economics as 'the study of mankind in the ordinary business of life'. So he set his arguments out in mathematical equations first to ensure their rigour, then replaced all the formulae with real-life examples. One important question, mattering to lots of people's lives, was why firms choose to bunch together in particular towns or cities. Marshall describes how historically, places became specialized in a particular industry because of their proximity to a raw material – Sheffield, for example, is famous for cutlery because of the quality of its grit, used to make grindstones. But the advent of better transport links had loosened these ties, he said, meaning that factories no longer needed to be right next to the mines or forests they relied on for inputs. Owners of heavy industry could locate anywhere, yet they often chose to be close to other factories in a specialized industrial town. This huddling, Marshall argued, was driven by three forces, today referred to as the 'Holy Trinity' of agglomeration.

CITY ECONOMICS. ALFRED MARSHALL'S THREE 'AGGLOMERATION ECONOMIES'	
Labour pools	Clustering makes hiring easier. The owner of an isolated factory finds it hard to attract skilled labourers; locating in a town with a specialized industry offers a 'constant market for skill'.
Technology spill-overs	Proximity boosts innovation. In concentrated industrial towns technology diffuses, and amplifies as new ideas are 'taken up by others and combined with suggestions of their own'.
Supply chains	Bunching makes inputs easier to access. Once one factory is up and running, 'subsidiary trades grow up in the neighbourhood'; other factories locate near by to be close to suppliers of tools and materials.
Alfred Marshall, *Principles of Economics*, 1890, pp. 221–5.	

In a way the three forces are obvious: that a well-trained pool of staff, innovative technology and reliable supply chains are beneficial to firms in an industrial city is common sense. But the forces influence a city in subtle ways. They do not benefit one firm in particular, nor is any one firm responsible for producing them. They are somewhat hidden from view – as Marshall put it, a specialized town's industries are 'in the air' so that local children learn them 'unconsciously'. External to any one factory, they are properties that belong to a city or town as a whole. Marshall's three forces, in economic terms, are 'externalities', but whereas in the Darien Gap externalities meant free trade caused damage, in Glasgow's pomp they created huge value.

In the Darien Gap, an externality occurred when a logger decided to fell a tree but did not take account of the impact the decision would have on others that valued the rainforest. With a whole group of loggers acting in the same way, the externality amplified something negative. The result was environmental degradation far greater than any one logger could have imagined. But externalities can be positive too. Imagine a shipyard owner considering where to locate along the banks of the Clyde. By choosing Govan they have a series of positive impacts on other yards: rival firms can hire laid-off workers or poach the best ones, can imitate and improve on the new-comer's technology, and benefit when new suppliers set up to provide inputs. Just as the individual logger does not see the full damage he does, the individual yard owner does not appreciate the extent of this positive impact. The result is the amplification of something positive – pools of labour, technology, and supply chains – that every firm benefits from. Benefit builds on benefit, resulting in a city like Glasgow, far stronger than any one individual's plans would have suggested.

AGGLOMERATION IN ACTION

To talk to the people of Glasgow is to understand what Marshall meant by an industry being 'in the air'. Shipbuilding is deeply ingrained in the city's identity, says Colin Quigley, a Govan-born local historian. 'It used to be easy to define and explain life in this city,' he says. 'The message was simple: "Welcome to Glasgow, we build ships here."' Mr Quigley takes me on a tour of Govan, pointing out sites of yards, theatres and cinemas all long gone. At the very centre of the borough we reach an intersection called Govan Cross that has an iron monument in the middle. On it, here in what was once the epicentre of British shipbuilding, Govan's motto appears: 'Nothing without work.'

Govan certainly had the pool of labour Marshall talked about, and its people knew how to work hard. The standard working week in the 1950s was six days and ran to 48 hours (the term 'week-end' traditionally referred to Saturday lunchtime). This is a religious city and many would take Sunday off to attend church, but it was also common to work seven days a week to take advantage of the overtime pay. Boys worked a five-day week in their main jobs, giving their unopened pay packet to their mothers each Friday and taking extra work to earn cash they were permitted to keep. Jim Craig delivered milk on weekday mornings before his shift at the shipyard started, and helped his uncle deliver coal at the weekend. In its heyday, ship-building employed 100,000 on the Clyde, and a 60-hour week was common for men and boys alike.

Glasgow is also a prime example of how technology diffuses and amplifies through mimicry and improvement. The world's first steamboat, the *Charlotte Dundas*, was launched on the Clyde in 1801. Wooden-hulled, with steam-powered paddle wheels, she was 56 feet long and travelled at six miles per hour. With the concept of steam-powered water transport proven, the world's first passenger steamboat, *Comet,* soon followed. And in 1818 Robert Wilson built the first metal-hulled boat, which was also the first to be propelled at the stern. This little vessel, the ancestor to the massive ships that reshaped global trade, had a suitably big name: they called her *Vulcan.* The refinement of shipbuilding innovations all along the Clyde was an example of Alfred Marshall's second agglomeration force, and put Glasgow decades ahead of other cities. When the *Margery,* a Clyde-built steamer, travelled to London in 1814 it was described as an 'extraordinary apparition' resulting in a 'great commotion among officers and men' – no one on the Thames had ever before seen a steamer.

With shipbuilding at its core, a vast range of subsidiary industry sprang up – Marshall's third explanation for specialized cities. The yards required huge amounts of raw materials, with Glasgow's metal and coal companies growing as they supplied the rapidly expanding shipyards. Shipping stimulated lighter industry too. Samuel Cunard, a Canadian, set up his company with investment from wealthy Glas-wegians in 1837 and became a pioneer of luxury travel. The Cunard Line's posters advertised its glamorous voyages from Glasgow to New York and Bombay. In Manhattan, residents were lured to Glas-gow and Scotland's 'land of romance'. While these cruises were far out of the reach of working-class Glaswegians, the luxury ships cre-ated thousands more jobs for carpenters and carpet fitters, and for firms selling everything from furniture to brass furnishings, glass and tableware.

Life for Glasgow's shipbuilders was not all hard work, recalls Govan shipbuilder Jim Craig. When the steam whistle blew at 5.30 p.m., signifying the end of the dayshift at the Fairfield yard, Govan would grind to a halt. The local police force, staffed by large Highland men, would have to stop the traffic and trams because moments later the streets would be full of workers in overcoats and bunnets (flat caps) marching out. For many the first stop was the pub. Jim recalls some of his colleagues' favourite establishments: Number 1, Mack's; Number 2, Harry's Bar – his list runs to 17 watering holes. There were four cinemas, and always a queue in front of them. Today, all of this is long gone.

While pay was tight, Glaswegians would scrimp and save for important items – many working-class families would own a good-quality musical instrument, for example – and Govan's high street became a destination in its own right, with department stores selling luxury goods. Today the road is a stark example of the death of the high street: there are a few convenience stores with boarded-up windows, a bookmaker's and a tanning shop; the remainder of the space is taken up by charity shops or community projects. It is hard to believe that in the 1950s this was a place where you could buy a mink coat.

THE FALL OF GLASGOW

The problem – and the warning Glasgow represents for all modern cities – is that any economic effect that exists 'in the air', as Marshall put it, creates fiendish problems. In the Darien Gap, a negative externality degraded the environment, hurt everyone, but could be pinned on no one in particular. As a result, too little is done to stamp them out. With a positive externality, the logic is reversed. The benefits of labour pools, technology and supply chains benefit everyone in a city but no one in particular is responsible for maintaining them. The risk Glasgow shows is that too little is done to protect them.

The demise came rapidly. In 1947 British shipyards were responsible for 57 per cent of new ships by tonnage in the world. The end of the Second World War was a boon: rival yards in Germany and Japan had been destroyed; allies who had lost liners and tankers in the war needed new ones. Peaceful seas meant global trade flourished, driving up demand for cargo ships, with the capacity of the world merchant fleet doubling between 1948 and 1965. But the Clydeside yards failed to grab the opportunity and started to lose market share. By 1962 the UK's slice of global shipping was a thin 13 per cent, and by 1977 the industry had been nationalized, becoming British Shipbuilders, a conglomerate that was quickly defunct. Two centuries of world-beating shipbuilding had collapsed in less than 20 years, ending up as a state-run husk.

The lesson of Marshall's three agglomeration forces is that when one firm sets up in a city it creates unseen benefits for all others. This works in reverse: every time a firm leaves a city it means a shallower pool of labour, less technological innovation and thinner supply chains – these impact everyone that remains. The logical conclusion is that cities should take anything that harms even one of their firms – including foreign competition – ultra seriously.

Britain, Glasgow included, badly under-estimated the threat from overseas. In part this was down to a failure to recognize something that Aceh showed more recently – that physical infrastructure can be reconstructed quickly and when it is it often improves on what went before. Yards at Hamburg and Bremen had been decimated by Britain's 'thousand-bomber' raids and important Japanese yards at Nagasaki were destroyed. But these competitors rapidly rebuilt, and in doing so made huge improvements to their yards.

The new yards in Japan used dry docks: this method involved constructing vessels in a cavity next to a river which is then flooded once the ship is ready to launch. On the Clyde, ships were still built on riverside slipways with an incline, so that Glasgow's shipbuilders could not use spirit levels, but had to line everything up using a special tool set to the 'declivity' of the ship. Japan's new yards were also far bigger, allowing them to operate at a larger scale and achieve cost savings. Japan started to win contracts, eroding Glasgow's market share.

Where the Clyde had once been an innovation hub, the workers on the river got stuck using old technology. Foreign competitors developed new welding methods to join together pieces of hull, while Clyde yards often stuck with time-consuming, costly (and heavy) rivets. In 1965 the UK government sent a ministerial delegation to Japan to inspect the country's new facilities. What they found must have been disturbing: workers at the Aioi shipyard, located 100 km west of Osaka, had produced 182 tonnes of ship per person that year. This was 22 times more than a typical British yard.

Once, the best ideas in the shipbuilding industry had flowed naturally in Glasgow, as foremen looked up the banks of the Clyde to see what their competitors did. But the industry was now international and the Clyde yards failed to respond to important changes. Customer demand shifted towards long-haul cargo ships and tankers propelled by diesel-powered engines and away from the coal-fired steamships that Glasgow was known for. The emergence of air travel and restrictions on mass emigration meant a drop in the need for large passenger liners, another Clyde speciality. All of these trends had been spotted years earlier, but while foreign firms had professional managers Glasgow's yardmasters were often men from the shop floor – excellent at what they currently did, but not experts in tracking the latest foreign techniques or developments.

The shipyard owners failed to invest too, taking out healthy dividends but ploughing less than 5 per cent of earnings back into new machines and technology (by contrast, car manufacturers reinvested over 12 per cent). The shipyards were being milked for cash at a time when they should have invested to stay at the technological frontier. The ideas in the air along the Clyde had once led the world; now the entire city was out of date.

CALL DUNLOP

Successive British governments played a role too, running a disastrous industrial policy built on poor economics. Shipping was tossed around the government departments like a hot potato, producing reams of studies and reports but few innovative ideas. Unable to decide what to do, politicians appointed an independent commission, chaired by Reay Geddes, in 1965. The commission included no experts on shipping (Geddes was a managing director at Dunlop, a tyre manufacturer) and they visited no shipyards. The grand idea after months of deliberation was to attempt to mimic the larger Japanese yards using a policy called 'grouping'. Geddes concluded that there were too many separate yards on British rivers like the Clyde and they should be bundled into bigger units through forced mergers. Each of the shipbuilders would be allowed to keep their own sites, but they would act as if they were part of a larger group.

Even on its own terms this plan made no sense. The Japanese yards with which the Westminster mandarins had become infatuated were massive single sites; Geddes' plan simply relabelled existing facilities, calling them a conglomerate. Glasgow was the most extreme example of this, with the formation in November 1967 of Upper Clyde Shipbuilders (UCS) as a grouping of the Fairfield, Alexander Stephen, Charles Connell, John Brown and Yarrow yards. The relabelled infrastructure looked nothing like a large Japanese yard – these separate yards didn't get any bigger and they remained miles apart. Common sense tells us that this is not the way to achieve economies of scale.

The only way to compete with a large Japanese yard would have been to build one, perhaps a public facility that the individual yards could bid to rent depending on the contract they had won. Alongside this, following Marshall's ideas about the spill-overs between firms in a successful city, Glasgow needed policies to re-ignite the positive externalities that had run dry in the city – a massive scheme of investment in training and tools to create a pool of skilled labour that was once again operating at the frontier of shipbuilding technology.

None of this happened, and over the course of four years UCS received £70 million of taxpayers' money but failed to find the efficiencies Geddes had promised. By the summer of 1969 the group was on the edge of bankruptcy, limping along on government handouts until it was broken up in 1972. As ship manufacturing sank, unemployment in Glasgow rose, rocketing from virtually nil in 1947 to 18,000 by 1966 and to 96,000 in 1983. Today, 59,000 Glaswegian households – a quarter of the total – have no adult in work; a rate far higher than the UK average.

DEATH AND INDUSTRY

CALTON TALES

Craigie, in his mid-fifties, was 'born and bred in the Calton' – the area of Glasgow's East End that has recorded some of the lowest life expectancies in this city. He grew up in a home on London Road, at the junction with Welsh Street, right in the middle of the district, and remembers the way the loss of employment affected the area. In his childhood the East End was a bustling place: 'You were busy, busy, busy – you were poor but you were working, and your mum or dad would get you a job.' Craigie started work in the Barras fruit market in 1972, moved on to selling firewood and evening editions of newspapers in local pubs, before getting a job in the local bakery. His friends worked as children and teenagers too, some making Jacob's Cream Crackers, others canning pickles.

Craigie and his cohort turned 16 in 1978 and by then everything had changed. Marshall's third force – the effect firms have on the network of suppliers and associated industries in a city – had transmitted the painful loss of shipping throughout Glasgow. The Parkhead Forge in the city's East End would have been a natural employer for Craigie: at its peak 20,000 worked there, many making steel components for ships. But with the shipyards failing, the forge closed in

1976. The Dalmarnock Works established by Sir William Arrol in 1872 had been pioneers in infrastructure construction, making the massive 'Titan' cranes used to lift train locomotives on to ships; the works struggled on, making steel bridges for a few years, but collapsed in 1986. With the area's historic employers of young men gone, the 1980s and most of the 1990s were defined by unemployment, alcohol and heroin for Craigie, and many of his friends.

Clean for over a decade, today Craigie works as a drug counsellor at a drop-in centre in the Gorbals, another deprived area just south of the Clyde. The centre is busy when I visit, reflecting the high and rising number of serious drug users in Glasgow. As he recalls the way he slipped into addiction, Craigie reflects on the low expectations people living in Calton had. His father, a roofer, was a tough and potentially violent man who 'worked hard, drank hard, fought hard and died easy,' Craigie says. Both his father and uncle died at 55, and his aunt at 56. 'The thing is, you knew your age of death was low in Calton.'

GLASGOW'S DARK MYSTERY

Drinking, smoking, a bad diet and little exercise – chronic factors that experts call 'health behaviours' – all shorten lives in Glasgow. This city was built on tobacco, and in Parkhead and Dalmarnock (a suburb next door to Calton in the East End) recent data shows that 44 per cent of people smoke, including 36 per cent of pregnant women. Deaths from alcohol abuse are many multiples of the Scottish average, itself high by European standards. Glasgow is hilly and green, with miles of cycle tracks offering great views, but in the poorer districts more than a quarter of all adults are limited by a disability. On weekday afternoons the Gallowgate – a historic thoroughfare running east from the city centre – has corner after corner of unemployed men and women standing smoking outside pubs, many of them propped up by crutches or walkers.

A second group of more acute factors – drugs, violence and suicide – are the big killers of those under 50 in Glasgow. In 2016 the city recorded

257 drug-related deaths, which is far higher as a share of the population than anywhere in the UK. Alongside the statistics for deaths of drug addicts, both the suicide and murder rates in Glasgow are far above the Scottish average. Men are most at risk, accounting for 69 per cent of suicides, 70 per cent of drug-related deaths and 75 per cent of homicides. Craigie survived his years as a heroin user, but for many other Glaswegian men the drugs, violence and self-harm prove deadly.

All of these factors are linked to economic deprivation. Statistical analysis of the impact poverty has on health is another Glaswegian innovation, going back to the groundbreaking studies of the cholera epidemic of 1843 here. Today Glasgow has in-depth data on 61 micro-regions of the city. The statistics show that in places like Calton, Gorbals and Govan – the districts hit hardest by loss of industry – people's incomes are lower and the likelihood of being out of work higher; they are more likely to smoke, drink and be addicted to drugs and die young. In other words, the death of industry itself – ultimately an economic failure – goes a long way to explaining why people die so young in Glasgow.

But this purely economic account does not go all the way, falling short as a full explanation of Glasgow's premature death problem. Looking at Liverpool and Manchester is one way to see the puzzle. These cities, not Edinburgh, are viewed locally as Glasgow's peers – all large west-coast cities, they share an industrial history, Irish and religious heritage, and historic football teams. The idea that the three are alike stands up in more rigorous statistical comparisons: data on everything from employment to diet, income deprivation to drugs, suggests the three places – all struck by de-industrialization – are a close match. Yet one statistic stands out: premature deaths are 30 per cent more common in Glasgow than in Liverpool and Manchester. And in-depth studies that take account of economic and social deprivation fail to explain the mystery away: when all is taken into consideration, people still die too young in Glasgow.

This 'excess' of deaths, over and above those that health experts can explain, was spotted in 2010. Known as the 'Glasgow effect', it

Scotland: drugs and death

Annual deaths attributed to drugs in Scotland, NHS data

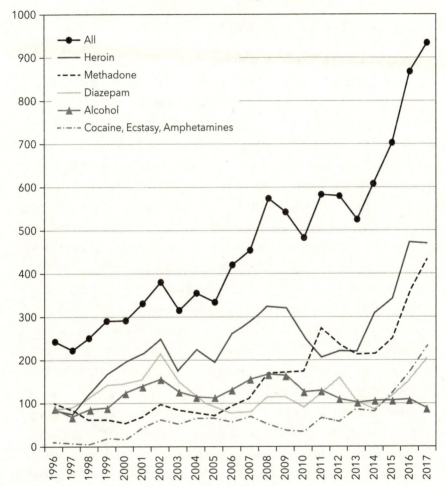

accounts for around 5,000 deaths a year. It's thought to have appeared around 50 years ago and to be getting worse over time. The mystery of early death suggests some hidden factor – something that damaged Glasgow – is being missed in most studies. Logically, that damaging force must be something that made the people here vulnerable but did less to harm people in Manchester and Liverpool. Whatever that hidden factor was, it started to take its toll in the 1970s.

HIDDEN CAPITAL

INTEGRATION, REGULATION AND RISK

My discussions with people who experienced Glasgow's decline convinced me that the solution to Glasgow's puzzle lie in another book published in the city's heyday, this one written by Emile Durkheim, a poor French academic, and ignored by economists. After a beloved friend took his own life, Durkheim became determined to understand France's high suicide rate. The nation had blossomed in the late nineteenth century, with leaps ahead in the arts and sciences, a fast-growing economy and peace after decades of war. But along with the belle époque came another statistic – a boom in suicides – that was hard to understand. So Durkheim set out to find out why, publishing a monograph, *Le suicide*, in 1897. A foundational work of sociology, it is also the root of an overlooked strand of thinking that helps explain what went wrong in Glasgow.

The patterns Durkheim found were too strong to be pinned on the typical explanations – depression, or debt – that centred only on an individual's circumstances. The data showed that the suicide rate was more than just the sum of a country's depressed or indebted individuals – it was a social phenomenon stemming from deeper problems he called the 'disease' or 'infection' of society. The cause of the disease was often a lack of 'social integration', with suicide higher in places where people set individualistic goals and, as a result, were left feeling apathetic and desperate if their plans went wrong. By contrast, he observed, societies in which people were bound together by a team ethic were stronger because goals were shared. When things go wrong in these places there is a 'mutual moral support' that benefits everyone. Just as Alfred Marshall's beneficial economic forces could be 'in the air', for Durkheim this protective safety net was something each citizen in a city shared.

THE CALABRIA EFFECT

To see how this links to Glasgow's demise, we need to take a brief detour through Italy via a groundbreaking modern study which builds on Durkheim's. In 1970 Italy devolved power from Rome, setting up 20 new regional government assemblies able to control everything from health and education to public works and economic development. Sensing an interesting experiment to track, US sociologist Robert Putnam started to make road trips up and down the country, interviewing hundreds of officials and voters as he went.

The performance of the new regional governments varied hugely. Politicians and civil servants representing Emilia-Romagna did what everyone had hoped for, pioneering innovative new laws to promote trade and protect the environment. Citizens were happy with their politicians and the economy bloomed. Calabria, the southern 'toe' of Italy's boot, was the other extreme. Here, government officials did virtually nothing except take a paycheque (the bureaucrats were so prone to slacking off, it was often impossible for Mr Putnam to find people to interview). Economically, Calabria flagged, with the lowest level of development of any EU region – in some villages the Calabrese still lived in stone hovels. By 1990 Italy had fragmented: the strongest regions were competing with Germany, the weakest stuck in poverty.

To understand Italy's polarization, Putnam followed Durkheim's lead, collecting reams of data to supplement the personal accounts and stories he heard on his trips across the country. He found huge differences in the level of social interaction. Emilia-Romagna and its neighbouring regions in the north had a vibrant social life, with thousands of football, hiking and hunting clubs; groups went bird-watching or that read books together, along with local choirs and bands. As well as such active social lives, people were engaged in civic life, turning up to vote in referenda, reading local newspapers that held politicians to account, and setting up credit unions to lend to those in need of cash. In the north of Italy people said they felt connected to a larger group; on Durkheim's 'integration' radar the region would have scored highly.

The south of Italy – Calabria, Campania and Sicily – is a place that conjures romantic images of craggy coastlines, amiable fishermen and farmers chatting in olive groves. In fact, what Putnam found were villages and towns with a nasty underbelly. Civic activity was paper-thin: there were few social clubs or sports teams, and most people did not keep up on local news and did not vote. They took decisions that were short-termist, selfish and often corrupt. Putnam was struck by the depressing proverbs the Calabrese used, including 'He who behaves honestly comes to a miserable end'. Unsurprisingly, the informal economic support mechanisms like the credit unions of the north were unheard of in the untrusting villages of the south.

Putnam's conclusion from all this was that the wellbeing of a community, its democracy and economy, rested on what he called 'social capital'. The clubs, groups and societies of the north both reflected and generated norms of trust, a culture of giving and receiving favours, and a tradition of taking part in civic life. Put together, these traditions, informal institutions and cultural norms – the north's social capital – helped trade and politics flourish, and enabled ad hoc support schemes such as the provision of emergency credit to those in need. The south, by contrast, had little social capital, instead running on a damaging cultural norm referred to as 'amoral familism', a code of conduct that says grab what you can for your family and screw your neighbour. This was the opposite of social integration, and people in the south reported feeling exploited, powerless and as if their lives did not count.

The problems that Durkheim and Putnam reported on – feelings of rudderlessness, a lack of integration, helplessness and loneliness for not being part of a wider group or project – are exactly what many people in Glasgow talk about when asked about their city's demise. The most surprising thing is that this comes up not when discussing industrial decline, but the demolition of their traditional tenement homes.

GLASGOW'S LOST CAPITAL

THE OTHER TENEMENT STORY

When you are hunting for an expert on tenement life in Govan, all roads seem to lead to Jean Melvin: at the library, at local museums and at local history groups her name comes up. Jean, a lifelong Govanite with a crystal-clear memory, is 93 years old. She tends to wear a silk scarf, held together with a brooch or toggle, and has a shock of white hair. 'I don't know much about shipbuilding,' she says when we first meet, 'but I know all there is to know about tenement life.'

Housing in Glasgow, unique in the UK, is another reflection of the city's outlier status. Between 1707 and 1901 the Glaswegian population grew from 13,000 to 960,000 – the fastest rise in the UK – and a tailored form of architecture was needed. The traditional Glaswegian tenement is three or four storeys high, made of sandstone, and contains apartments that share a common front door and a shared stairwell with communal toilets. Many of the homes were tiny, including 'single-ends' – one room where the whole family would cook, eat and sleep – and the slightly larger 'room and kitchen'. Adults slept in cavity beds (a sort of fold-out sleeping cupboard), children on the floor. Tenement living meant Glasgow was incredibly dense: in 1860 there were 330 people per acre, almost double the concentration of Dhaka in Bangladesh, the most cramped city of modern times.

Glasgow's tenement buildings have an awful reputation, famous for crowding, squalor and the shared toilets. Yet clues that there might be another side to the tenement story jump out when you visit the city. Some tenements in the original style remain. They are handsome, built from expensive sandstone, and have tall ceilings and large windows. Glaswegians who remember tenement life agree that overcrowding was a problem, but still talk with fondness about their buildings.

As well as being dense, tenements were home to a thicket of clubs, groups and societies: there were bands, football teams, the Boys' Brigade, camera and cycling clubs. In Govan, the summer fair held on the first Friday in June drew huge crowds, as floats paraded down the high street led by the police pipe band. 'The procession seemed to go on for ever,' recalls Colin Quigley, the local historian. Each end of the city had its own unique events and celebrations.

The milestones of life were marked by traditions that encouraged neighbours to play a role in one another's lives, explains Jean Melvin. A new baby in the building would encourage other young children to hang around on the stairways, eagerly awaiting the 'christening piece' that new parents would give to the first child they met of the opposite sex to their own. 'You'd get two buttered Abernethy biscuits, with a shilling wrapped in greaseproof paper between them,' says one Govanite, recalling the prize. A neighbour's nuptials were even better, as the father of the groom would throw pennies and threepenny bits in the street, creating a 'wedding scramble' as children rushed to scoop the coins up.

In addition to knowing what was happening in your neighbours' lives, you knew what was expected of you in a tenement building – there were roles and responsibilities that everyone adhered to. In many buildings cleanliness was close to an obsession, with women taking it in turn to scrub the tiled floors of the close, and the whole family pitching in when houses were given a deep clean on Friday evenings. A strict rota for washing set out whose turn it was to use the communal washhouse located in the shared spaces – 'the backs' – behind the tenement buildings. Women would often pitch in to help on another's wash day. And while today much is made of the horrors of sharing a toilet, people in Glasgow tend to recall these shared facilities as being spotlessly clean.

SANDSTONE VILLAGES

Life in Glasgow's tenements shows why social capital has real economic effects. The account Jean Melvin gives is one in which trust and reciprocity feature heavily. The entrances to tenement homes tended to have two locks, Jean explains: a large deadlock operated by a heavy key and a smaller 'penny check' – a tiny key that released a small latch. But the big locks were never used, says Jean, 'Those big keys sat rusting in drawers.' In many buildings, including Jean's, the latch key was left in the door when no one was at home; in other tenements keys were tied to a piece of string that was looped through the letterbox, so that anyone could retrieve it. While leaving doors unlocked was once common in the UK, these Glaswegian norms went further: an unlocked door means you trust your neighbours, a key left in the latch means you are inviting them in.

With doors open to them, neighbours would nip into each other's kitchens, borrowing some staple – flour, salt, butter – and leaving a note to say they had done so. Repayment would not be precise, but the expectation was that the deal was reciprocal. This fundamentally alters the economic set-up of the building: while each family may have been renting only a single-end or a room-and-kitchen, they could often access the entire building if they needed to. What was formally a collection of small private spaces became, in practical terms, a much larger semi-public one.

One of the surprising things about talking to shipbuilders like Jim Craig is to hear how volatile employment was, even in the good times. It is fashionable today to bemoan 'on-call' or 'zero-hours' contracts in the service sector and compare them to the steady work that manufacturing once offered. But that view is rose-tinted: unless you had a rare 'staff' job – perhaps a fifth of the workforce, Jim says – shipbuilders were on-call workers, employed only when there was a ship to build. The implications of this were most stark on launch days. Yard workers and locals would gather round to celebrate the ship slipping into the Clyde, but the celebrations were short-lived and bittersweet: if the launch was in the morning, lucky men were back at work on another ship by the afternoon; unlucky ones were laid off.

For many men there was no commute as the streets next to the yards were lined with densely packed tenement buildings, so that workers could head home at midday for lunch. The extensive informal networks within neighbourhoods helped men find work. Many, like Jim, were in 'father-and-son' jobs, a boy working as an apprentice to his dad. This meant the end of a contract on a ship cut at least two incomes, hitting a family hard, but information about other yards was soon gleaned from neighbours 'on the stairs'. A man laid off at Fairfield would soon hear about work further down the Clyde at Stephen's shipyard, or upriver at Harland and Wolff, says Jim. This fluid pool of skilled labour – a 'constant market for talent' – was Alfred Marshall's first force for city success in action, and it rested directly on social capital.

Women ran the household budget, and relied on other norms to manage families' turbulent incomes. Some were very simple: a woman whose husband was known to be out of work would receive discreet food parcels containing bread and soup from tenement neighbours. Others, including the way pawning worked, were more complex, Jean Melvin explains. Pawn shops' service – swapping valuable items for cash with an agreement to swap back later – was useful given the volatile nature of shipbuilding jobs. The practice was common, with shops everywhere, but had its problems. Some families lacked items that the pawn shops would accept as collateral and even if they did, it was embarrassing to be seen pawning wedding gifts or children's musical instruments. So, on hearing a man was out of work, neighbours would lend a woman their pawnable items (a new set of linen was a common example). Then another neighbour would pawn the goods. Often a building had a go-to person who pawned items regularly, was in good standing with lenders and was unafraid of stigma. One neighbour provided the collateral, a second arranged the pawn-shop loan, and the third – in distress and short of cash – received the funds.

GOVAN FINTECH

Just as Robert Putnam found in rural Italy, the trust prevalent in Glasgow's tenements supported unique financial innovations. Another tradition was a lending system known as a 'ménage'. A typical ménage involved 20 people and ran for 20 weeks. A value for the pot was set, often at £2, and each week members would pay in one-twentieth of this amount. At the end of each week a number would be drawn from a hat to determine which member had won. There was no risk involved: you could only 'win' once, so everyone was guaranteed a pay-out at some stage.

The ménage, a kind of no-lose lottery, was a piece of financial wizardry. Those that got an early win received the £2 lump sum up-front, the equivalent of a small-scale interest-free loan. Those that got a late win would not lose any money, and found it a useful commitment device – a way to lock away some cash each week. In addition to this, ménage members would often fix the outcome based on need, says Jean: 'You would swap around your numbers to make sure women needing the cash got it early.' Men would run separate ménages using a £5 pot to fund the purchase of tools. The ménage system was an innovative way of generating a lump sum without taking on debt, and only worked because neighbours trusted that everyone would pay their dues and the organizer would not abscond.

As well as standing behind Glasgow's labour market and innovative local financial arrangements, these norms and traditions provided a form of social safety net. Before Aneurin Bevan forced UK doctors to become employees of the National Health Service, a trip to see a medical professional meant paying. 'It was one and ninepence before 6 p.m. and two and sixpence afterwards,' recalls Jean Melvin. 'And the first thing the doctor would ask was "Do you have any money?" '* Families sought to avoid medical bills, with women developing all

---

* One shilling and ninepence was 21d, a little under 9p in today's money. Two and sixpence was 30d, or 12.5p.

sorts of remedies for aches and pains. This culture persisted long after the NHS was set up in 1948 and came to the fore when a child was born. Women in a tenement building would act as midwives for their neighbours. Most children were born at home, often on the kitchen floor. This safety net extended to outsiders, with families often permitting homeless people – 'lobby dossers' – to sleep in the stairwell, the coal fires dotted throughout the building providing some comfort on cold Glaswegian nights.

In southern Italy, where social capital was at its lowest ebb, Robert Putnam had found that civic life collapsed to 'amoral familism' – people living in a cynical and short-term way, acting only to further their own interest, or for the benefits of their immediate relatives. For many of the people I spoke to in Glasgow, the story of tenement life is of the opposite extreme: of the kind of 'mutual moral support' Durkheim identified and of a safety net that was like a huge extended family. 'You were a child of your close,' recalls Colin Quigley, explaining how any adult would help or chastise a child, as if they were its parent. Another local tells me that after an accident on the back-court, children with cuts and bruises would run inside to find 'a mammy' – your own mother was best, but any mother would do. 'I ran up to find my auntie,' says Jean Melvin, recalling one such incident. 'Well, she wasn't really my auntie, but they were all your aunties up the stairs.' The benefits of Glasgow's neighbourhoods were informal, unseen and unmeasured. The fact that they were hidden put them at grave risk.

UP AND OUT – RESHAPING GLASGOW

The third force that has shaped the Second City of Empire, after tobacco and shipbuilding, was the Glasgow City Council (GCC). The private market for housing had failed in the nineteenth century, with landowners building too little and landlords leaving one in ten homes empty rather than reducing rents to fill them. By 1895 Glasgow's City Improvement Trust had stepped in, constructing 46 tenement buildings that included 415 homes and nearly 100 shops. The trust also built the first not-for-profit homes that were available to rent, a first step towards the social housing that would become a foundation of the UK's welfare state.

The radical measures were not enough. In parts of the city rents jumped 25 per cent in just one year between 1914 and 1915 – around 20,000 tenants in Glasgow went on strike. (The rebels, led by Govan activist Mary Barbour, used the tight-knit neighbourhoods to their advantage: one woman acted as a lookout, carrying a bell to sound the alarm, and any approaching bailiffs would be pelted with flour bombs.) The 1915 rent strikes started a housing revolution: by 1939 the GCC provided around 17 per cent of housing and, after the Second World War, became the dominant builder, constructing 2,000 houses for every 50 built by private companies. The GCC also started to take decisions on architecture and design that had a visionary and futurist flavour. By the mid-1970s no city outside Russia would see greater state involvement in housing.

The contrast with the timid and backward-looking shipbuilding policies was stark. The UK's leading town planner, Sir Patrick Abercrombie, and a home-grown visionary, Robert Bruce, provided the ideas. A delegation was sent to Marseilles to see the revolutionary new high-rise development by Le Corbusier, *Cité radieuse*. The GCC decided to build skyscraper homes too: starting in 1960 more than 300 towerblocks went up, with most completed by 1968. The Red Road Estate, a pod of eight huge blocks, was built to house 4,700 people. Rising to 30 floors, they were the tallest residential buildings in Europe. Locals who were allocated a new home during this period remember the excitement; moving from a one-room single-end in a tenement to a high-rise flat was like 'winning the lottery'.

At the same time as the GCC turned Glasgow into a city of high-rise apartments, it also built out, constructing new estates at Castlemilk, Drumchapel, Easterhouse and Pollok. At the outer edge of each of the city's quadrants and known locally as the 'Big Four', the developments were designed to house almost 150,000 people. The first families moved to the peripheral estates in the late 1950s when shipping was still going strong and, as with the high-rise homes, locals remember being moved to these estates as an exciting step – there was more space, with your own garden and private toilets.

CAPITAL FAILURE

The economic plans to revive shipping were sluggish, backward-looking and modest, containing economic flaws that should have been spotted at the time. The housing plans were different: the country's best minds propelled the city towards a radical and modern plan, with cutting-edge towerblocks and peripheral housing estates going up so that cramped tenement homes came down. In the Gorbals every Victorian tenement building was demolished; in others the vast majority were razed. The loss of shipping had been bungling; this was intentional, well funded and meticulously planned.

With the benefit of hindsight, the rehousing plans look like a recipe for destroying the fabric of a community as fast as possible. The people who were moved had little agency: with 98 per cent of the new dwellings council-owned, families could be shifted on a whim. The Big Four peripheral estates meant communities were scattered to the corners of Glasgow, breaking neighbourly links and creating a long commute for those who worked in the centre. The high rises in Castlemilk became the subject of a famous folk song lamenting the separation of mothers from their kids playing below. On top of this, for years they were not connected by bus to the city centre, creating a population that was, in economic and social terms, stranded.

The housing schemes also revealed a sharp new political view on the role that local trade, shops and the informal neighbourhood economy play in the fabric of a place. Glasgow's earliest foray into public housing implicitly identified that trade was important, and tenements with dedicated space for shops on the ground floor were built. But that view had died by the 1960s. The Big Four peripheral estates were shopping deserts; they had hundreds of streets but no high street, meaning a long commute into town for basic staples.

The approach to pubs was even more stark: Gorbals, a central tenement district home to 40,000 people, had around 200 pubs before its
buildings were demolished; Drumchapel, a peripheral estate built to
house 34,000 relocated Glaswegians, had none at all.

The results were disastrous. Lacking ongoing investment, Glasgow's high-rise towers quickly became dilapidated. Unpopular with
families, residents reported feeling cut off and lonely. By the early
1990s the landmark buildings were starting to be demolished. The
peripheral estates were just as bad: by 1991 a map of deprivation in
Glasgow showed dark blotches at its four corners, marking out these
peripheral estates as its bleakest places. Gang culture, historically
strong in Glasgow, flourished. The Easterhouse site had been selected
because the surrounding lush green farmland meant inner-city kids
were once taken there on school trips to take in the air. By the 1990s
things were so bad in Easterhouse that foreign dignitaries were visiting to see what to avoid in their own social-housing developments.

'I broke down crying the day they tore our house down,' says
Colin Quigley, recalling the demolition of the tenement he grew up
in. Jean Melvin's daughter, Sandra Kane, describes a 'lingering sadness' as she recounts the destruction of the homes she lived in as a
child. Jean herself recalls a recent trip taken to her old neighbourhood, Teucher Hill, with the last of her living siblings, George. The
tenements, streets and shops were all gone, the school her children
had attended flattened too. They spotted just one relic of their past –
an old lamppost that had once marked the end of their street. With
nothing else by which to remember their previous life, they took a
photograph together standing next to it.

DEAR GREEN PLACE

It is hard to prove that an ambitious housing policy explains the
mysterious 'Glasgow effect' but the pattern certainly fits. While
Manchester and Liverpool, Glasgow's best comparators, both saw a

sharp de-industrialization neither experienced the same degree of mandatory resettlement or house demolition. Once a city where keys were left in doors, recent surveys show that a lower share of those in Glasgow than in Liverpool or Manchester agree that people can be trusted. Once a place where births, weddings and deaths were communal events, today almost 10 per cent of people in Glasgow feel isolated and lonely (the average in England is 4 per cent). These feelings are all associated with the kind of health behaviours, including the abuse of drink and drugs, that kill people. It is a complex story, and an active field of research, but the circumstantial evidence is strong and the locals' stories compelling.

The wider lesson of Glasgow is that there is much of value in a city economy that we cannot see, count or measure. Strong economic forces that lead a city to succeed – Alfred Marshall's agglomeration externalities – are, as he put it, 'in the air'. In this sense, they are like Emile Durkheim's concept of a 'mutual moral support', the kind of implicit and informal help that underpins an economy's success and can help soften its failings. None of these things are privately owned, they are shared by everyone in a city. And none of these things can be measured with any accuracy: they are in the ether, the philosophy, the tradition of a town. The city of Glasgow, whose name means 'Dear Green Place', shouts a warning to the cities of the future that three-quarters of us will live in: when an economic force is shared, unseen and hard to measure, you will do too little to protect it.

British shipbuilding started in Glasgow, with Govan its heart and Fairfield its leading yard. This city's achievements changed the modern world, but now are long gone. Still, Govan shipbuilder Jim Craig is proud and loyal and determined to be optimistic, telling me about a plan to build a new bridge over the Clyde that would connect the depressed Govan high street with Glasgow's affluent West End. As we discuss the scheme, Jim explains that it was once much easier to cross the river, pulling out his smartphone to find pictures of the small ferries that took commuting workers across the Clyde in Fairfield's heyday.

Jim's camera reel is full of shots of his grandchildren and, in among them, photos of the huge boats he worked on. He stops at a picture of the MS *Norsea*, a 588-foot passenger ferry made for P&O and launched at Govan in 1987. 'That was a great boat,' he says, zooming in to show the details: 'We beat the Japanese yard that was building her twin, and she handled like a gem.' I later looked the vessel up. Now renamed the *Pride of York*, this Glaswegian ship still sails between Hull and Rotterdam, with space for up to 850 cars. Set to finish service in 2021, she was the last large passenger boat the UK ever built.

FUTURE

THE ECONOMICS OF TOMORROW

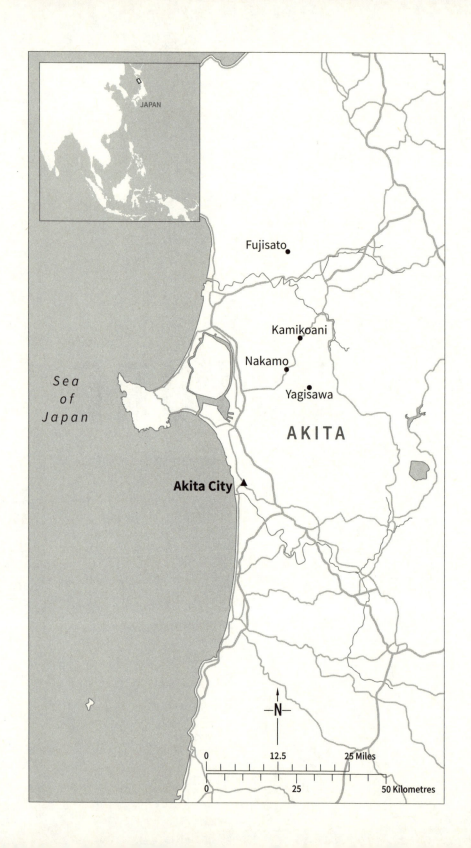

JAPAN

Fujisato

Kamikoani

Nakamo

Yagisawa

AKITA

*Sea
of
Japan*

Akita City

—N—

| 0 | 12.5 | 25 Miles |
| 0 | 25 | 50 Kilometres |

7

Akita

It's wonderful to live long.

Shigeaki Hinohara,

1911–2017

SILVER CITY

THE GAME CHANGES

Winter months in Akita bring bitter cold and plenty of snow, covering the whole of the city in a thick white blanket. The football pitches outside the headquarters of the Japan Football Association (JFA) are buried and hidden apart from the rusty goalposts that sprout up through the snow every 100 yards or so. Soccer is a summer sport here, and inside the building members of the JFA-70 league, a competition for players aged 70 or above, are mulling over the previous season and planning the coming one. 'There are so many messages when you manage a football team, and so many emails!' sighs Isamu Sugawara, the team's 83-year-old head coach. 'In the end I had to get two phones,' – he points to two smartphones on the table – 'One is just for football, the other just for my girlfriends.'

The team and their coach have been playing together for more than 60 years and reflect on how their style of football has adapted as they have grown old. 'The game changes,' says Shunetsu Suzuki, 73, the team's star attacker. Mr Sugawara nods and explains by tracing a line through the air with his finger to show the arc a ball might create when struck from the back of the field right up to the striker. Then the coach moves his arms suddenly to make an X across his chest: 'No! No more,' he says, looking sad. Mr Suzuki expands: in the JFA-70 league the players can't kick the ball very hard, so long passes are impossible. And since no one can run very fast, short and highly accurate passing is the key to success in their league, allowing the team to keep possession and conserve energy.

'Life changes too, as you get old,' says Mr Sugawara. 'You alter your aims and goals.' Like the head coach Mr Suzuki is single, a widower. 'Your plans, they become smaller and simpler. The main thing now, the main goal, is simply to stay alive.' Anything that gives you a routine is good, the men say, explaining how they train twice a week, on Wednesdays and Sundays, competing in the league and playing in three tournaments per year. But the most important thing is communication, says Mr Sugawara, showing me his smartphones more closely. They are simplified devices for the elderly with just four large buttons: email, contacts, call and text. If a player does not show up for training or a match, his team-mates get in touch immediately. The football team is a lifeline, says Mr Suzuki, 'because the real risk for men like us is suicide'.

Within Japan, Akita is seen as a bit of a backwater. It is an agricultural place with modest claims to fame for its *onsen* (hot springs), its fluffy white dogs and its sake, so good because it is kept cool by the copious snowfall. Akita is also Japan's most aged region: with an average age over 53 it was the first prefecture where more than half of the population is over 50 and more than a third is over 65. Visit Akita and after just a few minutes you realize the statistics don't lie: the train drivers, ticket collectors, the staff at the tourist information centre, the couples eating in restaurants and the waitresses serving them, the construction workers, the taxi drivers, the chambermaids and the chefs – they are all noticeably old.

In this – its demographics – Akita is far from a backwater. It is at the cutting edge; a trend-setting city of the future. The world is ageing fast, with many countries following the lead Akita sets. South Korea is behind Japan, but ageing faster: by 2050 both nations will look similar to Akita today – the average age will be 53 and more than one-third of people will be over 65. The world's most populous country, China, will see average ages rise from 35 to almost 50 during this time. In the west, Italy, Spain and Portugal lead the pack, all set for Akita-like demographics within 30 years too. (The UK and US are ageing more slowly but the trend towards an elderly economy is evident in both countries.) Brazil, Thailand and Turkey are all ageing fast too. The only places this trend is not seen are the very poorest countries, including the

The rise and rise of the over 65s

Proportion of the population aged over 65. UN data and projection for 20 major countries 1950–2100

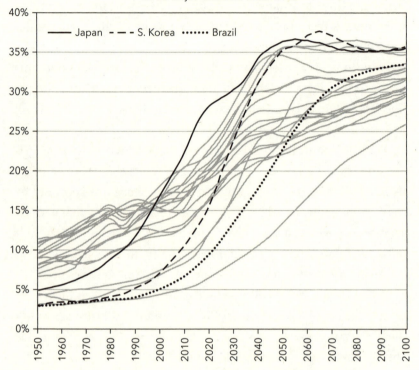

Congo. Today 85 per cent of the world's 7.6 billion inhabitants live in a country where the average age is rising.

The fact that we are heading for an Akita-like world causes considerable anxiety. Elderly people's needs create public costs – chiefly pensions and healthcare – that countries will need to fund, the economic pressure that this will bring leading the IMF to warn that 'countries risk growing old before they grow rich'. I travelled to Akita to talk to its residents old and young about the way ageing affected their lives in this extreme economy. I wanted to see how ageing tested not just the government coffers but also the deeper economic fabric seen at work in the first two parts of this book. Will our aged societies of the near future be places where people cooperate, using informality and tradition to solve economic problems, or be places where the fight to survive is self-defeating and ends in failure?

THE HYPER-AGED SOCIETY

Two factors are driving the world towards what some researchers call the 'hyper-aged society'. The first is how long people live. In 1960 the life expectancy for the average baby across the world was 52, according to World Health Organization data. By 2016 it had risen to 72, with the WHO finding higher life expectancy in every one of the 183 countries it holds statistics on in recent years. Longer-run data from Japan shows how it has led this trend: in 1900 the life expectancy for someone born in Japan was 45 and the average person was 27 years old. Today life expectancy is 84 and the average person in Japan is 47.

Another way to see this shift is in the numbers of extremely old people. The Japanese government started tracking centenarians in 1963, and that year found 153 of them. Back then, reaching 100 was often reported in the local press and marked by the receipt of a special sake cup, the *sakazuki*, made of solid silver. By 2016 the number of Japanese citizens aged 100 or older had risen to 65,000 and the rude health of those in their eighties and nineties means that by 2040 the government predicts there will be 300,000 of them. Reaching a century no longer gets you in the local news in Japan, and the celebratory *sakazuki* cup is now silver-plated.

The second factor that pushes up the average age of a place is a low birth rate. Here, there has been another global shift: WHO data shows that the birth rate has fallen by over 40 per cent since 1960. Long-run data explains the trend in Japan: in 1900 there was a population of around 44 million, families with five children were common and 1.4 million children were born. By 2015 the population was three times larger – 127 million – but large families had become a rarity so that fewer babies – just over one million – were

Japan's centenarian club
Number of people in Japan aged 100+, 1963–2016

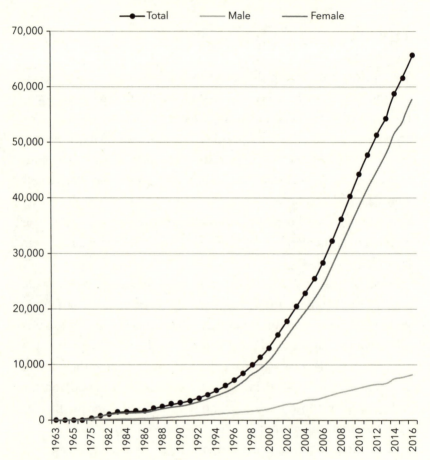

Source: Health and Welfare Bureau for the Elderly, Japan

born. As well as having the highest share of old people, Akita is the Japanese prefecture with the lowest share of children, with just one in ten people here below the age of 15. (In New York City, by contrast, around a quarter of people are under 15.) When the fertility rate drops there are fewer babies, toddlers and children to lower the average age – so when families have fewer kids a country gets old.

THE SHOCK OF THE OLD

I meet Kiyoko Ishii and her friend Shizuko Takasugi at a *Yugakusha* – a community centre for 'leisure and learning' – in a suburb of Akita City. Ms Ishii is 77 and has a youthful style: she wears a Patagonia jacket and hiking boots with a courier bag slung across her shoulder. As she leads a tour of the centre she points out a large modern hall where the activities take place; its walls are covered in photographs of locals taking all sorts of classes – dancing, playing the *shakuhachi* (a traditional wooden flute), reading poetry, debating and cooking. This is a facility for all ages, not just the elderly, yet everyone in the photos is old. This suburb, like so many in Akita, is dominated by the *koreisha* – the elderly.

'One of the main problems was that we had no role models,' says Ms Ishii, explaining the challenges of ageing as she guides us towards an older pagoda-style building where formal meetings take place. It is a traditional structure in Japan's *washitsu* style, with translucent sliding *shoji* doors and straw tatami mats as flooring. But it has been adapted for the elderly: it is warm, with mini heaters dotted around, and four chairs around the low central table: 'The elderly cannot kneel any more,' the women explain. Ms Ishii looks back on her life and the difficulties retirement has brought to her and the community: 'We were not prepared to live this long,' she says, 'because most of our parents died younger.'

This is a sentiment shared by most of the elderly people I met in Japan and reflects the fact that many have surpassed the ages to which their parents lived by 20 years or more. The country's demographic data shows what a shock such long lives have been. When the current cohort of Japanese 100-year-olds were born, life expectancy was 44 for men and 45 for women (for their parents, born in the late nineteenth century, living to 60 would have been considered a feat). But huge improvements in sanitation, healthcare and income meant that life expectancy shot up within their lifetimes so that the predictions for this cohort were badly wrong. Their lives have been far longer than they or government statisticians expected. When I ask Shunetsu Suzuki, the star striker of the local over-70s football team, what has surprised him about his old age, his answer is simple: 'Everything – I had no idea I would live this long!'

That feeling – that ageing was a shock – lies at the heart of the problems that Japan is facing and is something an influential idea in economics known as the 'life-cycle hypothesis' can help illuminate. In the 1940s a Jewish-Italian economist in his thirties called Franco Modigliani began to obsess about how an individual's tendency to save money changes over their lifetime. Modigliani thought that none of the popular economic theories of the day properly took into account the fact that humans dislike – and therefore take steps to avoid – large fluctuations in lifestyle. So, working with Richard Brumberg, a PhD student, he came up with a new one. Their idea was to start with the phases of adult life, which Modigliani described as 'dependency', 'maturity' and 'retirement'. Their insight was that while income varies greatly with these phases, our needs and desires – for clothes, food, fuel and entertainment – are much more stable. The economic challenge the individual faces is to look ahead and prepare, saving and borrowing in a way that ensures their spending – the satisfaction of their needs – is smooth even though income may dip and rise.

The predictions of the model for the individual are simple. Economic 'dependency' defines early adulthood where young people, still studying or on low wages, borrow to meet their needs. Then in the prime working years – Modigliani's 'maturity' phase – income is higher than spending, with spare cash saved each month. The pot allows a pleasant retirement during which income can fall sharply but a person's lifestyle can be maintained as they call on the assets they have accumulated. Since income and spending follow these predictable patterns the implication is that a person's wealth over their lifetime would look like a hump, as economic assets are built up and then drawn down.

On its own this seems like little more than common sense, but when you add together millions of people behaving in the same way to consider the system as a whole, Modigliani's model makes subtler predictions. One key insight is that countries where people are planning long retirements will appear rich, having both high savings rates and greater stocks of wealth – the result of citizens preparing for their twilight years. A more pessimistic lesson to take from this is that countries where people's retirements end up being longer than they planned will have wealth levels that are too low. A long life is typically seen as a good thing, but the life-cycle model shows that an unexpected jump in life expectancy can shock individuals and the entire economy.

In Japan, many people's retirement has been far longer than they imagined. Today workers retire at 65 but when the state pension was established in the 1940s the retirement age was just 55 – this was higher than male life expectancy, so the average man would die before he retired. Someone born in 1920 might have started work in 1940 expecting to retire in 1975 and having a handful of years to enjoy. But with many Japanese starting to live to 90 or 100 their retirements have actually been 35 or 45 years long. Some of this cohort have been retired for longer than the years they worked, and retired for longer than some of their parents lived. Many of the country's elderly did not expect to be around today and had no generation before them to pave the way. It is little surprise that few of them planned for it.

OLD-AGE TENSIONS

'It is tough to get by on the state pension,' says Mrs Takasugi. The average pension income in Japan is around $1,700 per month, but since it is based on lifetime contributions many elderly people – particularly women – have monthly incomes well below $1,000. While this is good by international standards it is not when Japan's high cost of living is taken into account, and more than half of the country's pensioners have no other regular cash coming in. The number of pensioners reliant on welfare has almost doubled over the past decade, and research suggests that close to 10 million pensioners may be living in poverty. For many, there is no private nest egg: 17 per cent of Japan's elderly have run down the 'hump' of assets the life-cycle model predicted they would need and are left with no savings at all. Despite the bitter temperatures, many pensioners in Akita grow vegetables to sell, Mrs Takasugi says, as a way of generating a little extra income.

The problem is that pensions in Japan are at once too low and too high. At the same time as Akita's *koreisha* scrimp, save and farm their way through retirement, longevity is putting intense pressure on Japan's government finances. In 1975 social security and health-care spending commanded 22 per cent of the country's tax revenue; by 2017 the figure, driven up by elderly care and pensions, had risen to 55 per cent. By the early 2020s the figure is set to hit 60 per cent. To look at it another way, every other public service in Japan – education, transport, infrastructure, defence, the environment, the arts – could rely on almost 80 per cent of tax revenue in 1975, but the increase in elderly-related spending means that only 40 per cent is left for all other national public expenditures. In budgetary terms, ageing is eating Japan.

This is a universal problem that South Korea, Italy and all the other countries following Japan on the road to a hyper-aged economy will have to face. Ageing came as a shock for a whole generation of elderly people who are unprepared and will need their pensions topping up. The young will have to pay, raising the prospect of tensions between young and old.

Japan is an interesting place to put intergenerational solidarity to the test because the notion of 'respecting your elders' does not quite cut it here. The traditional culture is one in which elders are worshipped: a central plank of Confucian ethics – the concept of *oyakoko* – demands filial piety and respect for one's forebears. Other ancient norms survive – like the protection of the dynastic ancestor household – in which appreciation of parents and care for elders are given great weight. This is a country where respect for the elderly is not just polite but is interwoven tightly with ancient history and philosophy.

There is plenty of opportunity for showing respect to the elderly in a hyper-aged place like Akita. At the local university I meet a group of students to discuss their thoughts on ageing, and discover that many either live with or spend significant time caring for their grandparents despite full-time study. On local buses the concept of the *shirubu shito* (silver seat) means that the young should always give way to an elderly person needing to sit down; and another scheme – the 'bus-coin' rule – means that Akita's *koreisha* can travel anywhere in the prefecture for a token 100-yen piece (around 80¢, or 65p).

But friction between the age groups is starting to build. Some of the grumbles you pick up are low level: the elderly are known to be a menace on the roads, for example. Other frustrations are more serious. 'They go to hospitals and just congregate there sitting and talking,' explains one student, 'and they don't take into account the costs of this.' This is such a common complaint that the Akita students explain there are jokes about it (Q. Why wasn't the elderly person at the hospital today? A. Because they were at home ill). They then take me through the kanji symbols used in a familiar phrase, *sedai-kan kakusa*, that keeps coming up. The symbols – 世代間格差 – mean 'generations', 'between' and 'disparity' – Japan's version of inter-generational inequality. The young people of Akita are aware of the costs the elderly impose, and that they are the ones expected to foot the bill.

A new vocabulary is appearing, and it is a long way from the respect that *oyakoko* demands. The word *rojin* (an aged person) has been adapted to produce *rojin boke* (a senile old person) or *rojin mondai* (the problems associated with old people). *Kareishuu* is the smell of ageing, applied particularly to old men, and *ojinkusai* is to behave like an old man. Young people might call their friends a *shobukure* (a dull old man) during an argument. Old women get abuse too: an *obatarian* is a pesky middle-aged woman, the type that elbows her way to the front in a department store sale but then demands to be given a *shirubu shito* on the way home. Family-based nursing care can be a decades-long burden in Japan, hence women (who bear the brunt of it) complaining of *kaigo jigoku* (nursing-care hell).

Many of these terms were first coined or popularized in the past 20 years and are one of many signs that ageing will be a real test of cohesion between the generations. Attitudes towards pensions are another. The state system was founded in 1942 and, as in most countries, works on a pay-as-you-go basis. This means there are no individually earmarked pots of money that are saved up; instead, the contributions a worker makes are used immediately to pay the pensions of the country's elderly. Pay-as-you-go pensions are an intergenerational pact: young workers pay today's pensions in the expectation that they will get the same deal when they retire.

But with *sedai-kan kakusa* – a common point of discussion in Japan – the system is becoming unstuck. Those in their forties and fifties have already been put on a less generous system, and young workers I meet expect it to be pared back even further, leaving them paying ¥15,000 (around $140) a month to fund a benefit they doubt they will receive when their time to retire comes. Their scepticism is justified: the vast majority of advanced economies plan to ease the pension burden by cutting the amounts paid and making pension ages higher. European countries have moved first, with the value of pensions trimmed in Italy, Spain and Germany. The most forward-thinking countries – the Czech Republic and Denmark – have set pensionable ages for their youngest workers at 70 and 72 respectively.

These reforms mean that, over the next 30 years or so, many countries' pension systems will require young workers to fund a system that everyone knows will be far less generous by 2050. It is hardly a way to generate confidence in public policy. Official statistics for Japan show that two-thirds of people do not trust that the pension system will cover them through their retirement, with the worry more acute among the young. For now, few students in the UK or US think much about pensions, but for those I met at Akita University it was a persistent concern. As Kana Sasaki, one 20-year-old, put it: 'pensions are constantly on my mind'.

The risk is that people choose to opt out of pension systems. While Japanese employees make payments automatically via payroll, the self-employed pay their contributions directly. In 1990 over 85 per cent paid their pension dues but by 2017 just 60 per cent did so, and among the young the number has fallen below 50 per cent. At the same time, long-running government surveys that track social solidarity (*shakai rentai*) by asking questions about social contributions and intergenerational harmony show that young people feel far less positive about Japan than older ones do. For a country built on the concepts of duty and collectivism these are worrying trends.

DOMESTIC BLISS TURNS SOUR

As well as angst between the generations, ageing is causing new tensions between the sexes in Japan. The post-war Japanese family had specific roles for men and women, the young and old. The budget was controlled by the wife, who took decisions on household maintenance, repair and upkeep, tracking it all in a special book, the *kakeibo*. Women also ensured the children did well at school, budgeting for private classes in the evenings, hence the nickname 'education mama'.

All of this required funding and set the expectation for the perfect husband, a 'salaryman'. Ultra-reliable, the salaryman's task was to hold down a steady job either in a big company – a member of the Nikkei 225 like Honda, Mitsubishi or Olympus was ideal – or as a bureaucrat. Once in his position the salaryman would stick like a limpet: allegiance to the company was sworn on 1 April each year, with switching firms regarded as treason. Salarymen would be promoted via the *nenkojooretsu* system which gives merit for years of service, rather than performance. Steady men like this were sought after as husbands: 'All I wanted was a salaryman,' explains one woman in her late seventies, thinking back to her teenage years.

Today the concept of the salaryman is unravelling. 'We had a model of the successful man,' says Kiyoko Ishii. 'His job was to work hard and earn money; and to spend his free time drinking, playing golf and singing karaoke,' she explains. All the *koreisha* I meet, brought up on the concept, agree: the duty of a salaryman was to work, or to engage in work-related leisure time. Hours were long – 16 a day was normal – and weekends were often taken up by mandatory 'away days' at camps with colleagues. With work taking up so much of his time, the salaryman would rarely be seen at home.

Salarymen and their wives were not prepared for decades of retirement. I hear of salarymen adrift: 'Company friends were not real friends,' is how one elderly man describes it; others are lonely, their lives devoid of a social network and structure. Retired women describe husbands who mope around the house, with few hobbies and who are unable or unwilling to cook. This annoys their wives so intensely that a new vocabulary chastising them has arisen. Retired men can be described as *sodaigomi* (a large garbage bag that is hard to dispose of) or *nureochiba* (fallen and rotting autumn leaves that stick annoyingly to footwear); their wives complain of *otto zaitaku sutoresusho* (retired husband stress). Elderly divorce has surged over the past 25 years.

'Ageing well is difficult for men,' says Mr Suzuki, the footballer. Loneliness is a risk when you have no network to fall back on, he explains: 'This is why so many people my age are committing suicide.' Mr Sugawara, the head coach, recalls a clever high-school classmate who became a salaryman and devoted his life to his company. 'He worked too hard, had no real friends, was too involved with competition at work.' There is a lesson in the lives of two samurai, he says: 'Nobunaga was clever and bold, but he was a lone wolf and was murdered at a young age. Tokugawa made alliances and friends, and he lived until his seventies.' Too many Japanese men were like Nobunaga: individualists scrabbling desperately for promotion. Surviving old age goes beyond saving a pot of retirement money: you need to invest in vital social assets – friends, sports networks – too. The team look on at their octogenarian leader with adoration as he concludes: 'As a man you must do your best at work but you need a private life – to be with friends and just do nothing, to do silly things, and to talk.'

SUICIDE AND LONELINESS

The Japanese reputation for formality and politeness is well deserved. In Akita meetings start with bowing, handshakes, the exchange and careful examination of business cards, before more formal introductions and biographies, copious expressions of thanks, the pouring of green tea and often the exchange of gifts. But pleasantries are not used to mask tough topics and after ten or fifteen minutes of an interview with an elderly person two words – *jiatsu* and *kodokushi* – will tend to come up. The words mean 'suicide' and 'lonely death' and have become part of the everyday vocabulary of ageing here. It seems that if you are over 70 in Akita the chances are that someone you know has met one of these fates, often pretty recently.

Suicide became worryingly common in Japan in the mid-1990s and its prevention has been a major goal of Japanese public-health policy since the mid-2000s. Government-funded counselling services and mental-health hotlines have helped combat the problem, with reams of data collected on suicides outlining the latest patterns. (For example: there has been a shift in the way people commit suicide, with fewer burning charcoal to produce carbon monoxide and more mixing bathroom chemicals to make deadly hydrogen sulphide gas.) Another new trend is the elevated elderly suicide rate: there were over 12,000 suicides of those aged 50 or over in 2016, which as a share of the population is much higher than in other countries. Most of the cases are of 50- to 69-year-olds and the vast majority are men. Here too Akita is an extreme: Japan's most elderly prefecture also has its highest official suicide rate.

The actual rate of elderly suicide may be far higher since many of those who take their own lives are isolated and their corpses can remain undiscovered for months, or even years. There were an estimated 46,000 *kodokushi* in 2016; the vast majority were elderly people and the number is thought to be rising fast. Many lonely deaths are suspected suicides and the two phenomena are now so common that companies dedicated to dealing with the aftermath have been set up. Masura Nishimura, a director of one of these specialist outfits, explains that it is a complex job combining administrative duties (collecting deceased persons' belongings and papers) and specialist cleaning tasks (the company uses a secret mix of chemicals to get rid of the smell and stains).

Mr Nishimura's company deals with on average five or six *kodokushi* per month and are busiest in the early summer, when the stench of a corpse kept chilled through the winter months alerts neighbours to the decaying body. He says there are suicides among the lonely deaths and that a typical case is a single man, often divorced, between 50 and 70 years old. This is the dangerous age, he explains: with people regularly living into their nineties or beyond, those below 70 are considered young and rarely receive extra support from the state or their peers. The most common reason for these lonely deaths, where suicide notes are found or a person's papers assessed, he says, seems to be poverty.

VANISHING VILLAGES

The global trend towards lower birth rates means that entire countries are starting to shrink. Unlike ageing this trend is not seen everywhere – slightly higher birth rates and inward migration are keeping the population up in the US, UK and France, for example – but it will reshape a host of nations across the globe. Japan, the world's trendsetter, has been shrinking for a decade, its population peaking at 128 million in 2010 and falling to 126 million by 2019. Southern Europe, in particular, is following fast with Italy, Spain and Portugal already experiencing population decline. Germany will start to shrink in 2022, Korea in the early 2030s. Akita, Japan's cutting edge of ageing economics, has experienced population decline for over 25 years and offers a valuable window on the future.

The main strip in Fujisato is what people in rural Japan call a 'shutter street'. Every shop is closed, with neat metallic roll-down shutters pulled over the windows. Faded kanji letters above the doorways reveal that one was a bakery and another a shoe shop, and across the road is a large frontage of a defunct women's clothing store. Further on, as the main road reaches a junction, there is a closed-down petrol station and garage.

Fujisato is around 90 km north of Akita City, and sits at the edge of the huge Shirakami-Sanchi beech forest that separates Akita from its neighbouring Aomori prefecture. It is a place in decline. Ten years ago the population was close to 5,000 but today only 3,500 people live here, making it one of Japan's most rapidly vanishing places. Numbers are set to decline by more than 40 per cent over the next 20 years. With too few customers to serve, the shops have closed. Just one store, a junk emporium selling and recycling huge box televisions, rusty refrigerators and filing cabinets – all of them obsolete 15 years ago – is open. As I wander the streets looking for the town hall, a single elderly lady cycles past, on her way to the modern garage on the outskirts of town that sells a few basic household items. The Japanese have a new term for this too: she is a *kaimono nanmin* – a 'shopping refugee'.

Fukami Sasaki, 61, is the town's mayor and has lived in Fujisato his whole life. Having spent most of his career as a local bureaucrat he rose to lead the council in late 2016. The mayor has the town's declining population on his mind and at his fingertips: at a snap of his fingers an assistant rushes off to fetch a data sheet on Fujisato's demographics. The print-out that returns is incredibly detailed, dividing the residents of this tiny place into five-year cohorts. His overriding aim, Mayor Sasaki says, is to ensure that there are at least 20 children in each grade at the local school, and 100 in each five-yearly cohort. But the data sheet shows the scale of his problem. Fujisato is precariously top heavy: there are hundreds of people over 90 years old here, but just 77 children under the age of five. Unless people move to the village, bringing toddlers with them, the mayor is going to miss his target in coming years.

Elsewhere in rural Akita, places are even further along the road to extinction. Yagisawa in deep winter is as picturesque a scene as you could hope for: nestled between mountains, the village is divided by a bubbling wooden bridge joining its two halves. The village once had a population of over 200, but there are just 15 people living here now, explains Mr Morimoto, a local guide. Many houses are boarded up, and there are a few deserted properties that have been left open to the elements. A large central building – a school – sits in prime position near the river, but classes have stopped. In the nearest large village, Kamikoani, the small library holds archive pictures of Yagisawa 60 years ago: it is summer and the village is staging a sports day, with at least 17 children taking part. Today there are none.

THE GOLD-DUST GENERATION

If grumpy old salarymen have become a point of mockery in Akita, another demographic group has become hugely popular. The vital role families with children play in keeping a village or town alive is often mentioned by shopkeepers, local politicians and restaurateurs alike who all talk glowingly of *kosodate sedai* – the 'child-rearing generation'. Young couples in their twenties and thirties are like gold-dust here – they spend money locally supporting shops, and their kids keep the local schools going.

Fujisato is at the frontier of Akita's long-life trend, with 52 per cent of the population over 65 years old already. The mayor has ideas to help offset the costs that this causes for the town: 'I want people to work until 75,' he says, explaining that he has attracted industry, in the form of a potato-processing factory, to the town as a way to boost elderly employment and earnings. But his big push as mayor is to make life in Fujisato as attractive as possible to young families. The plan involves education: investing in the kindergarten and repurposing a deserted building as a new high school. There are ideas on housing schemes too: the mayor wants to identify deserted homes that young couples could buy cheaply, or be allocated free of charge. Recognizing the lack of local employers, the mayor is pinning his hopes on those able to work remotely, and wants to boost the town's Wi-Fi signal to accommodate this.

The raw calculus of Japan's demographic change suggests that this project is destined to fail. Fujisato is a nice enough spot: the nearby Shirakami-Sanchi is the largest virgin forest in east Asia and home to species of bird seen nowhere else on the planet; there are beautiful paths to hike and natural hot springs that draw tourists. But the fact that Japan's population is shrinking means there are pretty villages all over the country that are dying out. A recent report suggests there are 869 municipalities – 50 per cent of the total – that are due to 'disappear' over the next 21 years if current trends persist. In the fight to attract young people the mayor has a lot of competition, and the experience others have had is not encouraging.

With its population nose-diving, the town of Tsuwano in southern Honshu has been even more proactive in its attempts to attract young workers. I meet Hidekazu Miyauchi and Kenji Hiyashi, representatives from Tsuwano, in Tokyo; Mr Miyauchi, in his fifties, presents me with statistics showing the town had a population of 13,400 in 1980, which had dropped to 7,600 by 2015. 'In many years the population was falling by 11 per cent,' he says. In response they have set up a marketing office in Tokyo called the Tsuwano Hub to extol the town's virtues; they have invested in a cool logo, a slick website and a press campaign that aims to attract young people disillusioned by city living to their town. They have had some success: Mr Hiyashi is 31 years old and moved to Tsuwano when he got fed up with cramped Tokyo, he explains. He commends the cheap housing, a close-knit community and the absence of a daily commute. 'You see we have had some success,' laughs Mr Miyauchi: 'Last year our population only fell by 8 per cent!'

SHRINKING PAINS

The main worry in places such as Fujisato and Tsuwano is that public services such as schools and hospitals are becoming harder to sustain. This has made village mergers a hot topic in rural Japan, with the government encouraging shrinking places to unite. This is the kind of policy to look out for soon in Italy and Portugal, where deserted villages are starting to become a point of public concern. Merging is a good idea, one local explains: if towns and villages share public services – buses, schools and libraries – there is a better chance of keeping more of them open.

The problem Akita faces is that proposed mergers consistently fail. One basic disagreement is what the name of the new place should be. Towns here have important historical or naturalistic references in their names: on the way back from Fujisato I drive through Ikawa (cherry blossom), Nagamote (long face) and Gojome (five castles). Merging towns often means bringing together the kanji symbols, producing names that look ugly and mean little. One example close to Akita City is Katagami, a merger of the towns of Showa, Itagawa and Tenno – its name is a portmanteau word, a mishmash of kanji with no real meaning. One local puts it to me in a way that expresses the sense of loss: 'The old towns had deep names. The modern names are a sadness point.'

Local rivalries and pecking orders also get in the way of rural mergers. By tradition, the high-ranking villages and families in an area are those that founded the place, or that fed the people with the produce of their hunting and fishing. Yagisawa, for example, is a famous home for bear hunters who were held in high regard for their ability to supply meat and traditional medicines made from parts of bear carcasses. People from these families and places have huge clout, albeit informal, and can delay merger plans that elected mayors and bureaucrats put together.

Another difficulty is debt. Heavily indebted villages are often keen to merge, while those in a stronger financial condition want to retain independence. Kamikoani, a large village near Yagisawa, is set to shrink by 40 per cent over the next 20 years and is known locally to be ready to merge with another village, but its debt makes it an unattractive partner. A recent proposed merger would have united Fujisato ('God-living town') with five other small towns to create a new conglomerate settlement taking the forest's name, Shirakami. But in addition to names, debt and power differences, there are fine varieties of culture and tradition between even the smallest hamlets in Akita, with each having specific gods and dances, festivals and recipes. The merger failed. All the while the schools in these places have tiny classes and are slated for closure, local doctors are moving away and more shopkeepers are rolling down their shutters.

MARKET FAILURES

As Japan's most aged villages begin to vanish, political and economic structures taken for granted elsewhere start to fail. Take local politics. In one sense the mayor of Fujisato's ambitious ideas are justified: local authorities across Japan have been given more autonomy in the past 40 years as Tokyo has sought to decentralize, allowing some tax and spending decisions – setting teachers' pay, for example – at a local level. But in another sense they are pipe dreams: when a village or town is set to die out grand visions for reform become pointless. The idea that politics really doesn't matter when a place is shrinking is sucking the life out of local democracy. Across Japan, one-fifth of seats in the 2015 local elections were uncontested due to lack of candidates. Despite the fact that devolution of power was warmly supported, many villages are now so short of willing politicians that proposals to abandon local democracy altogether are being considered.

Vital markets stop working in places that are dying out. Perhaps the best example is housing. The deserted villages of Akita are far from alone – there are thought to be 8 million *akiya* – 'ghost homes' – in Japan, with over 40,000 sq. km of abandoned land. One recent study estimated that this wilderness will double in size by 2040, by which time it will cover a land mass the size of Austria. Ghost homes, once a rural phenomenon, are starting to appear in major cities and within 15 years could account for 35 per cent of all houses, according to another study. The result is very different from the kind of housing slump or downturn seen in the UK and US a decade ago. It is not that prices in Japan have tumbled. With no one to live in these houses there is no price, however low, at which they can be sold. With no trading at all the concept of their 'price' becomes irrelevant. Parts of Japan's housing market have completely frozen.

The shutter streets and ghost houses in Akita's vanishing towns and villages create a sense of grief and mourning, locals say. 'The loss of tradition is difficult,' says Masaru Kaneya, a 70-year-old retiree who lives in a small village on Akita's coast. At least five homes in his small village are abandoned, he explains, and although he is worried about the future, as the eldest son in his family he is bound by a special duty – *hakamairi* – to visit and maintain the family's ancestral grave. The responsibility is a serious one, meaning that eldest sons find it hard to move away even if a village is dwindling rapidly. If the decision to leave – to find work, or a school – is finally taken the head of the household can feel a shame so deep that they will often refuse to tell their children where the family originally came from: the rural root is cut completely. As Mr Kaneya puts it, 'Dealing with a long life is OK; dealing with the end of a place is harder.'

Life in ageing Akita offers a series of warnings to the places that will come to mirror it, demographically, in the near future. The old-age economy brings new tensions – not just concern over government budgets, but stresses between husbands and wives, and between the young and old – that Japan's closest followers, including South Korea and China, may experience. Partly driven by low birth rates, it also brings an acute sense of loss, akin to that seen in Glasgow, as towns and villages dwindle and die as they are beginning to in Italy and Portugal. Yet despite all these concerns, there is another side to the economics of ageing, and to travel in Japan's most elderly places is also to discover a world of new, surprising and positive angles on this defining trend of the future economy.

GOLD, NOT SILVER

Despite the concern about pensioner poverty, for the retired *koreisha* I meet in Akita low income is rarely the primary concern. 'Remember that today's elderly are the "last war generation",' says Kiyoko Ishii, explaining the hardships that were endured after the Second World War: 'They lived truly poor – hungry, with not enough to eat.' As you travel through rural Akita you realize that a culture of make do and mend is in the DNA here – the wooden houses are held together with boards, planks and plywood patches, just as the cars – predominantly Toyotas built in the 1990s – are kept ticking over and gleaming by their careful owners. The elderly vegetable-growing business I was told about is a major operation: even modest houses have decent gardens, most of them dominated by a huge metal frame over which thick transparent plastic has been stretched to make a sizeable greenhouse.

Just like economies in the first two sections of this book, Akita is another place where the informal economy has kicked in. Many of the elderly couples here are more than self-sufficient, taking the fruit and vegetables from their greenhouses to local *michi-no-eki* – roadside rest stations where boxes of produce can be left for sale by locals under a kind of honesty system. At these markets in Akita local delicacies include the 'love thief', a fruit midway between a tomato and a plum whose sweet and sour taste is said to steal the hearts of those who taste it, along with a jam made from the fruit, which is called 'cheeks enthusiast'. Next to each box the seller leaves a photo of themselves, creating a montage of hundreds of small-scale farmers well into their eighties.

LIFE BEGINS AT 75

'I am very pleased,' says Natsue Hyakumoto, 'to have finally become a *proper* elderly person.' Mrs Hyakumoto had just turned 75, she explained, meaning that she had become a member of the so-called *koki koreisha* – or 'later-term' elderly, now distinguished in Japan from the *zenki koreisha*, or 'early' elderly. I had come south from Akita to visit a group of actors working at the arts centre in Saitama, a suburb on the northern fringe of Tokyo. Competition for roles at the theatre is intense, she explained, and since many of her friends and rivals are older than she is, being part of the *koki koreisha* club is like a prize. 'Being 75 or older is something we wear with pride,' she says.

Acting in Saitama is a world away from the elderly amateur dramatics of the English village hall. Performances are taken seriously, explain Sachiko Ukegawa and Hiroshi Watanabe, the artistic director of the company and head of the Saitama Arts Foundation. This starts with the name: the company is called Saitama Gold. The idea is that elderly people in Japan are fed up with the constant use of 'grey' and 'silver' as references to their hair – so when naming the theatre they deliberately avoided anything patronizing or that seemed to confer second-class status. The facilities here are top notch – it is all brushed concrete, polished steel and sleek lines reminiscent of London's South Bank.

Most importantly, the artistic credentials are unquestionable. The Gold Theatre was founded in 2006 by Yukio Ninagawa. One of Japan's most highly acclaimed theatre directors, he staged many plays in London and received a CBE in 2002. Ninagawa, who died in 2016, wanted to experiment with elderly actors who had rich life experience yet were hampered by physical and mental frailty. The quality of the plays, in which all players are over 65, has taken the Gold Theatre on tours of Paris and Bucharest in recent years. The main theatre in Saitama has a capacity of more than 750, and regularly fills it.

'I come from a theatrical family, but never acted,' says Natsue Hyakumoto, sitting up perfectly straight, as if well drilled in holding the perfect posture. Her father, a famous kabuki actor, was on tour so much he was rarely seen at home and she decided as a young woman never to be involved with actors, setting her heart on settling down with a good salaryman. 'My dream came true,' she says, beaming – Mr Hyakumoto was an engineer at Nissan. But later in life, once her husband had retired, she became restless – 'something was missing', she says – and she found her way back to the stage.

Fellow actor Kiyoshi Takahashi is 90. He wears a saggy black beanie hat hanging off the back of his head and a youthful puffer jacket that doubles as a blanket used to keep his knees warm when inside. Mr Takahashi served in the Japanese Army and later worked under the Allied occupation of the country. He has a rebellious air, explaining that after the military he became a technician, 'But I made my money from gambling.' Yoichi Tomaya, 81, is another big character: a union man, he had never acted before retirement but is now the star of the theatre group and puts his success down to the activism of his youth, which involved standing in stations shouting political slogans. 'I'm quick at learning my lines,' he says, 'and get all the best roles.'

The striking thing about the actors of Saitama is not so much their commercial or critical success but the fact that these people from diverse backgrounds have all started a new and successful phase of life, and one that began a decade or more after they retired. Mr Takahashi retired at 65 and started acting at 75; Mr Tomaya retired at 60 and started in his seventies. Their aim, as with the Akita over-70s football team, is to age with purpose, taking on new hobbies and challenges. Acting is a new vocation they want to sustain: the goal for all elderly thespians is to be on stage as much as they can, they say. The two limiting factors are memory and mobility. 'I know my limits and the roles I cannot play,' says Mr Takahashi, who walks slowly and with a stick. 'But I can remember my lines . . . and acting is a way of staying alive.'

REBRANDING OLD AGE

Turning age from something to fear into something to cherish is the idea behind Ryo Yamamoto's estate agency, R65. The branding is a reference to the R18 ratings given to films that are restricted to adults: just as teenagers aspire to their eighteenth birthday, so Mr Yama-moto wants to make reaching *koreisha* status an achievement that confers privileged access. The 27-year-old entrepreneur started out as an employee in a real-estate rental agency, but soon found a problem – and an opportunity: landlords were so fearful of elderly suicide and lonely deaths that they would refuse to accept retirees as tenants. The landlords' concerns were genuine: when a client dies it takes time to find a new one, and a *kodokushi* adds a negative stigma to the building, making it hard to rent out. After calling 200 land-lords, Mr Yamamoto found just five that would entertain the idea of renting to a client in his eighties.

This is a big market failure, explains Mr Yamamoto, since there are many reasons that active and reliable elderly people might want to rent: to get closer to grandkids, to downsize, following a divorce, or simply to get away from a traditional wooden house that needs upkeep and into a modern apartment that doesn't. So Mr Yamamoto called thousands of landlords, building a new database of those that would accept *koreisha* tenants. Next he set up seminars to teach property owners about the benefits of elderly renters. Landlords' thinking was outdated, he says. Even a 75-year-old will now live for ten or more years independently in a property, making them more reliable and less hassle than students or young adults who will move on after four or five years. Each time Mr Yamamoto convinces a new landlord that it is in their interests to rent to the elderly, his database grows.

The young entrepreneur has also set up a kind of early warning system to spot signs of *kodokushi*. 'You can't spot one hundred per cent of lonely deaths,' he explains, 'but there are signs.' His colleagues scan for tell-tale clues that a client has fallen or is unwell: the accumulation of newspapers outside a property, or a path covered with fallen leaves raise a red flag. Really helping people requires knowing about goings-on inside the home, he says. One idea his company considered – installing cameras in rented properties– was seen as a step too far, but electronic movement sensors that send an alert when someone inside a property is unusually still strike the right balance between care and privacy. And when an elderly tenant makes a rental payment one of the R65 team calls to say thank you in person. The call is a polite gesture and an important way to check that a living person made the payment: with both pension income and rental payments often automated, a person can continue receiving cash and spending it for months after they die.

The shock of ageing in Japan has driven a rapid shift in demands, tastes and needs. The natural economic reaction to all this is adaptation, and it can be seen everywhere in Akita. Men's urinals reflect the stages of life: there are the usual low ones for boys next to regular-height ones for men, but there is now always a third type surrounded by a frame that helps elderly men steady themselves. The ATMs in Akita have a small green plastic clip protruding from the wall next to them: a kind of docking station that holds your walking stick in place while you tap in your pin code. Car bumpers and bonnets carry colourful stickers shaped like a four-leaved clover with leaves of orange, yellow, mint green and racing green. This is the 'elderly driver mark' that tells people there is a *koreisha* at the wheel. The sticker itself has adapted: it was previously two-tone, yellow and orange, and became known as the 'autumn leaf' or 'fallen leaf' mark.

The addition of two shades of green is a reference to spring and summer, a modern assertion of elderly vitality.

AS BIG AS CANADA

For all the concerns about intergenerational inequality and unfairness satisfying the needs of the elderly, solving the problems they face is creating a huge amount of economic activity. Japan has 13 million late-stage elderly of 75 years or above, more than the entire population of Sweden (9 million), Portugal (10 million) or Greece (11 million). Add in the more youthful *zenki koreisha* (those aged between 65 and 75) and the number rises to 33 million – almost as many as the entire Canadian population. Elderly consumer spending is worth close to ¥120 trillion (around $1 trillion), making it similar in size to the Mexican or Indonesian economy. To put it another way: if the Japanese elderly formed their own country they would be able to claim a seat on the G20 group of rich and powerful nations that takes decisions on how the global economy is run.

This creates opportunities for the young who, like Ryo Yamamoto with his specialist estate agency, are tapping into what the Japanese call the 'silver-market phenomenon'. Many of the students I meet are looking ahead to working lives in which they will provide goods and services for the elderly. In Akita, Hikari Ishizuka, 19, explains she would like to become an entrepreneur running businesses that help the elderly in some way. Kenji Kajiwara, based in Tokyo, has developed the *Chikaku* ('near') TV set-top box, which allows grandchildren to broadcast from their smartphones direct to their grandparents' televisions. There are companies making specialized golf clubs (easier to hit the ball), special shoes that offset hip pain, elderly foods (easier to chew), elderly fitness clubs, elderly toy dolls for companionship, and elderly video games. The continued growth of the elderly in Japan is not just doom and gloom – they are a huge consumer group in their own right.

Brought together by these new intergenerational trades, Japanese young and old are forming new bonds. Many single people in Japanese cities live in 'share houses'. Communal buildings with 15 or more inhabitants, they were first set up by foreign travellers wanting to avoid Japan's complex tenancy rules in the 1990s and have since caught on with locals. There are now an estimated 30,000 across Japan. 'Each share house has its own concept,' says Ryo Yamamoto, explaining that these mini communities have a collective ethic, goal or aesthetic: 'You get houses where people like to spend money, where they are trying to save money, where they like to be arty and stylish, where they like to be quiet.' Advertisements for share houses set out the goal explicitly: houses for learning English, for losing weight and for setting up a business are all popular.

Conforming to the concept, goal or spirit of the house is a vital requirement and is more important than the age of a resident, says Mr Yamamoto (his own housemates range from 27 to 62 years old with every decade in between represented). And new types of share house are being set up that actively promote intergenerational living. In Akita, Kiyoko Ishii explains the rise of 'single-mother share houses', places where single mothers live together with their children and a number of shared 'grandmothers'. These elderly women are not relatives, and are most often widows or divorcees; they do some childcare and in return pay a lower rent. The ageing society is certainly creating tensions between the generations in Japan, but it is building new types of bond too.

DRESSING FOR DAY-CARE

Kazuko Kikuchi is the queen of her gaming table and she knows it. She wears a thin silk coat cut like a smoking jacket and covered with bright butterflies in yellows, blues and reds; her hair is dyed hazelnut brown and she wears deep-red lipstick and tinted spectacles. Sitting with three friends, she dominates both the game and conversation. First I ask the women's ages: 'No idea, I forgot in my sixties,' is her quick-fire response. Her friend Yoko Kumakawa timidly reveals that she is 87. 'You told us you were 82!' her pal screams. (Mrs Kikuchi later confides that she is 86.) Next I ask how often the women play together: 'Oh, not very often, just every Tuesday, Thursday, Friday and Saturday,' she chortles, without looking up.

The ladies are all locked into a serious game of mah-jong, taking it in turn to place the white tiles – a bit like dominos but smaller and chunkier – on the green baize that covers the table in front of them. When the game ends, a large hole automatically opens up in the middle of the table and the players shunt their pieces forward so they drop into it. The trapdoor then closes, the table whirs for a second and a new set of tiles pops up in front of each player, allowing a new game to begin. A leaderboard on the wall shows that Mrs Kikuchi is the highest-scoring player in Adachi, the suburb where this gaming room is based.

The room where the elderly gamers spend so much time looks like something between an illicit speakeasy and a Nevada casino. The entrance hall is minimal, with a metallic keypad on the wall. After a code is entered a door slides open and the decor changes: the shag-pile carpets are Bordeaux red, the wallpaper is chocolate brown with a gold-leaf motif and the gamers' padded seats are covered in cream imitation leather. There are local twists on the decor: a wall of pachinko machines – the Japanese cousin of pinball – bleeps, chimes and buzzes as the silver balls bounce around inside. On the other side of the room there is a large blackjack table where two elderly gentlemen are trying to beat the house while a young croupier in a black silk waistcoat deals the hands. A waitress tours the room serving drinks in wide glass tumblers. To the side of the room a door left ajar reveals a massage table and a neat pile of white towels. Parked outside the building there is a fleet of black minivans with tinted windows, gleaming rims and 'Las Vegas' emblazoned on the side, waiting to drop the gamers home after a day's fun.

This is government-funded elderly day-care, Japanese-style. 'It is based on the big American casinos,' says Kaoru Mori, who manages the centre and helped design it. Mr Mori, sharp-suited and businesslike, took a research trip to Las Vegas and carefully noted how things were done there. He then took everything a day-care centre in Japan must do by law and fused them with what he saw at Caesars Palace and the Bellagio. The croupiers here are qualified carers and the staff sitting behind what looks like a cashiers' desk are typing up medical notes. The speakeasy-style sliding door with its secret code is there because clients with dementia often feel the urge to wander off. The masseuse is really a physiotherapist and the cocktails, served in their chunkily appealing tumblers, are juices or medicinal supplements.

The approach is clever – the provision of basic medical needs clothed in activities, and an environment that gives purpose, competition and social interaction. The place feels like a real casino rather than an old people's home having a cards day. The only sign is that since gambling is illegal in Japan all transactions take place in the 'Las Vegas dollar'. Elderly visitors receive a daily income of these fake dollars, with which they pay for games of mah-jong, blackjack and pachinko (budgeting is good brain training, the staff here say). The catch is that they must earn their money by completing tasks: stretching, finger and shoulder exercises, and brain-training puzzles. Apart from this there are no toys or gimmicks: the blackjack table is a permanent structure, heavy and wide; the pachinko machines are the type you see in a Tokyo gaming hall. 'All the equipment here is professional grade,' says Mr Mori.

THE VALUE OF RIVALRY

There are at least 50,000 day-care centres in Japan, Mr Mori explains, and people can choose which one to go to from a list of local options. The elderly person pays 10 per cent of the cost up-front, and the remaining 90 per cent is picked up by the state. For ACA Next, the parent company behind Las Vegas, the idea of themed rooms has worked well: they are so popular with residents that they are planning a major expansion of the concept across the country.

Themed day-care also seems to work for the Las Vegas players. These people are old, deep into the later stage *koki koreisha* years – at one point a lady playing blackjack begins to wobble and a croupier-carer rushes over to lift her on to a bed and take her blood pressure. But they are also noticeably alert, focused on their games, and seem happy. The company is convinced about the therapeutic benefits of gaming. Its brochures are full of facts and figures about improved cognitive function and communication. The dollars-for-exercise income scheme has benefits, explains Mr Mori: the average resident here exercises for over 40 minutes per day, well above the national average. And the fact that the gamers look so smart is surely important: day-care is a place where there are friends and rivals to impress, an event that is worth dressing for.

For Japan as a whole, the real test of all this is cost. Long-term elderly care is one of the reasons the social security budget has ballooned, and there are reasons to worry that the burden may soon shoot up even more. Japan is going to need millions more carers in coming years but the work fits into a category of employment known as '3K' that people here seek to avoid. The term stems from 汚い (*kitanai*), 危険 (*kiken*) and きつい (*kitsui*) and translates roughly as 'dirty, dangerous and demeaning'. Recruiting enough young Japanese workers to undertake these 3K roles could send wage bills, and government spending, spiralling up.

'We need to make care work a more attractive job,' says Mr Mori, explaining that a key challenge for any day-care-centre manager is staff retention. At Las Vegas day-care the carers have the usual, unglamorous duties – for instance, helping the elderly clients visit the bathroom – but they also spend a good chunk of their day playing games, and the young blackjack croupier seems to be having a great time at his work. The staff carefully match players of a similar cognitive function and on many tables the players are so focused that the carers are hardly needed at all. Kazuko Kikuchi's table is bubbling away and as I say goodbye the octogenarian mah-jong master summons me to her table, looking over her glasses: 'Tell me: if the elderly in the UK don't have Las Vegas, what on earth do they do?'

ROBO-CARER

Life enters its last phases eventually, even in Japan, leaving many unable to attend day-care, and needing full-time personal nursing and observation instead. Here, the country faces another crunch. Late-stage care often requires one-on-one tasks such as feeding patients and lifting them from bed to bath. This is another 3K job, hard for recruiters to fill, and even if it were not it is hard to see how the numbers will add up. Medics in Japan predict that a four-fold increase in the number of personal carers will be needed by 2040. Others will face similar needs: taken together, Italy, Spain and Portugal will see the number of people aged 65 or over rise by 3.2 million between 2020 and 2030 – since around 20 per cent of this age group currently needs full- or part-time assistance, this suggests 640,000 new care workers will be required. But the working-age population will decline in all these countries – so there simply may not be enough people to provide tailored late-stage care. The question inventors, medics and carers across Japan are asking is whether personalized care really needs to be given by a person – and whether robots might be the answer.

The patients at the Silver Wings medical facility in Tokyo are similar in age to the Gold Theatre actors and the Las Vegas day-care gamers, but are at a later stage of life. They have conditions including Alzheimer's disease and other forms of dementia, and are here receiving treatment. Taneko Nanako is 90 and is slumped so low in her wheelchair that the table opposite her is at eye level. Sitting on the table there is a large white cuddly toy in the shape of a seal. Mrs Nanako has few teeth and her eyes are cloudy, but she smiles and is talkative. I ask her what she calls her pet. 'Boy,' she says. 'He's my boy!' She reaches forward, grabbing him from the table and dragging the seal into her lap, her face lighting up like a child given a gift at Christmas.

Boy's real name is Paro and at $5,000 he is an expensive toy. Developed by the Intelligent System Research Institute, a government-supported laboratory, in 2009 Paro became the first robot to be classified as a therapeutic aid: Paro, in other words, is proven to make patients better. The seal is covered with tiny sensors – under his fur, on the tips of his whiskers, on his nose – that allow the computer housed inside to assess the behaviour of the elderly person holding him, and react to it. The robot makes pleasant sounds and move-ments if treated well – cooing and gently wriggling – but recoils and makes sharper noises when struck or dropped. This helps to counter the sudden bursts of anger that are one symptom of dementia.

Next to Mrs Nanako two more women in their nineties are play-ing with their own Paros. But while the seals all look the same on the outside, the robot inside each of them has learned from repeated interaction with its owner, subtly changing the way it responds to being stroked or struck. This artificial build-up of knowledge is known as 'machine learning' and means that after a while no two Paros are the same because they have evolved, becoming tailored to their owner. In clinical trials elderly patients using Paro have been better able to communicate verbally and are more facially expressive than control groups. The symbiosis of patient and robot is evident: Mrs Nanako gives me permission to play with her Paro but the seal does not respond to the foreign hand. She shows me how to do it and he springs to life. The carers here say the benefits are unquestionable. 'It has helped Mrs Nanako hugely,' says one. 'When she came to us she was completely mute.'

The Silver Wings centre is at the cutting edge of research into the use of care robots and uses a range of different specialized machines. Sitting at a neighbouring table are three elderly ladies who are a little more physically stable – they can sit unassisted in chairs – and they are playing with robotic dogs. Yoshizawa Toshiko and Kisa Ohkubo, both 90, are engrossed, looking at, talking to and petting the canine bots. The machines are called AIBO and are made by Sony. They are louder, more physical and more mobile than Paro, roaming the table, bleeping and barking as they go.

The artificial intelligence inside AIBO is some way from perfection – a large rubber barrier surrounds the table, preventing the dogs from falling over the side. But like Paro these robotic pets can learn, picking up an owner's accent and dialect, responding to both touch and sound. As with Paro, interacting with AIBO seems to help brain function. Mrs Ohkubo's short-term memory is severely diminished and when she first came to the centre she would forget she had been bathed, spending all day asking to be washed again and gradually becoming more distressed. One of her carers says that the stimulation and focus provided by the robotic dogs have stopped this. Ayako Kotajima, who is 99 years old, tells me she is looking forward to her one-hundredth birthday but is sad because she can no longer walk and misses the dogs she kept as a younger woman. Her AIBO is an imperfect substitute, but it helps.

ROBO-COLLEAGUE

'Working with the elderly is tiring,' says Takashi Sugimoto, a care worker in his forties. Using an empty bed he mimics lifting an infirm patient and demonstrates how by leaning forward to scoop them up out of bed it is easy to injure the lower back. The problem is so common that a whole range of competing contraptions – essentially exoskeletons – are being developed to protect care workers. The smiling and excitable Mr Sugimoto is clearly a great carer. He is also a massive fan of the technology and keen to show it off.

The first robotic aid he puts on is a 'muscle suit' made by Innophys, a firm spun out of Tokyo Science University. It looks like a climbing harness and is powered by compressed air with inflatable chambers that pass around the carer's hips, running up the lower back and down along their quadriceps. When a care worker puts

their hands under an elderly patient to lift them up they simultaneously blow into a small tube, sending the suit a signal to inflate.
Another option is the 'robot suit' made by Cyberdyne Inc – a huge
white plastic hinge that is worn around the hips and lower back. This
one requires no manual signal; it reads electric waves sent by the brain
that tell it the caregiver is about to lift and powers up accordingly.
Both suits can reduce the burden on the lower back by two-thirds,
the team here say.

Pepper is the machine here that looks most like a classical robot.
He is a diminutive chap – perhaps 4 feet high – covered in a skin made
of white plastic. From the waist up his shape is humanoid: Pepper has
a torso, arms with fingers and thumbs, and a head and face. The Pepper
robot here works on the second floor of Silver Wings, which is more
like a day-care than residential-care ward, treating patients well
enough to sit together in a central common room. Pepper's task, like
that of the exoskeletons, is to work alongside the carers, saving them
time and making them more productive.

At the Silver Wings medical centre Mr Sugimoto turns Pepper
on, and a second later the robot's eyes light up and it stretches its
fingers. Without prompting, the female patients nudge their seats
and wheelchairs into a semi-circle and face him as he begins to
talk. The robot first demonstrates some arm movements and
stretches, talking the group through them step by step. Then he
starts to sing 'Haru ga kita' ('Spring Is Coming'), a nursery rhyme.
When the second verse kicks in Pepper begins to repeat the arm
stretches as he sings and most of the women who have gathered
around copy the robot, while the others smile and clap. Most of the
men seem unconvinced and sit at the back of the room looking
annoyed. But with Pepper leading the activity and entertaining
more than half of the patients, Mr Sugimoto is free to move quickly
between those not taking part, asking them how they are and
encouraging them to stretch.

The economic challenges ageing has brought to Japan – a labour
shortage and tight budgets – show why the robotic approach to care

is a decent idea to try, and is likely to catch on as Europe ages. Pepper robots can be rented for under $6,000 per year, and as competitors enter the market, prices are falling. In 2019 the average salary for care workers in Japan was a little over ¥3.5 million (around $32,000), with wages in the sector rising steadily. The huge price differential means a facility manager finding it hard to fill two slots on a care team could instead hire one human and rent two Peppers, and still save $20,000 a year. As long as robots like Pepper can do useful work, they can help fill the gaps left by Japan's labour shortfall, while soothing its budgetary pressure at the same time.

THE WORLD-LEADING BACKWATER

Akita, the remote Japanese prefecture at the very extreme of ageing, is a demographic trendsetter. Here, the factors that cause an economy to age – longer lives and lower birth rates – have created an economy today that others will experience tomorrow.

The first lesson to take from Akita is that the ageing economy is a paradox – we can see it coming, yet it is still a shock. In Japan, the elderly people I spoke to described their old age as unexpected because it was something they had not seen in their families, towns and cities before. The jump in life expectancy happened within a lifetime and meant today's cohort of *koreisha* had no role models for how to live productively into their nineties and beyond. Population decline is so new it has not yet happened in many places and is only 10 years old, even in cutting-edge Japan. The shrinking and elderly world is on the horizon: South Korea has a decade or so of population expansion left; Germany has just a few years.

The ageing economy is a slow-moving trend that will hit people unprepared. The pressures that it brings can be seen through the intuitive 'life-cycle' of economics. Unexpected ageing means that stocks of assets built up over a lifetime to fund retirement are too meagre, leaving pension shortfalls and care costs that put pressure

on government coffers and creates the frictions of a new faultline –
intergenerational inequality. The stories of Akita's most elderly
residents show that the life-cycle idea – of building a buffer to survive old age – applies in non-financial ways too. The rise in lonely
death and suicide, seen through the fate of Japan's once-successful
salarymen, points to the importance of personal reserves other than
cash, and the role that clubs, networks and social groups play in sustaining life after work.

The concern that so many people and countries may be unprepared is compounded by the fact that anxiety-generating statistics
are easy to come by when you start to consider the implications of
ageing. The sheer number of old people and the huge costs of caring
for them seem to suggest a challenge that will be impossible to meet.
Yet my time in Japan clarified some reasons for hope.

The first two parts of this book showed that the dividing line
between resilience and failure was often the unseen economic fabric
of a place, the informal markets built on trust, cooperation and shared
goals. Despite the frictions I heard about between students and pensioners, ageing seems to be a shock that – like a war or disaster – is
creating shared challenges for everyone. The other extreme economies
show this is the type of problem that the unmeasured economy – the
natural human disposition to invent and come up with goods and
services – is best at tackling. Travel in Akita and you see masses of
economic activity, from vegetable swaps to informal markets to
generation-spanning 'share houses' where childcare and rent are
implicitly traded, that is missed in gloomier reports.

On top of this collaborative approach to ageing sits a formal elderly economy that is huge – as big as Mexico's – and is creating
millions of new jobs. Japan's long lives mean its senior citizens need
new types of mobile phones, ATMs with walking-stick clips, and
elderly-friendly urinals. Its shrinking population means developing
advanced robotic carers takes on a critical importance. These are the
tasks in which the young are making their careers. The concerns
about pensioner poverty and the creaking welfare state are real,

but the story of ageing in Japan is also one of people coming up with ingenious ways to make elderly life cheap, fun, healthy and productive.

Yet as I travelled around Akita I came to think that one risk is being underplayed. In a country where the population is declining, the natural consequence is that many villages, towns and cities will cease to exist. I looked hard for a fightback, but it was impossible to find any real counter to the negativity and anguish people in these places felt. In the very long run, the fact that humans might take up less of the planet may be a good thing, but the shrinking and deserted communities of rural Akita are desolate, depressing and ghostly places. Again, this seems to go back to a fundamental idea in economics: that humans are forward-looking. When it becomes clear that a place is heading for extinction, markets – and local democracy – break down completely. What is happening in Japan today is rapidly catching on in Portugal and Italy and will affect Germany by 2030. For many places the economics of the future will be one of managed decline.

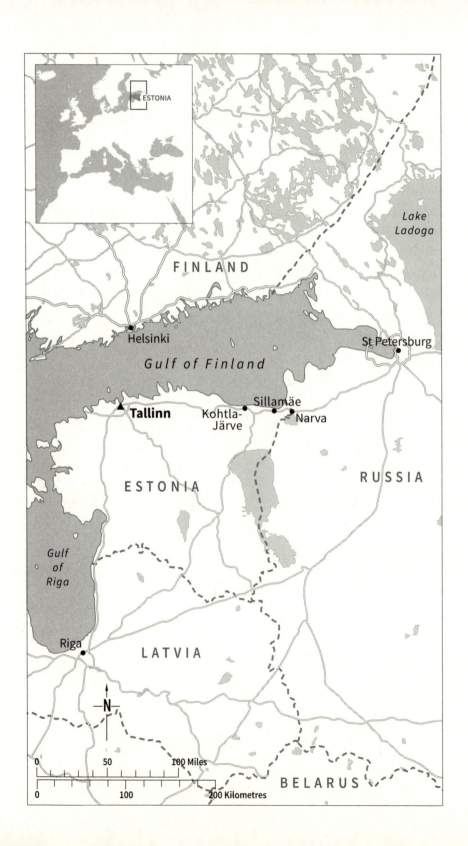

8

Tallinn

In transportation and agriculture, machines by now have practically
eliminated the need for human muscle power. Man has all but ceased
to be a lifter and mover and become primarily a starter and
stopper, a setter and assembler and repairer.

Wassily Leontief,
'Machines and Man', 1952

TECH ON THE BALTIC

A CRAZY OLD GUY WITH A SEED IN A POT

If you take the risk of entering a televised talent contest embarrassing things can happen. Every show has its jester: the crooner who turns out to be tone deaf, the dancer with no sense of rhythm. The awful realization that he might be destined to play this part started to sink in when Mattias Lepp, then 34, met the other competitors in the 2010 heats of *Ajujaht*, a popular Estonian TV show. 'Everyone else was younger, in their twenties,' he recalls. 'I started to think I was a joke contestant – here I was, this crazy old guy – and all I had was a seed in a little pot.' It is the stuff of anxiety dreams but Mr Lepp persevered and a few months later was crowned *Ajujaht* champion.

Sitting behind a sleek minimal desk in his office in Estonia's capital, Tallinn, Mr Lepp does not look like a typical talent-show contestant: his floppy grey shirt matches his tousled hair. Nor does he behave much like one: he likes to read the works of Plato and Seneca, enjoys thinking about botany, and says his favourite holiday is to walk in the Siberian wilderness alone, so that he has time to clear his mind. What made him a winner was his big idea – a new way to grow plants – and the fact that Estonia is a country that loves innovators: *Ajujaht* is one of many inventors' contests and translates roughly as 'brain hunt'. The victorious Mr Lepp received a prize of €30,000, and significant media coverage. Seven years later his company, Click and Grow, has 35 staff and recently raised $9 million in funding, including investments from Y Combinator, an influential Silicon Valley investment fund.

Mr Lepp shows me the first part of his invention. It looks like a massive pack of paracetamol designed for giants – flat tinfoil on one side with a series of large plastic bubbles on the other. Rather than holding a pill, each of the capsules contains a clump of soil, shaped like the root ball that comes out when you empty a dried plant pot. A user takes this 'smart soil' and slots it into the second part of his new system, a sleek machine in which plants – in this case, basil – will grow. Once plugged in, the Click and Grow incubator does all the work. Life for the plant is not cosy: the machine applies stress as the basil grows, starving it of water and light at crucial moments in order to stimulate reactions that produce desired chemicals.

This modern way of growing produces better food, Mr Lepp explains, bringing up a chart on his laptop to demonstrate his point. The analysis is chromatography, a technique that separates and tracks the levels of chemicals in his plants. In the case of basil, the important compound is rosmarinic acid, an antioxidant with potential health-giving effects. The computer's screen shows the graph for shop-bought basil, with a small hump indicating the rosmarinic acid content. The graph for basil grown in a Click and Grow machine shows a massive spike. Mr Lepp calls his invention a Smart Garden and, in terms of flavour and health, basil grown in this Estonian machine is better than plants bought from a shop or grown in a herb garden outside.

TREMBLING OVER TECHNOLOGY

Technology optimists like Mr Lepp and the care-robot inventors I met in Japan think their inventions will solve the challenges of our future economies. But around the world technological advances are also causing fear and uncertainty, with worries about elections, privacy and ethics, and alongside these political fears two deep economic concerns. The first is the prospect of mass unemployment, the idea that labour-saving technology – which could be software or machines – will make human workers redundant. Estimates of the likely job losses as automation looms vary, but the latest studies suggest that 25 per cent of workers in the US and 30 per cent in the UK are at risk of being replaced by a machine. The robots are coming, the story goes, and they are going to take our jobs.

The second fear is that technological advances will be unfair, generating a new type of inequality some call the 'digital divide'. The core of this worry is that the benefits technology brings will favour some groups – the young, the urban, the educated and the wealthy – at the expense of others.

Concerns over the impact of technology make Tallinn an interesting test case. Just as Akita offers a glimpse of the economics of ageing we will all soon experience, Tallinn is a technology frontier, and has already adopted many technologies that look set to catch on in our own economies. The capital is famously home to Skype, and pushed as a 'start-up paradise' by the government with some justification (the number of new companies established per head of population is one of the highest in the world). But what makes Estonia stand out as a leader in a

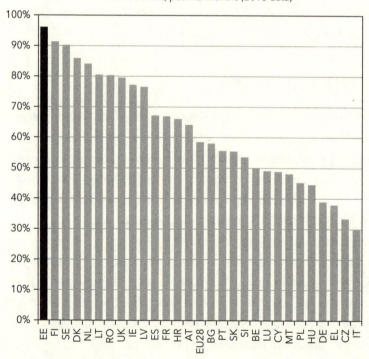

Estonia – leader of the digital pack

Percentage of people that use eGovernment,
EU countries, past 12 months (2018 data)

Source: European Commission

way Silicon Valley does not is the role of technology in the government. Tallinn is the seat of the world's first digital state, with more government services provided online than anywhere else in the world, and is the first country to establish a completely digital citizenship.

On its own, Estonia's embrace of technology across the economy and state would make it a trendsetter worth studying. But there is a fault-line here that makes it doubly interesting. In addition to being recognized by technologists as a global hotspot, Estonia has a lesser-known claim to fame as one of the most divided countries in the world. Part of the communist USSR between 1944 and 1991, the country retains divisions of language, race and culture. Relative to its population, Estonia is home to one of the largest groups of stateless people in the world. How did this tiny and divided state make such a giant technological leap forward, and will its future really be the utopia its brainiest residents are seeking?

COMPUTERS AND DREAMS

THE ANYWHERE GARDEN

Mr Lepp's aim is not just food that is tastier and better for you than the competition, he also wants to make it cheaper to grow. His original Smart Garden was a small unit designed for home use, allowing herbs to be grown on windows or bookshelves. The unit sells for $60 and a year's supply of capsules (allowing 18 plants to be grown) costs the same. The next stage is to supply huge factory-scale units – the Smart Farm. A blueprint of the new system shows plants growing on a series of racks that will travel slowly under banks of lights, like a many-layered conveyor belt. At one end of the machine new capsules of soil pre-filled with seeds are fed in; by the time they get to the other end the rack is full of mature plants ready for picking.

The idea was first inspired by NASA but their soil system, designed to grow plants in space, needed improvements, Mr Lepp says, explaining how he tinkered with the process for three years to perfect it. His system is adjustable so that as plants pass through it they are subjected to stresses tailored to each species. This means a user can simultaneously grow a huge range of edible plants, from salad leaves and mini tomatoes to chillies and strawberries. The Click and Grow version is not designed for use in outer space, but its in-built lights do mean that someone living in a high-rise flat in northern Europe could grow Mediterranean plants such as mimosa, peppermint and oregano.

Estonia's technologists all have a rosy endgame in mind and Mr Lepp is no different. He says he is motivated by food waste and food poverty, citing the poor diet of low-income communities in rich-world countries. He is critical of the huge agriculture companies that sell 'kamikaze seeds' in vast quantities to developing world countries. (These seeds have been bred to grow just one plant and leave no seeds for further cultivation, ensuring that the customer must buy more from the provider.) He also laments about the loss of plant varieties: 'We used to know of and eat one hundred and fifty wild plant species in Estonia, but now there are around thirty left, and we understand how to use only fifteen.' He would like to reintroduce lost species using his system, which he says should mean that anyone in any climate can grow their own healthy food. The long-term goal is to make ever larger machines, driving down the cost of his system and eventually making a machine that is perfectly efficient and completely automated so that vitamin-packed foods would be available to everyone free of charge.

BACK IN THE ESSR

Estonia is a tiny country, in headcount terms ranked 155th in the world, its population of 1.3 million close to that of small island nations like Mauritius or Cyprus. Yet in terms of digital technology and innovation it is a heavyweight, with the government leading the way. The tax system is close to paperless, with 94 per cent of filings

made online. Estonians can vote from their laptops and can be anywhere in the world when they do so. Politics is paperless, with all
cabinet documents electronic since 2000 (the UK's Parliament uses
1,000 tonnes of paper a year). Legal documents too can be signed
digitally using a smartphone. The only official things you cannot do
online in Estonia are marry, divorce and buy a house. In Tallinn I meet
Linnar Viik, a government adviser and one of the early architects of
Estonia's digital state. To understand the country's bold adoption of
technology, he says, you first need to realize the psychology that
drove it and the fact that it was born of necessity.

Previously an independent republic, Estonia was annexed by
the Soviet Union in 1940, then occupied by the Nazis before being
returned to Stalin's hands in 1944. In terms of land mass, the Estonian
Soviet Socialist Republic (ESSR) made up just one-five-hundredth –
0.2 per cent – of the USSR, but the little nation quickly became a vital
cog in the Soviet economic system. The shift was not smooth: agriculture changed most drastically, with private farms converted to
the *kolkhoz* (collective ownership) system. Land was appropriated by
the state, and any peasant running a successful farm was branded a
kulak, meaning tight-fisted, or selfish. Over a period of just four days
in March 1949 over 20,000 *kulak* Estonians were rounded up, put on
special trains and deported to Siberian cities such as Khabarovsk
and Krasnoyarsk over 5,000 km away.

The Estonian industrial base changed too, with factories set up all
along the north-east coast: Kunda was the site of a huge cement factory and pulp mill; Kohtla-Järve had plentiful oil-shale deposits and
became an important source of energy; Sillamäe, once a peaceful
resort where Russia's cultural elite, including Tchaikovsky, had vaca-
tioned, was repurposed as a centre for uranium enrichment, the nature
of the work so secretive that the town was removed from maps.

The economic model, planned from Moscow, was catastrophic
for Estonia. Agricultural collectivization was supposed to reduce the
number of farms by amalgamating small homesteads into large estates
and thus deliver efficiency gains; instead it resulted in agricultural

output falling by half. The resulting food shortages undermined the communist model in Estonia from its inception: during this period people survived only through a network of (illegal) privately run farms, with this informal agricultural output running alongside the official state system. By the late 1980s as the Soviet empire began to fray, the factory and military cities of the north-eastern ESSR were being allowed to decay and rust.

Estonians tend to look across the narrow Baltic channel to Finland when assessing their lot. Under Soviet rule comparisons were painful: in 1939 the two countries had a similar standard of living but by 1987 national income per person was $14,000 in Finland and just $2,000 in Estonia. When the country gained its independence in 1991 it inherited inefficient farms and defunct factories. With stores almost empty, prices soared as desperate shoppers bid up the price of basic goods: inflation in 1992 was over 1,000 per cent. In Sillamäe, the beach once loved by the poets, painters and composers of St Petersburg was left poisoned by nuclear waste from the secret uranium programme.

THE BLIND BET

The new country that emerged turned out to be daring and bold. In part, embracing radical new ideas was made easier by a desire to forget the past: many Estonians in their forties and fifties refer to 1991 as a 'clean break', with people wanting to shake off any memory of the old regime. In the ESSR the political class had been picked by Moscow and were party men with KGB links; to thrive, you had to work with them. 'That meant a distrust, not just of those who were in power, but anyone who had been a successful adult under the old regime,' recalls a Tallinn-based investor.

Boldness also came from the fact that the new country fell into the hands of young people. Estonia's first prime minister, Mart Laar, was 32 when he took the helm. A historian and philosopher, he had spent his twenties lecturing and writing books. 'When we started, politics here was like a zoo, with all sorts of people involved,' Linnar

Viik explains, thinking back to the diverse group of experts that drafted Estonia's constitution: 'We had composers and artists and writers and engineers and chemists and nuclear physicists and poets. We had very few people who had studied politics.' It sounds excellent.

Their problem was that expectations in the country were sky high, even though the region was in crisis. 'The Estonian people quickly expected a fully fledged country,' says Siim Sikkut, the country's head of information technology, explaining the challenge. There were lots of demands on the state in the post-Soviet Baltic. Defence was (and remains) important and expensive in this part of the world. Voters looked north to the Nordic countries, demanding a sound welfare system, high-quality public education and good healthcare. But at the same time years of Soviet rule had left Estonians wary of an overly large state, making it impossible to get public support for Swedish-style taxation. And all around it Estonia's neighbours were crumbling. Every one of the 15 post-Soviet states went into recession in 1992. By 2000, GDP per capita had fallen by an average of 30 per cent in Estonia's newly independent neighbours; in Ukraine it had been halved.

The youthful team running Estonia needed ideas fast. Some of their policies followed sound and well-worn economic advice: the new tax system was one of the simplest in the world, and they set up an independent monitor to oversee state spending. The more striking move was to commit fully to embracing technology across the state and in every part of the economy. 'We essentially made a blind bet on technology,' says Mr Viik, recalling the economic strategy of the early government. By the late 1990s Estonia had connected 97 per cent of its schools to the internet, was teaching coding at primary age, was investing heavily in digital infrastructure, and had adopted a host of initiatives to support companies making technology investments. Estonia was the only post-Soviet country to grow in that first decade, expanding by 14 per cent, and this Baltic tiger has continued its ascent since. GDP per capita has risen from $2,000 in 1987 to $22,000 by 2018, with Estonians starting to catch up with their Finnish rivals.

Looking back on the bet Estonia made and its impact on the

economy, Mr Viik, one of the project's early designers, sounds a word of caution: 'Technology is just an accelerator, so if you apply it to your old ways of doing things it can just amplify inefficiency.' As a political and economic force, the digitization of an economy is subtle and complex. 'Technology is not good and it is not bad,' he says, 'and it is definitely not neutral.'

TAMING BIG BROTHER

Ask an Estonian to show you their government ID and they tend to pull it out with a smile. The pale-blue plastic cards are not particularly striking to look at – like a UK or US driving licence but with an embedded chip, akin to a debit card. But the power of the ID is huge – it provides access to all online government services – and the reason for the grin is that it saves Estonians a lot of time. For older people the comparison is with Soviet times: 'I remember queuing for everything,' says one Tallinn resident. 'You would stand for hours only to find the government officials had gone for a long lunch or were demanding a bribe to hurry up.' Young Estonians say they really notice the benefit when they travel overseas and find that in other countries selling a car, opening a bank account or signing a tenancy agreement is painful, slow and paper-based. By comparison, doing these things at home using a laptop and the ID card is simpler and much faster.

'Estonians are an impatient people, and get bored easily,' says Rait Rand, a Tallinn-based inventor who won the country's 2017 *Ajujaht* competition with a new type of medical device. The ID card plays well with that part of the national psyche, he explains. A founding rule of the system is that the government is permitted to ask a citizen for a piece of data – for example their date of birth, blood type, address or driving-licence number – only once. If an Estonian has ever entered this information on any government website the state is never permitted to ask for it again and must instead retrieve the data from its own records. The contrast with attempts at state digitization in the US and UK, where queues at government offices have been swapped with lengthy online forms, is stark. In Estonia, by law, the government's computers fill out the forms for you. When technology saves people time in this way, they tend to embrace it.

Estonia also shows how to build trust in technology that runs on personal data, something at the heart of many controversies in recent years. The extensive tentacles of the system – the ID card is linked to every interaction with the state – seems Orwellian and risky: what if the system fails, or is abused? Estonians are not too worried about this: 97 per cent of them carry the card, and most understand and can explain the system's safeguards. The first buffer against attack is that there is no central repository of data because the system is 'disaggregated'. This means that each bureau holds only the data it collects and there is no central hub that pools it all together. Instead, when an agency needs a piece of data about you, it must request it from the government department that first collected it. The data is transmitted at the moment that it is needed via a system called the X-Road, and then deleted. This means that if the transport department wants to send you a speeding fine, it must ask the postal registry to supply your address via X-Road and must then destroy the data. This all happens in an instant, and means there is no central treasure trove for hackers to raid.

The second safeguard is that anyone using the system leaves a digital footprint. Every time a person's data is searched for, used or exchanged, a record is made in a personal 'data log' that can be checked online. This allows any citizen to look up all the queries that have been made about them, including who asked for the information. Finally, every agency holding a piece of data about an Estonian is required to link it to their ID number and display it in the citizen's private data log. As one young Tallinn resident explained to me, 'This is a way for me to control government, because I know exactly what the government knows about me.'

There have been teething pains along the way. One problem was that the system became faddish. With ministers and bureaucrats keen to use it, 'People were digitizing all over the place,' Mr Viik says, sometimes with no idea why. And there have been mistakes. In the early 2000s the Estonian border guards' computer system failed, for example. Most worryingly, there have been conspiracies. In the 2007 local elections, pensioners with Russian heritage in a Tallinn suburb were targeted with direct mail by a candidate in the election. The pamphlets went only to this specific type of household, suggesting that someone had illegally retrieved a list of addresses and ethnic backgrounds. This was a serious breach but it also proved how the system's safeguards work. It took less than an hour for officials to scan the data log and identify who had looked up the information, allowing the police to arrest them. 'In the digital world there is always a trace,' says Mr Viik, recalling the incident.

But not everyone in Estonia is happy about the role technology plays in the economic and political system here. Asked about the state of the economy, some are dismissive: 'Technology and tourism – this is all,' responds one shopkeeper. And while Tallinn residents seem to like their ID cards, they also know that automating and digitizing public services means fewer government roles. By building software that replaces functionaries and robots that replace bus drivers, technology companies seem to be a force for job destruction. These are global worries, as stark predictions of job losses in the US and UK show. By making its 'blind bet' on technology, the Tallinn government has made Estonia a kind of sacrificial lamb, sent first across the torrent of technology, those of us in countries that are following should eagerly watch how it fares.

THE END OF WORK

THE LAST MILE

Parked outside an office block in Mustamäe, a suburb to the west of Tallinn's old city, I meet a robot that goes to the heart of the debate about the impact of technology on jobs. Built by Starship

Technologies, the machine looks like the offspring of a cooler box and a remote-control car. The robot's body is a knee-high white container with rounded corners that runs on six wheels with black tyres. On the back-right corner an antenna rises to just below head height, with a tiny orange triangular flag flying at its tip. The styling of this little bubble car is the friendly side of futuristic – more Jetsons than Terminator. On closer inspection the sophistication of the machine starts to emerge: the front lip of its body hosts a bevy of sensors: eight cameras, radar, microphones and other sensors that Ahti Heinla, founder of Starship Technologies, says are too secret to divulge. It needs all of them because it is a delivery robot: seeing where it is going is essential.

While he has never entered Estonia's *Ajujaht* contest, Mr Heinla is certainly one of the country's top minds. He began writing computer code at ten and in his twenties he and his business partner Janus Friis helped found Kazaa (an early illegal file-sharing site, similar to Napster) and, later, Skype. Well over six feet tall, with sharp features and a shock of blond hair, he could only be northern European; he wears tailored trousers from an expensive suit with a faded T-shirt. Mr Heinla appears half nerd, half businessman and it is a lucrative combination: Skype was sold to eBay in 2005 for a reported $2.6 billion and, after being bought back by private owners, sold once more to Microsoft for $8.5 billion in 2011. Having got in early and retained stakes in the company through its rise, Mr Heinla is thought to be a millionaire many times over; his co-investor Mr Friis is worth over $1 billion.

Their deep pockets give the Tallinn innovators the resources needed to chase big ideas. 'The vision starts from the fact that logistics are still largely human based,' Mr Heinla says, running through the journey that an item bought via the internet typically makes: our online shopping is picked at a warehouse by a human, put on a truck driven by a human, sorted at a depot by humans and then put on delivery vans that are driven by humans. 'But in 20 years, every step in that chain will be robotic,' he predicts. The big question for companies like Starship is whether the final link in the chain – the journey from a local depot to the customer's door – can be automated. Logistics experts call this the 'last-mile problem' and are racing to solve it. (The last-mile problem is why Amazon and Uber are investing in delivery drones.) 'It is the hardest part of a journey: the last mile is the most complex to automate, simply because there is more unpredictable stuff that can happen on the street,' says Mr Heinla. The last mile is also the dearest – the costs of running a lorry are spread across hundreds of packages carried on it; by contrast, when a human must carry a single package to a consumer's front door there is no sharing of costs. If the complexities a small delivery robot faces can be cracked, and if Mr Heinla is right that trucks and vans will be relatively easy to automate, the era of humans delivering things will soon be over.

The prospect of a world of automated delivery is exciting and terrifying. Studies of the risks of automation predict scarily large numbers of job losses. Transport and logistics are big employers: in the US 4 million people currently do the kinds of jobs Mr Heinla predicts will be automated in the near future. This is 4 per cent of the workforce and includes 1.5 million people working in trucking, 630,000 couriers and messengers, 140,000 school and passenger bus drivers, and 75,000 who drive taxis and limousines. In the UK an even higher share of the workforce (6 per cent) does this kind of work. Automating logistics would be a huge shock to the economy, radically altering the working lives of millions of people.

Estonia is no different: almost 39,000 people (again 6 per cent of the workforce) have jobs in some kind of transport or logistics trade. Tallinn is full of middle-aged taxi drivers, and hundreds of young men buzz around the capital on bicycles delivering takeaway meals for Wolt, the Estonian version of a fast-food ordering app. If robots take over so that no one is needed to drive vans, deliver letters or courier curries, these people will need another way to earn a living. As I head back to the centre of town from the Starship Technologies offices a tram zooms past – it is automated, with no human driver. Is Estonia's blind bet on technology genius or madness?

MAN VERSUS TURNIP

The trend towards the Akita-like pensioner economy is relatively new, a phenomenon of the late twentieth century. By contrast, the question of technology and the workforce is at least three centuries old. If Estonia is a Petri dish for the study of modern inventions, the fields and factories of Britain were the past ones. Where those in Akita rightly complained they had no role models, here the experience of generations before sheds light on how technology affects workers, the types of innovation that did and didn't cause anger, and what might be expected in Estonia.

In the early eighteenth century, more than 80 per cent of the workforce in the UK had jobs in agriculture. Food shortages and famines were still common, and men, women and children spent their days ploughing, harvesting and looking after animals.

They were limited by their tools: the short-handled sickle was used by 90 per cent of harvesters in the late eighteenth century, for example. An ergonomically woeful device, the sickle forced the harvester to crouch while cutting a crop. The scythe had a similar blade but its longer handle allowed workers to cut while standing. As harvesters shifted from sickle to scythe, the time taken to cut an acre was halved. The turnip made the soil more productive, breeding made animals more productive and tools made humans more productive. These improvements all meant fewer man hours were needed to complete a task, and were a threat to farm hands just as Estonian delivery robots are to postal workers. Perhaps it was their simplicity, perhaps it was that these technologies met such a clear need, but no one got angry with the promoters of scythes or turnips. Instead, farm output rose, food shortages became less common, and the population began to rise.

CAPTAIN SWING

The tension between man and machines we see today began to build with the invention of more advanced machines. Joseph Foljambe and Disney Stanyforth patented the Rotherham Plough: a cheaper, lighter and stronger version of its predecessor the 'heavy' plough, it needed one man instead of two to operate. The 'seed drill' attributed to Jethro Tull was a multi-purpose machine that ploughed a groove, sowed seeds into it and then covered them with soil so accurately that 70 per cent fewer seeds were needed to sow a field. And Andrew Meikle's steam-powered threshing machine, invented in the late 1780s, reduced the time taken to clear an acre to just half a day – a 90 per cent improvement on labourers using sickles. By the early nineteenth century a torrent of agricultural engineering was in full flow, with farmers introducing mechanical reapers, haymakers, turnip cutters, winnowers and chaff machines. As the new technologies spread across the British countryside productivity jumped: by 1850 farms were producing two and a half times more than a century previously.

But many farm workers hated the new labour-saving technology and violence erupted in Kent in 1830 as they started destroying threshing machines. The anger spread, with hundreds of incidents becoming known as the Swing Riots (threatening letters sent to farmers using threshing machines were often signed by a common pseudonym, Captain Swing). Thousands of rioters were jailed, almost 500 were sent to penal colonies in Australia and hundreds were sentenced to death (in the end 16 rioters were publicly hanged). The Swing Rioters had some initial success: demands for higher wages were often met and investment in threshing machines was held back. But the riots did little to slow the march of technology. From the threshing machine to the tractor (1896), the combine harvester (1911), automation in slaughter houses (1960s) and milking machines (1970), to the Smart Farm (2015), promoted by an Estonian start-up, the advance of agricultural technology never really stopped.

Fears over the impact of technology on jobs morphed into anger at inventors and violence against machines in the Industrial Revolution too. Take the case of Lancashire-born James Hargreaves. In the early 1700s spinning – twisting natural fibres together to create the yarn used in weaving – was the bottleneck in cloth production:

weaving was so much faster that five spinners were needed to supply each weaver. Clothing was labour-intensive and costly to make: a shirt took around 580 hours, 500 of which was spent spinning. (If a shirt were made in the US at today's minimum wage using the technology of the eighteenth century it would cost more than $4,000 to produce.) Hargreaves' machine, the Spinning Jenny, was a frame on which one spinner could fill eight spools of yarn, boosting their output hugely. Fearful about their jobs and wages, a group of spinners in nearby Blackburn found out where Hargreaves lived, broke into his house and smashed up all his machines.

The fear that fewer spinners would be needed per yard of cloth was justified. While early versions of the Jenny had eight spindles, by 1784 the number rose to 80 spindles and around 20,000 of the machines were in use across England. The Jenny was then combined with other inventions – Richard Arkwright's water frame and Samuel Crompton's mule – which slashed the manpower needed to make a yard of cloth still further. A few thousand workers could now produce what millions had before, but rather than plummet, employment rocketed. Cloth prices fell, demand expanded and exports boomed. Far from shedding labour, textiles became a magnet for workers. Farmers who had previously used weaving as a side job gave up their land and switched to full-time cloth production. Lancashire became the Silicon Valley of its time, with families from outside the county drawn to it, and inventors from France and the US relocating there.

THE WORLD OF SERVICE

The fact that modern agriculture and industry rest on centuries of labour-saving technology explains why in 2019 employment in farming is below 5 per cent and manufacturing below 10 per cent in both the UK and US. Having been chased off the field and out of the factory by productive machines, more than 80 per cent of people now work in the services sector.

The definition of 'services' is wide and includes jobs in shops, hotels and restaurants, the provision of professional services such as accountancy and architecture, as well as publicly provided services like teaching, lecturing or occupational therapy. Trades in the services economy are often about saving time or avoiding chores – cooking, cleaning, driving, or washing. Or they involve paying others to complete tasks we lack the ability to do ourselves: translate texts, draw up architectural plans, design websites. In the modern economy very few people grow or make things: eight in ten of us spend our days trading time, effort, skill and knowledge.

On one hand, it is tempting to conclude that this should provide a modicum of safety against job-grabbing machines, since humans seem uniquely good at providing services. And there is a more optimistic reading of the scary-sounding automation studies: if a quarter of jobs are at risk then three-quarters are not, and that rump of human work is relatively evenly spread across workers with skills, and wages, of all levels. After all, there are so many things a shopkeeper, waiter or hairdresser must do that we find easy – walking, seeing, understanding customers' emotions – that machines find hard. When it comes to providing services of all types, humans are naturals.

NEVER RACE A ROBOT

On the other hand, 'All of the assumptions about things that robots cannot do are wrong,' says Ahti Heinla, pointing out that machines can now walk up a flight of stairs, process 3D images, and recognize human moods and feelings. The reason they are able to do this is down to a technique called 'machine learning', a technical term for learning from experience and the process that creates artificial intelligence, or AI. The idea is to set the computer or robot a task – ask it to identify an image, pick up an item from a shelf, navigate its way around obstacles in a room – and then give it feedback on what it got right and wrong. As this 'training' is repeated, often hundreds of thousands of times, the robot makes adjustments to avoid its past mistakes and gets better at performing a task correctly.

These ideas are not new: they were first demonstrated by US computer scientist Arthur Samuel, who coined the term 'machine learning' and used the technique to teach a computer to play draughts in the 1950s. But in the past decade improved computer power has allowed AI to become more sophisticated. Computers are now much better at image recognition, regularly beating human lab technicians in tests to spot cancerous cells. Robots are getting better at interpreting more than just pictures and videos: a Tallinn-based software start-up, RealEyes, has used webcams and machine learning to create AI that can read users' emotions. And developments in labs are far ahead of what is seen publicly, Mr Heinla says. So far Starship Technologies' robots have completed 100,000 miles of training as they test drive in Tallinn, London and California, the data from each outing feeding back into a massive shared brain in the Estonian nerve centre.

The warning from Estonia's leading inventors is not to take false comfort. The basic technology underlying AI shows that it is one to take seriously. Robots' artificial brains are powered by transistors that sit on computer chips and, just as the Spinning Jenny did, chips are improving at an astonishing rate. In 1965 Gordon Moore, then 36, predicted that computer chips would double in power every two years. The forecast, now known as Moore's Law, was remarkably accurate: between 1971 and 1989 the number of transistors on Intel chips (a company Mr Moore helped found) rose from 2,300 to 1.2 million. Recently, there has been evidence the pace may be slowing a little, but even if power doubles only every three years, say, the chips of 2030 will be 16 times more powerful than those of 2018. Vastly more advanced artificial intelligence is on the way, and will be seen in our working lives. The only prudent bet to make is that the machines it controls will be able to do anything we can, and more.

Those working at the cutting-edge of technology offer a lesson to the rest of us following in their wake: don't underestimate the

The expanding brains behind artificial intelligence

Transistors per computer processor, 1970–2017, thousands

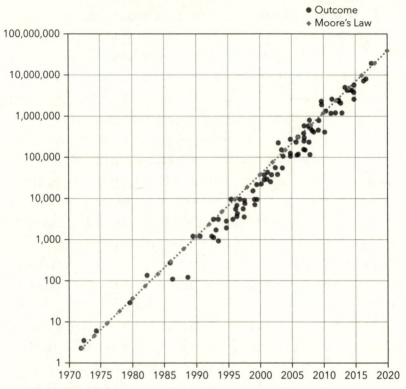

Source: Rupp (2018)

machines. Life in Estonia offers a second warning too, one linked to my travels in the first two parts of the book: the potential for new divisions and damage to the social fabric of a city. Tallin has many districts that are tech hubs, places where the city gleams and locals see no end of opportunity. As one entrepreneur put it to me, 'If you work in technology and are even half decent it is impossible to be unemployed here.' But other parts of the capital are depressed, still reeling from the eurozone crisis a decade ago. And it is not just the odd shopkeeper complaining about the bias towards IT companies and the government's bet on technology: young and highly educated people have concerns too. 'At first it is easy to assimilate here,' explains one Tallinn resident, a recent émigré from Russia. 'But after you have been here for a while you realize that inside one country there are two separate worlds.'

ESTONIA'S SECOND WORLD

STRANDED AND STATELESS AT EUROPE'S FRONTIER

The city of Narva, 200 km east of Tallinn, is the capital of Estonia's second world. Home to a little under 60,000 people it is the easternmost place in the European Union, closer to St Petersburg than Tallinn, a frontier city in which Russian influence is strong. The roads are lined with freight trucks waiting to cross the border and even those with Estonian number plates have Russian drivers – the name cards displayed in the front windows read 'Mihail', 'Sergei' and 'Alexei'. The adverts on billboards are written in Russian and placards in shop windows advertise Radio Eli 95.6 FM, a Russian station. The town's art gallery is largely filled with bequests from the collection of Peter the Great and Sergei Lavretsov, a Russian merchant; the paintings depict seascapes and mountain passes by Ivan Aivazovsky, Aleksandr Makovsky and Ivan Shishkin, all of them Russian. In a 1993 referendum in the city, 97 per cent of those who voted supported autonomy from Estonia (the government in Tallinn threw out the result). Today, over 90 per cent of the people living here are ethnically Russian.

With a good arm you could throw a stone into Russia from Narva. The old town is built up to the bank of the fast-flowing Narva River, the mid-point of which marks the unofficial external border of the EU (agreement on the exact point that Estonia ends and Russia begins has never been reached). The scene is dominated by two huge castles: Hermanni Linnus (Hermann Castle) on the Estonian side and Ивангородская крепость (Ivangorod Fortress) on the Russian. The Estonian riverbank is lined with fishermen using weighted lines to lob their bait into the deep waters. On the far bank three Russian fishermen each stand chest-deep in the water casting their own lines with the walls of Ivangorod – Russia's biggest fortress – rising steeply behind them. Atop its easternmost turret a group of elderly tourists look over into Europe, their white hair fluttering in the wind. It is all pretty tranquil.

But Estonia carries deep scars, says Marianna Makarova, who leads research at Integratsiooni Sihtasutus, the Estonian 'Integration Foundation'. Many of the problems stem from the way people were moved around by state decree under the Soviet system. 'You had no choice over where you went,' she explains. Young Russian engineers who had completed degrees in nearby St Petersburg would be sent to work in the factories and oil-shale plants in Narva and the easternmost county of Estonia (Ida-Viru) that was home to these facilities. These were not the plum jobs – the standard of living in Moscow was then far higher than in Estonia – but an energy worker with no family connections took what they were given (jobs at the coal mines of Karaganda and Vorkuta, both north of the Arctic Circle, were far worse gigs). With the Soviet system deciding where people would live, the ethnic make-up of the ESSR changed. Following the Second World War at least 210,000 people arrived from other Soviet states (the vast majority were from Russia, with some from Ukraine and Belarus) with the share of Estonian natives in the total population falling from 94 per cent in 1945 to 72 per cent in 1953.

Today 330,000 people with Russian heritage make up 25 per cent of the population of Estonia. They are the main group in Narva and Ida-Viru county, and there are 155,000 in Tallinn (40 per cent of the city's population). They live in two main districts in the capital. Lasnamäe is unremarkable, a suburb east of the old city with rows of high-rise towers thronging a dual carriageway. But Väike-Õismäe could only be Soviet: every block here has a very slight curvature and the buildings appear in a regular sequence – three low-rise grey, then one high-rise colourful – which repeats as you walk the streets, the precise geometry turning the roads in the neighbourhood into a series of huge and perfect concentric circles.

Immigrants who ended up in places like Väike-Õismäe did well, so when the USSR collapsed in the early 1990s they were faced with a stark choice. Only 5 per cent returned to Russia, but those who remained say they do not feel Estonian either. Many of those I talk to describe themselves as stranded. 'I don't really know where I fit,' one Russian-Estonian tells me, 'or what to call myself.' Another local explains a complicated phrase that translates as 'I'm too cold to be Russian, too warm to be Estonian' and refers to the stereotypes of national psyche: the fiery and impulsive Russian temper versus the cool and rational Estonian one.

For around 80,000 of the ethnic Russians, statelessness is not just a feeling but a matter of law. Getting hold of formal Estonian citizenship requires an application and a language test that many have not passed. So rather than holding mauve Estonian EU passports, people in this group hold light-grey ones embossed with gold lettering that reads 'VÄLISMAALASE PASS', and below it a translation, 'Alien's Passport'. Anyone possessing this document is a citizen neither of Estonia nor of Russia. They can access public services in Estonia and must pay tax here, but they are ineligible to vote in national elections. This bizarre situation also exists in Latvia; ethnic Russians stranded in the EU are one of the largest groups of stateless people in the world.

The average ethnic Russian in Estonia fares badly and is more likely to be unemployed. Those with jobs are on less secure contracts and easier to fire in a downturn: following the 2008 financial crash the unemployment rate for ethnic Estonians rose to 17 per cent; for ethnic Russians it hit 27 per cent; and for 'alien passport' holders it was over 30 per cent. This raises red flags when thinking about the looming threat from job-stealing technology.

This is also a group that might miss the opportunities in a forward-looking country bent on a high-tech economic strategy. Ethnic Russians have already been left behind in many ways: they are more likely to suffer from alcoholism and have a lower life expectancy than Estonians, particularly the men. In Narva, away from the tourist attractions of the river, there are rows of backstreets lined by Soviet-era tenement buildings that are badly run down. In Tallinn's old town those doing unskilled or low-paid work – the taxi drivers, the chambermaids and cleaners in the hotels, and the shelf stackers – all of them are Russian speakers. The real tragedy, Marianna Makarova explains, is that among the lowest-paid workers there are women in their fifties and sixties with advanced degrees from Russian universities who were sent here to manage Soviet energy facilities.

Unsurprisingly many ethnic Russians appear to have given up. A friendly local guides me to the vast pond at the centre of Väike-Õismäe's circular neighbourhood, where a crowd of men in their late fifties and sixties gather each day. They are 'fishermen', my friend says, using his fingers to make the quotation marks, winking and subtly pointing to a bag holding a large cache of strong lager tucked under some rocks. It is 10 a.m. on a weekday morning and many of the cans have already been drained.

A NEW BRIDGE

IT STARTS WITH THE STATE

After 25 years of betting on technology, the Estonian economy shows where the threats and opportunities of digitization show up. A technology pessimist can certainly make a case: the X-Road data-exchange system is now seen as the 'backbone' of the country and is like a threshing machine or Spinning Jenny for the modern economy. The digitization of government services means that human-to-human interactions – which involve booking appointments, travel and queuing – have been cut out of life here. Studies suggest that this generated an annual saving of 6,400 working years by 2014, with an ever-upward trend. The fearful interpretation is that this undermines 6,400 jobs, putting more than a quarter of the country's

25,000 administrative staff at risk. The number of central government posts – a core group affected by the X-Road – was down 2,450 between 2015 and 2018 alone.

Yet the optimistic case is easier to make. The loss of central government jobs is part of a wider plan. Like Japan, Estonia's ageing workforce is shrinking, and unless the government finds a way to trim its payroll by 750 people every year, its share of employment in the workforce will rise. Seen through this lens, automation is a need, rather than a risk. And across the economy, there are few signs of technology-induced slack. Unemployment is just 4.4 per cent, while labour-market participation of 72 per cent is the highest for 20 years and far above the rate in the US or the average EU country. Nor do robots and software appear to be hurting the average Estonian worker's pay: inflation-adjusted wages have risen 4 per cent in recent years. An official study for 2018 showed big demand for nurses, teachers, computer programmers, and bus and lorry drivers. Seen from the bird's-eye view such aggregate statistics provide, things appear to be going well.

Estonia's economic revival starts with the state, says Rait Rand, inventor and recent *Ajujaht* champion. Successive governments have adopted policies that actively create opportunities for inventors, he says, giving the system of unemployment benefits as an example. Anyone who decides to pursue a career as an inventor or entrepreneur can collect unemployment benefits in Estonia as long as they have a clear business plan and can prove they are making progress against it. This was important in his own case, says Mr Rand, emboldening him to take a risk and leave his steady job.

Mr Rand, in his early forties, spent much of his career designing gizmos. After studying electronic design and physics he became an in-house inventor at big companies, designing steering locks for General Motors, wind turbines for ABB, a renewable energy company, and electronics for Eriksson, a telecommunications company. In early 2017 he was asked to speak at the teaching hospital of Tartu University, his alma mater, about electronic sensors, and while being shown around noticed that nurses were spending a lot of time writing down observations rather than caring for patients. The most common reading – temperature – was being taken four times a day, more often for small children in neonatal care. At the end of his talk Mr Rand asked the audience whether it would be helpful if he automated the process. The response was so positive that in March 2017 he quit his job to pursue the idea full time. He came up with the solution in months and calls it the TempID.

Rait Rand laughs as he retrieves the tiny gadget from his trouser pocket: 'This is a great product – most of my previous inventions you would have to bring in on a tractor.' The TempID is a thin pink disc, which is stuck to a patient's skin and left there while they are receiving treatment. Mr Rand swipes the disc against his phone and a minute-by-minute chart appears, showing his temperature over the past four weeks. There are competitors, but the existing US-made sensors run out of power after 24 hours and transmit data via Bluetooth, something hospitals are wary of (TempID links directly to its user's phone, and its battery will last a year). Weeks after winning the *Ajujaht* competition, which is sponsored by the Estonian government, Mr Rand signed deals to supply the device to the country's three largest pharmaceutical chains.

Estonia's digital democracy helps support inventors in indirect ways. The TempID generates data – a person's temperature log – that is highly personal but becomes valuable only when shared and discussed with clinicians. But in 2018 data security concerns meant it became illegal to share confidential patient information via email, even with the patient and clinician concerned. In response, the TempID team is working on a secure channel that will allow patients and clinicians to communicate directly. This new pathway, more secure than email, will use 'Mobile-ID', a government-backed smartphone version of the physical ID card Estonians carry. 'The government's channel is the basis of our secure channel,' Mr Rand explains, reflecting the benefits of piggybacking on the state: 'For technology developers in Estonia the ground has often been prepared already.'

DIGITAL CITIZENS

The success of the digital ID card created a new problem, recalls Siim Sikkut, the government's head of IT. As Estonia's economy improved it started to attract outside investment and foreigners began taking up positions on the boards of Estonian companies. The efficiency of the ID system meant that many big companies had switched to signing and sharing all board documents digitally, but the foreign board members were unable to provide the government-verified e-signatures that were needed. Estonian firms had to go back to the old ways, explains Mr Sikkut: 'Companies had to revert to paper, and it was a hassle.'

The initial solution was to provide major foreign investors in Estonia with an ID card on an ad hoc basis, so that they too could sign board documents digitally. But then a bigger idea struck the team that developed the ID card: if the country was opening up its identification system to investors, why not just make it available to anyone? They had a hunch this might bring benefits: perhaps new 'e-Residents' would end up as customers for Estonian firms and spend money on professional services such as accountancy or website design. Since the idea was totally new there were no case studies to evaluate, and they took another punt. 'We just threw it out, to see if there would be any traction,' Mr Sikkut recalls, 'and after 24 hours it had gone way beyond what we expected – in a way the market was telling us: "go for it!"' Today Estonia has 35,000 e-Residents from 138 countries. They are all members of what the government's promotional blurb calls a 'New Digital Nation'.

Becoming an Estonian e-Resident is easy: you enter some basic information on a website, upload a photo and a scan of your passport, pay a €100 fee and finally select the Estonian embassy from which you would like to pick up your card. It all takes under five minutes. The real question is why you would bother. There are various categories of user, says 29-year-old Ott Vatter, who now runs the e-Residency programme. Some people are simply fans: they like the idea and get the card as a bit of fun, and as a symbol of cross-border solidarity. Others are driven by business consider-ations: e-Residents can open bank accounts remotely, allowing them to transact in euros. And some seem driven by anxiety and the desire for a foothold, albeit electronic, in a stable country. There has been interest in the scheme from Britons working on EU-funded research projects, perhaps fearful that the UK's exit from the EU might lead to pressure on their funding and seeing the e-Residency as insurance against this.

BETS AND JOBS

Estonia's radical experiments with policy to stimulate innovation seem to be creating jobs, explains Harry Tallinn, a local entrepre-neur who helps run the *Ajujaht* competition. By tracking the fortunes of five recent winners Mr Tallinn knows they collectively already employ 250 people and paid €1 million in tax in the first half of 2017. And those numbers will surely rise: start-up firms featuring on *Ajujaht* have raised over €30 million in funding from investors in recent years. When they spend the cash, revenues for suppliers, wages for staff and taxes received by the government will all increase.

Estonia's new category of citizen seems to be creating jobs too: by the end of 2017 the country's overseas e-Residents had set up almost 3,000 companies in Estonia, with the programme on track to boost GDP by over €30 million in the next four years. The main challenge is not demand for the e-Residency card but ensuring supply, explains Mr Vatter: since the card counts as an official government document it is only available for collection from Estonian embassies and the country has only 34 of them around the world. When I met Mr Vatter's team they were exploring partnerships with reputable overseas orga-nizations to ensure at least one pick-up point in every country. The government's target seems wildly ambitious – to attract 10 million e-Residents by 2025. If it gets even halfway the economic impact would be huge.

One lesson from Estonia's success is the importance of making a bold commitment that goes right across an economy, from the way a state shares data to the fine tuning of unemployment benefits to incentivize entrepreneurs. At the heart of this is the X-Road, the digital foundation the Tallinn government has built, and which private companies are now building services atop. The potential savings in time and public funds, together with the prospect for new private-sector jobs, explains why ideas from Estonia are diffusing fast. Some regional neighbours are partnering directly with the government in Tallinn: Finland started using the X-Road system in 2017, the Faroe Islands and Iceland have since announced they will do the same. Other countries are sending functionaries to visit Estonia to find out how the digital ID, X-Road, i-voting, and e-Residency work. An office set up to facilitate this, the e-Estonia Briefing Centre, received 800 official delegations in 2018.

While technology has never caused mass economy-wide unemployment, it has often driven big changes in the jobs that are available. This process, the churning of workers rather than their replacement, can be seen in Estonia: the plans of many firms here imply the destruction of some jobs and simultaneous creation of others. Click and Grow is a good example: its Smart Farm cuts the need for human labour in one way – it takes one adult less than two hours per week to oversee machines producing thousands of plants. At the same time, the technology is creating jobs employing people to design the machines, to make them, market and sell them, and then service them. As with previous technologies the result is a shift in the type of work being done, rather than the number of hours worked. And it is hard to question Mr Lepp's motives as he sets out his case: Click and Grow recently opened an operation in the US, a country where a staggering 40 per cent of food is lost or wasted through transportation and storage. As well as being local, growing food in your home requires 40 times less water than farmland does and no pesticides. Hundreds of years after the crop rotation system and the threshing machine, there are clearly still big gains to be made from getting farming right.

A related fear for our economic future is that while the quantity of jobs may hold up, their quality will be eroded: robots will do all the valuable work, while humans will be left doing repetitive, dull and cheap tasks. Estonia offers a counter here too – working alongside robots in technology companies offers posts for people with a range of skills, and they look quite fun. On my way out of Starship Technologies I am shown around the floor where the team overseeing the company's delivery-bots work. Inside a large room geeky-looking young men sit observing arrays of computer screens. Each of them is overseeing a single robot: the screens relay pictures of everything the robot picks up with its cameras and radar, and plots a path on the display to show the human where the robot is planning to drive next. As it reaches a road crossing, the robot stops and waits – at this stage in its development the human controller must give it permission to cross. The team observe the planned route, giving the robot feedback and improving its artificial brain.

The jobs in the control room are like being paid to play a computer game, albeit a rather boring one. And as I leave the main gate of the building one of the six-wheeled robots trundles up and waits to enter through the main reception. As well as an overseer in the control room the robot is accompanied – as they all are during this 'training' phase – by a minder who walks alongside it. He looks like a young James Bond: in his early twenties, wearing a company-supplied leather bomber jacket, and dark sunglasses. Other jobs are available in Estonia as the country's labour shortage – including the deficit of lorry and bus drivers – shows. Instead of becoming drivers, the staff here are teaching robots to drive: work that involves gaming with them, and walking around Tallinn wearing shades and a cool jacket. The new jobs are clearly more attractive than the old ones.

A NEW LANGUAGE

Even if digital technology does not eradicate jobs, it could cause damage if it adds new economic divisions to societies or widens existing ones. One of Tallinn's main tech hubs, Ülemiste City, is a reminder of the ethnic and linguistic fault-lines that make Estonia such a valuable test case. The recently completed business park is close to Lasnamäe, a region where Russian speakers are the main residents, and is a place where Tallinn past and future co-exist in one spot. Re-branded as the 'Silicon Valley of northern Europe', the park sits on the vast site of the Lenin National Union Factory, a state-owned railcar-manufacturing plant that operated here until 1991. Ülemiste City is home to hundreds of technology companies located in new office blocks that stand beside massive Soviet-built ware-houses. Above huge doorways of the old buildings deep-red bricks have been used to insert metre-high slogans into the walls: there is one for the Russian speakers – *СЛАВА КПСС!* (Glory to the Com-munist Party of the Soviet Union!); and one for Estonians – *ELAGU NLKP!* (Fly Communist Party of Estonia!). The large car park, packed with employees' shiny new vehicles, has a French-style kiosk in the corner that sells glossy magazines, and tucked behind it a memorial that carries a lengthy elegy to the Lenin factory railcar workers. If you are interested in a new digital divide in society, this is your place.

The employment record of firms based in Ülemiste City is an ini-tial clue that while technology might cause rifts, it can help heal them too. There are plenty of ethnic Russian innovators and entrepreneurs here, many in senior management positions. Playtech, a company that writes the software behind many gambling and gaming sites, was founded in Estonia in 1999 and now employs 5,000 people in 17 countries; there are lots of Russian speakers in its Tallinn office – essential, given that hundreds of coders work further east in its Ukrainian operation. Parallels, another software company, has built a kind of bridge for Mac and PC users, to ensure their work is always compatible. It has 800 staff working in its Tallinn base, with another office in Moscow. At Helmes, the software company next door, they say they hire people here and in Minsk, Belarus. Astrec Data, a com-pany that warehouses the reams of data needed by firms engaged in machine learning, has servers here in Tallinn and in St Petersburg.

Under the company's main logo is the strapline 'Connecting east and west'.

If anything, jobs in technology firms here appear slightly biased towards those from or with connections to former USSR countries including Russia. I ask leading technology innovators why: surely a group that is marginalized in general is going to fare badly in a new industry? The answer, in part, is education. There was a strong emphasis on mathematics and technical skills under the Soviet system, says Ahti Heinla, who warmly remembers battling against Russian schools in physics competitions. Ethnic Russians had a reputation for being highly numerate; they were in great demand as coders and developers as the industry began to flourish in the 1990s. This echoes today, with Russian-speaking Estonian parents valuing technical education highly and emphasizing its importance at home.

Others say the key is not the mathematics per se but the ability to communicate. Language is a major topic of debate in Tallinn and a political hot potato. The fundamental problem is that this country's two tongues are fundamentally incompatible: they are not even distant cousins, they have different alphabets and hardly any shared words. The political problem is that there are two parallel school systems here – one Estonian, the other Russian – which means that children and families mix relatively little. The single university system does force the two groups to integrate, explains a Tallinn professor, but before and after lectures the students divide along linguistic lines to talk in two separate groups. Technology companies are different because they run on what one Tallinn inventor calls 'three international languages' – mathematics, computer code and English – removing local language barriers completely.

While the government's educational policy – the twin-track school system – maintains divisions here, its innovation-supporting policies seem to help bridge them. The state-supported *Ajujaht* contest has had lots of Russian-speaking teams in recent years, explains Harry Tallinn. In 2017 contestants presented their inventions in Estonian, Russian and English; the competition included a team from

Moscow and a group of Russian-speaking Estonians – Poirot Systems – who lost out to Rait Rand's TempID in the final. (The young men, who had worked as bartenders, came up with a gizmo that automates stock control, ordering supplies to ensure that a cocktail bar never runs dry.) As with the X-Road and e-Residency the news about *Ajujaht* has travelled, and Mr Tallinn is helping the Moldovan government run a similar programme. Narva, the Russian-speaking city at the far east of the country, has hosted the TEDx brand of seminars since 2014. The theme for the 2017 event was 'without borders' and included technology inventors and scientists from Estonia, Russia and Ukraine.

This is not to say that Estonia's blind bet on technology has healed the divisions here. Almost 30 years after independence the country still has a deeply segregated labour market with many professions, such as law, public administration and the arts, seen as closed to ethnic Russians – a viewpoint backed up by employment statistics for these sectors, which are all tipped towards Estonian natives. In 2018 the unemployment rate for those unable to understand Estonian was more than double that for those with the language as their mother tongue. The most recent concern for marginalized Russians has been the prevalence of heroin and fentanyl addiction, and a corresponding rise in HIV rates and drug overdoses.

Yet Tallinn, a city that is 40 per cent Russian-speaking, offers grounds for hope when it comes to the role technology can play in a divided society. The optimistic case starts with the observation that the workplace is Estonia's best bet as a way to dissolve pre-existing cliques of language and ethnicity: across all industries those with Russian and Estonian heritage are more likely to make connections at work than they do in leisure time. The technology industries, running on the 'international languages' of maths, code and English, are thought to be relatively fair, with ethnic Russians well represented in this sector. Of course, not everyone gets these jobs – as a rule of thumb only around one in ten university students goes on to work in technology companies. But there is a huge unmet demand for talent in the ICT sector and, unlike the law or public administration, these industries are open to Estonians whatever their heritage. What matters for a country this divided is the addition of a sector where jobs are allocated based on ability rather than ethnicity or language.

THE BALTIC EXPRESS

Expect to hear more about the Estonian economic model in coming years: ideas from Tallinn, with their promise of cost savings and more employment, are diffusing fast. At the e-Government academy in Tallinn there is a huge map of the world on the wall, dotted with hundreds of tiny LED lights that show the cities with whom Estonians are working. Next up for the team here is a project with the Nigerian government in Lagos – a city that sees 2,000 new arrivals every day. The programme will track smartphone use as a way of spotting population growth, allowing energy supply, sanitation, transport and policing to be adjusted accordingly.

'In the end inventing is about freedom,' explains Rait Rand, touching the TempID disc in the palm of his hand. 'If you come up with the new idea and you set up the company then you are in charge.' In a country where corporate decisions were made from Moscow in living memory, this means a lot. Far from undermining it, others see technology as an important way to protect and enhance their democracy. By making the ballot box obsolete, Estonia's e-democracy has drawn young people into voting, and since a politician's assets are all traceable via the system, it cuts the potential for graft. As Siim Sikkut, the government's top tech guru, puts it, 'You can't bribe a computer.'

The aim for many of those seeking to crack the holy grail of artificial intelligence is to use computers to strengthen democratic systems too, says Ahti Heinla, inventor of the delivery robot. Teams across the world are racing to create something known as an artificial general intelligence, or AGI. This would be a computerized mind so powerful that it could reason, planning what to learn and building its own digital brain in a strategic way, rather than being taught what to do by its human masters. People pursuing this kind of research think an AGI might help humans solve intractable problems such as the politics of nuclear disarmament or the economics of trade deals.

For technologists the aim is not just for better-functioning democracies but more egalitarian economies too. Mr Heinla describes a future in which a blue-collar worker in need of some much-needed staple – a carton of milk or a toothbrush – will be able to order it online and have it delivered cheaply by the time they get home. This, he says, will be an equalizing step. 'Kings have always been able to afford servants, but common people have not – and this fact will not change.' Employing a human to ferry items around means paying their wage and creates a floor under which delivery costs cannot fall. Employing a personal human courier means it will always cost $5 or $10 to deliver a small package within a day, but, Ahti Heinla says, 'This is too much – the robots are the answer.' Robots earn no wages so their time is cheap. In Ahti Heinla's vision of the future the delivery-bot becomes a kind of everyman servant. Robots make us all kings.

MYTHICAL WAVES, IMAGINARY STORMS

Predictions of how technology will soon affect our economies can make for extremely worrying reading. Within ten years, the story goes, we are set to see a new breed of intelligent machines specifically designed to eviscerate the human workforce. That so many millions could see their roles automated will be a drastic shock, a point hammered home by the terminology used: the crashing 'waves' of technology, the 'perfect storm' of automation. The huge numbers and disaster-laden words paint a terrifying picture: when automation strikes it will be sudden, cause widespread damage and be completely out of our control.

My trips to Estonia, together with discussing stresses and strains with people living in the other extreme economies in this book, convinced me that to tell the story of technology in this manner is to see the challenge and risks in the wrong way. Start with the question of timing. Perhaps the most impressive idea I came across in Tallinn – to move farming into the homes of people eating the food – is a radical step that could have huge environmental benefits. At the same time, Mattias Lepp's Smart Farm is just another agricultural machine, a direct descendant of the seed drill and the threshing machine introduced centuries ago. The use of automated machines in industry is centuries old, and the technology of the moment, machine learning and artificial intelligence, recently turned 70. The invention, diffusion and application of technology is chronic rather than acute, slow burn rather than sudden, and has been changing the way humans work for centuries. Automated machines are old news; technology in the workplace, a trend of tomorrow, is also something we are more familiar with than we may understand.

Tech-savvy Estonia, in its own unique way, is a reminder of where some of the stresses of technology are likely to lie. The automation of a job, or of an important task within a job, alters human responsibilities; with this comes a change in the nature of roles and their societal ranking. The lesson from history is that while technology has not caused mass unemployment, it has caused mass shifts – from farming, to manufacturing, to services – in what humans do. Cutting-edge Estonia seems to show history is repeating itself: rather than job shortages, the nature of work is changing. The warning from previous parts of this book is that this kind of economic shock – a jolt to people's roles, responsibilities and status – is important. Flux in these higher needs, to use Abraham Maslow's hierarchy, can be just as costly as the raw economic destruction of a natural disaster. Economic flux, the changing and churning of work, can cause harm even in an economy where growth is strong and there is a shortage of workers.

For technologists bent on disrupting old ways of doing things, this is a blind spot. Travelling through the Russian-speaking suburbs of Tallinn and the entirely Russian town of Narva at the EU's eastern border was a stark reminder of what it means to be left behind by a new economic paradigm. While there is plenty of evidence that technology is drawing in high-skilled young Russian workers, 25 years after a 'blind bet' on a technology-driven growth model, many are still left behind. And the assumption that artificial intelligence will somehow solve all problems political and economic is unnerving. Estonia is a country whose citizens can vote from anywhere on the planet and which sells an e-Residency to foreigners with €100 and five minutes to spare. Yet the world's first digital democracy is also a place where 80,000 people are stateless. The Russian speakers with their grey 'alien' passports are taxpayers who may not vote and their situation is a fundamental violation of democracy. Even the fastest and most powerful artificial intelligence is not going to help with problems like this.

Estonia dispels a final myth of technological change – the notion that it comes from some uncontrollable and external force. In Tallinn, the technology is not coming from a faceless corporation sending armies of robots to eat our jobs. Rather it is the result of government-led industrial strategy that aims to tackle fundamental problems: tight budgets and a shortage of workers. Many of the automated machines people are most excited about – from farming and fruit-picking to delivery and nursing – are being designed for sectors where there is a shortage, rather than an excess, of workers. Facing the future in a prudent way means taking the labour-market threat from automation seriously – a spike in unemployment might happen. But technology is a solution to many problems that are already happening today, and we can be close to certain will continue. Robots can help with the challenges of the ageing economy, environmental degradation and shortfalls in countries' budgets. Prudence also means taking seriously the notion that we might not be automating fast enough.

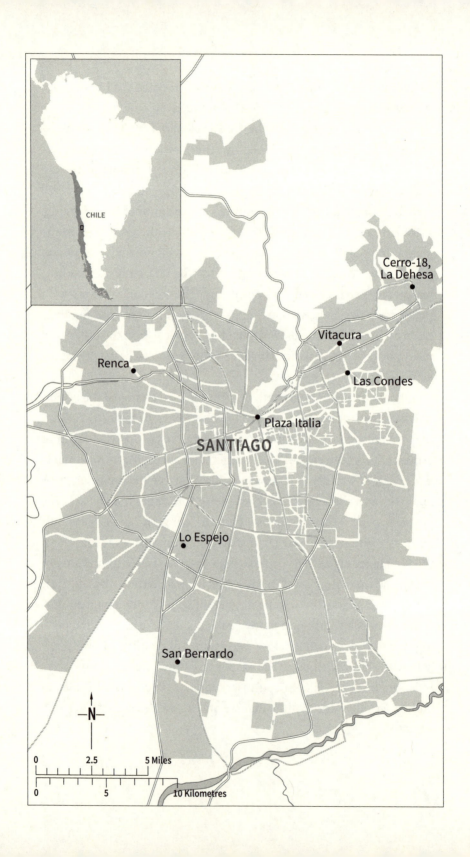

CHILE

Cerro-18,
La Dehesa

Vitacura

Renca

Las Condes

Plaza Italia

SANTIAGO

Lo Espejo

San Bernardo

N

| 0 | 2.5 | 5 Miles |

| 0 | 5 | 10 Kilometres |

9

Santiago

One of the great mistakes is to judge policies and programs
by their intentions rather than their results.

Milton Friedman,
1975

THE PIN-UP ECONOMY

TOP OF THE HILL AND BOTTOM OF THE PILE

For a view of Santiago, the neighbourhood of Cerro Dieciocho is hard to beat. Often written 'Cerro-18' (Hill 18), it is a small suburb that looks like one of the famous favelas that rise up the mountains around Rio de Janeiro. Here, the colourful makeshift homes climb a hill so steep that they appear to be stacked upon one another. The bus that links this hillside settlement with the centre of the city stops halfway up, leaving a climb up narrow flights of stairs that wind and weave between the dwellings. The ascent is punishing but worthwhile: from the top you can see how the tin-rooved shacks merge into the clean square blocks of neighbouring La Dehesa, a suburb built for the newly rich, and further on to the leafy gardens of Vitacura and Las Condes, and the city homes of the established Chilean elite. A shanty-town nestled among wealth, Cerro-18 offers a unique perspective on the capital of the world's most economically unequal developed country.

These hillside neighbourhoods are not slums. The roofing may be tin but the walls are often brick, and some of the homes are large and impressive. Self-built on land too hilly to develop commercially, each dwelling is unique, tucked into whatever space was going spare. At the very top of the hill the buildings stop, giving way to waste-ground used as a football pitch on which a couple of locals have also built a makeshift garage, upgrading a humble Renault Clio by adding shiny rims and a fat exhaust pipe. One side of the hill is too steep for building homes, playing football or tuning up cars – here there are just shrubs, detritus and, walking with a pink hessian sack in his hand, Christian Aravehala, 43, an unemployed construction worker.

Mr Aravehala is here collecting aluminium cans and the top of Cerro-18 is a decent spot to do it. As well as car maintenance and ball sports the locals use this spot for fly tipping, so there are plenty of rubbish bags to pick through. The fine view over Santiago's wealthi-est districts also attracts teenagers who come to light fires and drink, and as Mr Aravehala strolls around every so often he hits a mini jackpot – a blue plastic bag containing five or six empty lager cans. He crushes them with his foot and puts them into his bag, explain-ing that each kilo of cans will earn him 300 pesos (around 45¢, or 35p) and that his plan is to collect 6 kilos today – enough to buy some food and fund a bus trip to see his elderly mother who is in hospital in Providencia, a suburb around 45 minutes away. He moves steadily and his sack is filling up – but it is noon, 31 °C and rising, and with each can weighing just 15 grams he needs to collect 400 to reach his target. The heat is unrelenting, his nails are falling off and the ends of his fingers are badly swollen.

Like Akita and Tallinn, Santiago is an extreme economy that offers a window on the future. The capital is by far the biggest eco-nomic hub in Chile: with a population of 5.2 million it is home to a third of the Chilean population, is ten times the size of the next larg-est city (Antofagasta) and is the source of almost half of the country's economic output. A poor country in the 1970s, Chile had a national income per person half of that in Argentina. Today national income is almost $14,000 per person, the highest in Latin America, and not far behind Greece or Portugal. Reflecting its exceptional performance, Chile was accepted into the Organization for Economic Cooperation and Development (OECD) in 2010, becoming the first South American country officially to graduate from 'emerging' to 'developed' status. The rapid growth and eradication of poverty that came with it meant Chile was seen as an 'economic miracle' and made a poster child for development by influential international agencies that urged others to replicate 'the Chile model'.

The wrinkle in the success story was the fact that with Chile's miraculous growth came extreme inequality. As well as being the OECD's newest and best-performing member, Chile was also the most unequal economy in the rich-world club, with huge disparities.

One popular measure of inequality, the share of income going to the best-paid tenth of workers, rose from 30 per cent in the early 1970s to almost 50 per cent by the late 1990s. It has since edged higher, meaning that everyone outside the top tenth – nine out of ten people in Chile – now share less than half of the national income among them.

Today the path Santiago has already taken – fast growth with sharply rising inequality – is becoming the best-trodden route to development, with the Chilean level of inequality fast becoming a global norm. Together, India and China account for more than a

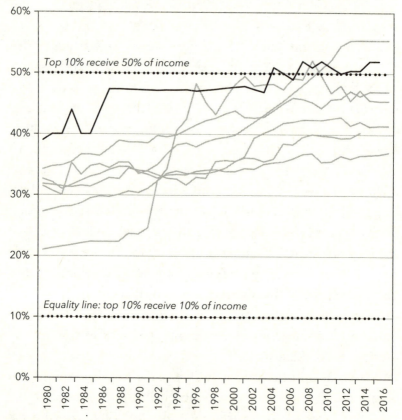

Income inequality – following Chile's lead

Income share of the top 10 per cent of earners, selected major economies

Source: World Inequality Database (2018). The black line shows Chile, the other lines are for the US, China, India, Russia, Germany and Europe.

third of the world's population, and both have become more unequal over the past 30 years as their economies have expanded. The world's fastest-expanding cities, from Lima in neighbouring Peru, to Lagos in Nigeria and Kuala Lumpur in Malaysia, are becoming the most unequal on the planet. The economies of the future are old like Akita, digital like Tallinn, and unequal like Santiago.

I went to Santiago to meet those at the top and the bottom of the city's income scale, and the controversial policymakers who had designed its extreme economic model. Chile-style economics had been praised and then pushed on others to copy and I wanted to understand ordinary Chileans' views on their country's development: if growth eradicates poverty, does inequality really matter? And if it does are there, as in Akita and Tallinn, reasons for optimism, signs of pushback, cooperation and resilience at the leading edge of this global trend?

THE EXPERIMENT

THE RISE AND RISE OF THE CHICAGO BOYS

'Back then we thought that inequality would, in the end, disappear.' Rolf Lüders sits in his apartment in Las Condes and casts his mind back to events in the early 1970s that still echo in Chile today. Santiago is divided into 32 districts or *comunas* and this is the plushest: across the road there is an exclusive golf club and the streets around the local El Golf subway station are lined with embassies with lush green lawns. Now 83, Mr Lüders wears an open-collar shirt and a simple grey cardigan, looking very much the academic he has become in recent years, but he sits surrounded by fine art, figurines and rugs from a previous life of international travel. As a younger man Mr Lüders pulled all the strings of Chile's economy, running both the finance and economy ministries in the early 1980s. He is also one of a small group responsible for a unique economic experiment.

The Chilean experiment had its roots in a policy set out by Franklin D. Roosevelt in his 1933 inauguration speech. The US president described his hatred of war, and promised that his country would no longer attempt to intervene militarily in the affairs of its neighbours on the American continent – it would become neutral. Instead, US attempts to influence its neighbours became softer and subtler. Starting in the late 1930s a body called the International Cooperation Administration (ICA) began to fund the sharing of skilled instructors and trained personnel with Latin American countries, a policy known as 'technical assistance'. ICA funding meant that US experts were involved in projects across the continent from trials involving new pesticides to help Ecuadorian banana growers to steps to improving sanitation in El Salvador, and hundreds more including Peruvian bean cultivation, policing in Honduras and teacher training in Guatemala.

Another project aimed to boost the quality of Chile's universities, and as part of this the University of Chicago and the Catholic University of Chile signed an ICA-sponsored technical assistance agreement in 1955. The formal plan was that Chilean PhD students would go to Chicago for two years and study economics, then return home and teach in Santiago. This student exchange would improve the standard of economics in Chile and would encourage the country's lecturers and students to move away from left-leaning and socialism-inspired ideas. The eventual impact went far beyond these modest aims: the exchange students, now known universally in Chile as the 'Chicago Boys', ended up with complete control of the country's economy.

MILTON AND ALITO

The blend of economics taught in Chicago in the 1950s was already famous by the time the Chilean students arrived: a system with its own methods, attitudes and interests that set it apart from thinking elsewhere. Methodologically rigorous, with a commitment to testing theories against data, the so-called Chicago School developed conclusions with big political implications. Their analysis led them to trust markets as a way to allocate scarce resources and be wary of politicians and the state. The best person to spend a dollar, the Chicago economists reasoned, was the person who earned it – and since state spending rested on taxes that drained workers' pockets and entrepreneurs' tills, Chicagoans thought government should be small and its involvement in the economy limited.

Two Chicago School academics stood out as the preeminent influences on the exchange students and, later, Chile. One was Milton Friedman, who by the mid-1950s was in his late forties and had been a leading light in the economics department for a decade. All the Chilean exchange students took classes with him and say that he was respected and liked, but that he was aloof and scary too. Mr Lüders had Friedman as a thesis adviser and recalls lectures of a striking clarity, with complex theory often explained through simple everyday stories. The other influence was Arnold Harberger who, like Friedman, was interested in practical economic questions, from the regulation of monopolies to the taxation of companies. Mr Harberger – who became known as 'Alito' – was the Chicago Boys' day-to-day adviser, adopted uncle and drinking companion.

The first group of exchange students trained in Chicago returned to Santiago in 1958. Brimming with ideas and plans, their main achievement in the first few years was to earn a reputation for setting exams that were far too hard, their Chilean colleagues and students unable to meet the exacting standards they had picked up in the US. Over time the roster of Chicago Boys began to grow, most of them returning to jobs in academia and think tanks. Measured against its stated aims, the educational exchange had worked: Santiago economics was now more rigorous, and its socialist bent tempered by an infusion of market-friendly ideas from Chicago. But this was all in the world of academia: for more than 15 years the real-world impact of the Chicago Boys on the average Chilean was zero.

THE FIRST EXPERIMENT

Everything changed in Chile in the early 1970s. Salvador Allende, the 62-year-old leader of the country's left-wing Socialist Party, was elected as president by a narrow margin at the beginning of the decade. In part Allende saw himself as continuing Chile's liberal tradition, promising a country of 'unlimited cultural, religious and ideological tolerance' in a 1972 speech at the United Nations. He was also a committed Marxist and ran on a ticket promising economic policies that would improve the lives of blue-collar and agricultural workers. In order to guarantee the fair outcomes the free market could not, the state would need to take control, nationalizing industry and 'collectivizing' farmland.

Allende made good on this manifesto. Soon after his election the assets of two US-owned copper mines and Chile's main telephone company were taken into state hands, with the foreign owners receiving nothing in return. The government took over the financial system. By the end of 1971 the state had bought up every foreign bank and controlled 90 per cent of domestic credit provision too. Loopholes in long-forgotten laws from the 1930s were used to force entrepreneurs to sell their companies, allowing direct state control of 40 per cent of industry. Any farm bigger than 80 hectares (around 200 acres) could be bought by the government at a price of its choice, with 10 million hectares from over 5,800 large estates – around 60 per cent of Chile's farmland – expropriated in this way. Allende set new, higher minimum wages for both blue- and white-collar workers, and took control of prices, with state-employed observers – the *Junta de Abastecimiento y Precios* – making sure that no shop deviated from the prices set by the government.

All this – the state control of companies, markets, prices and output – was the opposite of what the Chicago Boys had been taught. At first it was hugely successful and popular in Chile. Government spending rose by over a third as a huge programme of house building was launched. Economic growth jumped from 3.6 per cent to

8 per cent in 1971, the best year since the 1950s. Unemployment fell sharply and workers' buying power rose 22 per cent in a single year as price controls ensured that inflation fell. Chile's growing economy was more equitable too: mandatory wage increases for low-paid workers were 56 per cent, higher than the (still generous) 23 per cent rise that professional Chileans received. The wage gap between the skilled and unskilled fell and income inequality was driven down. In just a year Allende's promises seemed to be paying off.

But the success of such a huge shift in economic approach should be measured in decades not years, and the short-term boom Allende delivered was both artificial and unsustainable. Rampant spending on house building and the public sector meant the government deficit soared from 3 per cent in 1970 to over 30 per cent by 1973. Unable to pay their rocketing wage bills, firms began to cut back production, and strikes meant that many factories lay dormant. With the economy beginning to contract and unemployment rising, Allende was hit by the same global shock that undid Mobutu Sese Seko's economic plans in Kinshasa in the 1970s: the tumbling international price of copper starved Chile of export earnings. Inflation had always been high – around 25 per cent per year was normal – but as the central bank printed money to support Allende's spending, it rose to 250 per cent in 1972 and to over 650 per cent in 1973. With prices growing faster than wages, Chilean workers' buying power fell almost 40 per cent in 1973. The informal economy kicked in, with pirate vendors selling goods on black markets; in response, the government announced a plan to ban the sale of 30 key staples. Things such as oil, rice, sugar and meat were to be taken out of the market economy completely and would be provided directly by the government based on a family's need, rather than income.

With prices rising much faster than wages, Chileans were becoming poorer. Understandably, the promise of government-supplied rice and oil did little to soothe workers' concerns, and early 1973 saw a general strike. At the same time, a concerted newspaper campaign – which declassified documents now show was partly funded by the CIA – criticized Allende and his Marxist policies. Unrest began to build and June saw an attempted coup, in which the army surrounded the presidential palace, La Modena, with tanks. The plan failed, but on 11 September 1973 the Chilean Air Force bombed the palace, and the army stormed its grounds. Salvador Allende took his own life, apparently shooting himself with an AK-47 machine gun that had been a gift from Fidel Castro. The same day a military junta led by the head of the army, General Augusto Pinochet, took power, promising to rid Chile of the 'Marxist cancer'. Chile's short experiment with socialism was over and a new phase of extreme capitalism, one that would deliver rapid growth and sharp inequality, was about to begin.

CAMPING IN THE CITY

The district of San Bernardo, the southernmost *comuna* in Santiago, is one of the city's poorest. On Sundays, close to the town's central square, a huge market springs up under a vast canopy 10 metres wide and perhaps 500 metres long; the permanent structure creates a kind of open-air shopping street, offering welcome shade for stallholders and shoppers alike. The pre-Christmas shopping period coincides with the arrival of hot weather here in the southern hemisphere. Red triangles of Christmas-themed bunting flicker in the breeze while locals inspect the late-spring produce – huge watermelons, bulging red peppers and giant bulbs of garlic.

Away from the shade of this market the sun is punishing and a water vendor, Angela Silva, offers me a seat under her umbrella. I make a comment about how pleasant the stalls and central square are. 'It is a different world where I live,' she replies. 'Go to our market and you will see.' In her neighbourhood the people live *'asinado'*, Angela Silva says, translating the word with hand gestures implying that she and her neighbours live on top of one another. Shoppers from the middle-class market stroll past in imitation Ralph Lauren polo shirts and joke with Angela that she should be selling piña coladas in the unrelenting heat.

San Bernardo's other market is called Lo Blanco and takes its name from the street it is held on. There is no public infrastructure to assist stallholders or shoppers here; the very best stalls have blue tarpaulin roofing but many are simply tables covered with goods, with the odd umbrella attached acting as a parasol. At the fringes of the markets illegal vendors – known as *coleros* – huddle together setting out goods for sale on rectangular plastic sheets the size of pool tables. The vendors' business model is the same as the '*marchés pirates*' in Kinshasa, and I notice some sheets have long strings attached to each corner, which can be tugged together to create a bag if the trader needs to make a quick getaway. In central Santiago the *coleros* sell cigarettes and iPhone chargers and do well, but at this market these pirate vendors are old, thin and look desperately poor. No one is interested in buying their dusty old clothes, broken plastic toys or chunky chargers for long-defunct 2G phones; many of the *coleros* in Lo Blanco have no strings on their sheets; there are no police here, and no one bothering to carry out checks.

Lo Blanco feels edgy, and locals offer warnings about theft as we go in. But the people are friendly, and lots of Haitian couples promenade in smart Sunday clothes, chatting with friends they bump into. (Chile has seen increased immigration from disaster-stricken Haiti in recent years, with many of the new arrivals working in the construction sector.) Towards the edge of the market Jessica Villar, a 48-year-old woman, runs a tiny shop where she sells socks, underwear and Disney-themed children's swimming towels ahead of the coming summer season.

Jessica recalls moving to Santiago from the Chilean countryside and arriving at the neighbouring suburb, El Bosque, with her parents in 1979 when she was nine years old. Their home was a *campamento* – a kind of makeshift camp that sprang up as Chile rapidly urbanized. 'The reality of the *campamentos* was that we were cold, and we were hungry,' she says. The dwellings were informal – built using tarpaulins stretched over a frame made from sticks, held in place by string and rocks – and the family had to move constantly. Later, as the inhabitants invested in their makeshift homes, Jessica's camp was reclassified as a *población* – a more formal place with permanent structures, like a shanty town or favela – but that took a decade and the homes were still flimsy and cold.

Since then things have changed hugely, Jessica says. Having grown up in tents and rickety shacks, housing is her primary measure of economic success. 'Today I have a house, and my mother has a house,' she says, explaining that in 2004 she was able to buy a small plot with a dwelling already built on it. As we are talking, a young Haitian immigrant covered in concrete dust from work on a building site inspects the boxer shorts she has for sale. By contrast with the latest arrivals in Santiago, Jessica looks established and comfortable: she wears a deep-mauve top studded with sequins, Jackie Onassis-style sunglasses and diamante earrings. 'We are lucky in Chile,' she says.

These stories of escape from poverty and improved living standards are what the architects of Chile's remarkable development point to as their legacy. All of this was down to a plan – a radical new blueprint designed by Chile's young crop of Chicago-trained economists.

DICTATING THE FREE MARKET

Following the military coup, Pinochet warned that he had a 'strong fist' and that any Chilean stepping out of line would receive military justice. The media was immediately censored: anything put out by newspapers, television or radio needed military approval. Then a law, 'Operation Silence', decreed that only two papers, *El Mercurio* and *La Tercera*, could be published; at least 11 left-leaning newspapers, along with magazines and radio stations, were closed. Dissent was dangerous, with Pinochet and his underlings quick to detain and torture their critics. During his 17-year dictatorship some 40,000 Chileans had suffered human rights abuses ranging from imprisonment to torture. At least 3,200 are known to have died. In Santiago's central graveyard the face of a vast grey monolith is engraved with their names: those whose bodies were found on one side, those who are still missing on the other, Salvador Allende in the middle.

When it came to the economy, Pinochet took a different tack. The dictator knew nothing about economics but rather than control and plan Chile's markets in meticulous detail as his military training might have suggested, Pinochet turned to the Chicago Boys and their free-market ideas. The men, dismayed by Chile's shift towards Marxism, had been working on policy briefings for right-wing candidates since the 1970 election and, as Allende's socialist presidency had begun to sour, they had continued to work on their own alternative blueprint. (While their work is rumoured to have received indirect CIA funding, the men involved deny knowledge of this.) By 1973 the Chicago Boys' plan ran to a 200-page tome so fat that it became known as *El Ladrillo* ('the Brick'). The men delivered *El Ladrillo* to Pinochet who decided to adopt it wholesale. At first, the men acted as advisers but in 1975 Sergio de Castro, one of the first Chileans to be trained under the ICA's exchange programme, was made economy minister. In the space of 18 months the Chicago Boys had rocketed from academic backwaters to become a dictator's economists with near-total control of the Chilean economy.

El Ladrillo diagnosed many problems in Chile including inflation, volatility and poverty, but the big discussion was of *estatismo exagerado* – the bloated state. Reducing the role of the government in the economy meant unwinding everything Allende had done, and then going further. Take the ownership of private industry: between 1970 and 1973 the number of state-controlled companies had risen from 46 to 300 as Allende's socialist government nationalized industries. By 1980 the number had fallen to 24 as the Chicago Boys pushed a privatization agenda. The financial system saw the same pattern:

nationalized Chilean banks were sold to private buyers and international lenders were allowed back in; previous rules on interest
rates were scrapped, allowing the banks to set their terms freely.
Government spending was pared back, with big cuts to budgets for
infrastructure, housing, education and social security. In the 1980s
Ricardo Ffrench-Davis, the sole Chicago-trained economist critical
of the project, called it the world's 'most outstanding case of an
extreme market economy model'.

The initial results were mixed. Shoppers' options widened: quotas
on goods like cigarettes and chickens were abolished and Chile opened
its doors to trade, cutting import taxes from 90 per cent to 10 per
cent so that products from the US, Germany and Japan suddenly
became affordable. (Imports of cameras duly jumped by 200 per cent,
radios by 870 per cent and televisions by over 9,000 per cent.) Growth
was much worse than expected though: the economy expanded by
a little under 3 per cent, better than under Allende but behind the
country's long-run average.

The first decade of Chicago School economics was capped by an
acute slump: when a financial crisis swept Latin America in 1982
it was Chile, run by these superstar economists, that fared worst.
Output fell by 14 per cent, manufacturing shrank by a quarter and
unemployment rose to 27 per cent. Despite the economic slump,
prices still rose by over 20 per cent that year with inflation-adjusted
pay taken all the way back to its value in 1973. Unable to find jobs and
housing, many Chileans who had moved to Santiago in search of
work ended up living in makeshift camps – the *campamentos* Jessica's
family lived in – on the outskirts of the capital.

The lacklustre first decade and the crash at the end of it were put
down to the teething pains of opening a country to international
trade and finance and, untroubled by democracy, the Chicago Boys
pushed on. The pension system, education, healthcare, and low-
income housing all saw decentralization, reduced government control
and privatization. Finally, Chile started to bloom, growing at an
annual average of 7 per cent between 1985 and 1997. Such a fast

expansion can stoke up inflation, but in Chile price rises were small and steady. The country's investment and export rates, previously lagging its peers, became the best in South America. Neighbouring countries such as Peru and Ecuador, which had long been comparable in economic terms, were left in Chile's wake. Argentina, a historically far richer country, had income almost double Chile's in the mid-1970s, but by 1996 Santiago had bested Buenos Aires too.

THE MIRACLE OF CHILE

The first pages of *El Ladrillo* had set out precisely this aim: 'This project includes measures that guarantee high and sustained rates of economic development in the shortest possible period.' And the nation built on the mantra of growth started to win international admirers. As early as 1982 Milton Friedman had written in *Newsweek* that 'Chile is an economic miracle' and, despite the crash that year, the stellar growth that followed meant the term stuck. By the late 1990s Chile had become the darling of international bureaucrats based in Washington, DC, and Geneva who advise countries on growth, development and trade. Conferences were held in honour of Chile's take-off, with the International Monetary Fund saying that Chile was now in the 'home stretch' of economic development, the World Trade Organization saying that liberal trade had made its economy 'one of the most resilient', and the World Bank publishing a 450-page book on the 'pioneer' country and recommending that other countries follow Chile's 'replicable lessons'.

The importance of economic growth, the Chicago Boys say, is that it pulls up incomes for the poorest, ensuring that poverty falls. This was certainly true in Chile: in 1987 official data showed that 45 per cent of Chileans lived in poverty (meaning their income was below the level needed to cover basic needs like food, clothing and shelter), while 17 per cent were recorded as indigent (meaning they could not afford food). By the year 2000 poverty had fallen to 20 per cent, with the indigence rate falling to 6 per cent. Poverty reduction was greatest in years of fast growth and lowest during more sluggish years, and these improvements in the nation's statistics have shown up as real changes in people's lives. 'Children used to run around barefoot here,' says one stallholder at the market when pressed on the benefits of economic growth. 'Now they have shoes.'

The fact that inequality was simultaneously rising was seen as a snag, but not a fundamental problem. 'Relative versus absolute incomes,' says Rolf Lüders, from leafy Las Condes, 'this is the key question.' Chile's 'miracle' years show how these measures, key to debates of inequality, can move in opposite ways as an economy grows richer. Between 1973 and the late 1980s the incomes of the poorest tenth of Chilean workers rose so that in 'absolute' terms they were better off: this explains the impressive drop in poverty. But high incomes rose much faster over the same period, with pay for the top tenth of earners shooting from seven times the average Chilean's, to almost 35 times. The pie in Chile was now bigger, but the slices of it going to everyone outside the richest tenth had fallen. In 'relative' terms, those on lower incomes had become worse off.

For the Chicago Boys the fact that poverty fell was proof that their model of economic development worked. Santiago had been a city where children in poor districts ran barefoot and many families lived in tents. It became a city where kids wore shoes and people lived in houses. Set against this, an increase in inequality seemed to them like a price worth paying. And while their view on inequality may seem harsh, the Chicago economists had another big idea they thought would help those at the bottom. Their Chicago-inspired blueprint, *El Ladrillo*, contains much discussion of how steps to guarantee *igualdad de oportunidades* (equality of opportunity) would unleash Chile's 'innate potential'.

The policy that would deliver this was a radical reform of educational policy that would make it easier to get a degree. The benefits of higher education fell primarily to graduates, the thinking went, and so should no longer be state funded. Instead, student loans should be made more generous so that young people from poorer families could fund themselves. With raw talent evenly spread across society, boosting access among the poor would harness Chile's latent human capital: it would be fair, and growth enhancing too. The university sector was seen as outdated and inefficient, with the Chicago economists recommending the central government cede control to local politicians and to the universities themselves. Pinochet duly granted these new freedoms for regional lawmakers and deregulated the sector.

The result was an education boom. In the 1970s there were eight universities in Chile, all government funded. By 1990 there were 60, two-thirds of them private, along with almost 250 professional and technical institutes. The total number of Chileans receiving higher education more than doubled, rising from around 120,000 to almost 250,000 in a decade. Higher education was no longer free, but the courses being offered were more diverse and more young people were gaining degrees. The pattern – more universities and more students – has continued and seems to suggest that the goal of *igualdad de oportunidades* as set out in the original 1973 blueprint has been met.

Today the Chicago-trained economists are octogenarians who still see their system as complete, coherent and fair. By following their market-oriented blueprint Chile has grown fast, its poverty rate has fallen and many more university places mean enhanced educational opportunities. Yet despite being lauded by institutions such as the World Bank, today in Santiago the Chicago Boys' brand of economic development is the subject of regular demonstrations. The men are puzzled by this and cannot understand why their lives' work is not valued. Mr Lüders says he does not understand the protests: 'It must come from envy,' he suggests. Reacting to protests in 2011, their mentor Arnold Harberger was flummoxed too: 'This is the best economy in South America, but the people don't appreciate it.' For these men the job of modernizing Chile is complete. They can't see what people are complaining about.

HIDDEN CITY

SANHATTAN VIEW

The architectural icon of upmarket Chile is a 64-floor tower – the *Gran Torre Santiago*. Standing at 300 metres it is the tallest structure in Latin America and dwarfs every other building in this relatively low-rise city. A key attraction at the *Gran Torre* is shopping – six floors devoted to South America's largest mall have become a magnet for the region's aspirational middle classes (the place is so popular with cash-rich Brazilian tourists that descriptions of items are listed in Portuguese as well as Spanish). As its gleaming blue-green glass catches the warm evening light, the tower glows and twinkles like the New York City skyline, earning Las Condes the nickname 'Sanhattan'. The tower's elevation means a clear line of sight to anywhere in this city: wherever you live in Santiago you can see the tower, so you can see Sanhattan.

Nuevo 14, a district 12 km to the south, is a very different kind of neighbourhood: there is no brushed concrete, steel or glass, only cheap buildings made of breeze blocks with roofs of corrugated iron. For some in this suburb housing is even more basic. A group of 40 families have settled on a patch of waste ground that had become an informal dump, used by locals to fly tip their waste. The people living here have converted the site into a tiny hamlet, constructing makeshift dwellings that nestle around a central building which serves as a community hall and kitchen-canteen, housing the single fridge and gas stove the families share.

The residents live communally and the walls of the central hall carry various important lists: one is a daily rota with names and dates setting out responsibilities for keeping watch at night (the families explain they need to guard the dump against drug dealers and addicts who try to break in). There is also a longer list – a ledger of debts – showing IOUs both in terms of Chilean pesos and informal swaps and trades of food and chores. Outside the main hall there is a single toilet and shower that the families, who have 56 children among them, share. Next to this communal bathroom there is a pile of rubbish, perhaps 8 feet high. In the far distance the *Gran Torre* glows like a shining platinum ingot.

Everything here is strung together, recycled or borrowed, and this makeshift approach to life, together with the shared communal space and the rotas setting out chores, gives the community the feel of a New Age hippie encampment. But the people of the Nuevo 14 dump are not economic outsiders seeking a new way of living off-grid: all the men and women here work, holding down full-time jobs in rich neighbourhoods such as Las Condes and Vitacura.

SANTIAGO'S NEW MIDDLE CLASS

'We live here because it is our best option to be close to work,' says 24-year-old Melissa Neira. Santiago is a sprawling commuter city and travelling to jobs in the central districts takes around 90 minutes by bus (Nuevo 14 takes its name from stop number 14 on a 'new' bus route launched many years ago). Chile does have state-subsidized housing but these homes are on the outer fringes of the city, making travelling to work impossible, says Melissa. The hall has been filling up as people return from work and the other residents nod in agreement. 'And we are too rich for state support anyway,' she says. 'We are considered middle class, not poor.' They all laugh.

Sergio Munioz is a rotund Manchester United supporter who tells me he is 43 when we meet at the dump. 'You are 44, Sergio!' chortles his wife, Bertha. His job as an electrician in a small city-centre store earns him 400,000 pesos per month (around $600, or £460). Mandatory deduction of tax, pension, health and unemployment insurance means Sergio takes home 320,000 pesos a month. Bertha works as a gardener in an upmarket suburb. When I ask her salary she looks across at the other women and they all laugh, shouting '*la mínima!*' (the minimum wage in Chile was 250,000 pesos in 2018). The pattern is common among couples here. Ernel Gomez, an aluminium and glass recycler wearing a Pink Floyd T-shirt, earns 420,000 pesos a month while his wife Marguerite is an assistant to a salon stylist and, like Bertha, earns the minimum wage. The joint income for couples here tends to be around 700,000 pesos per month.

The poverty line for a Chilean family is set at 600,000 pesos per month and since Sergio, Bertha and all the other couples here are above it they are, in official terms, not poor. Yet their incomes are a stark example of the inequality that exists in Santiago: if Chilean national income were divided equally the average family would receive 2.8 million pesos – four times higher than the dump residents earn. And despite the communal approach to buying things the families here have little to show for their full-time work. The community has no electricity or gas connection: the few bulbs and the single refrigerator in the central hall have been rigged up via a long orange cable that runs outside the perimeter of the camp to an illegal supply. The chipboard houses are tiny (most are just 2 metres by 3 metres and have no windows) and while three of the perimeter walls of the compound are secure the fourth is just a pile of rubbish. The homes Zaatari's refugees have built themselves in the Jordanian desert are better made.

THE HIGH PRICE OF LIVING ON A TIGHT BUDGET

Of the ten adults I talk to at the dump community none complains that the wages for those who live in the city's rich neighbourhoods are unfairly high. Nor, surprisingly, are they clamouring for more pay. Even though so many – including all of the women – earn the minimum wage no one believes a hike in the country's baseline pay is the answer. 'It is no good doing that,' says Melissa. 'All that will happen is that our costs – our food, our bus journeys – will go up by the same amount.' They are angrier about prices. 'In this neighbourhood we are poor, but the prices we pay are high; in the Las Condes shops the prices are lower,' says Marguerite. She is talking about staples – food, simple household products – and her complaint is that the rich live cheaply while the poor pay more. A host of economic problems in Santiago suggest she is right.

Santiago's low-wage earners live hand-to-mouth, spending everything they earn and often a little more. Lacking formal credit facilities, Sergio explains, they often take on informal debt by buying on tick at local stores and clearing their accounts at the end of the month when their wages come in. This adds, they reckon, around 20 per cent to the prices they pay. Buying on credit is common in Chile: the country's current president, Sebastián Piñera, made his name and fortune introducing credit cards here, and credit-card debt has rocketed in recent years, but this form of credit has not reached Nuevo 14. Santiago has plenty of malls with big-box stores and discount supermarkets but because the people here survive paycheque to paycheque they are unable to buy in bulk. In the local markets of the poorest areas people buy in tiny amounts: toilet tissue is sold by the roll, hawkers sell individual cigarettes. The families at the dump know the savings they could make by avoiding expensive credit and buying in bulk but earn too little to take advantage of them.

The residents of Nuevo 14 also say they buy expensive things that they probably shouldn't. 'We definitely make bad choices,' volunteers Melissa, who has two young children. She explains her weakness for a place called Kidsmania, a theme park for young children. 'I know it is expensive and a waste of money,' Melissa says, explaining that nonetheless a cash windfall, tip or bonus is more likely to be used to fund a day out than be tucked under the bed and saved. Her partner Emmanuel Neira observes that low incomes make it hard to live well: 'Just look at us – we are all kind of chubby,' he says. (Chile has seen a jump in obesity in recent years with over a quarter of adults and one in five children classified as obese. The trend has not missed Nuevo 14: the men here in particular are strikingly overweight.) 'I know that they eat quinoa in Las Condes,' Emmanuel says, with a smile. 'And I know that I should eat quinoa, but when you have just finished a twelve-hour shift you want to eat something that makes you feel full.'

The Chicago Boys' idea that education should act as an equalizing force in Santiago makes Melissa and her neighbours bristle. Along with unaffordable prices in the shops, the cost of education is the group's main complaint. Getting a place in a state-funded school means demonstrating that you are economically vulnerable and cannot afford to pay for a private one, explains Bertha. The process is time consuming – there are lots of forms and meetings – meaning a loss of earnings for whichever parent takes it on. And the price of mandatory textbooks can be crippling – a basic schoolbook in Santiago can cost 20,000 pesos, the equivalent of two days' earnings for a minimum-wage worker. (If UK textbooks were priced comparably they would cost over £100.) As a reaction to unaffordable books an informal market has sprung up, with traders offering neatly bound black-and-white photocopies that sell for 10 per cent of the price of an official copy. The pirate booksellers are pursued by the police but are defended by the cash-strapped parents. 'You see,' says Bertha, 'even free education in Chile is not so free.'

After night falls on Nuevo 14, Emmanuel and Sergio chaperone me to the main road to pick up a taxi home. 'If you want to understand Santiago you should think of it as a human heart,' says Emmanuel, with a glint in his eye. 'Dirty blood goes into the heart from below; the clean blood circulates up and out of the top.' It is a reference to the well-known correlation between income and altitude in this city. Poor commuters travel uphill into the city centre from the low-lying neighbourhoods to the south while the rich travel down from the Barrio Alto, higher land that rises to the north. Emmanuel's joke is clever, dark and delivered in perfect English, the gallows humour of a talented man consigned to unskilled work who spends his nights guarding a dump against burglars and drug addicts. When an Uber finally arrives, the driver confesses he is relieved to get a client to take him away from Nuevo 14. It is dangerous here, he says.

EDUCATIONAL APARTHEID

'We face a brutal inequality,' says Carmen Matemala, 61. We are sitting in the principal's office of Escuela Domingo Santa María González, a school in one of Santiago's poorest neighbourhoods, Renca, where Ms Matemala is the director of studies. The school's principal, Lucy Nieto, nods vigorously in agreement. They teach 650 boys aged five to eleven here, of whom 80 per cent are classed as vulnerable students, the women explain – kids who cannot get places at other schools due to poor educational performance, or who have been excluded due to bad behaviour. Theirs is the sink school in a neighbourhood where the people are poor, and this tempers educational objectives here. 'We aren't really thinking about college or university,' says Ms Nieto. 'Our job here is simply to ensure we turn out decent young men that stay out of trouble.'

Ms Matemala offers a tour of the grounds. She is a tiny woman, wears a simple navy pinafore and is steely but with a soft and somehow saintly aura. Architecturally, the school seems a decent place to learn: the classrooms are well built and form a ring around a central courtyard which hosts a vast mesh of interlocking football games at lunchtimes. 'Only the boys know who is playing in each game,' Ms Matemala says. The school's problems don't show up in decaying buildings and classrooms, she says, but in educational attainment: many of the little boys here cannot talk, let alone read. 'When they come to us all they know how to do is point at something they want.' It is another paradox of Chilean development that official poverty statistics obscure: decades of growth have ensured that Santiago's schools have decent buildings yet the city still produces cohorts of school-age children who cannot speak yet.

Inequality starts before the boys she teaches are born, Ms Matemala explains. Many come from homes where the adults are unemployed, where there are no male role models and no books or newspapers to read. In response the school has put together an emergency package for the toughest cases, involving intensive lessons and speech therapy. 'The results are truly incredible,' she beams, describing how quickly boys dealt a tough start in life can catch up. The top students go on to Santiago College, the best state-funded high school in the country. Isn't this the system working, I ask, equalizing opportunity through education? 'No,' the women say, these boys are rare cases. In Chile education is a commodity that is bought and sold, 'with one system for rich and one for poor'. Far from being an equalizing force, these experts say, the education system takes the lottery of life and hard-wires it.

The Santiago subway: stations, income and educational attainment

Monthly income per capita and SIMCE scores at stops along Line 4 of Santiago's subway

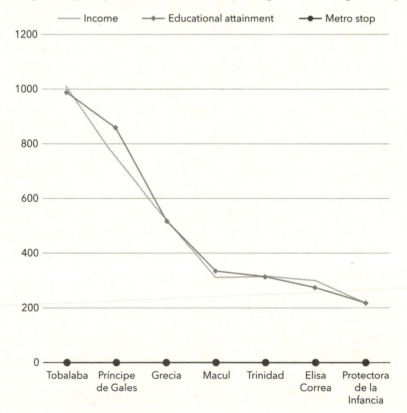

Source: Education 2020

At Educación 2020, a local think tank, I meet researchers who have come up with an astonishing analysis of this problem encapsulated in a single chart. Along a horizontal axis they plotted the stops on Line 4 of the city's metro, which starts at Tobalaba (close to Las Condes and the core of rich 'Sanhattan') and then travels downhill and south to Puente Alto, a much poorer neighbourhood. They plotted incomes at the district around each stop, which fall as the train heads south. And they plotted educational achievement, measured by local children's scores in the SIMCE test, an exam that will determine whether or not students will get into university or technical college. Test results fall with each stop on the metro line, resulting in a near-perfect correlation between income, location and attainment. The pattern is absolute: there are no rich areas where students flunk the SIMCE tests, and no poor neighbourhoods where kids ace the exams. It shows that Santiago is a city of divisions: just by knowing where someone lives you can accurately predict their educational outcome. The result is what Mario Waisbluth, the director of research at Educación 2020, calls 'educational apartheid'.

EDUCATIONAL WARFARE

'The education market in Santiago is a cake with many layers,' says Mr Waisbluth. 'There are schools for rich kids, schools for half-rich kids, schools for less rich kids, lots of layers for the middle class, and then schools for the poor.' The base layer is made of the 34 per cent of students who attend schools like Domingo Santa María González in Renca – fully funded by the state with education free of charge. Then there is a middle-class layer, which covers 60 per cent of children who attend schools that are state subsidized but also require co-payment by parents. There are hundreds of thin sublayers here with fees ranging from token payments of a few thousand pesos, to more than 240,000 pesos (around $350) a year and every price in between. The top layer is the 6 per cent that attend privately funded schools, with the icing on the cake being The Grange, a

British-style public school universally regarded as Santiago's best. A year at The Grange costs parents close to $20,000.

The amount you spend on education matters. Employers in Santiago ask potential hires to list the high school they attended on job applications, even when the applicant has completed an advanced university degree. This makes business sense, locals say: a manager hiring someone educated at The Grange is also buying their contact network. Hire an equally talented person from a less prestigious school and you get less for your money. If you want your kids to do well in Santiago, aggressive educational competition is a must. 'Let's say there are ten levels of private high school in this city,' explains one middle-class parent. 'Well, then everyone despises the people at the level below, and will do everything they can to get to the level above.' Another parent describes it as 'educational war'.

The middle layer – the co-payment schools – are the key players in this battle. Introduced in the 1980s the co-payment policy provides parents with an educational voucher, which can be 'spent' with a school of the parents' choice; these vouchers are then used by the schools to claim a monthly payment from the government, on top of which they are able to charge additional fees. The SIMCE system was introduced at the same time to provide a transparent measure of each school's performance. This was more Chicagoan thinking at work: with parents given the freedom to choose where to send their kids, and making that choice based on reliable data, schools would compete to raise standards. The market would regulate itself.

Today the vast majority of 'voucher' schools are not free, and require co-payment. And despite being state subsidized, three-quarters of these school-companies are run for profit. The publicly available SIMCE results are used as a kind of share value, telling prospective parents whether a school's stock is high or low. The idea was that teachers would redouble their efforts to improve children's grades, focusing special attention on those who are struggling. In reality Santiago's schools work hard to select the best-performing students, using entry exams and trying to weed out underperformers in order to protect the school's aggregate SIMCE score. A similar filtering happens with teachers: the best trained go to private voucher schools that offer higher salaries; the underqualified and underperforming teachers end up at the municipal sink schools.

School leaders at both extremes of Chile's education market agree this stratification is a problem. From her tiny office in Renca, principal Lucy Nieto says that teacher quality is the key challenge: when we met she was pinning her hopes on a new programme to invest in teacher training and limit the extent to which schools are allowed to select their pupils. From his plush office at The Grange, Rachid Benammar, the school's rector, says that the best way his school can help is by providing pro bono teacher training in a new academy they have set up. They are worthy ideas but the challenge is huge: despite its 'growth miracle' and new advanced-nation status, Chile's high-school kids perform at the level of much poorer Latin American countries like Colombia.

The way high schools in Santiago work cements economic stratification rather than churning it up. This is a challenge to the economic programme set out in *El Ladrillo*, which relied on education as a type of insurance. The Chicago Boys' blueprint aimed for sustained growth that would counter poverty, and open access to high-quality education that would deliver equality of opportunity. To reform education they relied on Chicagoan ideas: the importance of choice and competition, the freedom to innovate that deregulation and privatization bring, and above all on the role of the market. But as the damaging and self-defeating trades seen in Darien and Kinshasa show, markets do not guarantee good outcomes. The market for Chilean education is another example: it is bad at high-school level, and when it comes to the market for university degrees things are worse still.

GRADUATE TAX

Any student who manages to navigate the stratified high-school market enters a wild west if they go to university in Santiago. The Chicago

Boys' plan was for a private system with little state spending but lots of choice, and it has been followed to the letter: Chile commits just 0.5 per cent of GDP to higher education, the lowest in the OECD; the expansion of the university sector has continued with over 150 institutions offering degrees, two-thirds of which are for-profit outfits run by private companies. There are universities everywhere in Santiago: on main roads, up side streets, and between car showrooms. Metro stations and bus stops in the city are plastered with posters showing beaming students from one university or another, many promising improved employment prospects.

Melissa and Emmanuel, the young couple living at the encampment on the Nuevo 14 dump, both believed that university degrees would lead to well-paid jobs. Melissa completed a course in psychology but it has helped little: she works as the assistant to a childminder in Las Condes. Her husband completed three years of an information technology course, but when the couple's second child was born he dropped his studies, taking up work as a security guard. Emmanuel tells me he would like to finish the course when the kids are older; Melissa says she is looking for something better. Until then, both earn the same working-class salaries as the members of their community who have no higher education. The only difference is that they now shoulder student debts that will take years to pay off.

When market competition works effectively, rivalry between firms should drive prices down and quality up. In Chile's education system, built on free-market ideals, the ratio of the cost of the average university course to average incomes is 41 per cent, the highest in the OECD. This means students who complete their degrees must make massive debt repayments – 18 per cent of income for 15 years for the typical graduate. The profit motive ensures prices are high and costs, including pastoral care, are cut: Chile has a 50 per cent university dropout rate. In this troubling statistic the country is a world leader, with Santiago full of people like Emmanuel with half-baked degrees but fully loaded debts.

While the prices are high, the quality is not. The *Comisión*

Nacional de Acreditación is supposed to regulate things but accreditation is voluntary and around 70 per cent of courses don't have it, meaning there is no vetting or quality control. Part of the problem is a lack of experience: most students are the first generation of their family to attend university and the sector is characterized by cynical behaviour that takes advantage of the naive or credulous. As one senior ex-minister described it to me, 'The best business in Chile in recent years has been to set up a university, collect the fees and then simply strip the place of assets.' Some of the scandals have been tragicomic. At one university, eventually shut down for money laundering, the owners brazenly pocketed student fees, offering scant tuition in return. At another the students completed lengthy degrees in dentistry, architecture and law only to find that they were not actually qualified to work. Education – more, cheaper, better – was central to the Chicago Boys' plan. With hope and promises leading to disappointment and debt, education has become the totemic issue in Santiago. In this trendsetter city, I found that inequality of income and opportunity had already revolutionized politics, and may well give birth to an entirely new brand of economics.

THE NEW SCHOOL

FROM PENGUINS TO PRESIDENTS

The fightback started with a strike staged by almost 800,000 high-school children in 2006 that became known as the Penguins' Revolution (the white shirts and black blazers Chilean children wear mean 'penguin' is a friendly nickname for a schoolkid). By 2011 the student movement had grown: large demonstrations involved 600,000 marching in Santiago, carrying posters decrying the Chicago Boys and their market-orientated policies. The 2011 protests (known as the 'Chilean Winter') catapulted the students' leaders – Camila Vallejo at the University of Chile and Giorgio Jackson at the

Catholic University – into the public eye and in 2013 both were elected as national politicians. Ms Vallejo joined the Communist Party, which supports Chile's centre-left coalition. Mr Jackson was more radical. He remained independent, founding a new party – *Revolución Democrática* – and coaxing other small parties to create a new coalition, *Frente Amplio*. In 2017, the first general election it fought, *Frente Amplio* won 20 per cent of the vote. Mr Jackson received 60 per cent of the votes in his constituency, making him one of the best supported of the country's 120 senators.

Giorgio Jackson's constituency office offers an excellent perspective on inequality in Santiago. On the top floor of an eight-storey block it has a large balcony that faces Santa Lucia park, a public garden full of ancient trees and colonial statues. To the right a wide avenue slopes up through wealthy Providencia and Vitacura with the gleaming *Gran Torre* shining in the sun. To the left the road slopes down towards Plaza Italia, known by everyone in the city as an unofficial borderline between rich and poor, a spot from which buses start the long trek to neighbourhoods such as Renca. The senator arrives on a fixed-wheel bicycle, has a straggly beard and carries a small rucksack full of books – something of a trademark – on his back; now in his early thirties, he is losing his hair and covers his scalp with a black baseball cap. Mr Jackson could easily be mistaken for a graduate student. He is seen by many in Santiago as the most important politician in a generation and a future Chilean president.

Born to an upper-middle-class family Mr Jackson attended a private school in wealthy Providencia. A talented athlete, he represented Chile in volleyball as a teenager and went on to study computing and engineering at university, funded in part by a sports scholarship. He did not intend to go into politics, he says, but was drawn to it by the education demonstrations and a sense of the growing injustice of the economy in Santiago. Feelings of guilt and anger started to build inside him, he confides, so he decided to do something. While many of the politicians propelled to power by the student movement want to swing Chile back towards Allende-inspired socialism, Mr Jackson is offering something new, and it is catching on.

Mr Jackson has the presence of a politician – he stands tall and somehow fills the room – but is mathematical and nerdy too. The old spectrum of left-wing and right-wing ideas has failed, he says, and a new politics is needed that must be 'n-dimensional not two-dimensional'. Free from party line and intellectual baggage he is refreshingly honest and admits that *Revolución Democrática* is developing its policies on the fly. There is not yet a new version of the Chicago Boys' *El Ladrillo*, but his team are working on a suite of new policies that could form one. Keen to know what Chile's future economic playbook might contain, I asked the senator what he likes to read.

The thinkers he cites as influences are an eclectic bunch, ranging from classical philosophers to modern political theorists. He is particularly impressed by the recent work of Byung-Chul Han, an academic born in Korea and based in Berlin. Mr Han is a modern-day pamphleteer, producing scores of thin books that have made him a star of German philosophy; he is a critic of Milton Friedman, and by association the Chicago Boys and the Chilean economic model. Under modern capitalism, Mr Han argues, people are told they are free to choose the goods they buy and the careers they pursue. In fact, we are 'slaves' to consumerism, enticed by markets that exist to create false wants. Fashion exists, for example, to make people feel they have a deep need – in a Maslow sense – for the latest cut of jeans or pattern of dress. The economics of data are the same, in Mr Han's view. Our data is in mass supply and freely supplied by us. But we are slaves here too, chasing tokens of approval – likes on Facebook and Instagram – that we mistakenly feel are valuable.

The big idea Mr Jackson takes from all this is the notion of 'false scarcity' – markets where prices are so high they exclude many people when it should be possible to provide the underlying resource to everyone. This comes about, he says, because of 'facilitated monopolies' that control supply of goods. He is particularly critical of the patent system, intellectual property rules, and anything else that shields markets from competition. Once you understand how vital industries work in Santiago's free-market economy – from banks to booksellers, from pensions to pharmaceuticals – you can see what he is getting at, and why his ideas strike a chord with the public.

MARKET FAILURE, SANTIAGO-STYLE

In the neighbourhood of Lo Espejo the market happens every Sunday. It is vast – one stallholder claims it is the largest in Latin America – and has no real centre, sprawling through the backstreets of this dusty and poor suburb and out to the railway tracks that fringe it. There are fashion stalls selling clothes including counterfeit Premier League football shirts and a vast selection of electronics: phones, chargers, together with CDs and DVDs of pirated albums, films and software. There are hundreds of stalls selling food: green-grocers' tables are weighed down by massive green *zapallos*, a pumpkin-like vegetable that is hacked open to reveal bright golden flesh used to make *sopillas* – a savoury pastry. People eat while they shop: there is grilled chicken, freshly made ceviche salads and the ubiquitous *italiano*, a foot-long hot dog taking its name from the green, white and red of the avocado, mayonnaise and tomato dolloped on top.

The stalls at Lo Espejo show how a well-functioning market is supposed to work. Take fish. A fishmonger, Carlos, de-heads, guts and fillets white fish in seconds with a few quick flashes of his sharp knife, piling up the flesh of *jurel* (jack mackerel) and *merluza* (hake) that sells for 2,000 pesos a kilo. Carlos says that if he could get hold of prized fish – *congrio* (similar to monkfish), *corvina* (a type of bass) or perhaps *centolla* (king crab) – he could sell his goods in a more affluent district and make more money, but since these species are bought up by big fishing companies he gets what he can and comes here. As we talk he is constantly filleting while an assistant makes the sales.

Another stallholder is offering massive boulders of chocolate, which is being chopped up into rocks the size of cricket balls and sold wrapped in clear plastic. The brand – 'Nestle' – is scrawled on a piece of cardboard next to it: this is waste chocolate from a local factory, sediment that is scraped out when the chocolatiers clean their machines. In affluent Las Condes it would be discarded but here in Lo Espejo it has value. This market is playing its proper role, matching low-priced, no-frills products with shoppers' tight budgets, meaning buyers and sellers make a trade that works for both sides. Goods are graded, sorted, and sold; the market stalls are left clear. This, the way markets line up shoppers and stallholders to ensure nothing goes to waste, is why economists like them.

New entrants find it easy to start up in Lo Espejo's vast market. Hernan, 58, explains how he lost his job at the local bicycle factory when the manufacturer shifted production abroad. Using a small lump-sum redundancy payment as working capital, he set up a stall that specializes in just two products – toilet roll and detergent – outside his home. Hernan explains how he stocks a range of qualities and prices for his customers, from the cheapest 'Noble' (1,100 pesos for five toilet rolls), through 'Confort' and 'Favorita' up to the expensive 'Elite' at 1,700 pesos. Hernan points out that each of his prices offers a significant saving on the local supermarket (where Elite would cost 2,400 pesos, for example). Prices are a problem, he says, 'but customers know they can trust me'.

Trust is important in Santiago since the markets for many simple goods are biased against the average Chilean. This includes toilet roll: in 2015 it was discovered that two manufacturers controlling 90 per cent of sales had secretly been colluding to raise their prices; they had extracted $460 million over a decade. The case forms part of a pattern, with another investigation finding that cartels had inflated the price of bus tickets – doing serious damage in this city of commuters. Yet another had found that three firms controlling 90 per cent of the market for chicken had colluded, abandoning their rivalry and raising prices instead.

COSY CAPITALISM

Expensive chicken, costly bus tickets and overpriced toilet paper make life harder for Chilean families with low incomes, and there are also problems in markets that play a deeper role in the fabric of a country. The same two companies control 85 per cent of the market for newspapers, 85 per cent of online news and 80 per cent of advertising revenues. Healthcare is concentrated too: a small number of health insurance providers control the markets. Just three pharmacy chains handle 90 per cent of drug purchases – all three of them involved in recent collusion cases.

'The market does not care,' says Daniel Jadue, 'the supply of prescription drugs shows this.' Mr Jadue, 46, is the mayor of Recoleta, a poor district to the east of the city, and is a representative of the Chilean Communist Party. The problem, he explains, is that the residents in his district are just not worth supplying with medicines because their incomes are too low, so the pharmacies don't bother. Las Condes, he maintains, has a ratio of one pharmacy per 20,000 people, while in Recoleta there is just one between 140,000, and across Chile millions live in places where there are no pharmacies at all. This means, as Melissa Neira of the Nuevo 14 community had pointed out, that poor people pay more. The cost of medicines is higher in Recoleta as locals must travel by bus to get them; this makes things particularly hard for the elderly and those with chronic conditions.

In response Mayor Jadue has taken matters into his own hands, opening a *Farmacia Popular* or 'people's pharmacy'. Located on the ground floor of the town hall, and named after Ricardo Silva Soto, a pharmacist murdered by Pinochet's secret police, it sells prescription antibiotics, antihistamines and a wide range of products for the elderly, from eye drops to incontinence pads. To escape the grip of the collusive Chilean market the outlet imports drugs from abroad and can pass on savings of up to 70 per cent compared with the price in Santiago's private pharmacies.

Eyeglasses are another problem – there are no opticians at all in Recoleta – so the *Óptica Popular* has been set up to fill the gap in the market. They sell glasses for 6,200 pesos (around $9, or £7) and prescription sunglasses for 8,800. This saves locals a costly journey, says the manager proudly, and their imported goods offer savings of 90 per cent on the prices charged by private opticians outside Recoleta. The fact that a communist mayor is forced to import basic goods suggests that those that lauded Chile and sought the 'replicable lessons' from its model of capitalism might have missed something.

THE OIL AND WATER CITY

PUBLIC PARKS, PRIVATE SPACES

The encouraging thing about visiting Akita and Tallinn, the frontier economies at the global extremes of ageing and technology, were the signs that these international trends, which can be so worrying, were also bringing people together. As well as tough times there was plenty of evidence of trade, cooperation and understanding between the young and old, and between groups divided by history, heritage and language. Those collaborative approaches used human and social capital, both using and refreshing norms of trust, favours and shared effort. While I saw plenty of informal cooperation in Chile – the *campamento* on the dump, the informal market for school textbooks – I left Santiago thinking there were more reasons to worry.

Start at the top. In private, members of the Santiago elite worry about the state of their city: look harder, they say, and there are cracks that affect both rich and poor. Many are concerned about the lack of diversification of the formal economy: having experienced striking development, Chile is now seen as resting on its laurels. The country is still as dependent on mining as it was in Salvador Allende's time, with copper providing 30 per cent of government revenues a year. Plans set out in the Chicago Boys' blueprint, *El Ladrillo*, to diversify away from basic activities such as mining and build up more advanced industries, have come to little, making the country vulnerable to swings in global commodity prices.

A proud local will explain this away with two stories: their country is small, and in practical terms it is an island. (Chileans see themselves as hemmed in by the Atacama Desert and Antarctica to the north and south, and the Andes and Pacific to the east and west.) Chile's size and hard-to-reach location make diversification hard, the story goes. Immigrants and more critical locals say these excuses are nonsense: Chile is easily in the world's top third of countries by population and has been trading successfully by sea since the early 1800s. The real reason for the reliance on copper and the failure to diversify is related to inequality. There is no reason to rock the boat here: for those managing established businesses, many of them in cosily concentrated industries, life is a little too good.

Parents among the elite – the people who send their children to The Grange – chatter too, privately, about the effect that extreme comfort can have on their kids, often raising a new upper-class archetype known as the 'Zorrone' as a concern. Essentially a US frat-boy with a twist of grunge, the Zorrone wears chinos and cashmere sweaters but has tattoos and greasy hair too. They have no aspiration to attend old elite universities and instead attend new private ones with middling academic performance and ultra-high fees. A Zorrone need not compete with his cleverer countrymen because jobs in companies their parents own or manage have already been lined up. 'The Chilean elite does not expose its kids to the tests that those in the US and Europe do,' says one worried father.

Inequality in Santiago also affects how public space is used. 'The social layers here do not mix at all,' explains one foreigner, recalling a failed attempt to organize a summer picnic as an office outing. The problem was an unwritten division that delineates places and activities as '*cuico*' or not. (*Cuico* loosely means higher class and can be used negatively by the working class or endearingly by the wealthy.) 'People could not meet outside work, because there are *cuico* parks, and non-*cuico* parks, and people from one class will not visit the other.' In formal terms, Santiago's parks are public spaces funded through general taxation and accessible to anyone; in practical terms inequality has turned them into private places with access based on income.

With resilience in mind this is concerning. Recent studies have shown that 'social infrastructure' – places like libraries and parks – are a kind of insurance policy against bad times. This chimes with what I saw in Glasgow: when people mix and know their neighbours' challenges and talents, they are better at dealing with a shock or setback. But in Santiago the public sphere has been closed off. The city's crime rate is low yet there is a huge investment in security in poor and rich neighbourhoods alike, with many homes encased in iron bars. The back roads running through neighbourhoods are sealed off, turning public thoroughfares into private spaces and making it hard to walk or cycle through the city. A huge helium balloon carrying CCTV cameras floats over Vitacura day and night, helping soothe the fears of its wealthy residents. Only one in five Chileans says they trust their countrymen, far lower than the developed-world norm.

While envy over pay seemed to be absent at the bottom of the Santiago income ladder, there is certainly some bad blood. 'The maids in Las Condes are expected to wear their uniforms outside, when they go to the shops on their lunchbreak or on the way home from work,' explains Melissa Neira of Nuevo 14. 'It is a way of showing that they are different – that they do not belong there.' It is not a rule or a law but a cultural norm, a way of maintaining the divisions of class and status. If social capital and social infrastructure matter for resilience, then Chile's economy is weaker than people think.

RESULTS NOT INTENTIONS

For many young people in Chile, men like Rolf Lüders and his fellow Chicago Boys are symbols of greedy capitalism and callous self-interest. Yet it is impossible to read *El Ladrillo* without concluding that its authors had the country's best interests at heart – the text brims with ideas and ambition. The young men could see the potential of their nation; they were tired of seeing Chile falling behind its neighbours. Their economic plan was based on what they had been taught by Friedman and Harberger in Chicago, and what they promised was a rising tide of poverty-eradicating growth.

But one of Friedman's most famous dicta was that when it comes to economic policy it is not intentions that should be judged, but results. Seen narrowly, the results in Chile mean it is still possible to view the country as a victory for the Chicago-inspired model of economic development. The nation remains the crown jewel of Latin America, and a favourite case study for supporters of reform through privatization. Indigence – the most acute form of poverty that means people cannot meet the basic need for food – has been almost eliminated. In the poorest parts of Santiago it is easy to find people who grew up cold, hungry and living in precarious *campamento* temporary housing. Decades of sustained growth drove down the poverty rate year after year, making basic needs easier to meet and vastly improving life in these neighbourhoods.

Chile's path – fast growth coupled with extreme inequality – is one that many emerging countries and their ever-expanding cities are following. For its followers on the same road Santiago offers a warning. Just as free markets do not always create value, strong growth does not always deliver the development that it seems to promise. In particular, Santiago has become a city where Maslow's pyramid has been stretched: while many basic needs are easier to meet, the higher needs – education, agency – have moved further out of reach. Chile has the highest per capita GDP on its continent. But within its developed-world OECD group, it has the fastest-rising obesity rates, the worst school results, the highest university costs and the worst dropout rates. My time in Santiago shows that all of this is linked to inequality.

These practical failures mean that Santiago has once again become a fascinating place, the site of a new battle for ideas. The Chicago Boys

took the helm after a period of tight economic control, in which artificial markets were tethered to socialist agendas; they wanted to show
that free markets were the best way to run an economy and the
'miracle' they delivered seemed to win the case. But on the ground
in modern Santiago it is clear that markets have delivered perverse
forms of competition, with the rampant yet corrosive rivalry in education being the most important example. Here, the market makes
delivering equality of opportunity impossible, entrenches inequality,
and has created neighbourhoods with such low incomes that shoppers do not matter, and basic goods must be provided by the state.
Pushed through this extreme system the young people of Santiago,
economic trendsetters whose path so many around the world will follow, are asking whether markets can be relied upon at all.

Conclusion

A rough guide to the future

I profess both to learn and to teach anatomy, not from books
but from dissections; not from positions of philosophers
but from the fabric of nature.

William Harvey,
De Motu Cordis, 1628

Economics is a study of mankind in the ordinary business of life . . . it is
on the one side a study of wealth; and on the other, and more
important side, a part of the study of man.

Alfred Marshall,
Principles of Economics, 1890

DESTINATION 2030

When you travel to a far-off, unknown and intimidating place, a good local guide is invaluable. You need someone who has been there already, can explain the terrain and the difficulties it will throw up, and advise you on how to prepare. My motivation with this book was to look for people alive today who are experiencing stresses and strains that might be relevant in a place we are all heading: the future. Rather than go to the typical countries and cities studied by economists, it meant getting off the beaten track to apply an idea – studying extremes – first championed 400 years ago, by William Harvey. The analysis of extreme cases has been widely used across the medical sciences and, following related ideas developed by David Kirkaldy, plays a foundational role in modern engineering and physics too. What do the world's most extreme economies say about the stresses and strains of 2030, and how we should prepare for them?

Start with the fact that we know a lot about where we are heading. Urbanization is an example. In 1950 more than 70 per cent of the world's population lived in rural areas. Economic challenges, for most people, were rural ones. Decades of migration then saw towns and cities swell and villages shrink, with 2007 the landmark year in which the world's urbanites first outnumbered its countryfolk. This trend is set to continue: between 2020 and 2030 the urban population is forecast to rise by almost 790 million – this is more than twice the US population and will result in 43 'megacities' of over 10 million people. By 2050 the pattern of a century earlier will have been reversed: 70 per cent of people will live in urban areas. The implication is that the economic forces of city life, resting on the three 'agglomeration' forces described by Alfred Marshall and seen in Glasgow, will come to the fore. Sustained trends point to where we are going and the type of economics that will be important there.

The most important trends of the next decade will be the three forces described in the third part of this book. They are global, they are currently causing great concern, and they are likely to intensify. By 2030 four countries – Japan, Italy, Spain and Portugal – will look like Akita does today, with more citizens over the age of 50 than under it. Technology – robots and automated software – will influence more workplaces, and digitization will diffuse through the state sector as governments seek savings by emulating steps taken in Tallinn. Santiago-style urban inequality will become more common as the top tenth of earners' share of income creeps towards 50 per cent in the world's biggest emerging economies. The year 2030, for most people on earth, will be a cocktail of these three cities: an urban society that is old, technologically advanced and economically unequal.

THE TREACHEROUS MIDDLE WAY

As well as helping to clarify the destination, extremes point to pitfalls along the way. Pressurized and damaged places pare economics back to a simple and raw form, often revealing modern examples of the central question in political economy – the role of free markets. As 2020 approaches, views on how to manage markets have become polarized. Parties of the left plan to give the state a greater role, controlling companies and engineering outcomes. Those on the right want to give entrepreneurs freer rein, betting that the hunger for profit will solve our challenges while relying on competition to provide discipline. Life in some of the world's toughest places shows why both poles should be avoided.

To remain resilient, as the first part of the book shows, a society often creates its own informal markets. Despite all the odds, trade and exchange sprang up quickly in tsunami-ravaged Aceh, in the Zaatari refugee camp and even in Louisiana's highest-security penitentiaries. The process was organic – these markets thrived without the assistance of the state, and often in the face of its considerable hindrance. Self-built financial systems also flower. America's underground prison economies use a host of parallel currencies, including mackerel, coffee and the newest digital 'dot' currency; the traditional gold culture of Aceh provides savings and insurance; in Zaatari, traders had turned powdered milk into a tradeable asset as a way to suck hard cash into the refugee camp. People are able to create markets, and have the ability to establish complex ways to transfer value – building the payment system their economy runs on – that is innate. Engineered economies stamp this out and waste these skills.

By holding back self-built trade, systems of tight control block more than just the exchange of goods. When you live on an economic knife-edge, you tend to see the value of being able to trade freely quite clearly. Throughout my travels, people discussed the economy as a place to get hold of goods and to make money, but also as an important source of identity. Producing things, and buying and selling them, generates responsibilities – to maintain quality, fulfil contracts and deliver on time. When done well this leads to a sound reputation and the respect that follows. Markets are places where goods are allocated between buyers and sellers, but they are also sites that support individuality and self-expression. The places where state control was so strong that free trade had no chance of sprouting were the bleakest and most forlorn that I visited.

The problem is that Daniel Jadue, the communist mayor of one of Santiago's poorest suburbs, is right: the market really does not care. Just as good markets create value, bad ones destroy it. Often, as seen in the Darien rainforest, the problem is an economic 'externality' arising because some actor – in this case loggers – ignores the costs imposed on others when making decisions. Darien is an unregulated place where the natural urge and ability to trade erodes the long-term prospects of those living there. The externality problem, which is common, means that a free market will produce too much of things that are bad, and too little of things that are good. Once you have seen the destruction this causes first hand, the idea that unsupervised markets can be relied on to deal with public policy problems appears naive, almost dangerous.

Nor do markets reliably spring up where they are most needed or bounce back when they are down. If ever there were two groups that could gain from trade they are the impoverished but knowledgeable guerrillas of the Darien jungle and the cash-laden and terrified migrants lost on a deadly trek through it. Yet no market for safe passage exists. The people of Kinshasa, failed by colonial and political leaders, have ended up stuck in a catch-22 of low-level corruption that holds up every daily transaction. The magnifying forces of agglomeration that made Glasgow rocket on its upswing also smashed the city on its downturn. As we saw, the core of these failures – the damage of externalities, the self-defeating implications of rational choice, the fragility of networks – was economic. These failed places had failed markets at their foundations.

The cities that are flourishing by 2030 will have found a middle way – a model that uses the natural human ability to create markets while mitigating the costly downsides of unbridled free trade. The extreme failures I encountered show why this will not be simple. Many of the breakdowns of resilience I encountered were the result of well-meaning policies: the model Acehnese village, high on a hill; the Darien teak subsidies; the plan to 'group' Glasgow's shipyards into more muscular competitors; even Mobutu Sese Seko's plans to turn Kinshasa into a hydro-powered industrial hub – all of this made sense on paper. Each of these ideas involved the state trying to tame or influence the market in some way, and each of them went terribly wrong. The future, and the middle path to it, is a rocky road. This puts a premium on a deeper understanding of economic resilience – not just the ebb and flow of GDP, but our ability to withstand catastrophic downturns.

INFORMALITY: THE ORDINARY BUSINESS OF LIFE

To understand resilience, we need to make parts of economic life that are currently hidden from view a central part of our statistics, debate and policies. The role of the informal economy, which is bigger, more sophisticated and more innovative than policymakers understand, is a huge gap. Wherever I went in the world, by spending time talking to people about how their economy really worked, I discovered a hidden system running in parallel to the one tracked by statistical agencies and covered by journalists. The city of Kinshasa is an example of how official data paints an incomplete picture. Home to millions of people, it is devastatingly poor, as official statistics suggest. It is also a buzzing place of informal trade and innovation – a giant village economy – something the data, which is the only picture most outsiders see, does not show. Refugee camps are another example: measured in terms of the official companies in the camps, Zaatari and Azraq are identical twins; seen on the ground, they are worlds apart.

Tracking informality through softer information gleaned on site would improve our picture of an economy and shed some light on how resilience works. Kinshasa is again a standout example: as the Catholic priest told me, it is only through informality – street hawking and the 'break-up' business – that the people survive there. In Aceh, the traditional system of wealth worn as gold bangles turned out to be a latent insurance mechanism. And the tough lives of Glasgow's shipbuilding families were soothed by informal safety nets – from the face-saving norms of pawning goods, to the 'ménage' saving pools – that were finely tuned to the difficulties of life in that city. At present, informality plays no role in mainstream economics. If we care about resilience, this will need to change.

A NEW STUDY OF WEALTH

We also need to take a fresh look at how we measure wealth. Economics focuses on a place's 'capital' – things that store value over time and can be used in the annual flow of output and income a village, city or country produces. The attention is on financial capital – assets such as cash, equities and bonds – and physical capital such as buildings, factories and machines. Both are vital, and the tragedy of economies like Kinshasa's and Darien's is in part down to their shortfall. Yet these forms of wealth are just part of the picture. Focusing on them to the exclusion of all else means our approach is narrow and simplistic, missing hidden assets that lie behind thriving and resilient economies.

Aceh, Zaatari and Louisiana are all very different places. But in each of them financial and physical capital was in scant supply, and people showed, in different ways, the importance of ideas, skills and knowledge. This, a country's 'human capital', has come to be recognized as an important source of economic growth over the past 30 years. Extreme economies add another angle: human capital does more than help an economy expand, it is also a way to insure against catastrophic decline. Human capital, like informality, is a pool of resilience. John Stuart Mill knew this in the mid-1800s; the people of Aceh showed it as they rebuilt following the 2004 tsunami. Yet most countries make no serious attempt to measure human capital, and the few that do (including the UK) treat it as a side project.

Yet the biggest gap in economics is the way it completely ignores social capital. In part, this is because the concept is controversial. Critics on the left say that an economic system relying on social capital would give right-wing politicians headroom to slash public services. Those on the right think it is best left to arise spontaneously, and not the sort of thing governments should interfere with or spend money on. Others regard the concept as too imprecise to be useful in any practical way. Hard to measure and easy to annoy, it is readily ignored.

But in places of extreme stress and change, the role social capital plays is crystal clear. It is a glue that binds a society's other assets together, squeezing more out of them. In places characterized by trust and reciprocal favours – places where social capital was high – I witnessed and heard about physical and financial capital being put to better use. From the sharing of motorbikes in Aceh to the way scales in Glaswegian tenement shops were used to weigh local babies, they were examples of a tool, machine or piece of infrastructure being used more intensively and effectively because a positive culture underpinned the society. As Robert Putnam's travels through

Italy showed, social capital also often stands behind informal financial arrangements. The remarkable resilience I saw on my journeys confirmed this. Local traditions and norms underpin the informal systems of payment, insurance, credit and saving that spring up in the most testing times. Social capital is pretty simple: it boosts productivity and makes an economy more resilient.

These missing pieces of economics – informality in our income, human and social capital in our wealth – can be shadowy and hard to measure. But by failing to take them into account we are missing huge chunks of the economy. Our economic picture is incomplete, inhibiting our ability to assess the trends set to shape the economy of the near future.

THE PATH AHEAD

Almost 400 years ago William Harvey argued that nature could best be understood in places 'apart from the beaten paths'. Harvey's advice was aimed at anatomists, but in the context of the modern economy it has never been more relevant. Over the coming decades, millions of people will take a path to an economy none of us has trodden before – to a world full of old people, of advanced software and machines, and of vast new megacities that are the most unequal places on earth. Today Akita, Tallinn and Santiago are odd and extreme places, marginal cities never part of the main script of economic discussions. Tomorrow, life in them will be the norm.

To navigate all this, we need a fresh economics. People like to trade and are good at it, but the markets we create can destroy value – the only way forward is a new middle way. Failure is possible, even where potential is highest, so we need greater focus on resilience. An economics of resilience recognizes that for many people and many countries, income starts with informal trade. It accepts that a society's wealth is built on human and social capital, with financial and physical capital sitting on top. Today these subtler and more human aspects of income and wealth play little part in economic measurement or planning. My travels suggest that if they did, we might see things we are missing: the powerful fightback against old age, the real locus of the pain from technological advances, and the hidden faultiness – the erosion of resilience – that inequality is creating in the world's most promising economies.

ACKNOWLEDGEMENTS

The first people to thank are all those who appear in the pages of this book. I travelled over 100,000 miles and spoke to more than 500 people during the research, and wherever I went people were happy to talk. From the freezing hamlets of Akita in midwinter to the sweltering backstreets of Kinshasa in summer, people took me in, showing me their homes and offices, churches and mosques, and offering food, drink and their stories.

The project would not have started or finished without the support of Caroline Michel and her team at Peters Fraser + Dunlop; Tim Binding gave me valuable advice and Alexandra Cliff offered encouragement and countless letters in support of visas. The book has benefited hugely from the expert editorial guidance of Henry Vines at Penguin Random House and Colin Dickerman at Farrar, Straus and Giroux. I am indebted to Doug Young, who first backed the idea, and to Stephen Morrison, who waded through a rough manuscript written on the road and offered valuable comments. Rahat Siddique was a tireless research assistant, finding countless papers, books, and out-of-print articles as well as helping set up interviews while I was travelling. Amy Sebire's wise counsel ensured that I got in and out of some of the trickiest places on the planet unscathed.

A group of local guides travelled with me, translated and ensured I got to the people with the most important stories to tell. In Aceh, Juik Furqan was a translator, mountain guide and nightly dinner companion. Jinan Naskabandi introduced me to Syrian families in

Zaatari and Azraq; Mohammed Shabana showed me his home and took me to see his friends and his mosque in the Zaatari camp. In Louisiana, Wilbert and Linda Rideau provided me with contacts and out-of-print copies of Wilbert's earliest articles; Kelly Orians introduced me to people with first-hand experience of the prison system. In Darien, Juan Velasquez explained his economic fears and let me sleep in one of his hammocks; Delifino Davies – no relation – of the Kuna tribe offered me help, advice and pickled fish when I was lost and alone. In Kinshasa, Sylvain Muyali was a skilled guide and translator, and Jean-Marie Kalonji introduced me to a host of young people across the city. In Glasgow, Abigail Morris of Fairfield Heritage provided useful contacts with local shipbuilders. In Akita, Milly Nakai provided translation and Mr Morimoto drove me through the snow to some of the abandoned rural villages he had discovered. Camila Cea and Francisco Ramírez were skilled translators in Santiago, able to reach all parts of that stratified city.

I am grateful to a group of colleagues who encouraged me to think about people's stories when covering economics. Zanny Minton Beddoes and Andrew Palmer first persuaded me to try my hand at journalism and taught me how to do it. My onetime roommate Anne McElvoy has always nagged me to explain economics in simple terms. Emma Duncan supported an early trip to Zaatari through her commissioning. Noreena Hertz urged me to write the book when I told her the idea. Soumaya Keynes offered her thoughts and contacts as I sat down to write the proposal. Edmund Conway and Will Page have been long-time sounding boards and sources of nuggets of data, ideas and reading.

I relied on my family from start to finish. Josephine Davies sowed the seed of an idea by telling me about the hidden prison economies she had encountered. Ian Booth provided articles and papers on William Harvey. Alexandra Davies gave me her sense of urgency. Peter Davies gave me many books that came in useful writing this one. My biggest thanks go to Frances Booth for giving me the confidence to go for it, and to Isabel Shapiro for being a reader, editor, travel companion, motorbike chauffeur and daily support without whom I would never have finished.

Finally, I owe a debt of gratitude to my early instructors and mentors: Oliver Board, John Tasioulas, Peter Sinclair, Paul Klemperer and Peter Davis. I am also grateful for the more recent support of Margaret Stevens, John Asker, and the late David Backus. The book is written with thanks to two university teachers – a medic and an economist – to whom I am eternally grateful.

NOTES AND REFERENCES

CHAPTER 1: ACEH

NOTES

The disaster

Banda Aceh was struck by what geologists call a 'near-field' tsunami. Scientists visiting the area combined eyewitness accounts with data collected on the ground (including damage to buildings and the location of debris) to work out how big the waves were. The north-west coast – places like Lhokgna and Lampuuk – was hit by waves more than 30 m high: Gibbons and Gelfenbaum (2005).

The changes in the earth's tilt and shape were picked up quickly by NASA scientists Dr Richard Gross and Dr Benjamin Fong Chao – see NASA (2005).

The number of fatalities has had to be estimated since so many people were missing presumed dead. Official figures and demographic models put the number between 128,000 and 168,000 in Aceh Province. The mortality rates were highest in Banda Aceh and Aceh Besar districts (around 23 per cent) – see Doocy et al. (2007*a* and 2007*b*).

History

The history of Indonesia is set out in Ricklefs (2001). A more detailed Acehnese history covering the sultanate, the wars with the Dutch and the independence of Indonesia and Acehnese exceptionalism (or isolation) is given in the collection of papers in Graf et al. (eds.) (2010). The importance of pepper, and the rise of Aceh to provide half of the world's supply, is described in Reid (2015).

On disasters and growth

One of the first modern studies of the economic implications of natural disasters was Albala-Bertrand (1993), who studied disasters in 26 countries between 1960 and 1979. A subsequent literature has examined whether a disaster might be 'good' for growth – a review is given in Cavallo and Noy (2009).

Researchers examining the impact of disasters use data from the publicly available Emergency Events Database (EM-DAT) compiled by the Centre for Research on the Epidemiology of Disasters (CRED) at www.emdat.be.

Petty, Stone and GDP

William Petty's works are set out in his 1662 book on taxation and in his 1676 *Political Arithmetick*; his contribution to the development of systems of national accounts is traced in Kendrick (1970) and more recently in Davies (ed.) (2015).

While other economists – notably Simon Kuznets in the US – helped develop modern GDP measures, Richard Stone was arguably the most important, winning the Nobel Prize for his work in 1984. His contribution is discussed in Johansen (1985) and much more detail on all the various contributors is set out in Studenski (1958), while an accessible modern history is Coyle (2014).

Economic impact of the tsunami

Estimates of damage in Aceh are set out in World Bank (2006), which also contains data on the localized inflation impact of aid-agency spending. In BRR (2009), the Indonesian agency that oversaw the relief work published its findings, setting out the scope of the damage and the rebuilding that took place between 2005 and 2009.

My GDP calculations were made using non-oil GDP at real terms, with the data taken from the official government agency, Statistics Indonesia.

The civil war, GAM and the peace process

The history of the war in Aceh is described by Graf et al. (eds.) (2010). Peace talks had failed in 2000 and 2002, and following this, the Indonesian government was seemingly committed to wiping out GAM completely. The new player in 2005 was the Crisis Management Initiative (CMI) run by former Finnish president Martti Ahtisaari. The 2005 MOU was signed by Indonesian minister Hamid Awaludin and GAM's leader Malik Mahmud, and witnessed by Mr Ahtisaari, who later won the Nobel Peace Prize. The peace process and the role that the CMI played in it is discussed in Daly et al. (eds.) (2012).

Sharia Law in modern Aceh

In 2016 over 300 people received public whippings. The majority (90 per cent) were men, mainly those accused of gambling. But those punished also included women accused of gambling and drinking alcohol, and couples accused of sex before wedlock – see Institute for Criminal Justice Reform (2017).

Petty and Mill on human capital

The modern term 'human capital' became popular only in the second half of the twentieth century, but it is clear that this is what Petty (1662) and Mill (1848) were talking about. Petty wrote that a state that kills or imprisons its subjects only harms itself, since these subjects – through their labour – are a source of wealth. Mill wrote about 'the great rapidity with which countries recover from a state of devastation' and explained that it is because humans constantly use, damage and rebuild physical capital (such as machines and factories) that the physical means of production can be rebuilt far more quickly that we might imagine, so long as human capital and the human population remain relatively intact.

REFERENCES

Albala-Bertrand, J. M. (1993), *Political Economy of Large Natural Disasters* (Oxford: Clarendon Press).

BRR (2009), '10 Management Lessons for Host Governments Coordinating Post-disaster Reconstruction' (Indonesia: Executing Agency for Rehabilitation and Reconstruction (BRR) of Aceh–Nias 2005–2009).

Cavallo, E., and Noy, I. (2009), 'The Economics of Natural Disasters: A Survey', Inter-American Development Bank Working Paper 124.

Coyle, D. (2014), *GDP: A Brief but Affectionate History* (Princeton: Princeton University Press).

Daly, P., Feener, R. M., and Reid, A. J. S. (eds.) (2012), *From the Ground Up: Perspectives on Post-tsunami and Post-conflict Aceh* (Institute of Southeast Asian Studies).

Davies, R. (ed.) (2015), *Economics: Making Sense of the Modern Economy* (London: Profile Books).

Doocy, S., Gorokhovich, Y., Burnham, G., Balk, D., and Robinson, C. (2007*a*), 'Tsunami Mortality Estimates and Vulnerability Mapping in Aceh, Indonesia', *American Journal of Public Health*, 97 (Suppl 1), S146–51.

——, Rofi, A., Moodie, C., Spring, E., Bradley, S., Burnham, G., and Robinson, C. (2007*b*), 'Tsunami Mortality in Aceh Province, Indonesia', *Bulletin of the World Health Organization*, 85 (4), 273–8.

Gibbons, H., and Gelfenbaum, G. (2005), 'Astonishing Wave Heights Among the Findings of an International Tsunami Survey Team on Sumatra', in *Sound Waves* (US Geological Survey).

Graf, A., Schröter, S., and Wieringa, E. (eds.) (2010), *Aceh: History, Politics and Culture* (Singapore: Institute of Southeast Asian Studies).

Institute for Criminal Justice Reform (2017), 'Praktek Hukuman Cambuk di Aceh Meningkat, Evaluasi atas Qanun Jinayat Harus Dilakukan Pemerintah' (Jakarta).

Johansen, L. (1985), 'Richard Stone's Contributions to Economics', *Scandinavian Journal of Economics*, 87 (1), 4–32.

Kendrick, J. (1970), 'The Historical Development of National Accounts', *History of Political Economy*, 2, 284–315.

Mill, J. S. (1848), *Principles of Political Economy with Some of Their Applications to Social Philosophy* (London: Longmans, Green & Co.).

NASA (2005), 'NASA Details Earthquake Effects on the Earth', Press Release, 10 January.

Petty, W. (1662), 'Treatise of Taxes and Contributions', republished in Hull, C. H. (ed.) (1899), *The Economic Writings of Sir William Petty Vol. 1* (Cambridge: Cambridge University Press).

———, (1676; published 1691), *Political Arithmetick* (London: Mortlock at the Phoenix, St Paul's Church Yard).

Reid, A. (2015), *A History of Southeast Asia: Critical Crossroads* (Chichester: John Wiley & Sons).

Ricklefs, M. C. (2001), *A History of Modern Indonesia Since c 1200* (London: Palgrave Macmillan).

Studenski, P. (1958), *The Income of Nations* (New York: New York University Press).

World Bank (2006), 'Aceh Public Expenditure Analysis: Spending for Reconstruction and Poverty Reduction' (Washington, DC: World Bank).

CHAPTER 2: ZAATARI

NOTES

Chart. Data on the number of refugees

Data on the sizes of camps are from the UNHCR. The populations of camps shift, and I have taken the peak year during the period 2010–15. Other large refugee settlements include Dadaab in eastern Kenya, which is a collection of five smaller camps, and Kutupalong in Bangladesh, home to Rohingya refugees fleeing Myanmar – see UNHCR (2016a). Data on refugees by country (of origin and host) are available from the UNHCR Population Statistics database.

Zaatari – key facts – founding, employment rate, start-up rate

The early years of Zaatari, including the informal situation in the camp, are set out in Ledwith (2014); other data including the revenue generated by unauthorized businesses in Zaatari are from the regular UNHCR factsheets, see e.g. UNHCR (2016c). The start-up rate is calculated as the number of new businesses established as a percentage of existing business. For a summary of the well-established markets that were built by the refugees during the first 18 months of the camp, see REACH (2014). Data for the number of shops for later years are tracked over time by the UNHCR, see e.g. UNHCR (2016c).

Negative interpretation of Zaatari

The lawlessness and lack of control in the early months of the Zaatari camp are discussed in Amnesty International (2013) and Ledwith (2014). See also Jordan Vista (2012).

Azraq – built by design

For claims about the improvements that Azraq would provide over Zaatari, see ReliefWeb (2014); for UN officials' views on the two camps, see Montgomery and

Leigh (2014) and Sweis (2014). On the steps taken to build a model camp at Azraq, see Gatter (2018). For an example of how this narrative influenced the initial reporting on Azraq, see Beaumont (2014).

Maslow's theory of motivations, and its application in disaster zones

The original hierarchy of needs is set out in Maslow (1943). For recent work testing the theory empirically, see Diener and Tay (2011), and for its use in the context of refugees, see Lonn and Dantzler (2017).

Depression in Azraq

The lack of work in the camp, and resulting depression, came from interviews with refugees there. For more on the divergence between the official view and the reality of life in Azraq, see Gatter (2018), and on Village 5 – the camp's jail – see Staton (2016). On official paid work ('incentive-based volunteering') in the camp and the huge supply of willing workers relative to positions, see UNHCR (2016d). On the importance of employment to refugee wellbeing, see Bemak and Chung (2017).

Child labour and the risk of a missing generation

On the risks and extent of child labour, see UNICEF (2014), and on the challenges of providing education in Zaatari, see Schmidt (2013).

REFERENCES

Amnesty International (2013), *Growing Restrictions, Tough Conditions: The Plight of Those Fleeing Syria to Jordan* (London: Amnesty International).

Beaumont, P. (2014), 'Jordan Opens New Syrian Refugee Camp', *Guardian*, 30 April.

Bemak, F. and Chung, R. C.-Y. (2017), 'Refugee Trauma: Culturally Responsive Counseling Interventions', *Journal of Counseling and Development*, 95 (3), 299–308.

Diener, E., and Tay, L. (2011), 'Needs and subjective well-being around the world', *Journal of Personality and Social Psychology*, 101 (2), 354–365.

Gatter, M. (2018), 'Rethinking the Lessons from Za'atari Refugee Camp', *Forced Migration Review*, 57, 22–4.

Institute on Statelessness and Inclusion (ISI) (2016), 'Understanding Statelessness in the Syria Refugee Context'.

Jordan Vista (2012), '26 Security Officers Injured in Zaatari Riots', 28 August.

Ledwith, A. (2014), *Zaatari: The Instant City* (Boston: Affordable Housing Institute).

Lonn, M., and Dantzler, J. (2017), 'A Practical Approach to Counseling Refugees: Applying Maslow's Hierarchy of Needs', *Journal of Counselor Practice*, 8 (2), 61–82.

Luck, T. (2014), 'Jordan's "Zaatari" Problem', *Jordan Times*, 19 April.

Maslow, A. H. (1943), 'A Theory of Human Motivation', *Psychological Review*, 50 (4), 370–96.

Montgomery, K., and Leigh, K. (2014), 'At a Startup Refugee Camp, Supermarkets and Water Conservation Take Priority', *Syria Deeply*, 6 May.

REACH (2014), *Market Assessment in Al Za'atari Refugee Camp, Jordan*, November.

ReliefWeb (2014), 'Opening of Azraq Camp for Syrian Refugees in Jordan', summary of ACTED report, April 2014.

Schmidt, C. (2013), 'Education in the Second Largest Refugee Camp in the World', *Global Partnership for Education*, 20 June.

Sherine S., Lachajczak, N., and Al Nakshabandi, J. (2014), *Exit Syria*, Film (SBS Online).

Staton, B. (2016), 'Jordan Detains Syrian Refugees in Village 5 "jail"', *IRIN*, 27 May.

Sweis, R. F. (2014), 'New Refugee Camp in Jordan Tries to Create a Community for Syrians, *New York Times*, 30 May.

UNHCR (2015), *Factsheet: Zaatari Refugee Camp*, February.

——— (2016*a*), 'Life in Limbo: Inside the World's Largest Refugee Camps', ESRI Story Map: https://storymaps.esri.com/stories/2016/refugee-camps

——— (2016*b*), *Factsheet: Jordan – Azraq Camp*, April.

——— (2016*c*), *Factsheet: Zaatari Refugee Camp*, October.

——— (2016*d*), *Incentive-based Volunteering in Azraq Camp*, October.

UNHCR Population Statistics, available at www.popstats.unhcr.org

UNICEF (2014), *Baseline Assessment of Child Labour Among Syrian Refugees in Za'atari Refugee Camp – Jordan*, November.

CHAPTER 3: LOUISIANA

NOTES

Statistics on global incarceration, in the US and in Louisiana

Statistics on global prison population are taken from Prison Studies (2016); data on the US prison population are taken from the US Bureau of Justice Statistics (2018). Data on length of sentence in Louisiana State Penitentiary are from Louisiana Department of Corrections (2010); further data on prison trends are taken from the DOC's 'Briefing Books'.

George Laval Chesterton

The quote on p. 81 is from George Laval Chesterton's *Revelations of Prison Life*, published in 1856. Chesterton was governor of the Middlesex House of Correction, Coldbath Fields, between 1829 and 1854. The prison, known as 'the Steel', was located at Mount Pleasant in Clerkenwell, central London. Chesterton's account makes clear that the prisoners had a good deal of autonomy in the prison, including ways of communicating with one another and a well-developed underground economy.

Wilbert Rideau

Wilbert Rideau's account of his crime, time on death row, and rehabilitation and writing is set out in Rideau (2010). The book is dedicated to C. Paul Phelps, a long-serving governor of Angola who supported and mentored Rideau's writing career.

The Angolite

Many US prisons have in-house newspapers, but *The Angolite* is probably the best-known and won a number of national journalism awards under Wilbert Rideau's editorship. Current copies of the magazine are available by subscription, or for purchase at the penitentiary's museum. Back copies of the paper are held by Louisiana State University. Some of Wilbert's earliest writings have been lost – his wife, Linda, kindly provided me with scanned copies of his work.

Data on Louisiana: income, poverty, obesity, graduation, murder rates

Data on income and poverty are taken from US Census Bureau historical income tables. Data on obesity rates in the US are from CDC (2017) and are available via the visualization site *State of Obesity*; data for educational attainment are from National Center for Education Statistics (2016); murder numbers and rates per 100,000 population are from FBI (2018).

The Kongo people

The Kongo people were part of a large kingdom with territory in west central Africa that spanned parts of the Republic of the Congo, Democratic Republic of the Congo, Gabon and Angola. The Kongo Kingdom was taken over by Portugal in the late nineteenth century. Kongo people speak Kikongo, one of the four official languages of the modern Democratic Republic of the Congo, and are one of the largest ethnic groups in that country.

Slave farming, history of Angola, Franklin and Armfield

Angola has a well-maintained museum that contains much of its history. The first published accounts of the Louisiana penal system and the importance of slave-leasing were by Carleton (1967, 1971). Recent work on the political economy of the use of enslaved prisoners as farm workers is set out in Forret (2013) and Cardon (2017). Information on the role of Franklin and Armfield is available from the Alexandria Black History Museum.

Prison Enterprises

The crops and output of Prison Enterprises are set out on its website, and its financial performance is included in the state's consolidated accounts, State of Louisiana (2016).

Pay rates in US prisons and in the UK

The rates for prisoner pay are set at a state level and not published in a US-wide format: Sawyer (2017) hand-collects and compares them. In the UK, prisoner pay is more opaque – the numbers are based on interviews. See HMPS (2004) for the latest publication on prisoner pay in the UK.

Jevons, money and the 'double coincidence of wants'

Jevons, along with Carl Menger and Léon Walras, is seen as the founding father of the 'neoclassical' school of economics. The quote on pp. 93–4 is from Jevons (1875).

Weird and wonderful informal currencies

The monetary system of Rossel Island has been extensively surveyed, starting with Armstrong (1924) and more recently by Liep (1983, 1995). The use of wood-pecker scalps is described by Buckley (2002); on the use of nzimbu shells in the kingdom of Kongo, and raphia cloth in Angola, see Vansina (1962). A more formal examination of primitive types of currency can be found in Pryor (1977).

Synthetic cannabis

On the synthesis of HU-210 in Israel, see Mechoulam et al. (1990). Hudson and Ramsey (2011) present more history and evidence on the search for synthetic versions of the main substances in cannabis; for a global picture the UN tracks the use and development of synthetic cannabinoids and presents some history, see United Nations (2011, 2013). The death of David Rozga and the legislation that followed (the David Mitchell Rozga Act) is set out in Sacco and Finklea (2011).

The Naval Criminal Investigative Service (NCIS) was aware of Spice by the late 2000s – see NCIS (2009) and *Naval Today* (2013). A case study of US Navy sailors who have used synthetic cannabinoids and complained of psychological problems afterwards is Hurst et al. (2011).

Drug busts in Angola; use in UK prisons

Scandals at the Angola penitentiary are regularly reported on by *The Advocate* (2017, 2018).

Dot money: store cards

Some of the history of electronic gift cards is set out in *Slate* (2005), the mid-2000s rise is traced in Dove Consulting (2004) and the recent surge in the number of pre-paid debit-card transactions is discussed in Federal Reserve System (2018). The demographic characteristics of users are surveyed in Pew (2015).

Spice in UK

On synthetic cannabis in the UK, see Her Majesty's Chief Inspector of Prisons for England and Wales (2014), Public Health England (2017) and Gauke (2018).

Voice of the Experienced and the First 72+
For the fight to reform the Louisiana justice system, see VOTE (2018), the First 72+ (2018) and Rising Foundations (2018).

REFERENCES

Adams, J. (2001), '"The Wildest Show in the South": Tourism and Incarceration at Angola', *TDR*, 45 (2), 94–108.

Advocate, The (2017), 'Department of Corrections: Cadet, Visitor Caught Smuggling Drugs into Angola', *The Advocate* Staff Report, 13 June.

—— (2018), 'Four Angola Employees Arrested, Two Sanctioned After Investigation into Drugs, Sexual Misconduct at Prison', author Grace Toohey.

Alexandria Black History Museum, www.alexandriava.gov/BlackHistory.

Alexandria Times (2017a), 'The Center of Alexandria's Slave Operations', 19 January.

—— (2017b), 'Franklin and Armfield Office', 20 May.

Angola Museum History, www.angolamuseum.org/history/history.

Armstrong, W. E. (1924), 'Rossel Island Money: A Unique Monetary System', *Economic Journal*, 34, 423–29.

Buckley, T. (2002), *Standing Ground: Yurok Indian Spirituality, 1850–1990* (Berkeley: University of California Press).

Cardon, N. (2017), '"Less Than Mayhem": Louisiana's Convict Lease, 1865–1901', *Louisiana History: The Journal of the Louisiana Historical Association*, 58 (4), 417–41.

Carleton, M. (1967), 'The Politics of the Convict Lease System in Louisiana: 1868–1901', *Louisiana History: The Journal of the Louisiana Historical Association*, 8 (1), 5–25.

—— (1971), *Politics and Punishment: The History of the Louisiana State Penal System* (Baton Rouge: Louisiana State University Press).

CDC (2017), *Prevalence of Obesity Among Adults and Youth: United States, 2015–2016*, NCHS Data Brief No. 288, October.

Chesterton, G. L. (1856), *Revelations of Prison Life* (London: Hurst and Blackett).

Dove Consulting (2004), *2004 Electronic Payments Study for Retail Payments Office at the Federal Reserve Bank of Atlanta*, 14 December.

FBI (2018), *Crime in the US 2017*, https://ucr.fbi.gov/crime-in-the-u.s/2017/crime-in-the-u.s.-2017.

Federal Reserve System (2018), *The Federal Reserve Payments Study: 2018 Annual Supplement*, Federal Reserve System, 20 December.

First 72+ (2018), 'Small Business Incubation', accessed December 2018: www.first72plus.org.

Forret, J. (2013), 'Before Angola: Enslaved Prisoners in the Louisiana State Penitentiary', *Louisiana History: The Journal of the Louisiana Historical Association*, 54 (2), 133–171.

Gauke, D. (2018), 'From Sentencing to Incentives – How Prisons Can Better Protect the Public from the Effects of Crime', Speech, Ministry of Justice, 10 July.

Her Majesty's Chief Inspector of Prisons for England and Wales (2014), *Annual Report 2013–14* (London: Her Majesty's Inspectorate for England and Wales).

HMPS (2004), 'Prisoners' Pay', Prison Service Order 4460, 30 September.

Hudson, S., and Ramsey, J. (2011), 'The Emergence and Analysis of Synthetic Cannabinoids', *Drug Testing and Analysis*, 3, 466–78.

Hurst, D., Loeffler, G., and McLay, R. (2011), 'Psychosis Associated with Synthetic Cannabinoid Agonists: A Case Series', *American Journal of Psychiatry*, 168 (10), Letters, October.

Jevons, W. S. (1875), *Money and the Mechanism of Exchange* (London: Henry S. King & Co.).

Liep, J. (1983), 'Ranked Exchange in Yela (Rossel Island)', in Leach, J. W., and Leach, E. (eds.), *The Kula* (Cambridge: Cambridge University Press).

——— (1995), 'Rossel Island Valuables Revisited', *Journal of the Polynesian Society*, 104 (2), 159–80.

Louisiana Department of Public Safety and Corrections (2010), *Annual Report 2009–2010*.

Louisiana DOC (2018), *La. Department of Public Safety and Corrections, Briefing Book*. Data available at https://doc.louisiana.gov/briefing-book.

Mechoulam, R., Lander, N., Breuer, A., and Zahalka, J. (1990), 'Synthesis of the Individual, Pharmacologically Distinct, Enantiomers of a Tetrahydrocannabinol Derivative', *Tetrahedron: Asymmetry*, 1 (5), 315–18.

Menger, C. (1892), 'On the Origins of Money', *Economic Journal*, 2 (6), 239–55.

National Center for Education Statistics (2016), *Digest of Education Statistics: 2016*, https://nces.ed.gov/programs/digest/d16.

Naval Today (2013), 'Naval Criminal Investigative Service Brings New Drug Awareness Campaign to NMCP', 27 March.

NCIS (2009), 'Introduction to Spice', Norfolk Field Office, 9 December.

Pew (2015), 'Banking on Prepaid: Survey of Motivations and Views of Prepaid Card Users', Pew Charitable Trusts, June.

Prison Enterprises, www.prisonenterprises.org.

Prison Studies (2016), *World Prison Population List*, eleventh edition. Statistics available at www.prisonstudies.org.

Pryor, F. L. (1977), 'The Origins of Money', *Journal of Money, Credit and Banking*, 9 (3), 391–409.

Public Health England (2017), 'New Psychoactive Substances Toolkit: Prison Staff', 1 January.

Rideau, Wilbert (2010), *In the Place of Justice: A Story of Punishment and Deliverance* (New York: Knopf).

Rising Foundations (2018), 'Our Small Business Incubator', accessed December 2018: www.risingfoundations.org.

Sacco, L., and Finklea, K. (2011), 'Synthetic Drugs: Overview and Issues for Congress', *Congressional Research Service*, 28 October.

Sawyer, W. (2017), 'How Much Do Incarcerated People Earn in Each State?', Prison Policy Initiative Blog, 10 April.

Slate (2005), 'Why Gift Cards Are Evil', 4 January.

State of Louisiana (2016), *State of Louisiana Comprehensive Annual Financial Report for the Year Ended June 30, 2016*, 30 December.

United Nations (2011), 'Synthetic Cannabinoids in Herbal Products', United Nations Office on Drugs and Crime, UN document SCITEC/24, April.

————— (2013), *World Drug Report 2013*, United Nations Office on Drugs and Crime (United Nations: New York).

US Bureau of Justice Statistics (2018), available at www.bjs.gov.

US Census Bureau, Historical Income Tables, www.census.gov/data/tables/time-series/demo/income-poverty/historical-income-households.html.

Vansina, J. (1962), 'Long-distance Trade Routes in Central Africa', *Journal of African History*, 3 (3), 375–90.

VOTE (2018), 'Advancing Justice in Louisiana: Policy Priorities', Voice of the Experienced, accessed December 2018.

CHAPTER 4: DARIEN

NOTES

The Gap, history, people and famous crossings

Burton (1973) discusses the native tribes of Darien, the vegetation and bird life, and the risk to them posed by the Pan-American Highway. A useful discussion of the challenge of completing the highway, including interesting maps, is given in Comptroller General of the US (1978). The Gap has been crossed by vehicles, with the aid of boats: in 1972 the Trans-Americas Expedition crossed Darien in the dry season assisted by the British Army major John Blashford-Snell. More information on the history of the Gap, including photos of the Blashford-Snell expedition, is in Miller (2014).

The Colombian civil war, FARC, right-wing paramilitaries

A huge document with facts and figures on the Colombian civil war was published in 2013 and is available in English as *BASTA YA!* ('Enough Already!') by GMH (2016); a much shorter new piece with numbers on the war is Miroff (2016*b*).

Buccaneer histories and tales: Henry Morgan, William Dampier and Lionel Wafer

The first account that set out the life of the British buccaneer Henry Morgan was Exquemelin (1684); the accounts that influenced public opinion in Scotland were Dampier (1697) and Wafer (1699). Versions of all can be found online. Of the three, Wafer's account is the most exciting and he gives lots of detail, including maps of Darien.

The Company of Scotland and the Darien Plan
The Company of Scotland was one of the world's first 'joint-stock' companies (a public company in which individuals can invest) and was later known as the Darien Company. An excellent account of its formation, investors and goals is set out in Watt (2007).

The Darien disaster
The tragedy of the Darien expedition is set out in detail in the classic modern account by Prebble (1968). A modern account of a personal journey to find New Caledonia is provided in McKendrick (2016). Diaries of survivors who experienced the disaster first hand are quoted in Watt (2007) and include Borland (1779). The ancestors of US president Roosevelt who were on the Scottish boats are traced in Millar (1904).

Yaviza: history, the museum, impact of the road
The area around Yaviza and the extent of the protected indigenous land is mapped in Herlihy (2003) – the paper also describes the history of the area, including the construction of the forts to protect the Spanish gold river transport route.

Aerial photos of Darien, evidence on the extent of Panama's lost rainforest
Figures on the rate of deforestation in eastern Panama are provided in Mateo-Vega et al. (2018). The conversion of rainforest to farmland and the policies adopted to prevent deforestation are discussed and evaluated in Nelson et al. (2001); maps of the forest cover over time and the impact of logging are provided in Gutierrez (1989); the problem of deforestation and the rise of cattle-ranching are discussed in Arcia (2017) and Belisle (2018).

The 'Tragedy of the Commons'
Ecologist Garrett Hardin coined the term 'Tragedy of the Commons' in the 1960s in a discussion of overpopulation and the environment – Hardin (1968).

Failures of free markets
The example of common ground that is damaged by overuse is set out in the first of William Forster Lloyd's 'Two Lectures on the Checks to Population' delivered in Oxford in 1832.

Ostrom's work, governing the commons, Törbel, Japanese villages
Ostrom's work is presented in her *Governing the Commons* – see Ostrom (1990). A discussion of the informal system used to manage resources in Japanese villages is described in McKean (1996).

Panama's Law 24, and the teak tree
The impact of the teak tree in homogenizing Panama's biodiversity is discussed in Griess and Knoke (2011). The impact of Law 24 in incentivizing the plantation of teak trees is discussed in Sloan (2016); on the 'teak fever' and how better reforestation could cure it, see Hall (2018).

The economic potential of Panamanian environment

On the diversity of bird life in Panama, see Ridgely and Gwynne (1992). The economic potential of the Panamanian environment, if protected, is assessed in Dorosh and Klytchnikova (2012).

The trouble following FARC demobilization

The rise in the cultivation of coca for cocaine production is traced in United Nations (2016). See also Miroff (2016*a*).

New migrant routes into the US

There is little official information on the migrant route into the US via Darien. One paper that describes the routes and numbers in more detail is Miraglia (2016).

Panama's cash-for-citizenship policy, the role of teak

On the 'citizenship for investment' policy, including the $40,000 reforestation visa programme, see Consulate of Panama (2018).

The global market for Embera wood

The international price of hardwoods on the open market is tracked in ITTO (2018).

REFERENCES

Arcia, J. (2017), 'Panama: The Ranching Industry Has Moved into Darién National Park', *Mongabay*, 26 June.

Belisle, L. (2018), 'Darien Suffers from Illegal Deforestation', *Playa Community*, 20 April.

Borland, F. (1779), *The History of Darien* (Glasgow: John Bryce).

Burton, P. J. K. (1973), 'The Province of Darien', *Geographical Journal*, 139 (1), 43–7.

Comptroller General of the US (1978), 'Linking the Americas – Progress and Problems of the Darien Gap Highway', Report to the Congress by the Comptroller General of the US, PSAD-78-65, 23 February (Washington, DC: General Accounting Office).

Consulate of Panama (2018), 'Panama Reforestation Visa Program', accessed December 2018.

Dampier, W. (1697), *A New Voyage Round the World* (London: Knapton).

Dorosh, P., and Klytchnikova, I. (2012), 'Tourism Sector in Panama Regional Economic Impacts and the Potential to Benefit the Poor', World Bank, Policy Research Working Paper 6183, August.

Dudley, S. (2004), *Walking Ghosts: Murder and Guerrilla Politics in Colombia* (New York: Routledge).

Estrella de Panama (2009), 'Deforestation Is Killing Darien', 13 April.

Exquemelin, A. (1684), *Buccaneers of America* (London: William Crooke).

GMH (2016), *BASTA YA! Colombia: Memories of War and Dignity* (Bogotá: CNMH).

Griess, V., and Knoke, T. (2011), 'Can Native Tree Species Plantations in Panama Compete with Teak Plantations? An Economic Estimation', *New Forests*, 41, 13–39.

Gutierrez, R. (1989), 'La deforestación, principal causa del problema ecología ambiental de Pánama', Dirección Nacional de Desarollo Forestal.

Hall, J. (2018), 'Curing "Teak Fever" in Panama through Smart Reforestation', UN-REDD, 4 September.

Hardin, G. (1968), 'The Tragedy of the Commons', *Science*, 162 (3859), 1243–8.

Harris, W. (1700), *A Defence of the Scots Abdicating Darien* (Edinburgh).

Herlihy, P. (1989), 'Opening Panama's Darien Gap', *Journal of Cultural Geography*, 9 (2), 42–59.

———— (2003), 'Participatory Research Mapping of Indigenous Lands in Darién, Panama', *Human Organization*, 62 (4).

ITTO (2018), 'Tropical Timber Market Report', International Tropical Timber Organization, December.

Lloyd, W. F. (1833), 'W. F. Lloyd on the Checks to Population', *Population and Development Review*, 6 (3), 473–96.

McKean, M. A. (1996), 'Common-property Regimes as a Solution to Problems of Scale and Linkage', in Hanna, S. S., Folke, C., and Mäler, K.-G. (eds.), *Rights to Nature: Ecological, Economic, Cultural, and Political Principles of Institutions for the Environment* (Washington, DC: Island Press).

McKendrick, J. (2016), *Darien: A Journey in Search of Empire* (Edinburgh: Birlinn).

Mateo-Vega, J., Spalding, A. K., Hickey, G. M., and Potvin, C. (2018), 'Deforestation, Territorial Conflicts, and Pluralism in the Forests of Eastern Panama: A Place for Reducing Emissions from Deforestation and Forest Degradation?' *Case Studies in the Environment*, June.

Millar, A. H. (1904), 'The Scottish Ancestors of President Roosevelt', *Scottish Historical Review*, 1 (4), 416–20.

Miller, S. W. (2014), 'Minding the Gap: Pan-Americanism's Highway, American Environmentalism, and Remembering the Failure to Close the Darien Gap', *Environmental History*, 19, 189–216.

Miraglia, P. (2016), 'The Invisible Migrants of the Darién Gap: Evolving Immigration Routes in the Americas', Council on Hemispheric Affairs, 18 November.

Miroff, N. (2016a), 'Peace with FARC May Be Coming, So Colombia's Farmers Are on a Massive Coca Binge', *Washington Post*, 8 July.

———— (2016b), 'The Staggering Toll of Colombia's War with FARC Rebels, Explained in Numbers', *Washington Post*, 24 August.

Nelson, G. C., Harris, V., and Stone, S. W. (2001), 'Deforestation, Land Use, and Property Rights: Empirical Evidence from Darién, Panama', *Land Economics*, 77 (2), 187–205.

Ostrom, E. (1990), *Governing the Commons: The Evolution of Institutions for Collective Action* (Cambridge: Cambridge University Press).

Paterson, W. (1701), *A Proposal to Plant a Colony in Darien*.

Playfair, W. (1807), *An Inquiry into the Permanent Causes of the Decline and Fall of Powerful and Wealthy Nations* (London: Greenland & Norris).

Prebble, J. (1968), *The Darien Disaster* (London: Martin Secker & Warburg).

Ridgely, R., and Gwynne, J. A. (1992), 'A Guide to the Birds of Panama with Costa Rica, Nicaragua, and Honduras' (Princeton: Princeton University Press).

Sidgwick, H. (1887), *The Principles of Political Economy*, second edition (London: Macmillan and Company).

Sloan, S. (2016), 'Tropical Forest Gain and Interactions Amongst Agents of Forest Change', *Forests*, 27 February.

United Nations (2016), *Monitoreo de territorios afectados por cultivos ilícitos 2015*, UNDOC, June.

Wafer, L. (1699), *A New Voyage and Description of the Isthmus of America* (London: Knapton).

Watt, D. (2007), *The Price of Scotland: Darien, Union and the Wealth of Nations* (Edinburgh: Luath Press).

CHAPTER 5: KINSHASA

NOTES

Facts and figures on the Congolese economy

GDP and unemployment figures in this chapter are taken from the World Bank Development Indicators database. The Congo's ranking of 184/190 in ease of doing business is explained in World Bank (2018b). The number of people living below the poverty line of $1.90 per day is from the World Bank Poverty and Equity database; data for the Congo are sparse, and available for only two years – 2004 (94 per cent) and 2012 (77 per cent) – both showing the most acute poverty in the world. On the prevalence of malaria, see WHO (2018), and on its treatment in Kinshasa see ACT watch Group (2017).

Verney Lovett Cameron's trips across Africa

Weymouth-born Verney Lovett Cameron described his pan-African expedition in Cameron (1877); his importance and his role as a campaigner for the abolition of slavery is discussed in Casada (1975).

Tax rates – official and actual – in Kinshasa

For a summary of the how the tax system is officially supposed to work, see PwC (2018). Information on how things operate in reality comes from interviews in Kinsasha; see also Nkuku and Titeca (2018a, 2018b).

Henry Morton Stanley – his books, his life

The popular account of Henry Morton Stanley's travels across Africa is Stanley (1878). Tim Butcher retraced the expedition in the 2000s and discusses Stanley's life and trip in his memoir – Butcher (2008).

For a modern biography, which includes discussion of both Stanley's brutality and his opposition to slavery, see Jeal (2007) and the op-ed Jeal (2011); see also Bierman (1990). For a Congolese perspective, see Mbu-Mputu and Kasereka (2012).

The Berlin Conference and the scramble for Africa

The defining event of the 'scramble for Africa' was the Berlin Conference of 1884. Fourteen countries attended and signed the resulting treaty. France and Britain ended up with the largest claims, followed by Germany and Portugal – see Pakenham (1991).

King Leopold II; humanitarian disaster in the Congo Free State

For a modern account of Leopold's rule, see Hochschild (1999) and more recently van Reybrouck (2015). The important contemporary accounts that raised awareness of what was going on in the Congo Free State are *Red Rubber* by E. D. Morel (1906) and the *Casement Report* of 1904, which outlined harrowing stories of ill treatment, especially in Leopold's private *Domaine de la Couronne* – see Casement (1904, in particular the interviews in 'Inclosure 1').

The Congo had no official census until the 1920s, when the population was 10 million. The lack of a census and of burial records means there is ongoing disagreement over the number of deaths attributable to the Congo Free State. Casement's report includes many accounts of villages that have collapsed or disappeared, with Morel putting the estimate of deaths at 20 million. Many others put the figure at 10 million – see Hochschild (1999) and Vansina (2010).

The Congo Crisis

For a contemporary review of booking and opinion at the time of the Congo Crisis, see Neff (1964); on the role of the US and Belgium in the crisis, see Kaplan (1967).

Mobutuism – the successful early years

On the shift from crisis to stability under Mobutu, and the success of the 1967 reform package, see Young and Turner (1985).

The crash in value of Mobutu's currency

Mobutu was forced to re-denominate the currency in 1993, with the 'new zaire' worth 3 million old zaires; the Congolese franc, launched in the summer of 1998, was worth 100,000 new zaires, or 300 billion of the original currency.

Agriculture and industry under Mobutu

On Mobutu's agricultural plans and their disastrous results, including data on crop yields and farm output, see Young and Turner (1985).

On the ideas behind the grand infrastructure plans, see Young and Turner (1985). The poor performance of the Maluku mill is examined in United Nations (1989). On the ongoing discussion and politics around the grand infrastructure plans – in particular the Inga dams – see Gottschalk (2016).

The two pillages of Kinshasa

The pillages are also sometimes called the First and Second Plundering. For contemporary accounts of Mobutu's failures and the two pillages, see Berkely (1993) and Richburg (1991); the events are discussed in Haskin (2005) and van Reybrouck (2015). The economic impact of the pillages, which can clearly be seen in the country's output data, led to Mobutu's decline; for an account of life in Kinshasa in the final years, see Wrong (2001).

Feeding the horse: public servants and informal taxation

The informal taxation undertaken by the police force is seen everywhere in Kinshasa; it is discussed in Eriksson Baaz and Olsson (2011). On corruption under Mobutu, see Reno (2006).

The pirate city

There are few modern estimates of the extent of the 'Article 15' informal economy, but its importance is discussed in Putzel et al. (2008), with some estimates given in IMF (2015). The Kinoise reaction – to build informal villages within Kinshasa – is discussed in de Boeck (2013). On the importance of illicit and informal activity to the economy in Zaire, see MacGaffey (1991). On the endemic system of informal taxation, see Nkuku and Titeca (2018a, 2018b). For the implications of this for data on the Congolese economy, see Marivoet and de Herdt (2014).

The educational system, privatization and motivation fees

The collapse of state spending on education is discussed in Brannelly (2012); the informal privatization of the state by Trefon (2009); and the privatization of public education in Brandt (2014), de Herdt and Titeca (2016), and Brannelly (2012).

The Office des Routes and public infrastructure (roads)

For the tribulations of the Office des Routes under Mobutu, see Young and Turner (1985); for a more recent analysis of the state of the Congo's infrastructure, see Foster and Benitez (2011).

On Kabila and post-Mobutu theft of state assets

On the wealth of the Kabila family and its sources, see Congo Research Group (2017). Estimates of funds that have gone missing due to theft of mining revenues are available in Global Witness (2017); the role of coltan in the conflict in eastern Congo is HCSS (2013); for a critique of Kabila, and the similarity of his methods with those of Mobutu, see Bavier (2010).

Catch-22 – getting stuck on 'Article 15'

The perplexing strength of the weak state is discussed in Englebert (2003). On the idea that corruption is so endemic that the economy could be harmed if it were stamped out, see Jeune Afrique (2013). On the way 'Article 15' and the culture of taking a little plays out in the context of modern payroll services, see Moshonas (2018).

REFERENCES

ACTwatch Group (Mpanya, G., Tshefu, A., and Losimba Likwela, J.) (2017), 'The Malaria Testing and Treatment Market in Kinshasa, 2013', *Malaria Journal*, 16 (94).

Bavier, J. (2010), 'Congo's New Mobutu', *Foreign Policy*, 29 June.

Bayart, J.-F. (2009), *The State in Africa* (Cambridge: Polity Press).

Berkely, B. (1993), 'Zaire: An African Horror Story', *Atlantic*, August.

Berwouts, K. (2017), *Congo's Violent Peace: Conflict and Struggle Since the Great African War* (London: Zed Books).

Bierman, J. (1990), *Dark Safari: The Life Behind the Legend of Henry Morton Stanley* (New York: Knopf).

Brandt, C. (2014), *Teachers' Struggle for Income in the Congo (DRC): Between Education and Remuneration*, thesis, University of Amsterdam.

Brannelly, L. (2012), 'The Teacher Salary System in the Democratic Republic of the Congo (DRC)', Case Study: Centre for Universal Education, Brookings.

Butcher, T. (2008), *Blood River: A Journey to Africa's Broken Heart* (London: Vintage).

Cameron, V. L. (1877), *Across Africa* (New York: Harper & Brothers).

Casada, J. A. (1975), 'Verney Lovett Cameron: A Centenary Appreciation', *Geographical Journal*, 141 (2), 203–15.

Congo Research Group (2017), *All the President's Wealth: The Kabila Family Business*, Pulitzer Center on Crisis Reporting, July.

Dash, L. (1980), 'Mobutu Mortgages Nation's Future', *Washington Post*, 1 January.

de Boeck, F. (2013), *Kinshasa: Tales of the Invisible City* (Leuven: Leuven University Press).

de Herdt, T., and Titeca, K. (2016), 'Governance with Empty Pockets: The Education Sector in the Democratic Republic of Congo', *Development and Change*, 47 (3), 472–94.

Englebert, P. (2003), 'Why Congo Persists: Sovereignty, Globalization and the Violent Reproduction of a Weak State', Queen Elizabeth House Working Paper 95.

Eriksson Baaz, M., and Olsson, O. (2011), 'Feeding the Horse: Unofficial Economic Activities Within the Police Force in the Democratic Republic of the Congo', *African Security*, 4 (4), 223–41.

Foster, V., and Benitez, D. (2011), *The Democratic Republic of Congo's Infrastructure: A Continental Perspective*, Working Paper 5602 (Washington, DC: World Bank).

Global Witness (2017), *Regime Cash Machine*, Report.

Gottschalk, K. (2016), 'Hydro-politics and Hydro-power: The Century-long Saga of the Inga Project', *Canadian Journal of African Studies/Revue canadienne des études africaines*, 50 (2), 279–94.

Haskin, J. M. (2005), *The Tragic State of the Congo: From Decolonization to Dictatorship* (Algora).

HCSS (2013), *Coltan, Congo & Conflict*, Hague Centre for Strategic Studies.

Hochschild, A. (1999), *King Leopold's Ghost: A Story of Greed, Terror and Heroism in Colonial Africa* (New York: Mariner Books).

IMF (2015), *Democratic Republic of the Congo – Selected Issues*, IMF Country Report No. 15/281 (Washington, DC: IMF).

Jeal, T. (2007), *Stanley: The Impossible Life of Africa's Greatest Explorer* (London: Faber and Faber).

———— (2011), 'Remembering Henry Stanley', *Telegraph*, 16 March.

Jeune Afrique (2013), 'RD Congo: la saga des salaires', 5 November.

Kaplan, L. (1967), 'The United States, Belgium, and the Congo Crisis of 1960', *Review of Politics*, 29 (2), 239–56.

MacGaffey, J. (1991), *The Real Economy of Zaire: The Contribution of Smuggling and Other Unofficial Activities to National Wealth* (Philadelphia: University of Pennsylvania Press).

———— (2018b), 'How Kinshasa's Markets Are Captured by Powerful Private Interests', *The Conversation*, 11 March.

Marivoet, W., and de Herdt, T. (2014), 'Reliable, Challenging or Misleading? A Qualitative Account of the Most Recent National Surveys and Country Statistics in the DRC', *Canadian Journal of Development Studies/Revue canadienne d'études du développement*, 35 (1), 97–119.

Mbu-Mputu, N. X., and Kasereka, D. K. (eds.) (2012), *Bamonimambo (the Witnesses): Rediscovering Congo and British Isles Common History* (Newport: South People's Projects).

Morel, E. D. (1906), *Red Rubber: The Story of the Rubber Slave Trade Flourishing on the Congo in the Year of Grace, 1906* (New York: Nassau Print).

Moshonas, S. (2018), 'Power and Policy-making in the DR Congo: The Politics of Human Resource Management and Payroll Reform', Working Paper, Institute of Development Policy, University of Antwerp.

Neff, C. B. (1964), 'Conflict, Crisis and the Congo', *Journal of Conflict Resolution*, 8 (1), 86–92.

Nkuku, A. M., and Titeca, K. (2018a), 'Market Governance in Kinshasa: The Competition for Informal Revenue Through "Connections" (Branchement)', Working Paper, Institute of Development Policy, University of Antwerp.

———— (2018b), 'How Kinshasa's Markets Are Captured by Powerful Private Interests', *The Conversation*, 11 March.

Pakenham, T. (1991), *The Scramble for Africa* (London: Weidenfeld & Nicolson).

Peterson, M. (ed.) (2015), *The Prisoner's Dilemma* (Cambridge: Cambridge University Press).

Poundstone, W. (1992), *Prisoner's Dilemma* (New York: Doubleday).

Putzel, J., Lindemann, S., and Schouten, C. (2008), 'Drivers of Change in the Democratic Republic of Congo: The Rise and Decline of the State and Challenges for Reconstruction', Working Paper No. 26, Crisis States Research Centre, London School of Economics, January.

PwC (2018), 'Congo, Democratic Republic: Corporate – Taxes on corporate income', PwC.

Reno, W. (2006), 'Congo: From State Collapse to "Absolutism", to State Failure', *Third World Quarterly*, 27 (1), 43–56.

Richburg, K. B. (1991), 'Mobutu: A Rich Man in Poor Standing', *Washington Post*, 3 October.

Stanley, H. M. (1878), *Through the Dark Continent* (London: Sampson Low, Marston, Searle & Rivington).

Stearns, J. K. (2012), *Dancing in the Glory of Monsters* (New York: PublicAffairs).

Trefon, T. (2009), 'Public Service Provision in a Failed State: Looking Beyond Predation in the Democratic Republic of Congo', *Review of African Political Economy*, 36 (119), 9–21.

United Nations (1989), 'Report on the Rehabilitation of the Mauluku Steel Mill (Sosider), Zaire', United Nations Industrial Development Organization, PPD.112 (SPEC.), 21 March.

van Reybrouck, D. (2015), *Congo: The Epic History of a People* (London: Harper Collins).

Vansina, J. (2010), *Being Colonized: The Kuba Experience in Rural Congo, 1880–1960* (Madison: University of Wisconsin Press).

Verhaegen, B., and Vale, M. (1993), 'The Temptation of Predatory Capitalism: Zaire Under Mobutuism', *International Journal of Political Economy*, 23 (1), 109–25.

WHO (2018), *World Malaria Report 2018*, 19 November.

World Bank (2018*a*), *Atlas of Sustainable Development Goals 2018: World Development Indicators* (Washington, DC: World Bank).

World Bank (2018*b*), *Doing Business 2019* (Washington, DC: World Bank).

Wrong, M. (2001), *In the Footsteps of Mr Kurtz: Living on the Brink of Disaster in the Congo* (London: Fourth Estate).

Young, C., and Turner, T. (1985), *The Rise and Decline of the Zairian State* (Madison: University of Wisconsin Press).

CHAPTER 6 : GLASGOW

NOTES

Glasgow, from high to low: Walpole to Walsh

The natural beauty of Glasgow was famously commented on by Daniel Defoe (1707), the city's industrial achievements set out by Walpole (1878). Discussion of the 'Glasgow effect' is in Walsh et al. (2010).

The Glasgow art scene, Alexander Reid and the impressionists

The statement about the superiority of Glasgow's art scene to London's is due to Hermann Muthesius, a German architect who worked as cultural and technical attaché at the German Embassy in London at the turn of the twentieth century, publishing *Das englische Haus* – see Muthesius (1904). The impact that Alexander

Reid had is described in Fowle (2011). Sir William Burrell consistently bought from Reid and credited him with creating a love of art in Scotland – many of their pieces remain in the Burrell collection, see Glasgow Museums (1997).

Glasgow's 'firsts': Watt, Kelvin, the subway

The history of physics and applied science in Glasgow, and the businesses that the scientific discoveries helped support (including Watt, Kelvin, Rankine and Logie Baird) are discussed in Johnston (2006). On the history and role of the University of Glasgow, see Coutts (1909) and Moss et al. (2000). The Glasgow subway, opened in 1896, came after those in London and Budapest, but it was the first to run trains that were pulled by wires powered by a separate engine room, meaning smoke-free travel – see Wright and MacLean (1997).

The rise and fall of the 'Virginia Dons'

The rise and fall of the 'Tobacco Lords' and their impact on the architecture of central Glasgow is described in Nichol (1966). The tobacco trading that Glasgow's merchants engaged in is set out in Devine (1990).

The height of Glaswegian shipbuilding

The investment in the river and the industry it supported is the basis of the famous local saying: 'The Clyde built Glasgow, and Glasgow built the Clyde.' The rise of Glaswegian shipping is described in fine detail by Bremner (1869), a modern history is Walker (2001), and a chapter on the making of the Glaswegian reputation for fine ships is discussed in Smith (2018).

Urban economics and agglomeration effects

Marshall's discussion of the economics of agglomeration is from his *Principles of Economics* (1890). For examples of recent work using Marshall's set-up, see Potter and Watts (2012), and Brinkman et al. (2015).

The rapid decline of shipbuilding

Histories of the decline of British shipbuilding typically start with, and focus on, the Clyde. The rapid decline of the industry, and the role of the state in managing, subsidizing and ultimately letting shipbuilding fail is set out in fine detail by Johnman and Murphy (2002); a personal account by the last manager of the Stephen's shipyard is Stephen (2015). The thesis that it was craft tradition in British shipyards – techniques that made it harder to achieve economies of scale – is Lorenz (1991); see also Burton (2013).

Britain looks to Japan

The active role the British government played in the decline of shipbuilding industry is set out by Connors (2009); the study of Japanese yards, including their productivity data, was published as Board of Trade (1965). The lack of investment is taken from Johnman and Murphy (2002).

The Geddes Commission, Upper Clyde Shipbuilders – its creation and demise
The formation and output of the Geddes Commission is discussed in Johnman and Murphy (2002), and Connors (2009); the report is published as Board of Trade (1966). A concise history of the formation and failure of the Upper Clyde Shipbuilders 'experiment' is Broadway (1976). Film footage of the yards at the time of the UCS plan can be seen in the documentary directed and narrated by Sean Connery, *The Bowler and the Bunnet*, available from the British Film Institute – see Connery (1967).

Health behaviours
Data on 'health behaviours' (diet, smoking and exercise) are taken from the Glasgow Centre for Population Health and publications by its researchers – see GCPH (2008), Whyte and Ajetunmobi (2012), and Dodds (2014). Maps and data on deprivation and health outcomes are available from the GCPH website – see also Carstairs and Morris (1991).

Violence and drugs
Data on drug deaths are taken from the annual publication *Drug Deaths in Scotland*, National Records of Scotland (2018); suicide rates are from NHS Scotland.

Durkheim and Le suicide
The French original of Durkheim's work is Durkheim (1897); the first English translation is the 1952 version, republished more recently as Durkheim (2002). For a biography of his life and work, see Lukes (1992), and for a discussion of the modern relevance of his work – including the importance of the concept of 'social facts' – see, for example, Berkman et al. (2000).

Putnam, Italy and social capital
Putnam's travels and investigation into social capital and democracy in Italy are set out in Putnam (1993); see also Pagden (1988). A formal and mathematical treatment of the concept is set out in Coleman (1990).

Criticisms of social capital from the left and the right
Criticisms of social capital from economists include Arrow (1999) and Solow (2000). An example of the argument that the concept supports neoliberal economic policies is the discussion by Ferragina and Arrigoni (2017).

Overcrowding and poor conditions in Glaswegian tenements
The linkages between cramped conditions, poverty and disease are set out in famous epidemiological studies – see Pulteney (1844) and Perry (1844).

The City Improvement Trust, Mary Barbour and the rent strikes
The history of the City Improvement Trust, together with a description of the first social housing built in Glasgow, is in Withey (2003). For information on women in Glasgow, including Mary Barbour and the rent strikes, see King (1993); see also the documentary film *Red Skirts on Clydeside*, Woodley and Bellamy (1984).

Bruce, Abercrombie, Spence, the dream and failure of Glasgow planning

The two plans to re-arrange Glasgow are Bruce (1945), and Abercrombie and Matthew (1949). Much of the Bruce plan – including the demolition of Glasgow's historic centre – was deemed too radical, but ideas in it influenced planning in Glasgow for decades. The Abercrombie plan – the 'Clyde Valley Regional Plan' – was hugely influential, see Smith and Wannop (1985). The plans are also discussed in Checkland (1976).

The Big Four – ambition and failure

Striking maps of deprivation that show the conditions in the Big Four estates are available in *Inquiry into Housing in Glasgow* (1986). Damer (1989) provides in-depth detail, interviews and a critique of inter-war housing scheme Moorepark, which became one of Glasgow's most infamous areas and known as 'Wine Alley'. Craig (2003) describes life in Drumchapel, with the problems at Easterhouse examined in CES (1985). The problems of the peripheral estates are ongoing, as set out in Garnham (2018).

History of tenements

On the history of tenements, their legal basis, architecture, furniture and impact on society, together with maps, plans and pictures, see Worsdall (1977). Recordings of those who lived in the tenements together are collected into themes in Faley (1990). Ralf Glasser's trilogy of books cover a life that started in the Gorbals, on the importance of retaining respectability while pawning goods – see Glasser (1986).

Songs and poems about life on the peripheral estates

'Jeely Piece Song' by Adam MacNaughton is also known as 'The Skyscraper Wean' and is about the plight of children sent to live in Castlemilk high-rise buildings.

Deaths from drugs and the rise of HIV in Glasgow

The number of deaths from drugs in Scotland has continued to increase. In 2017 it hit its highest level since comparable records started. Glasgow has a disproportionate share of these deaths, with the prevalence of injected cocaine appearing to cause many more deaths in the past two years – see National Records of Scotland (2018). On the related HIV epidemic, see Ragonnet-Cronin et al. (2018).

REFERENCES

AAPSS (1897), 'Notes on Municipal Government', *Annals of the American Academy of Political and Social Science*, 9, 149–58.

Abercrombie, P., and Matthew, R. H. (1949), *Clyde Valley Regional Plan 1946* (Edinburgh: His Majesty's Stationery Office).

Arrow, K. (1999), 'Observations on Social Capital', in Dasgupta, P., and Serageldin, I. (eds.), *Social Capital: A Multifaceted Perspective* (Washington, DC: World Bank).

Atkinson, R. (1999), *The Development and Decline of British Shipbuilding.*

Barras, G. W. (1894), 'The Glasgow Building Regulations Act (1892)', *Proceedings of the Philosophical Society of Glasgow,* xxv, 155–69.

Berkman, L. F., Glass, T., Brisette, I., and Seeman, T. E. (2000), 'From Social Integration to Health: Durkheim in the New Millennium', *Social Science and Medicine,* 51, 843–57.

Board of Trade (1965), *Japanese Shipyards: A Report on the Visit of the Minister of State (Shipping) in January 1965.*

———— (1966), *Shipbuilding Inquiry Committee 1965–1966 – Report* (London: HMSO), Cmnd. 2937.

Bourdieu, P. (1986), 'The Forms of Capital', in Richardson, J. G. (ed.), *Handbook of Theory and Research for the Sociology of Education* (New York: Greenwood Press).

Bremner, D. (1869), *The Industries of Scotland: Their Rise, Progress and Present Position* (Edinburgh: Adam and Charles Black).

Brinkman, J., Coen-Pirani, D., and Sieg, H. (2015), 'Firm Dynamics in an Urban Economy', *International Economic Review,* 56 (4), 1135–64.

Broadway, F. (1976), *Upper Clyde Shipbuilders – A Study of Government Intervention in Industry* (London: Centre for Policy Studies).

Bruce, R. (1945), *The First Planning Report to Highways and the Planning Committee of the Corporation of the City of Glasgow,* 2 volumes (Glasgow).

Burton, A. (2013), *The Rise and Fall of British Shipbuilding* (Stroud: The History Press).

Carstairs, V., and Morris, R. (1991), *Deprivation and Health in Scotland* (Aberdeen: Aberdeen University Press).

CES (1985), *Outer Estates in Britain: Easterhouse Case Study,* Paper 24 (London: Centre for Environmental Studies).

Chadwick, E. (1842, reprinted 1965), *Report on the Sanitary Condition of the Labouring Population of Great Britain* (Edinburgh: University of Edinburgh Press).

Checkland, S. (1976), *The Upas Tree – Glasgow 1875–1975* (Glasgow: University of Glasgow Press).

Coleman, J. (1990), *Foundations of Social Theory* (Cambridge, Mass.: Harvard University Press).

Connery, S. [director] (1967), *The Bowler and the Bunnet,* available on BFI (2018), *Tales from the Shipyard: Britain's Shipbuilding Heritage on Film,* DVD (London: BFI).

Connors, D. P. (2009), *The Role of Government in the Decline of the British Shipbuilding Industry, 1945–1980,* PhD thesis, University of Glasgow.

Coutts, J. (1909), *A History of the University of Glasgow from its Foundation in 1451 to 1909* (Glasgow: University of Glasgow Press).

Couzin, J. (2003), *Radical Glasgow: A Skeletal Sketch of Glasgow's Radical Tradition* (Voline Press).

Craig, A. (2003), *The Story of Drumchapel* (Glasgow: Allan Craig).

Damer, S. (1989), *From Moorepark to 'Wine Alley': The Rise and Fall of a Glasgow Housing Scheme* (Edinburgh: Edinburgh University Press).

Defoe, D. (1707), *A Tour Through the Whole Island of Great Britain*, Book XII.

Devine, T. (1990), *The Tobacco Lords: A Study of the Tobacco Merchants of Glasgow and Their Trading Activities, c.1740–90* (Edinburgh: Edinburgh University Press).

Dodds, S. (2014), *Ten Years of the GCPH: The Evidence and Implications,* Glasgow Centre for Population Health, October.

Durkheim, Emile (1897), *Le suicide: étude de sociologie.*

Durkheim, Emile (2002), *Suicide* [English translation] (London: Routledge Classics).

Faley, J. (1990), *Up Oor Close – Memories of Domestic Life in Glasgow Tenements 1910–1945* (Oxford: White Cockade).

Ferragina, E., and Arrigoni, A. (2017), 'The Rise and Fall of Social Capital: Requiem for a Theory?', *Political Studies Review*, 15 (3), 355–67.

Fowle, F. (2011), *Van Gogh's Twin: The Scottish Art Dealer Alexander Reid* (Edinburgh: National Galleries of Scotland).

Garnham, L. (2018), *Exploring Neighbourhood Change: Life, History, Policy and Health Inequality Across Glasgow*, Glasgow Centre for Population Health, December.

Garvin, E., et al. (2012), 'More Than Just an Eyesore: Local Insights and Solutions on Vacant Land and Urban Health', *Journal of Urban Health: Bulletin of the New York Academy of Medicine*, 90 (3), 412–26.

GCPH (2008), *A Community Health and Wellbeing Profile for East Glasgow*, Glasgow Centre for Population Health, February.

Glasgow Museums (1997), *The Burrell Collection* (London: HarperCollins).

Glasser, R. (1986), *Growing Up in the Gorbals* (London: Chatto & Windus).

Hill S., and Gribben, C. (2017), *Suicide Statistics: Technical Paper*, Scottish Public Health Observatory, NHS Information Services (ISD), NHS Scotland.

Inquiry into Housing in Glasgow (1986), Glasgow District Council.

Johnman, L., and Murphy, H. (2002), *British Shipbuilding and the State since 1918: A Political Economy of Decline* (Exeter: University of Exeter Press).

Johnston, S. (2006), 'The Physical Tourist Physics in Glasgow: A Heritage Tour', *Physics in Perspective*, 8, 451–65.

King, E. (1993), *The Hidden History of Glasgow's Women: The THENEW Factor,* (Edinburgh: Mainstream).

Lorenz, E. H. (1991), *Economic Decline in Britain: The Shipbuilding Industry 1890–1970* (Oxford: Oxford University Press).

Lukes, S. (1992), *Emile Durkheim: His Life and Work* (London: Penguin Books).

McArthur, A., and Kingsley Long, H. (1956), *No Mean City* (Neville Spearman).

MacFarlane, C. (2007), *The Real Gorbals Story* (Edinburgh: Mainstream).

Marshall, A. (1890), *Principles of Economics* (London: Macmillan and Company).

Morgan, A. (2010), 'Social Capital as a Health Asset for Young People's Health and Wellbeing', *Journal of Child and Adolescent Psychology*, S2, 19–42.

Moss, M., Forbes Munro, J., and Trainor, R. H. (2000), *University, City and State: The University of Glasgow since 1870* (Edinburgh: Edinburgh University Press).

Muthesius, H. (1904), *Das englische Haus* (Berlin: Ernst Wasmuth).

National Records of Scotland (2018), *Drug Deaths in Scotland 2017*, 3 July.

Nichol, N. (1966), *Glasgow and the Tobacco Lords* (London: Longmans).

Pagden, A. (1988), 'The Destruction of Trust and Its Economic Consequences in the Case of Eighteenth-century Naples', in Gambetta, D. (ed.), *Trust: Making and Breaking Cooperative Relations* (Oxford: Blackwell).

Perry, R., (1844), *Facts and Observations on the Sanitary State of Glasgow, Shewing the Connections Existing Between Poverty, Disease, and Crime* (Glasgow: Gartnaval Press).

Peters, C. M. (1990), *Glasgow's Tobacco Lords: An Examination of Wealth Creators in the Eighteenth Century*, PhD thesis, University of Glasgow.

Potter, A. and Watts, H. D. (2012), 'Revisiting Marshall's Agglomeration Economies: Technological Relatedness and the Evolution of the Sheffield Metals Cluster', *Regional Studies*, May.

Pulteney, W. A. (1844), *Observations on the Epidemic Fever of MDCCCXLIII in Scotland and Its Connection with the Destitute Condition of the Poor* (Edinburgh: William Blackwood & Sons).

Putnam, R. (1993), *Making Democracy Work: Civic Traditions in Modern Italy* (Princeton: Princeton University Press).

————, with Leonardi, R., and Nanetti, R. (1993), *Making Democracy Work: Civic Traditions in Modern Italy* (Princeton: Princeton University Press).

Ragonnet-Cronin, M., with Jackson, C., Bradley-Stewart, A., Aitken, C., McAuley, A., Palmateer, N., Gunson, R., Goldberg, D., Milosevic, C., and Leigh Brown, A. J. (2018), 'Recent and Rapid Transmission of HIV Among People Who Inject Drugs in Scotland Revealed Through Phylogenetic Analysis', *Journal of Infectious Diseases*, 217 (12), 1875–82.

Scottish Violence Reduction Unit (2018), 'SVRU Welcomes Formation of VRU in London', 18 September.

Smith, C. (2018), *Coal, Steam and Ships: Engineering, Enterprise and Empire on the Nineteenth-century Seas* (Cambridge: Cambridge University Press).

Smith, R., and Wannop, U. (eds.) (1985), *Strategic Planning in Action: The Impact of the Clyde Valley Regional Plan 1946–1982*.

Solow, R. M. (2000), 'Notes on Social Capital and Economic Performance', in Dasgupta, P., and Serageldin, I. (eds.), *Social Capital: A Multifaceted Perspective* (Washington, DC: World Bank).

Stephen, A. M. M. (2015), *Stephen of Linthouse: A Shipbuilding Memoir 1950–1983* (Glasgow: IESIS).

Valtorta, N. K., Kanaan, M., Gilbody, S., et al. (2016), 'Loneliness and Social Isolation as Risk Factors for Coronary Heart Disease and Stroke: Systematic Review and Meta-analysis of Longitudinal Observational Studies', *Heart*, 102, 1009–16.

Wainwright, O. (2018), 'Charles Rennie Mackintosh: "He Was Doing Art Deco Before It Existed"', *Guardian*, 7 June.

Walker, F. (2001), *The Song of the Clyde: A History of Clyde Shipbuilding* (Edinburgh: John Donald).

Walpole, S. (1878), *A History of England from the Conclusion of the Great War in 1815*.

Walsh, D. (2016), *History, Politics and Vulnerability: Explaining Excess Mortality in Scotland and Glasgow*, Glasgow Centre for Population Health, May.

————, Bendel, N., Jones, R., and Hanlon, P. (2010), 'It's Not "Just Deprivation": Why Do Equally Deprived UK Cities Experience Different Health Outcomes?' *Public Health*, 124 (9), 487–5.

————, Taulbut, M., and Hanlon, P. (2008), *The Aftershock of Deindustrialisation Trends in Mortality in Scotland and Other Parts of Post-industrial Europe*, Glasgow Centre for Population Health and NHS Health Scotland, April.

Whyte, B., and Ajetunmobi, T. (2012), *Still the 'Sick Man of Europe'?*, Glasgow Centre for Population Health, November.

Withey, D. (2003), *The Glasgow City Improvement Trust: An Analysis of Its Genesis, Impact and Legacy, and an Inventory of Its Buildings, 1866–1910*, PhD thesis, University of St Andrews.

Worsdall, F. (1977), *The Tenement – A Way of Life* (Edinburgh: Chambers).

Woodley, J., and Bellamy, C. [directors] (1984), *Red Skirts on Clydeside*, Sheffield Film Co-op.

Wright, J., and MacLean, I. (1997), *Circles Under the Clyde – A History of the Glasgow Underground* (Capital Transport Publishing).

CHAPTER 7: AKITA

NOTES

Shigeaki Hinohara

Shigeaki Hinohara was a doctor who became a longevity guru in Japan, dying in 2017 at the age of 105. He wrote hundreds of books, including the bestseller (in Japan) *Living Long Living Good*: Hinohara (2006). On his life, see Roberts (2017), and on the impact of 'Hinohara-ism' see Bando et al. (2017).

Japanese demographics

Data on Japanese demographics are from the National Institute of Population and Social Security Research (IPSS), see IPSS (2017*a*). For age by municipality and regional population ageing projections, see IPSS (2013). Data on the number of centenarians by sex is available from Japan's Health and Welfare Bureau for the Elderly (2017).

Life expectancy

The life expectancy of Japanese birth cohorts is set out in Japan's *Life Tables* – see Ministry of Health, Labour and Welfare (2015). Long-run life-expectancy projections for other countries are from *World Population Prospects* – see United Nations (2017).

Modigliani and Brumberg: the life-cycle model

On the origin of the life-cycle model, see Modigliani's essay in Breit and Hirsch (2009). On the implications and importance of the model, see Deaton (2005).

Pensions

Historical data on the share of social security spending in total government expenditure are available in Ministry of Finance (2016). On the burden of ageing on the healthcare system, see Reich and Shibuya (2015).

The ancestor household in Japan; respect for elders

On the concepts of *oyakoko* and *ie* in the ancestor household, see Yoshimitsu (2011). For the impact of Confucian concepts on economic outcomes – for example, corporation organization – see Nakane (1970) and Kumagai (1992).

Intergenerational inequality

A recent review of intergenerational equity is given by Motoshige (2013). An early paper on the risk pension reforms posed to Japanese notions of solidarity is Takahashi (2004). On government programmes that aim to bring generations together, see Larkin and Kaplan (2010).

The two samurai

Oda Nobunaga, born in 1534, played an important role in unifying Japan. A deft ruler also known as an economic strategist, he destroyed many opponents and competitors and was assassinated in 1582, aged 47. Tokugawa Ieyasu, born in 1543, was another of Japan's unifiers. Involved in plenty of battles, he also became known for alliances and avoiding conflict. He died of natural causes in 1616, aged 73. The Tokugawa clan then ruled for 250 years. On the unifiers of Japan, see Chaplin (2018).

Suicide rates

On the problem of suicide and the alarming rise in Japan as a case study, see WHO (2014). On suicide rates in Akita and the prevalence of economic concerns as a cause of suicide, see Fushimi et al. (2005). On the problem of elderly suicide across rural Japan, see Traphagan (2004).

Lonely deaths

Data on the causes of death are tracked by the Ministry of Health, Labour and Welfare (MHLW). The number of 'lonely deaths' is not a readily available statistic but see Ministry of Health, Labour and Welfare (2011) for a discussion, and Waterson and Tamura (2014) for some data. On social capital, connectedness and loneliness, see Hommerich (2014).

Disappearing Japan: Fujisato and Tsuwano

The data for Fujisato were provided to me in hard copy form by the mayor of the village; they are available on the book's website: www.extremeeconomies.com. For the rise of the concept of the 'shopping refugee', see Odagiri (2011).

Data on Tsuwano were provided to me in hard copy by the representatives of the town. For pictures and more data, see Barrett (2018).

Crisis of democracy – uncontested elections
The report that predicted so many villages would disappear in fast-ageing prefectures such as Akita was Hiroya (2014); on the related crisis of local government in rural Japan, see Yoshida (2015) and Hijino (2018).

Ghost houses – Akiya
On the rising number of 'ghost houses' and the implications of this for the wider housing market, see Nozawa (2017); for photographs of abandoned towns, factories and islands, see Meow (2015).

Ninagawa and the Saitama Gold Theatre
On Ninagawa and his role in Japanese theatre, see Billington (2016).

The power of the elderly consumer
The sizes of the elderly cohorts are from IPSS (2017a). On the implications of elderly consumers for marketing and product design, see Kohlbacher and Herstatt (2011). For other examples of elderly Japanese taking up non-traditional retirement hobbies, see Takahashi et al. (2011). On the role that elderly consumers are playing in stimulating new types of products, see Kumano (2015). For concerns that an elderly workforce may lead to lower productivity (and inflation), see Liu and Westelius (2016).

3K jobs
On the problem of unappealing 3K jobs and labour shortages in Japan, see Morikawa (2018). On the impact of this in the care system, and the offsetting role robots can play, see Ishiguro (2018); on the wider need for robots in Japan due to worker shortages, see Schneider et al. (2018).

Paro: its invention, costs and impact
There is a growing literature on the use of Paro in clinical settings; for the potential benefits in terms of anxiety, stress and pain, see Petersen et al. (2017), and for results on depression and social interaction, see Jøranson et al. (2016). Some studies have criticized the therapeutic benefits and the cost-effectiveness of the robots – see Moyle et al. (2017) and Mervin et al. (2018).

The race to 50
Data on population-ageing projections for other countries are from the UN's *World Population Prospects* database; see also United Nations (2017). Projections for 2050 are discussed in Pew Research (2014). On the looming challenge for Korea, and the lessons that the country may take from Japan, see Zoli (2017). For the concern that countries may 'grow old before they grow rich', see IMF (2017). A useful

discussion of the problem in the US is Poole and Wheelock (2005); for the financial impact of the type of 'longevity risk' now playing out in Japan, see IMF (2012).

REFERENCES

Allison, A. (2013), *Precarious Japan* (Durham, NC: Duke University Press).

Bando, H., Yoshioka, A., Iwashimizu, Y., Iwashita, M., and Doba, N. (2017), 'Development of Primary Care, Lifestyle Disease and New Elderly Association (NEA) in Japan – Common Philosophy with Hinohara-ism', *Primary Health Care*, 7 (3).

Barrett, B. (2018), 'When a Country's Towns and Villages Face Extinction', *The Conversation*, 14 January.

Billington, M. (2016), 'Yukio Ninagawa', obituary, *Guardian*, 16 May.

Breit, W., and Hirsch, B. T. (2009), *Lives of the Laureates: Twenty-three Nobel Economists* (Cambridge: MIT Press).

Chaplin, D. (2018), *Sengoku Jidai. Nobunaga, Hideyoshi, and Ieyasu: Three Unifiers of Japan* (CreateSpace Independent Publishing).

Coulmas, F. (2008), *Population Decline and Ageing in Japan – The Social Consequences* (Abingdon: Routledge Contemporary Japan).

Deaton, A. (2005), 'Franco Modigliani and the Life Cycle Theory of Consumption', Lecture, March.

Fushimi M., Sugawara, J., and Shimizu, T. (2005), 'Suicide Patterns and Characteristics in Akita, Japan', *Psychiatry and Clinical Neurosciences*, 59 (3), 296–302.

Gratton, L., and Scott, A. (2016), *The 100-Year Life: Living and Working in an Age of Longevity* (London: Bloomsbury Information).

Health and Welfare Bureau for the Elderly (2017), 'Hyakusai Korei-sha ni taisuru Shukujo oyobi Kinen-hin no zotei ni tsuite' (About the Celebration and Souvenir for Centenarians).

Hijino, K. L. V. (2018), 'Japan's Shrinking Democracy: Proposals for Reviving Local Assemblies', *Nippon*, 16 May.

Hinohara, S., (2006), *Living Long, Living Good*.

Hiroya, M. (2014), 'The Decline of Regional Cities: A Horrendous Simulation – Regional Cities Will Disappear by 2040, A Polarized Society will Emerge', *Discuss Japan*, Japan Foreign Policy Forum, No. 18, Politics, 20 January.

Hommerich, C. (2014), 'Feeling Disconnected: Exploring the Relationship Between Different Forms of Social Capital and Civic Engagement in Japan', *Voluntas: International Journal of Voluntary and Nonprofit Organizations*, 26.

IMF (2012), 'The Financial Impact of Longevity Risk', *Global Financial Stability Report*, April (Washington, DC: IMF).

—————— (2017), *Asia and Pacific: Preparing for Choppy Seas*, Regional Economic Outlook, April (Washington, DC: IMF).

IPSS (2013), *Regional Population Projection for Japan: 2010–2040* (Tokyo: National Institute of Population and Social Security Research).

—————— (2017a), *Selected Demographic Indicators for Japan* (Tokyo: National Institute of Population and Social Security Research).

———— (2017*b*), *Population Projection for Japan: 2016–2065* (Tokyo: National Institute of Population and Social Security Research).

Ishiguro, N. (2018), 'Care Robots in Japanese Elderly Care: Cultural Values in Focus', in Christensen, K., and Pilling, D., *The Routledge Handbook of Social Care Work Around the World* (London: Routledge).

Japan Times (2017), 'After One-year Hiatus, Akita Again Has Highest Suicide Rate in Japan', 23 May.

Jøranson, N., Pedersen, I., Rokstad, A. M., and Amodt, G. (2016), 'Group Activity with Paro in Nursing Homes: Systematic Investigation of Behaviors in Participants', *International Psychogeriatrics*, 28, 1345–54.

Keynes, J. M. (1937, reprinted 1978), 'Some Economic Consequences of a Declining Population', *Population and Development Review*, 4 (3), 517–23.

Kohlbacher, F., and Herstatt, C. (eds.) (2011), *The Silver Market Phenomenon – Marketing and Innovation in the Aging Society* (Berlin: Springer).

Kumagai, F. (1992), 'Research on the Family in Japan', in *The Changing Family in Asia* (Bangkok: UNESCO).

Kumano, H. (2015), 'Aging Consumers Reshaping Japanese Market: Consumption Patterns of Japan's Elderly', *Nippon*, 25 November.

Larkin, E., and Kaplan, M. S. (2010), 'Intergenerational Relationships at the Center: Finding Shared Meaning from Programs in the US and Japan', *YC Young Children*, 65 (3), 88–94.

Liu, Y., and Westelius, N. (2016), 'The Impact of Demographics on Productivity and Inflation in Japan', IMF Working Paper, WP/16/237, December.

Meow, J. (2015), *Abandoned Japan* (Paris: Jonglez).

Ministry of Finance (2016), *Public Finance Statistics Book: FY2017 Draft Budget* (Tokyo: Ministry of Finance).

Ministry of Health, Labour and Welfare (2011), *Creating a Welfare Society Where Elderly and Other People Can Be Active and Comfortable* (Tokyo: Ministry of Health, Labour and Welfare).

———— (2015), *The 22nd Life Tables* (Tokyo: Ministry of Health, Labour and Welfare).

Mervin, M., et al. (2018), 'The Cost-effectiveness of Using PARO, a Therapeutic Robotic Seal, to Reduce Agitation and Medication Use in Dementia: Findings from a Cluster-randomized Controlled Trial', *Journal of the American Medical Directors Association*, 19 (7), 619–22.

Morikawa, M. (2018), 'Labor Shortage Beginning to Erode the Quality of Services: Hidden Inflation' (Toyko: Research Institute of Economy, Trade and Industry).

Motoshige, I. (ed.) (2013), *Public Pensions and Intergenerational Equity*, NIRA Policy Review No. 59 (Tokyo: National Institute for Research Advancement (NIRA)).

Moyle, W., et al. (2017), 'Use of a Robotic Seal as a Therapeutic Tool to Improve Dementia Symptoms: A Cluster-randomized Controlled Trial', *Journal of the American Medical Directors Association*, 18 (9), 766–73.

Nakane, C. (1970), *Japanese Society* (Berkeley: University of California Press).

Nozawa, C. (2017), 'Vacant Houses Are Undermining Tokyo', *Discuss Japan*, Japan Foreign Policy Forum, No. 41, Society, 11 September.

Odagiri, T. (2011), 'Rural Regeneration in Japan', Centre for Rural Economy Research Report, Research Report 56 (Newcastle: CRE).

Petersen, S., Houston, S., Qin, H., et al. (2017), 'The Utilization of Robotic Pets in Dementia Care', *Journal of Alzheimer's Disease*, 55, 569–74.

Pew Research (2014), *Attitudes About Aging: A Global Perspective*, Pew Research Center, 30 January.

Poole, W. and Wheelock, D. C. (2005), 'The Real Population Problem: Too Few Working, Too Many Retired', *Regional Economist*, Federal Reserve Bank of St Louis, April.

Reich, M., and Shibuya, K. (2015), 'The Future of Japan's Health System – Sustaining Good Health with Equity at Low Cost', *New England Journal of Medicine*, 373, 1793–97.

Roberts, S. (2017), 'Dr Shigeaki Hinohara, Longevity Expert, Dies at (or Lives to) 105', *New York Times*, 25 July.

Satsuki, K. (2010), *Nature's Embrace: Japan's Aging Urbanites and New Death Rites* (Honolulu: University of Hawaii Press).

Schneider, T., Hong, G. H, and Le, A. V. (2018), 'Land of the Rising Robots', *Finance and Development*, 55 (2), IMF.

Statistical Handbook of Japan 2018 (2018), (Tokyo: Statistics Bureau, Ministry of Internal Affairs and Communications).

Takahashi, K., Tokoro, M., and Hatano, G. (2011), 'Successful Aging through Participation in Social Activities Among Senior Citizens: Becoming Photographers', in Matsumoto, Y. (ed.), *Faces of Aging: The Lived Experiences of the Elderly in Japan* (Stanford: Stanford University Press).

Takahashi, M. (2004), 'The Social Solidarity Manifested in Japan's Pension Reforms', *Shimane Journal of Policy Studies*, 8, 125–42.

Traphagan, J. W. (2004), 'Interpretations of Elder Suicide, Stress, and Dependency Among Rural Japanese', *Ethnology*, 43 (4), 315–29.

Ueno, C. (2009), *The Modern Family in Japan: Its Rise and Fall* (Melbourne: Trans Pacific Press).

United Nations (2017), *World Population Prospects: The 2017 Revision, Key Findings and Advance Tables*, ESA/P/WP/248 (New York: United Nations).

Wakabayashi, M., and Horioka, C. Y. (2006), 'Is the Eldest Son Different? The Residential Choice of Siblings in Japan', October, NBER Working Paper No. w12655.

Waterson, H., and Tamura, K. (2014), 'Social Isolation and Local Government: The Japanese Experience' (London: Japan Local Government Centre).

WHO (2014), *Preventing Suicide: A Global Imperative* (Geneva: World Health Organization).

Yoshida, R. (2015), 'Vanishing Communities Find Themselves Facing Shortage of Leaders', *Japan Times*, 24 April.

Yoshimitsu, K. (2011), *Japanese Moral Education Past and Present* (Cranbury, NJ: Associated University Presses).

Zoli, E. (2017), *Korea's Challenges Ahead – Lessons from Japan Experience*, IMF Working Paper WP/17/2, January.

CHAPTER 8: TALLINN

NOTES

Wassily Leontief

The quote at the start of the chapter on p. 263 is from an essay, 'Machines and Man', written by Harvard economist Wassily Leontief for an issue of *Scientific American* devoted to automatic control of machines – see Leontief (1952).

The two fears from technology: unemployment and division

On the risk that technological progress will lead to mass unemployment, see Keynes (1930) and Leontief (1952), and for a survey of the history of these kinds of concerns, see Mokyr et al. (2015). The prediction of 30 per cent automation – 44 per cent for the low skilled – is from PwC (2018); see also Muro et al. (2019) for a Brookings Institution report on the US. For recent discussion of a 'digital divide' or a new 'digital underclass', see World Bank (2016) and OECD (2018). Early concerns over the digital divide in the US are set out in FINA (1995, 1998).

Estonia's digital achievements: tax, political system, e-government

For dates and facts on the Estonian 'digital society', see the government website: www.e-estonia.com; for the government's long-term plan, see Ministry of Economic Affairs and Communications (2013) and State Electoral Office of Estonia (2017). Data for voting turnouts are available from the electoral office site: www .valimised.ee/en.

The economy under Soviet rule

For the economic impact of the Soviet system, including the rise of illegal farming as a response to food shortages, see Misiunas and Taagepera (1993); on the collectivization of farming, see Jaska (1952).

Estonia takes off

For a review of Estonia's 'take-off' in the mid-1990s, see Almi (1996), and for an account of the 'economic miracle' from one of its architects, see Laar (2007). On the wider reforms Estonia undertook in the context of other post-Soviet economies, see Roaf et al. (2014). The figures for 2018 are taken from the Statistics Estonia website: www.stat.ee.

The X-Road

The X-Road is often referred to as the 'backbone' of e-Estonia. Its name was changed to 'X-tee' in 2018, and information on its usage and status can be tracked in real time at www.x-tee.ee/factsheets/EE/#eng. On the role the system plays in allowing personal control of private data, see Priisalu and Ottis (2017); on the use of the system by private sector companies, see Paide et al. (2018).

Logistics and the labour market
Data on transport and logistics in the labour market are from Statistics Estonia, the Bureau of Labor Statistics (US) and the Office for National Statistics (UK).

The early agricultural revolution
On the importance of crop innovations and how these ideas diffused across the UK, see Overton (1985); on improvements to livestock breeding by Robert Bakewell, see Wykes (2004). On the importance of mechanization in farming and of how individual farmers are promoters of change, see Fox and Butlin (eds.) (1979). For recent work and data on the intensity of innovation in seventeenth-century Britain, see Ang et al. (2013); for estimates of agricultural productivity, see Apostolides et al. (2008). On how rising agricultural productivity supported a boom in the UK population, see Overton (1996).

The Swing Riots
The classic account of British agricultural labourers' reaction to the mechanization of farm work is *Captain Swing* by Hobsbawm and Rudé (1968); for a more recent account of the use of violence in this period, see Griffin (2010).

The Industrial Revolution
On the role of the Spinning Jenny in the Industrial Revolution, see Allen (2007). For a history of cotton innovation and the UK in the context of Indian and Chinese cotton production, see Riello (2013).

The decline of manufacturing employment
Changes in employment for the US are from the Bureau of Labor Statistics; for a 100-year view of the US, see Ghanbari and McCall (2016).

Arthur Samuel, and the origins of AI
On the origins and early development of artificial intelligence, see Nilsson (2009). The original paper by Arthur Samuel on machine learning and the game of checkers is Samuel (1959); for a short survey of Samuel's contribution, see McCarthy and Feigenbaum (1990). For artificial intelligence and robots in the longer history of 'technological transformations', see Ayres (1989).

The computer chip and Moore's Law
The original Moore's Law argument is set out in Moore (1965). On the recent slowdown in the rate of chip improvement, see Waldrop (2016), and on the way new types of chip mean Moore-like improvements will continue, see Simonite (2016).

Narva
For a study of Narva's unique role and history in Estonia, see Smith (2002); for concerns about Narva's geopolitical significance and possible invasion by Russia, see Trimbach and O'Lear (2015).

Estonians of Russian heritage

On the history and number of migrants from Russia to Estonia, see Sakkeus (1994); on the role that Soviet policy played, see Kahk and Tarvel (1997). For an introduction to the challenges faced, see Koort (2014); for estimates of labour market segregation and its impact on unemployment and wages, see Saar and Helemäe (2017). More recent research tracks integration through various social behaviours such as childbearing and school attendance – see Puur et al. (2017); for a global picture on stateless people, see UNHCR (2016). Contemporary data on the ethnic background of Estonians is from Statistics Estonia.

Economic statistics on Estonia: employment, labour market participation, wages

Data on the recent performance of the Estonian labour market are from Statistics Estonia – see Vannas (2018).

The impact of the ID card, entrepreneurs' challenges, and e-Residency

For a description of the e-Residency project by its architects, see Kotka et al. (2015), and on plans for expansion of the e-Residency system, see Korjus (2018). For independent research, see Tammpuu and Masso (2018).

Language barriers in Estonia

Estonian is a Uralic language, related to Finnish and Hungarian. Russian is Slavic, part of the Indo-European family, and is closer to English than it is to Estonian. Some say this is one reason Estonia was treated more harshly during Soviet occupation than Latvia and Lithuania, where the languages are closer to Russian. On the labour market as an ethnic mixer, see Saar and Helemäe (2017) and the discussion of Kruusvall (2015).

Countries copying Estonia

On the use of the Estonian digital government project overseas, see www.e-estonia.ee. For example, for the case of Canada, see Thomson (2019).

Latest on the risks to employment

For recent research on robots in the workplace, see Graetz and Michaels (2015); on the tendency to overstate the unemployment risks and the failure to predict new types of employment, see Mokyr et al. (2015).

REFERENCES

Allen, R. C. (2007), 'The Industrial Revolution in Miniature: The Spinning Jenny in Britain, France, and India', Economics Series Working Papers 375, University of Oxford, Department of Economics.

Almi, P. (1996), 'Estonia's Economy Takes Off', *Unitas*, 68, 16–18.

Ang, J. B., Banerjee, R., and Madsen, J. B. (2013), 'Innovation and Productivity Advances in British Agriculture: 1620–1850', *Southern Economic Journal*, 80 (1), 162–86.

Apostolides, A., Broadberry, S., Campbell, B., Overton, M., and van Leeuwen, B. (2008), 'English Agricultural Output and Labour Productivity 1250–1850, Some Preliminary Estimates', Mimeo, University of Exeter.

Ashton, T. (1948), *The Industrial Revolution 1760–1830* (London: Oxford University Press).

Ayres, R. U. (1989), *Technological Transformation and Long Waves*, International Institute for Applied Systems Analysis, Research Report 89–1.

Baburin, A., Lai, T., and Leinsalu M., 'Avoidable Mortality in Estonia: Exploring the Differences in Life Expectancy Between Estonians and Non-Estonians in 2005–2007', *Public Health*, 125, 754–62.

Brynjolfsson, E., and McAfee, A. (2012), *Race Against the Machine: How the Digital Revolution is Accelerating* (Digital Frontier Press).

Chambers, J. D., and Mingay, G. E. (1966), *The Agricultural Revolution 1750–1850* (London: B. T. Batsford).

Clark, G. (2002), *The Agricultural Revolution and the Industrial Revolution*, Working Paper, University of California, Davis.

————— (2005), 'The Condition of the Working Class in England, 1209–2004', *Journal of Political Economy*, 113, 1307–40.

Deane, P. (1969), *The First Industrial Revolution* (Cambridge: Cambridge University Press).

FINA (1995), *Falling Through the Net: A Survey of the 'Have Nots' in Rural and Urban America*, National Telecommunications and Information Administration, United States Department of Commerce, July.

FINA (1998), *Falling Through the Net II: New Data on the Digital Divide*, National Telecommunications and Information Administration, United States Department of Commerce, July.

Fox, H., and Butlin, R. (eds.) (1979), *Change in the Countryside*, Institute of British Geographers (Oxford: Alden Press).

Ghanbari, L., and McCall, M. (2016), 'Current Employment Statistics Survey: 100 Years of Employment, Hours, and Earnings', *BLS Monthly Labor Review: August 2016*, US Bureau of Labor Statistics.

Graetz, G., and Michaels, G. (2015), 'Robots at Work', *Centre for Economic Performance Discussion Paper No. 1335*, March.

Griffin, C. (2010), 'The Violent Captain Swing?', *Past & Present*, 209, 149–180.

Hobsbawm, E., and Rudé, G. (1968), *Captain Swing* (London: Lawrence & Wishart).

Jaska, E. (1952), 'The Results of Collectivization of Estonian Agriculture', *Land Economics*, 28 (3), 212–17.

Kahk, J., and Tarvel, E. (1997), *An Economic History of the Baltic Countries* (Stockholm: Almquist & Wiksell International).

Kattel, R. and Mergel, I. (2018), *Estonia's Digital Transformation: Mission Mystique and the Hiding Hand*, UCL Institute for Innovation and Public Purpose Working Paper Series (IIPP WP 2018-09).

Keynes, J. M. (1930), 'Economic Possibilities for Our Grandchildren', in *Essays in Persuasion* (1963) (New York: W. W. Norton & Co.).

Koort, K. (2014), 'The Russians of Estonia: Twenty Years After', *World Affairs*, July/ August.

Korjus, K. (ed.) (2018), *E-Residency 2.0, White Paper.*

Kotka, T., Alvarez del Castillo, C. I. V., and Korjus, K. (2015), 'Estonian e-Residency: Redefining the Nation-state in the Digital Era', Cyber Studies Programme Working Paper No. 3, University of Oxford, September.

Kruusvall, J. (2015), Rahvussuhted. Eesti ühiskonna integratsiooni monitooring. Uuringu aruanne.

Laar, M. (2007), 'The Estonian Economic Miracle', *Heritage Foundation*, 7 August.

Lebergott, S. (1966), 'Labor Force and Employment, 1800–1960', in Brady, D. S. (ed.), *Output, Employment, and Productivity in the United States after 1800* (Cambridge, Mass.: NBER).

Leontief, W. (1952), 'Machines and Man', *Scientific American*, 187 (3), 150–60.

McCarthy, J., and Feigenbaum, E. (1990), 'In Memoriam: Arthur Samuel and Machine Learning', *AI Magazine*, 11 (3), 10–11.

Ministry of Culture (2014), *The Strategy of Integration and Social Cohesion in Estonia, 'Integrating Estonia 2020'.*

Ministry of Economic Affairs and Communications (2013), *Digital Agenda 2020 for Estonia.*

Misiunas, R., and Taagepera, R. (1993), *The Baltic States: The Years of Dependence, 1940–90* (Berkeley: University of California Press).

Mokyr, J., Vickers, C., and Ziebarth, N. (2015), 'The History of Technological Anxiety and the Future of Economic Growth: Is This Time Different?', *Journal of Economic Perspectives*, 29 (3), 31–50.

Moore, G. E. (1965), 'Cramming More Components on to Integrated Circuits', *Electronics*, April, 114–17.

Muro, M., Maxim, R., and Whiton, J. (2019), 'Automation and Artificial Intelligence: How Machines Are Affecting People and Places', Report, Brookings Institution, 24 January.

Nilsson, N. (2009), *The Quest for Artificial Intelligence* (Cambridge: Cambridge University Press).

OECD (2018), 'Bridging the Rural Digital Divide', OECD Digital Economy Papers, No. 265 (Paris: OECD).

Overton, M. (1985), 'The Diffusion of Agricultural Innovations in Early Modern England: Turnips and Clover in Norfolk and Suffolk, 1580–1740', *Transactions of the Institute of British Geographers*, 10 (2), 205–221.

——— (1996), *Agricultural Revolution in England: The Transformation of the Agrarian Economy 1500–1850* (Cambridge: Cambridge University Press).

Paide, K., Pappel, I., Vainsalu, H., and Draheim, D. (2018), 'On the Systematic Exploitation of the Estonian Data Exchange Layer X-Road for Strengthening Public-Private Partnerships', in *Proceedings of the 11th International Conference on Theory and Practice of Electronic Governance*, ICEGOV'18, April.

Priisalu, J., and Ottis, R. (2017), 'Personal Control of Privacy and Data: Estonian Experience', *Health Technology*, 7, 441.

Puur, A., Rahnu, L., Abuladze, L., Sakkeus, L., and Zakharov, S. (2017), 'Child-bearing Among First- and Second-generation Russians in Estonia Against the Background of the Sending and Host Countries', *Demographic Research*, 35, 1209–54.

PwC (2018), 'How Will Automation Impact Jobs?', *Economics: Insights*, February.

Riello, G. (2013), *Cotton: The Fabric that Made the Modern World* (Cambridge: Cambridge University Press).

Roaf, J., Atoyan, R., Joshi, B., and Krogulski, K. (2014), '25 Years of Transition: Post-communist Europe and the IMF', *Regional Economic Issues Special Report*, IMF, October.

Saar, E., and Helemäe, J. (2017), 'Ethnic Segregation in the Estonian Labour Market', in *Estonian Human Development Report 2016/2017*.

Sakkeus, L. (1994), 'The Baltic States', in Ardittis, S. (ed.), *The Politics of East–West Migration* (New York: St Martin's Press).

Samuel, A. L. (1959), 'Some Studies in Machine Learning Using the Game of Checkers', *IBM Journal*, 3 (3), 211–29.

Simonite, T. (2016), 'A $2 Billion Chip to Accelerate Artificial Intelligence', *MIT Technology Review*, 5 April.

Smith, D. (2002), 'Narva Region Within the Estonian Republic. From Autonomism to Accommodation?', *Regional & Federal Studies*, 12 (2), 89–110.

State Electoral Office of Estonia (2017), 'General Framework of Electronic Voting and Implementation Thereof at National Elections in Estonia', Document: IVXV-ÜK-1.0, 20 June.

Study of Social Groups in Integration: Summary and Policy Suggestions (2013), (Tallinn: Tallinn University IISS).

Tammpuu, P., and Masso, A. (2018), 'Welcome to the Virtual State: Estonian e-Residency and the Digitalised State as a Commodity', *European Journal of Cultural Studies*, 1–18.

Thomson, S. (2019), ' "It's Got Us Very Intrigued": MPs to Study How Canada Can Learn From "Digitally Advanced" Estonia', *National Post*, 13 January.

Trimbach, D., and O'Lear, S. (2015), 'Russians in Estonia: Is Narva the next Crimea?', *Eurasian Geography and Economics*, 56 (5), 493–504.

UNHCR (2016), *Ending Statelessness Within 10 Years*, Special Report.

Vannas, Ü. (2018), 'Employment Rate at Record High in 2017', *Quarterly Bulletin of Statistics Estonia*, 7 June.

Waldrop, M. (2016), 'The Chips Are Down for Moore's Law', *Nature*, 9 February.

World Bank (2016), *World Development Report 2016: Digital Dividends* (Washington, DC: World Bank).

Wykes, D. (2004), 'Robert Bakewell (1725–1795) of Dishley: Farmer and Livestock Improver', *Agricultural History Review*, 52 (1), 38–55.

CHAPTER 9: SANTIAGO

NOTES

Chile as a leader on the road to global inequality
Historical inequality data for Chile are taken from Ffrench-Davis (2010) and Solimano (2012); cross-country trends are taken from the OECD and *World Inequality Report 2018*. Among newly developed countries, the other example of an extremely unequal country is Mexico, which in recent years has vied with Chile as the most unequal OECD country.

The Good Neighbor Policy, the ICA, and the Chicago exchange agreement
President Roosevelt outlined his Good Neighbor Policy in his first inaugural address and expanded on it in later speeches – Roosevelt (1933, 1936). The origins and working of the International Corporation Administration (ICA) and the Chicago–Chile exchange agreement that followed are discussed in detail in Valdés (1995). The philosophy and aims of the ICA in the mid-fifties are set out by its director in Stokes (1956); examples of the ICA across the Americas are in ICA (1959).

Friedman and Harberger, and their influence on the Chicago Boys
An important foundation of Chicago-school thinking is Henry Simons's essay 'A Positive Program for Laissez Faire', printed in Simons (1947). For overviews of Chicagoan thinking, see Miller (1962) and Reder (1982); for an introduction to Friedman, see his *Capitalism and Freedom* (1982a). For an account of the education of the Chicago Boys and their impact, see Valdés (1995). The recent film *Chicago Boys* has footage of the young men in Chicago and contemporary interviews – see Fuentes and Valdeavellano (2015).

Salvador Allende's economic plan
Allende's economic programme and results during the period from 1970 to 1973 are examined in detail in Larrain and Meller (1990). On the nationalization of copper, see Fleming (1973).

Human rights abuses under Pinochet
The original Chilean investigation on human rights abuses under the Pinochet regime was published in 1991 and is known as the Rettig Report – see Weissbrodt and Fraser (1992); subsequent official reports in 2004, 2005 and 2011 have increased the estimates of abuses. All this information is chronicled at a dedicated museum – the Museo de la Memoria – in Santiago. A summary of the CIA's involvement in the Pinochet coup, death of Allende and human rights abuses has been published as CIA (2000).

El Ladrillo – 'The Brick'

El Ladrillo was republished by a Chilean think-tank – see CEP (1992). For an early critique of the 'extreme experiment', see Ffrench-Davis (1983).

The miracle of Chile

The early success of liberalization of trade is set out in Ffrench-Davis (2010); see also Corbo (1997) on the removal of trade prohibitions.

The notion of the 'miracle' of Chile is from a *Newsweek* article – see Friedman (1982*b*). For an example of the praise given to Chile and the urge for other countries to follow its path, see World Bank (1999); and for Chile's 'exemplary' policies, see Brookings (2009).

Poverty reduction

For statistics on the reduction of poverty, see Altimir (2001) and Ffrench-Davis (2010); for the argument that official statistics mask hidden poverty, see Solimano (2012).

Income inequality and growth

On the persistent problem of poverty and increasing problem of inequality in Chile, see Ffrench-Davis (2010) and Solimano (2012). For a summary of the arguments that Chilean development and growth are not reaching the majority of its citizens, see COHA (2011). On the resilience of inequality in Santiago, see Fernández et al. (2016).

Equality of opportunity

For the importance of equality of opportunity in the Chicago Boys' plan, see CEP (1992). For information on the huge boost in university numbers and an introduction to the context of Chilean education, see Arango et al. (2016).

Education and segregation

The co-pay public–private system is highly controversial – see Bellei (2008). For a summary of research on critical findings, see COHA (2008); see also Hsieh and Urquiola (2006). Some still favour the system, though: Chumacero et al. (2016) has a clear background on the voucher competition system, arguing that it does lead to improved results. On economic and residential segregation, see Montero and Vargas (2012). On the cost of university courses and drop-out rates, see Arango et al. (2016).

Giorgio Jackson, the Penguins Revolution, the 'Chilean Winter'

On the 2006 protests – the Penguins Revolution – see Chovanec and Benitez (2008); and on the 2011 protests – the 'Chilean Winter' – see Bellei and Cabalin (2013), and Vallejo (2016). On the push for free college education that followed, see Delisle and Bernasconi (2018). For reporting on the impact of Giorgio Jackson and the *Frente Amplio* (the 'Broad Front'), see Mander (2017). For an example of the new philosophy Mr Jackson cites as influential, see Han (2017).

Competition scandals
On collusion in pharmaceuticals, see FNE (2012); for competition scandals and high concentration across Chilean industry, see OECD (2010).

Divisions in Santiago, social infrastructure and private security
The evidence of a link between social infrastructure that allows people to mix (including libraries and parks) is set out in Klinenberg (2018). On feelings of social cohesion, interpersonal distrust and personal insecurity, see Dammert (2012); and on the rise of the private security industry, see Abelson (2006). On the link between social capital and health, see Riumallo-Herl et al. (2014).

The future – the unequal world
On the drivers of rising inequality, see OECD (2011) and *World Inequality Report 2018*. On the trend towards urbanization, see United Nations (2018), and on urban inequality, see OECD (2018).

REFERENCES

Abelson, A. (2006), 'Private Security in Chile. An Agenda for the Public Security Ministry', Security and Citizenship Programme, FLACSO-Chile, August.

Altimir, O. (2001), 'Long-term Trends of Poverty in Latin American Countries', *Estudios de Economía*, 28 (1), 115–55.

Arango, M., Evans, S., and Quadri, Z. (2016), *Education Reform in Chile: Designing a Fairer, Better Higher Education System*, Woodrow Wilson School of Public and International Affairs, Princeton University, viewed 18 January 2019.

Bellei, C. (2008), 'The Private–Public School Controversy: The Case of Chile', in Chakrabarti, R., and Peterson, P. E. (eds.), *School Choice International: Exploring Public–Private Partnerships* (Cambridge, Mass.: MIT Press).

——, and Cabalin, C. (2013), 'Chilean Student Movements: Sustained Struggle to Transform a Market-oriented Educational System', *Current Issues in Comparative Education*, 15 (2), 108–23.

Brookings (2009), 'The IMF's Outlook for Latin America and the Caribbean: Stronger Fundamental Outlook', Washington, DC, 21 May.

CEP (1992), *'El Ladrillo': Bases de la Política Económica del Gobierno Militar Chileno*, (Santiago: Centro de Estudios Públicos).

Chovanec, D. M., and Benitez, A. (2008), 'The Penguin Revolution in Chile: Exploring Intergenerational Learning in Social Movements', *Journal of Contemporary Issues in Education*, 3 (1), 39–57.

Chumacero, R., Gallegos Mardones, J., and Paredes, R. D. (2016), 'Competition Pressures and Academic Performance in Chile', *Estudios de Economía*, 43 (2), 217–32.

CIA (2000), *CIA Activities in Chile*, Central Intelligence Agency, 18 September.

COHA (2008), *The Failings of Chile's Education System: Institutionalized Inequality and a Preference for the Affluent*, Council on Hemispheric Affairs, 30 July.

———— (2011), *The Inequality Behind Chile's Prosperity*, Council on Hemispheric Affairs, 23 November.

Corbo, V. (1997), 'Trade Reform and Uniform Import Tariffs: The Chilean Experience', *American Economic Review*, 87 (2), 73–7.

Dammert, L. (2012), *Citizen Security and Social Cohesion in Latin America* (Barcelona: URB-AL III).

Delisle, J., and Bernasconi, A. (2018), 'Lessons from Chile's Transition to Free College', *Evidence Speaks Reports*, 2 (43).

Díaz, J., Lüders, R. and Wagner, G. (2016), *Chile 1810 – 2010. La República en cifras. Historical statistics* (Santiago: Ediciones Universidad Católica de Chile).

Fernández, I. C., Manuel-Navarrete, D., and Torres-Salinas, R. (2016), 'Breaking Resilient Patterns of Inequality in Santiago de Chile: Challenges to Navigate Towards a More Sustainable City', *Sustainability*, 8 (8), 820.

Ffrench-Davis, R. (1983), 'The Monetarist Experiment in Chile: A Critical Survey', *World Development*, 11 (11), 905–26.

———— (2010), *Economic Reforms in Chile – From Dictatorship to Democracy* (London: Palgrave Macmillan).

Fleming, J. (1973), 'The Nationalization of Chile's Large Copper Companies in Contemporary Interstate Relations', *Villanova Law Review*, 18 (4), 593–647.

FNE (2012), *Competition Issues in the Distribution of Pharmaceuticals*, OECD Global Forum on Competition, 7 January 2014, La Fiscalía Nacional Económica.

Foxley, A. (2004), 'Successes and Failures in Poverty Eradication: Chile', Working Paper 30806, 1 May.

Friedman, M. (1982*a*), *Capitalism and Freedom* (Chicago: University of Chicago Press).

———— (1982*b*), 'Free Markets and the Generals', *Newsweek*, 25 January.

Fuentes, C., and Valdeavellano, R. (2015), *Chicago Boys*, CNTV, November.

Han, B.-C. (2017), *Psychopolitics: Neoliberalism and New Technologies of Power* (London: Verso).

Hsieh, C., and Urquiola, M. (2006), 'The Effects of Generalized School Choice on Achievement and Stratification: Evidence from Chile's Voucher Program', *Journal of Public Economics*, 90, 1481.

ICA (1959), *Working with People: Examples of US Technical Assistance* (Washington, DC: International Cooperation Administration).

Klinenberg, E. (2018), *Palaces for the People: How Social Infrastructure Can Help Fight Inequality, Polarization, and the Decline of Civic Life* (London: Bodley Head).

Larrain, F., and Meller, P. (1990), 'The Socialist-Populist Chilean Experience, 1970–1973', in Dornbusch, R., and Edwards, S. (eds.), *The Macroeconomics of Populism in Latin America* (Chicago: University of Chicago Press).

Mander, B. (2017), 'Leftwing Bloc Upends Chile's Traditional Balance of Power', *Financial Times*, 24 November.

Miller, H. L. (1962), 'On the "Chicago School of Economics"', *Journal of Political Economy*, 70 (1), 64–9.

Montero, R., and Vargas, M. (2012), *Economic Residential Segregation Effects on Educational Achievements: The Case of Chile*.

OECD (2010), *OECD Economic Surveys: Chile* (Paris: OECD).

———— (2011), *Divided We Stand – Why Inequality Keeps Rising* (Paris: OECD).

———— (2018), *Divided Cities: Understanding Intra-urban Inequalities* (Paris: OECD).

Reder, M. W. (1982), 'Chicago Economics: Permanence and Change', *Journal of Economic Literature*, 20 (1), 1–38.

Riumallo-Herl, C., Kawachi, I., and Avendano, M. (2014), 'Social Capital, Mental Health and Biomarkers in Chile: Assessing the Effects of Social Capital in a Middle-income Country', *Social Science & Medicine*, 105C, 47–58.

Roosevelt, F. D. (1933), First Inaugural Address, 4 March.

———— (1936), Address at Chautauqua, 14 August.

Sanhueza, C., and Mayer, R. (2011), 'Top Incomes in Chile Using 50 Years of Household Surveys: 1957–2007', *Estudios de Economía*, 38 (1), 169–93.

Simons, H. C. (1947), *Economic Policy for a Free Society* (Chicago: University of Chicago).

Solimano, A. (2012), *Chile and the Neoliberal Trap – The Post-Pinochet Era* (Cambridge: Cambridge University Press).

Stokes, J. M. (1956), 'The International Cooperation Administration', *World Affairs*, 119 (2), 35–37.

United Nations (2018), *World Urbanisation Prospects – Key Facts* (New York: United Nations).

Valdés, J. G. (1995), *Pinochet's Economists: The Chicago School of Economics in Chile* (Cambridge: Cambridge University Press).

Vallejo, C. (2016), 'On Public Education in Chile', *OECD Yearbook 2016* (Paris: OECD).

Weissbrodt, D., and Fraser, P. (1992), 'Report of the Chilean National Commission on Truth and Reconciliation', *Human Rights Quarterly*, 14 (4), 601–22.

Winn, P. (ed.) (2004), *Victims of the Chilean Miracle – Workers and Neoliberalism in the Pinochet Era, 1973–2002* (Durham, NC: Duke University Press).

World Bank (1999), *Chile: Recent Policy Lessons and Emerging Challenges* (Washington, DC: World Bank).

World Inequality Report 2018, World Inequality Lab., Paris School of Economics.

INDEX

Page numbers in *italics* refer to maps and charts.

A NOTE ABOUT THE AUTHOR

Richard Davies is a British economist and journalist. He is a fellow of the London School of Economics and has served as economic adviser to the chancellor of the exchequer and as chair of the Council of Economic Advisers at HM Treasury. He also served as the economics editor of *The Economist*.